Praise for *How to Make a Living as a Poet*, The [illegible] Poetry Project and the Precision Poetry Drill Team

"The book is a high-spirited combination of practical advice, interviews with other working writers and—of course!—poems. It's also an exceedingly generous book, shot through with passion and ideas. Subsequently Glazner's book is far more than another how-to book destined to disappear on a shelf. It is a manifesto on the rewards of finding ways to turn one's passion into work—an important message sure to resonate with anyone who reads it, poet or not."

—*Santa Fe Reporter*

"I am in love with a new book written by a poet. Here I am a nonfiction writer steeped in facts and reality, enthralled with the mission of a bona fide poet. *How to Make a Living as a Poet* by Gary Mex Glazner is just what the doctor ordered for the poet struggling to make a living. Frankly, it's good for the writer who wants to make a living."

—C. Hope Clark, www.fundsforwriters.com

"Poetry is perhaps the least remunerative of the literary arts. Even poet lauerate Ted Kooser has a day job. But Santa Fean Gary Mex Glazner *does* earn his daily bread with poetry. And this week he tells the rest of us how."

—*The Santa Fe New Mexican*

"It's poetry with a purpose."

—*Good Morning Memphis*, CBS

"The Precision Poetry Drill Team is coached by poet Gary Glazner who says he's trying to emulate the precision and competitive nature of those hot high-steppin' football bands from the south."

—*All Things Considered*, NPR

"Their effect really brightened. They smiled. Many of them began to move with the beat of the poem, which was exciting. Many of them responded with touch. They'd reach out and hold his hand as he approached them."

—Dr. Kristen Sorocco on the Glazner's Alzheimer's Poetry Project

"He whirled around the circle, repeating the stanza and hopping from one foot to the other. As he passed each person he pumped their hands up and down to the rhythm of the chant. And as he passed, he also pumped life into their faces. Formerly somber expressions became animated. Hands clapped. Feet stomped. Eyes shone with humor, recognition and, later in the hour, tears."

—*Northwest Arkansas Times* on Glazner's Alzheimer's Poetry Project

How To Make a Life as a Poet

How To Make A Life As A Poet

Gary Mex Glazner

SOFT SKULL PRESS
BROOKLYN, NEW YORK
2006

How To Make A Life As A Poet
ISBN: 1-933368-14-4
ISBN-13: 978-1-933368-14-6

Book Design by Anne Horowitz
Cover Design by Catherine Burke

Published by Soft Skull Press
55 Washington Street, Suite 804
Brooklyn, NY 11201
www.softskull.com

Distributed by Publishers Group West • www.pgw.com

Printed in Canada

Cataloging-in-Publication data for this title is available from the Library of Congress.

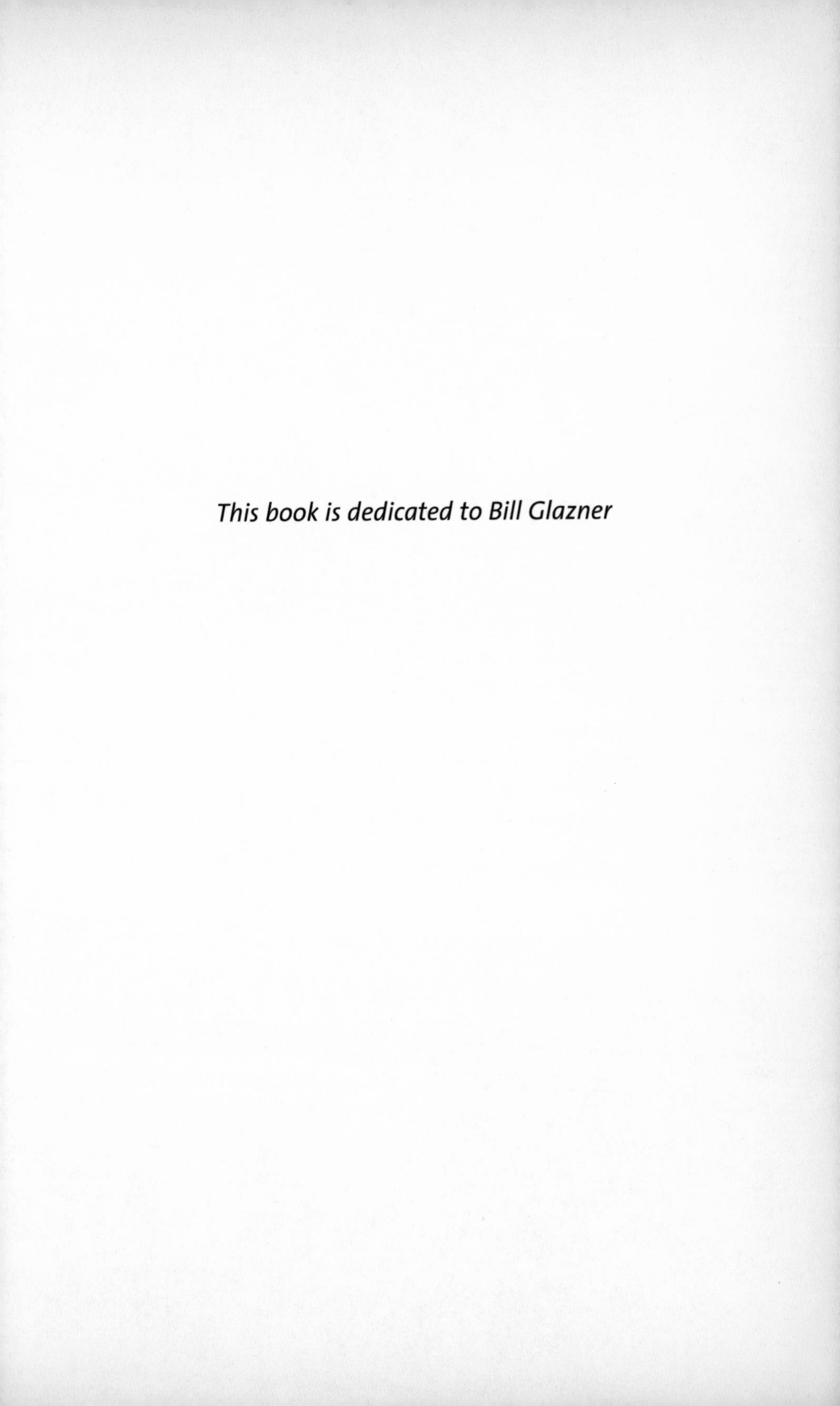

This book is dedicated to Bill Glazner

Contents

The Poem Factory Pledge

Often when **reading a book**

don't you just want to call up the author and say,

"What about this?" or

"This is my particular situation,

may you help me please?"

We here at *Poem Factory* pledge to help you with your **poetry problem.**.

Can't find the right word?

Poem Factory is full of words.

Need to brainstorm **potential sponsors** for your *poetry project?*

NO PROBLEM!

Need a *list of foundations* that you can write to for **grants?**

NO PROBLEM!

Need a **WACKY WAY** to promote your *poetry series?*

Poem Factory specializes in **WACKY**.

Need a new metaphor?

Metaphorically speaking, we've got you **COVERED!**

Poem Factory won't stop until poetry sales are soaring.

Won't give up until you can call

1-800-555-Poet and get an ANSWER.

Meanwhile you can contact *Poem Factory* at:

http://howtopoet.blogspot.com

Operators are standing by.

Here is a Partial List of our Departments and Services:

- For the unacknowledged legislators of the world—ask for Mr. Shelley.
- For the spontaneous overflow of powerful feelings—ask for Mr. Wordsworth.
- For the communication of pleasure—ask for Mr. Coleridge.
- For Negative Capability (that is, when man is capable of being in uncertainties, mysteries, and doubts, without any irritable reaching after fact and reason)—ask for Mr. Keats.
- For the reason bards love wine, mead, narcotics, coffee, tea, opium, the fumes of sandalwood and tobacco, or whatever other procurers of animal exhilaration—ask for Mr. Emerson.
- For a great poem for ages and ages in common and for all degrees and complexions and all departments and sects and for a woman as much as a man and a man as much as a woman—ask for Mr. Whitman.
- For a book and it makes your whole body so cold no fire can ever warm me, andknow that is poetry—ask for Ms. Dickinson (works from home).
- For the lover of life who makes the world his family, just as the lover of the fair sex enlists in his family all the beauties that he has captured, may capture or will never capture—ask for Mr. Baudelaire.

- For the psychic automatism in its pure state, by which one purposes to express—verbally, by means of the written word, or in any other manner—the actual functioning of thought—ask for Mr. Breton.
- For the intelligence that is often the enemy of poetry, because it limits too much, and it elevates the poet to a sharp-edged throne where he forgets that ants could eat him or that a great arsenic lobster could fall on his head—ask for Mr. Lorca, Dept. of *duende*.
- For scribbling about a new fashion in poetry—ask for Mr. Pound.
- For poetry that is prose bewitched, a music made of visual thoughts, the sound of an idea—ask for Ms. Mina Loy.
- For a rose is a rose is a rose is a rose—ask for Ms. Stein.
- For poetry, I, too, dislike it—ask for Ms. Moore.
- For Compose. (No ideas but in things) Invent!—ask for Dr. Williams.
- For a poem that is energy transferred from where the poet got it (he will have several causations), by way of the poem itself to, all the way over to, the reader—ask for Mr. Olsen, Head of the Parts Dept.

I pledge allegiance to Poetry—
all Words
and to the Breath for which they stand,
all silence, living, dead,
with listen and speak for all.

Introduction

Beware the Jabberwock, my son!

*The jaws that bite, the claws that catch!**

—Lewis Carroll

I was a florist for eighteen years, but I always wanted to do something more masculine, so I became a poet. This book is a follow-up book to *How to Make a Living as a Poet*, also published by Soft Skull. I see the books working together to help bring more poetry into your life. I have used writing the books as a way to explore making poetry more central to my life.

In the year since *How to Make a Living as a Poet* came out, I have been hired to teach a class on poetry slam at Desert Academy in Santa Fe. I have come up with the concept of the Precision Poetry Drill Team and have taken on the role of coach. I have used the book tour for *How to Make a Living* as an opportunity to bring the Alzheimer's Poetry Project (APP) to seven states. The concepts put forward in that book have helped me get funding for the APP from the City of Santa Fe Arts Commission, the Puffin Foundation, the State of New Mexico Arts Commission, and the National Endowment for the Arts. In June, I traveled to New Zealand, starting the APP in Wellington and speaking on New Zealand national radio. A *Voice of America* broadcast on the APP reached millions of listeners worldwide. Bread for the Journey funded the publication of *Sparking Memories: The Alzheimer's Poetry Project Anthology*. In short I have tried to use the ideas from *How to Make a Living as a Poet* to build the audience for poetry and to allow myself to be a full-time poet.

This book includes many interviews with poets who speak about how they bring poetry into their lives. We learn about Judith Tannenbaum's work with prisoners and the publication of her wonderful memoir of the experience, entitled *Disguised as a Poem: My*

Years Teaching Poetry at San Quentin. Marc Smith, inventor of the poetry slam, speaks about the early days of slam, using music with poetry, and his innovative project with the City of Chicago, which among other things put poems in one hundred thousand pizza boxes. We talk with Kim Addonizio about how she runs her poetry workshops and how she incorporates her love of blues and passion for playing the harmonica into her readings. Patricia Smith tells us how poetry saved her life. Eleni Sikelianos tells us why there had better be sex in heaven. Hettie Jones talks about Beat poetry and all the jobs she's had to take to keep her family together. Attlia the Stockbroker rants about being a punk poet—perhaps the original punk poet—and making his living as a poet for over two decades. Michele Tea dishes on touring with two vans chockfull of "Sister Spitters." Liz Belile gets us hot with her fearless, feminist porn. Tom Mayo talks about using poetry to remind medical and law students of their humanity. Dayvid Figler talks about being a poet and a judge. Beth Lisick talks about opening as a spoken word artist for Neil Young and how everyone kept asking, "Where is your guitar?" Quincy Troupe tells us how to put together a book of poems. Taylor Mali talks about touring and getting close to having a television show. Abraham Smith talks about getting paid to study poetry. Craig Arnold gives his take on what's good and bad about the poetry slam and some great tips on touring. John Tritica and Bruce Holsapple talk to Larry Goodel about, among other things, studying with Robert Creeley.

In the essay department, we have a wonderful piece by Logan Phillips and Suzy La Follette on thinking about the slam poem as just another poetry form. I give examples of how to write query letters for sponsorships and share some of my experiences coaching the Precision Poetry Drill Team. We have a section on insurance plans for writers. I talk to Bob Holman's mother about giving birth to a bard. I confess to being hit in the head with a rock by an angry poetry student. I reveal my secret identity as PoetMan and share some of my techniques for working with young children using poetry. I reveal how PoetMan is faster than a speeding simile, is able to leap tall metaphors with a single bound, and is more powerful than a speeding locomotive full of steaming hyperbole.

This series is meant to be interactive and lead to a third book, *Still Not Making a Living as a Poet? The Readers Respond*. Soft Skull and I would like to hear your stories about how you used these ideas. Did they work? Did you find funding for your poetry series? Did the CEO of the Corporation for Crushing the Spirit of America laugh at you and your poetry? Did wearing a giant P on your chest protect you from having a dull day job? What went right, what went wrong? Write to:

http://howtopoet.blogspot.com

and let us know. We will publish you on the blog site and collect the best of the responses in *The Readers Respond*, to be published in 2007. That means the deadline will be coming up soon, so get cracking!

Jabberwocky

by Lewis Carroll

'Twas brillig, and the slithy toves
Did gyre and gimble in the wabe:
All mimsy were the borogoves,
And the mome raths outgrabe.

"Beware the Jabberwock, my son!
The jaws that bite, the claws that catch!
Beware the Jubjub bird, and shun
The frumious Bandersnatch!"

He took his vorpal sword in hand:
Long time the manxome foe he sought—
So rested he by the Tumtum tree,
And stood awhile in thought.

And, as in uffish thought he stood,
The Jabberwock, with eyes of flame,
Came whiffling through the tulgey wood,
And burbled as it came!

One, two! One, two! And through and through
The vorpal blade went snicker-snack!
He left it dead, and with its head
He went galumphing back.

"And, has thou slain the Jabberwock?
Come to my arms, my beamish boy!
O frabjous day! Callooh! Callay!"
He chortled in his joy.

'Twas brillig, and the slithy toves
Did gyre and gimble in the wabe;
All mimsy were the borogoves,
And the mome raths outgrabe.

BUILDING THE AUDIENCE FOR POETRY

To have great poets, there must be great audiences too.
—Walt Whitman

I write for myself and strangers.
—Gertrude Stein

The people fancy they hate poetry, and they are all poets and mystics!
—Ralph Waldo Emerson

Poets are mysterious, but a poet when all is said is not much more mysterious than a banker.
—Allen Tate

My mouth blooms like a cut.
—Anne Sexton

Poetry is nobody's business except the poet's, and everybody else can fuck off.
—Philip Larkin

Put Down The Poetry Book and Back Away Slowly

I gave up on new poetry myself thirty years ago, when most of it began to read like coded messages passing between lonely aliens on a hostile world.

—Russell Baker

Poetry books don't sell. Poetry books don't sell, but how about books about poetry books not selling, will they sell? What about books about books about poetry books not selling, perhaps they will sell?[*] If you are holding this book and contemplating buying it, will you be sympathetic to the fact that poetry books don't sell? Will you buy it to help buck that trend? Or will knowing that poetry books don't sell make you put it back on the shelf and walk away?

How does poetry fare in the realm of phrases used, the currency of thought, and the impact on language? Where would movie reviewers be without Coleridge's idea of "suspension of disbelief?" Have you ever stumbled over Chaucer's "love is blind?" It's really "Child's play," once you get going—also Chaucer, also from *The Canterbury Tales*. Not knowing how much poetry affects the way we use language, we might say, "Ignorance is bliss," without knowing we owed a debt to Thomas Gray. Are you starting to feel Blake's "doors of perception" open up a little? Starting to feel like poetry might be a bit of an "albatross around your neck?"[†] We are back at Coleridge, who also was one of the first to make money from giving lectures, in his case on Shakespeare.

[*] I don't want to get all Gertrude Steinish on you, but she actually has sold quite a few poetry books, so perhaps what is needed is more repetition and very complex, convoluted grammar to help get people to buy poetry books by the bushel.

[†] Want to read more about poetry phrases in everyday speech? Check out *Brush Up Your Poetry* by Michael Macrone.

If poetry is so ingrained in the way we think and speak, why don't poetry books sell? All of the foregoing examples come from that golden period of poetry beginning with Chaucer and moving into the Romantic period, when the flowering of rhyming, rhythmic poetry was written—and rhyming, rhythmic poetry isn't written much anymore, is it? Whoa Nelly—what about hip-hop? What about the thousands and thousands of young men and women, boys and girls, all across the world who are working on their "flow?" Working on the next rhyme that shows us exactly what it's like to live their lives? I was in New Zealand last week and heard great Maori hip-hop, so if we count rap as poetry—just try to come up with a definition of poetry that would exclude rap—perhaps poetry books really do sell in the millions, and we are just slow to recognize that CDs and videos are also a form of book.

How about podcasts*, those lovely little blasts of spoken word audio popping up all over the internet now? They are perfect for poetry, and poets have been quick to adapt the technology. Ever notice how admen co-opt the latest visual presentation of text that arises in cutting edge poetry? Notice how commercials pick up the sound of rappers and spoken word performers?

Poetry is all around us, all the time: poetry in the way we think, the way we love—especially when it's fast love (remember Christopher Marlowe's "love at first sight?") Perhaps the strongest tie between those old classic poems and hip-hop is that those poets and rappers didn't get so caught up in saying something new that they forgot to say anything at all. Are you feeling me? Fo' shizzle?

I want to go out on a limb here and suggest that poetry books can sell, but we have to have a shift in cultural and societal thinking: we have to get people to believe that poetry can sell. Holy bat-guano, ¡Poetman!, we as poets have to believe poetry books can sell. We have to step outside the norm and find ways that poetry is of use to our communities, and when we do that, poetry will sell as rap sells, because hip-hop is community and rap documents that community.

* Check out http://performancepoetry.indiefeed.com

Am I suggesting that you start wearing baggy pants, drinking forties, and that you pull a drive-by on Jorie Graham? No, but one of the things rappers do that might be of use to poets is they tell stories that resonate with their hood. Do you have a hood? Are your poems written in such a way that they are understood? Good! Am I saying you have to rhyme? No, and I'm not saying you have to dumb down your work—just that identifying who you are writing for might help you reach those people.*

We as poets have to stop putting down hip-hop and understand that what is of use to a sixteen-year-old might not be the same thing that is of use to a forty-five-year-old and get over ourselves. Poets have to fire Emerson's "shot heard 'round the world." Wake up, poets! Stop thinking your work can't sell, and find ways that it *can* sell. Stop being so narrow minded in how you define "book." Stop looking to literary journals as your only outlet for your poems. So as Shakespeare kinda said, let's "strike while the iron is hot."

* It might help to adopt rappers' habit of taking on fancy names. Big Willy P-Speare, anyone?

The Precision Poetry Drill Team

I thought poems were songs for people with bad voices.

—Lorna Dee Cervantes

When I was hired to teach poetry slam at Desert Academy, an independent school in Santa Fe, I wanted to use the class as a laboratory for my group performance ideas. I wanted to bring the students up to a professional performance level and be able to include them in some of my poetry tours. The thing that clinched taking the job for me was when the head-of-school, Ray Griffen, said, "If you come up with cool ideas of where to take the students, the parents will pay for it." I have taught poetry under various poets-in-the-schools programs in seven states, and this is by far the most rewarding teaching experience I have had.

The class is an elective, so the students are self-selected and come into the class with an interest in, or, in some cases, a love of poetry. In my first year, the class consisted of seven students. Their level of interest was a great deal more appealing and easy to motivate than your usual poet-in-the-school class of twenty-five yawning, distracted, get-us-out-of-here kids.

I wanted the poetry slam class to have a unique name and identity. I had just seen the film *Drumline* and loved the energy of the high-stepping drum bands and thought "Precision Poetry Drill Team" might convey some of that intensity and energy. Here is the description blurb I use in publicity for the team:

> The Precision Poetry Drill Team performs multi-voiced classic poems such as Blake's "The Tyger," freestyle, hip-hop takes on Poe's "The Raven," a chilling version of Szymborska's "The Terrorist He's Watching," a jazzy version of "We Real Cool," by Brooks, and original spoken word. The ensemble draws inspiration from jump-rope rhymes, military chants, auctioneers, gospel call and response, and rap. It's synchronized swimming with words and modern Greek chorus and motor-mouthed youth spilling over with teenage angst. These kids are lettering in poetry! The Precision Poetry Drill Team is a rah-rah free zone.

As I write this piece on the PPDT, we have been hired by the Santa Fe Opera to put together a performance as part of the festival on the Spanish poet Federico Garcia Lorca. This caps off a wonderful first year that included traveling to New York to perform and take workshops at the Bowery Poetry Club and going to San Francisco to participate in the Youth National Poetry Slam. We were featured on NPR's *All Things Considered* in a broadcast that reached over two million people. Locally, we rewrote Gil Scott Heron's "The Revolution Will Not be Televised" as "The Television Will Not be Revolutionized" and performed in a Leave No Voter Behind event and were featured at the High Mayhem festival, an avant-garde music event with some of the nation's top jazz experimental improvisers. We also performed at the Zozobra Festival in Santa Fe in front of 20,000 people.

I became interested in group performances of spoken word when I took a class on experimental music with Norman Masonson at Indian Valley College in Northern California in 1979. We studied the music of John Cage and had Lou Harrison as a guest lecturer. We performed a piece Masonson had scored for multi-voice. In my senior project at Sonoma State University, in 1982, I included tape loops of poetry and the poems were choreographed for modern dance by Victoria Strobridge. When I met Marc Smith in 1989, in Chicago, he rekindled my interest in group poems with his talk about the work he had done with the Bob Shakespeare Band. In the early days of the National Poetry Slam, cities were encouraged to put together group pieces, and the San Francisco teams I was part of also included a few group pieces.

What follows in this chapter are two of the poems that the PPDT performs. I have scored or set them for multiple voices. The first, William Blake's "The Tyger," is an example of using the group to perform a repeated section of a poem as a chant, or it could also be thought of as functioning like a bass line underneath a main voice reciting the body of the poem. The second setting, Coleridge's "Kubla Khan," divides the poem among three or more voices and plays on the energy of having those voices double up on certain lines and of having the whole group recite other lines together.

A few thoughts on working with groups of poets reciting a poem. You want to have the poets articulate the words, paying attention to how they enunciate the consonants and making sure they are in unison. The dynamics of the poems are especially important. I worked for much of the year with the students on their ability to project and to speak the poems with resonance. We talked about supporting their breath with their diaphragms as singers do, and we used singing and acting warm-up techniques. We tried reciting the poems using different voice and accents to loosen the students up and expand their ideas of how poems can be recited. Because they love hip-hop, we often read the poems over rhythm tracks or "beats." I tried always to make the recitation of the poems fun, but at times the students were overwhelmed by how much we had to practice the poems. As we did more public performances, they started to understand the level at which they needed to know the poems to be able to perform for the public, and they grew less resistant to rehearsing. I also used the public performances as an opportunity to push them to work hard, and scheduling many performances helped develop and keep up their recitation skills.

Please let me know your experiences in working with students or adults with group poems, and don't hesitate to contact me at poetmex@aol.com if you have questions or want feedback on setting poems for groups.

THE TYGER—William Blake
(Scored by Gary Mex Glazner)

Group:
(*Loud*)
Tyger! Tyger! burning bright
In the forests of the night,
(*Soft*)
Tyger! Tyger! burning bright
In the forests of the night,

(*Soft*)
Tyger! Tyger! burning bright
In the forests of the night,
Tyger! Tyger! burning bright
In the forests of the night,

(*Soft*)
Tyger! Tyger! burning bright
In the forests of the night,
Tyger! Tyger! burning bright
In the forests of the night,

(*Loud*)
What the hammer? what the chain?
In what furnace was thy brain?
Tyger! Tyger! burning bright
In the forests of the night,

(*Very Soft*)
When the stars threw down their spears,
And watered heaven with their tears,
Did he smile his work to see?
Did he who made the Lamb make thee?

(*Crescendo to Very Loud*)
Tyger! Tyger! burning bright
In the forests of the night,
burning bright
burning bright
when thy heart began to beat,
burning bright
burning bright
What the hand dare sieze the fire?
burning bright
burning bright
In what furnace was thy brain?

(*Very Soft*)
When the stars threw down their spears,
And watered heaven with their tears,
Did he smile his work to see?
Did he who made the Lamb make thee?

(*Crescendo to Very Loud*)
Tyger! Tyger! burning bright
In the forests of the night,
Tyger! Tyger! burning bright.

Solo:
(*Loud*)
Tyger! Tyger! burning bright
In the forests of the night,

What immortal hand or eye
Could frame thy fearful symmetry?

In what distant deeps or skies
Burnt the fire of thine eyes?
On what wings dare he aspire?
What the hand dare sieze the fire?

And what shoulder, & what art.
Could twist the sinews of thy heart?
And when thy heart began to beat,
What dread hand? & what dread feet?

What the hammer? what the chain?
In what furnace was thy brain?
What the anvil? what dread grasp
Dare its deadly terrors clasp?

(*Very Soft*)
When the stars threw down their spears,
And watered heaven with their tears,
Did he smile his work to see?
Did he who made the Lamb make thee?

(*Crescendo to Very Loud*)
Tyger! Tyger! burning bright
In the forests of the night,
burning bright
burning bright
when thy heart began to beat,
burning bright
burning bright
What the hand dare sieze the fire?
burning bright
burning bright
In what furnace was thy brain?

(*Very Soft*)
When the stars threw down their spears,
And watered heaven with their tears,
Did he smile his work to see?
Did he who made the Lamb make thee?

(*Crescendo to Very Loud*)
Tyger! Tyger! burning bright
In the forests of the night,
Tyger! Tyger! burning bright.

KUBLA KHAN—Samuel Taylor Coleridge
(Scored by Gary Mex Glazner for three or more voices)

All:
In Xanadu did Kubla Khan

A:
A stately pleasure-dome decree:

B:
Where Alph, the sacred river, ran

C:
Through caverns measureless to man

All:
Down to a sunless sea.

A & B:	**C:**
Through wood and dale the sacred river ran,	In Xanadu
Then reached the caverns measureless to man,	In Xanadu
And sank in tumult to a lifeless ocean:	In Xanadu
And 'mid this tumult Kubla heard from far	In Xanadu

ALL:
Ancestral voices prophesying war!

C:
And all who heard should see them there,

ALL:
And all should cry, Beware! Beware!

B:
His flashing eyes, his floating hair!

A:
Weave a circle round him thrice,

C:
And close your eyes with holy dread,

A & B:
For he on honey-dew hath fed,

ALL:
And drunk the milk of Paradise.

It's a Bird . . . It's a Plane . . . It's ¡PoetMan! to the Rescue

American poetry now belongs to a subculture. No longer part of the mainstream of artistic and intellectual life, it has become the specialized occupation of a relatively small and isolated group.

—Dana Gioia, from *Can Poetry Matter?*

In working with Tom Leech, the printer at the press at the Palace of the Governors museum in Santa Fe, I found out about a grant that the museum had received from the Institute of Library Services. The grant covered programing around the museum's show on the history of printing in New Mexico, "Lasting Impressions: The Private Presses of New Mexico." Cheryl Mitchell was overseeing the programing and was looking for children's programing that the museum could use as outreach. I started thinking about how to use poetry in a fun way to reach kids and came up with ¡PoetMan!, the idea being a superhero poet who would recite poems, play word games, and talk about simple writing skills with young children in the twelve-and-under category. I also wanted to make the program hip enough for the parents.

What I want to do in this chapter is to show the package that I brought in to Mitchell. My goal was to provide her with a comprehensive idea so that she could see all the perimeters of the project at once and not have to wonder what it would look like, how it would work, or how it could be implemented. I have found that in making presentations, if you can cover all the elements of a project, you are more likely to get a "yes."

I began with the task of developing a catch-phrase that would convey the spirit of the project. In this case, I was looking for a playful way to introduce simple writing concepts to kids. The younger ones would not grasp the grammatical terms, but the older ones would be able to, and, with any luck, the parents would get a laugh. What I came up with was:

faster than a speeding simile,
able to leap tall metaphors with a single bound,
more powerful than a steaming locomotive full of hyperbole,
It's . . . ¡POETMAN!

I used this as the basis to draft a sample press release, create a simple threefold brochure, design a one-sheet flyer, and record a sample Public Service Announcement (PSA). I knew that Mitchell was interested in reaching rural libraries, so I drew up a list of libraries I could potentially take the project to. When I walked into the meeting she was immediately able to grasp the humor and depth of the program. Most radio stations have some policy whereby they play a certain number of PSAs, and these are a great way to get free publicity. They normally have to be sponsored by a non-profit, and in this case the museum was the sponsor. The PSA really brought home how dynamic the project was and gave Mitchell a great way of introducing it to the other museum staff. She committed to five presentations and gave me the go-ahead to start contacting the libraries to book an event with them.

As we go to press, I have completed all the readings. The audiences ranged in size from ten to over one hundred. The kids were fun to work with and came up with some great metaphors including, "Soccer balls are like floating cows," and "Vigas [the wooden beams in adobe houses] are like long wooden giraffe necks." Some of the kids read their own poems. There was a delightful one entitled, "Monkey Love." One girl made up a poem on the spot, asking for words from the audience to compose her poem. After she had gotten about two minutes into a fantastic poem about cheese, dogs, dragons and wagons, she said, "I'm getting a little nervous, could I take some more words from the audience?" "Of course." Then she added more animals to the story and finished with a big, "The End!" A very shy five-year-old repeated the lines to a seventeenth century Japanese haiku after me, softly and with great feeling.

We are waiting to see if, in the fall, more funding will become available to continue the program, and I am approaching a potential sponsor. What follows is the press release and a brochure, which may help give you ideas about how to set up a poetry project. To hear the PSA, surf over to: http://howtopoet.blogspot.com.

SAMPLE PRESS RELEASE

March 1st, 2005

Contact:

New Mexico Department of Cultural Affairs

228 East Palace Avenue

Santa Fe, New Mexico 87501

phone: (505) 384-9655

¡POETMAN! performs at the Estancia Public Library

On Saturday May 7th, at 10 am, poet Gary Mex Glazner brings ¡POETMAN! to life for children of all ages at the Estancia Public Library (10th and Highland in Estancia). The program is free and aimed at families coming together, playing word games and having fun while hearing and learning about great poems. Call (505) 384-9655 for information.

"Tell us more about ¡POETMAN! super powers!" Good question, young knowledge seeker. ¡POETMAN! is able to leap tall metaphors with a single bound. He is faster than a speeding simile, more powerful than a steaming locomotive full of hyperbole. Want to know more? He created the first known rhyme with orange. ¡POETMAN! puts the giggle in wiggle-worms and is the world's foremost authority on dog poems. And last but not least, he vanquishes boredom and the blah, blah, blahs.

"What about ¡POETMAN!'s alter ego, this Glazner character?" Again with the good question, young knowledge seeker. Gary Mex Glazner makes his living as a poet. He has worked with everyone from young kids in YMCA after-school programs to Alzheimer's patients. As poet-in-residence at a hotel, they put his poems on the guests' pillows and gave away over 40,000 poems. NO! Not 40,000 different poems! Glazner is the coach of the Precision Poetry Drill Team at Desert Academy in Santa Fe. His work has appeared on NBC's *Today* show and NPR's *Weekend Edition* as well as under-water on the Bay Area Rapid Transit system.

The ¡POETMAN! program is sponsored by the New Mexico Department of Cultural Affairs and the Palace of the Governors Museum. Cheryl Mitchell, Director of Grants for the Palace of the Governors Museum, says, "We were looking for something fun and unique to do for families and kids, something that had an educational component but wouldn't feel stuffy." ¡POETMAN! is on a mission to bring poetry to the kids of New Mexico and to all the rural libraries around the state.

¡Poet Man!

Pun for the Whole Family

Poetry for Kids
Hear a Rap version of "The Raven."
Rhyme along with "The Tyger."
You and your family will write poems.
Hear amazing stories.
Have fun with word games.
Come One, Come All,
Come Children of all Ages!
Come help put an end
to the tragedy of blank pages.

¡Poet Man! perfoming at the library in Las Vegas, New Mexico

Contact info:
Gary Mex Glazner
12 Highview Lane
Santa Fe, NM 87508
505-438-6607
poetmex@aol.com

What people are saying about ¡Poet Man!:

"In all the world of poetry, there is only one Gary Glazner, Minister of Fun of the National Poetry Slam."
—Bob Holman

"Sharp tongue and razor wit . . . a gestural genius."
—Dave Eggers on Gary Mex Glazner

"It's not just what you say it's how you say it,"
—*Newsweek* on Glazner's "Busload of Poets Tour."

¡Poet Man! Fans

Glazner's work has been featured on:

NBC's *Today* show,

NPR's *All Things Considered* and *Weekend Edition*,

and underwater on the Bay Area Rapid Transit System.

He has been published by

Haper Collins, W.W. Norton, and Salon.com.

Glazner is Poet-in-Residence for the 400-year old Palace of the Govenors Museum in Santa Fe.

About ¡Poet Man!

Gary Mex Glazner makes his living as a poet. He is the author of *Ears on Fire: Snapshot Essays in a World of Poets*, published by La Alameda Press. The book chronicles a year abroad in Asia and Europe meeting poets, working on translations and writing poems. His book *How to Make a Living as a Poet*, published by Soft Skull Press in March 2005, features essays on creative poetry programming and interviews with leading poets.

Glazner is the director of the Alzheimer's Poetry Project. The APP is a simple idea: read classic poems to the patients they might have learned as students. Even in the late stages of the disease, this helps to spark memories, and they often can say words and lines along with the poems.

Glazner is the coach of the Precision Poetry Drill Team at Desert Academy in Santa Fe. Glazner is the editor of the "Word Art: Poetry Broadside Series" at the Palace of the Governors Museum. This summer, Glazner will lecture for the Santa Fe Opera on the Spanish poet Federico Garcia Lorca.

Families have fun with ¡Poet Man!

WHO IS . . .

- Able to leap tall metaphors in a single bound?
- Faster than a speeding simile?
- More powerful than a steaming locomotive full of hyperbole?
- Who created the first known rhyme with orange?
- Who puts the giggle in wiggle worms?
- Who is the world's foremost authority on dog poems?
- Who is the utmost vanquishier of boredom and the blah, blah, blahs?

POET MAN THAT'S WHO!

Kids doing the ¡Poet Man! dance.

¡Poet Man! presents a fun program for the whole family. You will hear classic poems recited in an upbeat, high-energy fashion. Glazner brings 25 years of experience of reading and writing poetry to the program. He has worked with everyone from graduate students at universities to Alzheimer's patients to youngsters in YMCA after school programs.

You will write your own poems and play enjoyable word games. You and your children will find yourselves learning about poetry, while laughing and having a great time.

This program is about love of language, about playing with words, about hearing some of the world's most loved poems, about the joy of learning, about coming together as a family and a community to celebrate poetry and yourselves.

Sponsorship Query Letters

There's no money in poetry, but then there's no poetry in money, either.

—Robert Graves

The question I get the most in regard to funding for poetry projects is how to approach a sponsor. I have included two query letters here as examples of how I write to sponsors. Here are a few reasons I think trying for sponsorship, whether national or local, can be of great use in funding poetry projects. First, in general there is less competition in trying for a sponsorship than in trying for a grant. You might be one of hundreds of groups vying to receive a grant, whereas, even when trying for a national sponsor, you will be competing against a smaller number of groups. With a sponsor, you will get your response in a shorter time period than with a foundation or a city, state, or federal granting agency, who believe that if they respond to requests for proposals within six months, they are working fast. With sponsorships, especially on the local level, you can often meet the decision-maker and talk with that person about your ideas. Sponsorships often allow for a greater degree of input from sponsors: they can tell you what they need and work with you to build your event, program or tour.

The two letters that follow, one written to Jet Blue Airline and the other written to New Mexico Piñon Coffee, are real letters. In the case of Jet Blue, the letter was not successful, and I never heard back from them. In the case of New Mexico Piñon Coffee, I did not hear from them for months, generally a bad sign, and gave up hope. As I was getting ready for the tour I had asked them to sponsor, I resolved to call them. I got through to the owner and he said he "loved the idea" but was a new owner and "couldn't commit right now." I was shocked: after such a long silence, the plan had seemed hopeless. We had a great discussion and agreed to meet to see if there might be some way of working together now, with the idea of a possible sponsorship in the future. He offered to give me samples of coffee, which were a great hit at the bookstores and made great thank you gifts to tour hosts. I am looking forward to developing the sponsorship. In case you don't know, New Mexico has many piñon pine trees, the source of the flavorful piñon nut, and the coffee is a great conversation starter for a poet touring from New Mexico.

Feel free to use these letters as templates and inspiration for your own sponsorship requests. Don't forget we are looking for readers' responses and would love to know how this book and *How to Make a Living as a Poet* are used. Write to

http://howtopoet.blogspot.com/

and let us know what happened. Did you get the sponsorship? Did they laugh at you? Call you a crazy poet? Did you marry the boss's daughter? End up launching a hostile pirate poet take-over? We here at the Poem Factory want to know.

From: Gary Glazner

Dear Jet Blue:

Goodwill is often called "Blue Sky." I am writing to you with a unique opportunity to sponsor the "Blue Skies Poetry Tour." April is National Poetry Month, and this April my new book, *How to Make a Living as a Poet*, will be published. In order to help promote the book, I will be performing poetry around the country. This is where you and I can work together in getting publicity and generating goodwill for your airline.

Some of the companies I have helped to market are:

Pontiac
The Santa Fe Opera
Inn on the Alameda
Grand Marnier
Alzheimer's Poetry Project

Please consider allowing me to book four roundtrip flights on your airline during the month of April in exchange for Jet Blue being named the official tour sponsor. This twist on the idea of Poet-in-Residence becomes Poet-in-the-Sky and the core of our media campaign. At the start of each flight, I will offer to write a personal poem for any of the passengers and read a short poem on flying.

Does combining poetry with business really work? Good question! With the tour for Grand Marnier, we reached over ten million people, generating coverage in *Newsweek* and the *New York Times*. With Inn on the Alameda, we put poems on the hotel guests' pillows and gave out over 40,000 poems, got a front page story in the *Albuquerque Journal* and over thirty other stories written in travel magazines and newspapers. With the Santa Fe Opera, I am doing outreach and lecturing on the Spanish poet Federico Garcia Lorca, giving their upcoming presentation added value for opera clubs and fans. With Pontiac, I drove around the country in a new "Vibe" performing with a jazz trio, helping to brand the car as cool and hip. My Alzheimer's Poetry Project has been covered on NBC's *Today* and NPR's *Weekend Edition*, reaching over 9.5 million people and leading to major funding for the project.

Launching a "Poet-in-the-Sky" will be an irresistible human interest story, with special appeal to travel writers, business writers, radio commentators, and morning television shows. Let's work together this April to get some feel-good publicity for your airline. I will be happy to send info about my new book, *How to Make a Living as a Poet*. Thank you for your consideration.

All the best,
Gary Glazner

Poet-in-Residence and Coach of the Precision Poetry Drill Team • Desert Academy
505-438-6607 • poetmex@aol.com • 12 Highview Lane, Santa Fe, NM 87508

From: Gary Glazner

Dear Mr. Wolf:

Ever since the 1950s when Jack Kerouac hit the road, people have associated coffee with poetry. Today, most bookstores feature cafés and encourage people to linger over good coffee with a good book. I am writing to you with a unique opportunity to sponsor the "Piñon Coffee Poetry Tour." In March, my new book *How to Make a Living as a Poet* will be published. In order to help promote the book, I will be performing poetry around the country. This is where you and I can work together in getting publicity and generating goodwill for your company. Some of the companies I have helped to market are: Pontiac, The Santa Fe Opera, Inn on the Alameda, Grand Marnier, and the Alzheimer's Poetry Project. What you will get for your sponsorship:

- •Tastings of your coffee at the "How to Drink Coffee like a Poet" workshops.
- •A mailing to 100 leading bookstores with cafés, with a sampler of your coffee and book promo.
- •Promotional materials to the workshop participants explaining how to order your coffee online.
- •Working with the bookstores to add your coffee to their menus.
- •As sponsor of the tour, you will be featured in all press releases and mentioned in all media appearances, email blasts, and mailings.

Does combining poetry with business really work? Good question! With the tour for Grand Marnier, we reached over ten million people, generating coverage in *Newsweek* and the *New York Times*. With Inn on the Alameda, we put poems on the hotel guests' pillows and gave out over 40,000 poems, got a front page story in the *Albuquerque Journal* and over thirty other stories written in travel magazines and newspapers. With the Santa Fe Opera, I am doing outreach and lecturing on the Spanish poet Federico Garcia Lorca, giving their upcoming presentation added value for opera clubs and fans. With Pontiac, I drove around the country in a new "Vibe" performing with a jazz trio, helping to brand the car as cool and hip. My Alzheimer's Poetry Project has been covered on NBC's *Today* show and NPR's *Weekend Edition*, reaching over 9.5 million people.

Brewing up this "Piñon Coffee Poetry Tour" will be an irresistible human interest story, with special appeal to food writers, business writers, radio commentators, and morning television shows. Let's work together this March to get some feel-good publicity for your coffee. I have enclosed info about myself and my new book, *How to Make a Living as a Poet*. I am not talking about an arm and leg here—poets work cheap! Thank you for your consideration.

All the best,
Gary Glazner

Poet-in-Residence and Coach of the Precision Poetry Drill Team • Desert Academy
505-438-6607 • poetmex@aol.com • 12 Highview Lane, Santa Fe, NM 87508

INTERVIEWS

The poet prone to exaggeration sees clearly under torture.
—René Char

Marc Smith: Slam Papi

Marc Smith is the creator of the Poetry Slam. As stated in the PBS television series *The United States of Poetry*, a strand of new poetry began at Chicago's Green Mill Tavern in 1987 when Marc Smith found a home for the Poetry Slam. Since then, performance poetry has spread around the world, including more than 150 American cities that host their own slam performances. Each year, teams from these cities compete in the National Poetry Slam. The slam has also taken root internationally. He is the past president of Poetry Slam Incorporated, the non-profit that administers the National Poetry Slam. Smith has performed at the Smithsonian Institute, the Kennedy Center, the Art Institute of Chicago, and the Chicago Museum of Contemporary Art. Smith's poetry has been featured in his book *Crowd Pleaser* and the anthologies *Aloud! Voices from the Nuyorican Poets Café*, which won the 1994 American Book Award, and *The United States of Poetry*, a publication that accompanied the PBS television series. Smith was featured on the television show *60 Minutes* and in the film *Slam Nation: The Sport of Spoken Word*. Smith is the editor of *The Complete Idiot's Guide to Poetry*. He has performed in over 1000 shows at the Green Mill.

Poetry Investigator: You are working on a project with the City of Chicago. Could you tell us about that?

Lois Weisberg was important to us in the poetry slam because she gave me the money to fly out for your thing in San Francisco in 1990*. So I have always had a great relationship with her and she is still the Commissioner of Cultural Affairs in Chicago and she's done lots of great things for the city of Chicago. I happened to be at a function that she was at and we got to talking and she mentioned she had this food and the arts festival for the city of Chicago. I said, "I'd like to do something for the festival." We gave her a bunch of different ideas, from having poets as waiters in restaurants serving poems off a menu to write-offs in conjunction with cook-offs, a bunch of goofy ideas. The ideas that stuck were doing performance poetry with a food theme at different events around the city and a poetry hot dog cart.

* The first national poetry slam, held at Fort Mason with Chicago, New York, and San Francisco participating.

PI: How are you going to run the poetry hot dog cart?

The poetry hot dog cart will include the "Stirring Things Up, Eat Your Words Ensemble," that is a take-off on the festival name of "Stirring Things Up." We have a custom-made hot dog cart with a poetry menu and portable P.A. loudspeaker. We will push this cart through Millennium Park, in Chicago. I will be the barker and jump out to get the crowd's attention. The ensemble will do a piece, we will offer custom-made poems, like love links with gloom. They will be able to choose an entrée and two relishes. Three poets from the ensemble will sit in lawn chairs and write poems on the spot, giving their take on love links with gloom or whatever the people choose.

We will also offer a "Today's Special" menu so we don't have to write everything from scratch. We will mix in ensemble pieces and then move to another location in the park and repeat the effort. We will also have someone to render the poem on paper, so the participants can take home a souvenir.

PI: Tell us about the Pizza Poetry aspect of the project.

I got a phone call from my city contact Melissa Turner saying that Lou Malnati's Pizza wanted to sponsor something in the food festival. She said, "We need a poem right away for a press conference to announce the opening of the festival." They wanted the poem to be about pizza and the city, and Lou Malnati's Pizza was commissioning the poem. I thought, "Pizza and the city, oh, boy." I got lucky in researching the poem and discovered that Lou Malnati was the guy that invented deep-dish pizza. There was enough information on the website to get me clicking. I knocked it out pretty quick, the poem is a kind of Chicago booster poem. The city loved it and it ended up on an advertisement that gets sent out with all the Lou Malnati's Pizzas, so it is going out on one hundred thousand boxes of pizza this summer.

PI: Here are the opening stanzas of "Deep Dish Chicago."

Chicago. The deep dish city of deep dish people
Everybody's juices bubblin' and sizzlin' and spittin' inside:

And a crust that can be thick, when it needs to be thick
When it gets poked and fingered and belittled
And cast off as just another second-city helping,
a flatlander's windy cheese.

But we know better, we who live this city and love its people,
Know that it's second to none when it comes to a slice
Of authenticity, genuine no BS . . . "Skip the pretension, pal."

PI: That is a great connection between Chicago being the birth place of deep dish pizza and the birth-place of the poetry slam.

That is the theme I used, playing on my second city insecurities. How Chicago starts things and other cities try to pretend that they started them. That is kind of tongue-in-cheek, but Chicago is a great breeding ground for ideas and new things. Where sometimes Chicago falls flat is in supporting its artists after they have gained a little success, they don't take care of them as well as they should. Another thing about Chicago is people have to be genuine. If you live in Chicago you can't strut your stuff around, people say, "Who are you?" It's a Midwestern thing.

PI: I just saw a documentary on Howling Wolf and it showed how electric blues really took hold in Chicago, with Chess Records and all the great blues musicians, Muddy Waters, Little Walter and many others coming to Chicago and of course that leading to rock-n-roll.

People do recognize blues coming up the river to Chicago, which has its own style. That is like the slam too, every place the slam has been exported to gives it its own style, its own flavor, while retaining something of the Chicago style.

PI: Let's talk about the spread of the poetry slam. You have just been in Europe for six weeks touring and reading at festivals.

This was my sixth time going to Germany and my first time of going to France and Denmark. The interesting thing is even though there are local differences, they have the same struggles, the same internal conflicts, the same personalities show up, they have the same success of bringing all kinds of different people together into an audience for poetry and the same widening of the audience for poetry. Also expanding the boundaries of what is accepted as poetry. The European slams also connect people just like in the States who would never be connected. You have a real mix of cultures, ethnic backgrounds, and classes that come together in the poetry slam. The similarities far outweigh the differences that come up in the local slams.

What I really got a feeling for in this last trip is how huge the poetry slam has grown. People say, "It's bigger than the Beats." Well, it is much bigger than the Beats. It will go down—I might be full of shit saying this, with my narrow subjective viewpoint—but I think the poetry slam will go down as the biggest social literary movement of our times. There are so many people involved. In France I was at grade schools where poetry slam is being taught, being used as a teaching tool for poetry. With tenth graders slamming. In Germany there are hundreds of poetry slams.

PI: How many years have they been holding National Poetry Slams in Germany?

They will be celebrating their tenth anniversary next year, as the Green Mill is celebrating twenty years of poetry slams.

PI: What was it like working with the French kids? Do you speak French?

I had a translator with me. I never do this but when I went into the schools, I was a judge at their poetry slams. I had a translator whispering into my ear as they read the poems. I judged more on their presentation and performance. The kids that were at the French National Poetry Slam were phenomenal. A school that was from a poor neighborhood outside of Paris really nailed it—there were a couple of them that could perform with adults and hold their own and they were only ten or twelve years old.

There are so many people involved around the world, I don't know of any other thing that is not propelled by commercial interests that is so huge.

PI: What were the festivals like where you performed?

The festival in Germany was organized by Norah Gomringer, the daughter of the guy who invented concrete poetry. She battles being the daughter of a famous poet. She is only twenty-three years old and is a great organizer and poet. She is in the university system and doing her dissertation on poetry slam. The French National Poetry Slam had sixteen teams, five from Paris and the rest from around France. There was a spoken word tent at a rock festival in Denmark, with Snoop Doggy Dog and Black Sabbath music bleeding into the tent. So that was tough duty, but the poetry slam worked well. The tent ran from noon until ten p.m., with some of Denmark's best-known writers—it wasn't just the outsiders. I ran the slam with Fredrick Anderson. I was scared: it was the third day of a rock festival and everyone was drunk, but people stayed and listened the whole time.

PI: Here you are twenty years after inventing the poetry slam. Talk about how it feels to see the tremendous growth.

For years now I have had a humble and also neutral feeling about the poetry slam. I have never taken too much of this seriously. The last few years I have seen myself as a servant to the poetry slam. I have had so much conflict and disappointment, with how people have behaved, the uglier side of human behavior, what it has turned into for me, is I just do my job. I go to Europe so that they can see the principles that I believe in can get heard. When I wasn't active in going around to the various slams, a lot of people were trying to say it's "this." The most corrupting is the commercial aspect. Like other art forms get corrupted by a commercially motivated direction. I don't think that is what the poetry slam is about: there are too many poetry slam organizers who produce shows, who get very little in return. It is not the performance poet who goes from show to show that makes this movment happen. What makes this movement happen are the local orgainzers.

I like the respect I get in Europe. It's great to perform at these large events. I performed in front of a couple of thousand people at the German National Poetry Slam. I love to perform, but I am smart enough to know while I am in Europe it is not about me, it's about the poetry slam as a movement, about all those local organizers who make the shows happen.

PI: How do you make your living as a poet?

Well, the thing that enabled me to be free in the struggling times, when I was totally broke, was creating poetry shows. For a long time, and I still do, I looked at myself as a showman, that is my art. I enjoyed that much more than writing poems and performing poems. I was always a component of the show but the show itself was the greater art.

The shows I did for the summer solstice at the Museum of Contemporary Arts had some slam competition element. They always had audience interaction. I have done themes, like the "Mardi Gras, Fat Tuesday, Seven Deadly Sins Show." The motif was an ensemble group for each of the seven deadly sins. Each ensemble group was five to ten people. They created an ensemble piece that was like a float in the Mardi Gras parade, only with poetry.

The early shows were tremendous. People went so many different places. I got the reputation as a guy who created shows that were unique. You're not going to see anything like this. For instance we had a "Biker Day" at the Field Museum. Which was just nuts. There were Harleys in the museum. We asked about having the poets make their entrances on the motorcycles, but because of the carbon monoxide they wouldn't allow that to happen. But the bikers did make an entrance, all you needed was the motorcycles.

I had pretended that because they were bikers I didn't know whether they were going to show up or not. They came in from the stairways, you had Boy Scouts running around and yelling, "Here come the bikers." They had those air horns, "Honk! Honk!" Everybody knew the biker poets had arrived.

That is the kind of show that I became known for. If people sat down and said, "We want to do something different"—they would call me up. Because they were big institutions—when I look back on it they got a great fucking deal. If I did something like that now I would charge ten times more money. But it did sustain me.

PI: You have the Green Mill as a regular income.

The Green Mill is my regular gig. In the early years I was starving. One year I had to sell my jazz records to pay the rent. One year I had a voice-over job, but because I don't believe in that stuff, I would turn down commercial work. I had one company call me up—October was always was the worst month, because my car insurance came due, and health insurance came due and a couple of other bills were due. October came and I was broke. One year somebody from the East Coast called that had been to the Green Mill show and asked if I wanted to do a radio commercial. I took it. Fifteen minutes of work and I ended up making three thousand dollars from it after the royalties and everything.

Before Sandy and I got divorced she had an income so I didn't feel completely destitute. I had my savings, which became hers. After we got divorced, I was completely on my own and I wasn't doing the home repair work anymore. When we separated I was living on bowls of rice.

Even when I moved back to the Berwyn house and I had to assume all those bills, there were times when I didn't have anything. It didn't bother me. In the AA program you lose your fear of not having financial security. Let the universe take care of it, and I truly live that way. There was no money.

I tried one time to be like a local musician—I had a gig every day of the week. For twenty-five dollars, fifty dollars. It was the worst way to do it. No wonder some of these musicians get stuck, you can't live that way. You go from gig to gig with no time to create. What do you end up with at the end of the week? Three hundred dollars. So the big shows would get me a chunk of money here and there. I have humble desires so I don't need much.

PI: Now you work with your band and take your show into schools.

Getting Joan Sherman as my agent helped. She just happened to be the right person. Joan is from the hippie days. She worked with folk musicians and only took on clients she believed in. We don't have a contract. It hasn't been a lot of work, but for me it was just enough work so it made my nut. It was the big show that I had developed in Chicago—four poets, a band, and myself.

I designed that show to get my philosophy of what the slam was about out. Because a lot of what the slam is about has been lost, in the feeling that it is just about one person winning at the National Slam. It's about all the people in the room. That is what's important. To make another star is not important. That's what everybody does.

But if you bring different people together in a room, together they really do get to know each other and form a community. No bullshit, that is what happens in Chicago. From the beginning that was the important point to me. I was always that kind of a person.

Joan appreciated that. So that's the show we take around. We've done some big shows, the Kennedy Center. But it is mostly like Ida, Ohio or the Lebanon Opera house. It's the small communities. What I communicate is community. I connect with them and my troop connects with them. Fortunately it's a concert hall series and it's a chunk of change. The last few years I have not worried about money.

PI: How about sales of your book *Crowd Pleaser*?

I sold them all and he's got the second edition. I gave many away but the publisher got his money back. I think he printed two thousand. I'm sure I gave away three or four hundred books. Some I sold them for five dollars, below cost. But I made sure he got his money back.

Jeff thought this was going to be the book that went around the world. I don't think that anyone has figured out how to translate what slam poets do on the page.

The stories in the book are okay. I don't think anybody has been able to figure out how to transcribe the rhythms that slam poets have, how to put those rhythms on the page. When we put the book together I wanted it to be more of a souvenir than "the" book. I have never thought about doing another one. I can see that as you and other people tour it's a good way to make your money. I should certainly have a CD of the band.*

PI: What tips do you have for working with a band, on making the poet part of the ensemble?

That was a real conscious effort on the guitarist Mike Smith's and my part from the very beginning. From the very beginning we said we don't want the music to be background for the poetry. We did not want the poetry to be secondary to the music, the old Beat poet thing with the music being secondary to the poem. If it was just some rhythm going behind it, some base line, so what?

Both Mike and I worked to integrate the music and the words. When they come together it creates a new thing. Rather than creating an A, B form structure the pieces are structured on episodes. More like A, B, C, D, E, and F. We didn't want to be just rock or just jazz. Each poem should be its own form. Each idea has to be expressed in its own unique way. As we worked on it—because I'm such a bad musician I can never find the one—we had to create the loops that I could come in on. So if I didn't come in right on the one, it didn't matter. I'm much better now. There is a real precision on when the words come in and out.

When we create the pieces it's trial and error. I will throw out an idea of what I think the texture of the sound should be. Sometimes I can give them a rhythm but it is very difficult for me because I don't know the musical terms.

* Check out Slampapi.com. Smith completed the CD and might still have copies.

PI: Talk about working with classic poems. You perform a lot of poems by Sandburg and Wallace Stevens.

I started doing that because once again the poets inspired me. Everybody was always doing their own work and inferior work. With all this great poetry I became self-conscious about putting up another poem of mine that wasn't very good. Why not do other people's poems? The audience loved it. The audience is very moved when you do the great works.

PI: Let's take Sandburg's poem "Skyscraper." How do you approach that as you start to develop it as a performance piece for yourself?

The first step in the process is the selection.

PI: So you find something that resonates with you?

Right, it has to be a poem that moves me. Which is hard because in all the great collections you got—which is something poets never talk about—say we have a book of poems like this [*picks up large anthology off shelf*]. Poets that read know that out of this book of the great poets, there is gonna be 10 percent of them that are going to be good.

Something about poets, at least this is my opinion, they get success and all of a sudden they have to keep putting it out. They keep putting it out and putting it out and nobody ever says, "That's shit." And it is. A lot of stuff is just shit. So that's the first process. You go though and you try to find the work that is really good, something that connects with you in some way.

One thing you look for is archaic language in the poem that no one is going to get. What will the old metered verse sound like on the stage? Will it sound funny now? Metered verse has become such a cliché. Can I rewrite this to make it work? From the beginning I have been very cavalier about rewriting poems, I don't care. I think of it the way people think about folk music. No one cares that great folk songs have been rewritten over the ages and I look at poetry that same way.

Once I find something that I want to do, the first process is to memorize it. I have a lot of stuff I memorize that I never do. In the memorization process, then, I start to find the stuff that is just going to be a clunker on the stage. I either rewrite it or cut it down, retool it for my own purpose.

Then it becomes exactly the same process as me working on my own poems. Only it's a little more difficult to get it down, because it's not in your subconscious like your own work is.

All the poems I do on stage have been developed in stage time, which is really the only way to get there. I could see it from you last night reading at the Green Mill. You've got your act down and the stage time develops it, it comes alive.

I think that I'm very lucky in that I have a style that is very relaxed and very genuine. Much different than the kind of dazzle slam poets that are artificial. It's very interesting, but I can see in maybe seven years it will be just as artificial as all the other styles. Hopefully I don't have that and I am more genuine in my presentation. Maybe because I try to live the life that I write about. But I really believe what I am writing and what I say onstage. I don't think that's true for a lot of poets.

PI: Give us a description of the early days of the slam. Was the energy different from now? How has it changed?

Everything really started in at the Get Me High Lounge. Before I started doing the readings there was no audience for poetry in Chicago. Even if Ginsberg came to town, a hundred people would show up. The local luminaries would have their wife and five of their students.

The open mics were at the most thirty people. Every person was there to read their poem and leave. That's how it was. Read your poem and leave. You can still go to towns and find these god-awful, self-indulgent, terrible poets at open mics.

That immediately started to change when we started doing the poetry readings at the Get Me High. If the poets were boring in the least, I would get them off the stage quick. That's when the three-minute time limit came in. Previous to that there was no time limit for poets—people would go on for fifteen minutes in the open mic. That's where we started to introduce the audience reaction, my smart-aleck remarks after the poems, anything to keep people's attention, to build an audience.

The first half of 1985, I tried to do the old style of poetry reading and it turned into the same old shit. The poets complaining. That's when I got a distaste for the behavior of poets. I quit doing it at the Get Me High for a few months. People told me they wanted me back.

I came back at the beginning of 1986. A whole new regime. You're gonna pay first of all. Put fifty cents up on the bar. Just slap your fifty cents up on the bar, and I came around and collected your fifty cents. I also had a deal with Butchie the owner to get a cut off the drinks, and people drank a lot.

PI: Wasn't that when Ron Gillette would come in costumes? You expanded the normal reading by adding characters and sometimes people wouldn't even know it was him?

Right, Ron at that time was moving to Milwaukee, but he did do some of those early shows. That's when I became ruthless with the featured poets. Ten seconds of boredom, one person yawning and you were off the stage. They hated me.

At the same time Ron and I were really working it with costumes and characters. We learned what we did by trial and error. At the beginning of 1986 was when I started to collect people for the Chicago Poetry Ensemble. Which was Ron, Rob Van Tyle, John Shihan, Karen Nictripe, Mike Barret.

The focus then became completely on the audience, to serve the audience. You're here to communicate to the audience. This show is for the audience, it is not for you. You're just a participant. That made all the difference. Under my dictatorship they had to do what I told them to do. God bless them and how they put up with me. Of course, we just got roaring drunk at every rehearsal. It was fun at the end.

PI: Describe something you would do as the Chicago Poetry Ensemble.

Our great series was based on the Whitechapel Club, which was a bohemian, literary arts club. The club was in Piper's Ally in Chicago, where all the news guys would go, George Aid, Finley Peter Dunne, Wallace Rice, and Opie Read among others.

The Whitechapel Club's claim to fame—this was at the end of the nineteenth century—is that they would write news stories before they happened. Their greatest news story before it happened was that they cremated a man on Indian Dunes beach.

It was re-enactment of Shelley's funeral pyre. And the story was run before the guy even killed himself. We did a series of, I think, four or five episodes as the Whitechapel Club.

By this time we had moved to the Green Mill. I was Dr. Spray, the deranged doctor who worked out of the mental hospital. Mike Barrett and I were walking along the bar, like we were walking to the club. Dr. Spray would peel mozzarella cheese off of a skull like he's eating the flesh off the skull. Everybody wrote or selected poems, Shelley poems. It was a verse play in episodes. It was quite successful. People loved it. That was our greatest artistic accomplishment. Our worst was the "Send in the Clowns." We did this Christmas thing. The last episode we did a chorus of "Send in the Clowns." It was so bad we stopped after that one. At the Green Mill, for the first eighteen weeks, we created a new show every week, unbelievable. No wonder we had some dogs in it.

PI: Here is Smith's Slam Philosophy, reprinted from his website:

> The purpose of poetry (and indeed all art) is not to glorify the poet but rather to celebrate the community to which the poet belongs. (This idea is paraphrased from the works of Wendell Berry).
>
> The show and the show's effect upon the audience are more important than any one individual's contribution to it.
>
> The points are not the point, the point is poetry. (Alan Wolfe)
>
> The performance of poetry is an art—just as much an art as the art of writing it.

NO audience should be thought of as obligated to listen to the poet. It is the poet's obligation to communicate effectively, artfully, honestly and professionally so as to compel the audience to listen.

The Slam should be open to all people and all forms of poetry.

With respect to its own affairs, each Slam should be free from attachment to any outside organization and responsible to no authority other than its own community of poets and audience.

NO group, individual, or outside organization should be allowed to exploit the Slam Family. We must all remember that we are each tied in some way to someone else's efforts. Our individual achievements are only extensions of some previous accomplishment. Success for one should translate into success for all.

The National Slam began as a gift from one city to another. It should remain a gift passed on freely to all newcomers.

Such philosophies might sound a high tone in your head and leave your cynical self muttering, "What Bull!" Sometimes it is. The idealism and cooperative forces of the slam are in constant conflict with the competitive and self-serving appetites of its ambitious nature. This struggle has taught us much, but threatens to obliterate all that has grown to be. I, as surely you have guessed, am on the side of idealism and hope. Idealism and hope.

That's me. Along with whiny, jealous, bitter, where's mine, who does she think she is, "Fuck it, I quit."

Kim Addonizio: On Teaching Workshops and Combining Music with Poetry: A Booster Rocket on my Little Sailing Ship

Kim Addonizio was born in Washington, D.C., in 1954. She received her B.A. and M.A. from San Francisco State University. Her books of poetry include *Tell Me*, which was a finalist for the National Book Award; *Jimmy & Rita*; *The Philosopher's Club*; and *Three West Coast Women*, with Laurie Duesing and Dorianne Laux. Addonizio is also the author of *In the Box Called Pleasure*, a collection of stories. With Dorianne Laux, she is the co-author of *The Poet's Companion: A Guide to the Pleasures of Writing Poetry*. Addonizio was a founding editor of the journal *Five Fingers Review*. Among her awards and honors are fellowships from the National Endowment for the Arts, a Pushcart Prize, and a Commonwealth Club Poetry Medal. Kim Addonizio teaches in the M.F.A. program at Goddard College and lives in San Francisco, where she freelances as a teacher of private workshops in the Bay Area.

Poetry Investigator: What are the different revenues you have from poetry?

I teach private workshops. I have people over to my house, give them coffee and cookies. We sit around and talk about their poems. So I am completely freelance at this point. I was doing adjunct work in schools. I don't really want to be in academia—I've tried to run the other way as often as I could from those kinds of teaching jobs. I support myself with workshops. I also give readings, which is a good chunk of my income at this point. Giving readings at schools, festivals and wherever people will have me. I teach at writers' conferences, often in the summer. I do private consultations where I look at people's manuscripts. People come to me and I'll give them feedback on their poems or manuscripts. I cobble all these activities together.

PI: How about book sales?

Book sales I make very little from. I do make a little bit from royalties. With *Tell Me* getting so much attention from being a National Book Award finalist, it has sold a lot better than my other books. *The Poet's Companion*, which I wrote with Dorianne Laux, made me a few thousand over the years. I sell my books after readings, which is good for drinks afterward and maybe dinner.

PI: What is the structure of the workshops as far as how much you charge? How many students do you need for each workshop?

When I first started trying to hold workshops, I was teaching composition at San Francisco State, and that was a lower circle of hell. I was trying to get out of that, trying to write my way, feel my way to another way to make my living. The first workshop I offered I didn't get any people. Then I took a bartender course, thinking I would become a bartender to make money. Then I managed to get a couple of classes going, by consistent advertising. Finally I had advertised long enough that—the one or two people who responded to the first ad I had kept track of—as more people responded I finally reached critical mass and got enough people to make holding the workshop worthwhile.

Now my classes run around eight people and I am able to teach two to three groups a week and get enough people to fill the classes. I am averaging fifteen to twenty-five students a week. Two classes are no problem. Sometimes it is a stretch to fill the third class. I have been doing this long enough now and I have a website where I advertise, word of mouth, and I have been in the Bay Area for twenty-five years. I have been here long enough that people know my work and that I teach workshops, so I have people come to me. I think it would be very difficult to do this in an area that was not a literate, urban area, and you need to be there long enough to make connections in the community.

PI: How much do you charge for the workshops?

I just went up to forty dollars a session, so it depends on how many times we meet—somewhere between six and ten weeks. That makes the workshop anywhere from two hundred to four hundred dollars. People commit to the whole session, not week by week. If people have to miss, I give them feedback in writing so they get something from it.

PI: Do they pay in advance for the whole course?

Yes, they have to pay in advance for the whole course. I have a refund system that I have worked out, where if they drop the class after it starts I give back a certain percentage. I have a waiting list so I try to fill their spot and give back all their money if I can. If something happens—someone might have a sudden death in his or her family or they might move—if they have paid for the class and I can't fill their spot I will still give them written feedback so that they get something from it and don't just lose their money. I have to protect myself, because what I have found from doing this for a long time is that when I first started I would just ask people to pay the first class, or if they couldn't afford it they could pay me half then and half later. I ended up getting burned a lot from that situation. I had to make an organized and detailed policy, so people knew what the rules were up front, otherwise I would be the one losing money.

PI: Does having people pay for the workshops in advance weed out the less dedicated writers?

It is an interesting thing: when people make a financial commitment, they make more of a commitment on other levels. It is a way of them saying, "My writing is important to me. My writing is worth spending money on. If I am going to make this financial commitment then I am going to make a commitment in other ways. I am going to show up with a poem every week. I am going to make a commitment to the group." If there are ways that they cannot make that commitment then often they will drop the class or go elsewhere.

As a writer and someone who depends on that income to pay my rent or now pay my mortgage, when someone just flakes out and says I just changed my mind and I end up eating it—I just can't afford to do that. I am a little too hand-to-mouth to do that. I need to know I have the income coming in.

PI: In the workshops that you teach, how do you avoid what has come to be criticized as the workshop poem?

Well I'm not sure what that means, the workshop poem. I suppose it's a poem where everything that offends everybody has been edited out. A safe little technically-okay, essentially piece of crap. That no one cares about.

PI: Yes. I am thinking you've got ten people and they all say what works and doesn't work, and the poem gets flattened out.

I don't know that that process per se flattens poems out. I really think it depends on how you tackle it. What I talk about are ways of opening up possibilities for the poem, and I ask people if something is not working for them. I ask them to say why it is not working for them, and I ask them to offer a suggestion for them. It is always thrown back to the poet because it is their poem. I tell them to listen to what resonates and discard what doesn't. They are still going to have to find their way through. When people revise things, at least in my groups, they don't take everyone's suggestions and, hopefully, what they have done through that process is make some kind of discovery for themselves.

That may be a discovery that has to do a lot more with what they are trying to say, or what is the heart of my poem, what is the poem trying to do, than should it have this word in it or not. We do talk about the language of course, because that is what the poem consists of. But I also try to get to what are the issues in the poem and has the writer really sufficiently investigated those issues. What are some ways that they might do that. In that sense, I don't feel it is about writing something everybody is going to agree with.

PI: Perhaps setting that tone at the beginning, you can help avoid the workshop poem.

Some people just want to please so they are going to do it anyway. Even if you tell them not to take everyone's advice. It is always a balance between pleasing yourself and trusting yourself as an artist. But it's also when you are developing as an artist that you realize you are making something that is being read by other people, that is communicating to people, and it's important to consider what people are getting from your poem.

You have to consider the source, too. It is a fine balance, listening to criticism and hearing what is valuable criticism that is going to help you work on the weaknesses you have. To help you work on your craft so that you're not just shutting out all that, staying open because that is really important to development. Finding your inner source, finding what you are trying to do and the way that you need to make a poem, that is always a tricky balance I struggle with as a teacher.

PI: How do you judge success for the workshops? I would imagine that you have a range of interests in the class, from wanting to get better as writers, to wanting to publish, to perhaps as a step for them in becoming professional.

For me what the workshops are about is trying to write better. They are about exploring the art. Maybe write better isn't the right term. It is about going deeper into poetry. That is what I want people to do.

Whether they publish or not is incidental. Almost everyone in the workshop wants to publish. There are a few people who are not interested in that. They say, "I learn things about myself from writing, and I am fascinated to see what the next poem will say."

My focus is on the writing and not on will this be published or not. I certainly support my students who want to publish and help them figure out when the poem is ready and deal with rejection.

For me it is about going deeper into poetry, and the success for me is people keep coming back. For me, the success of the workshops is that I have students that I have had for years, sometimes year after year. Sometimes they go away and return years later. There must be something they are getting from this process, or they wouldn't come back.

I do have short-term students who are going into MFA programs that are working on a manuscript to submit, or they have come out of a program and need a writing community. Some people shop around—they will study with one teacher and then see what someone else has to offer. I feel it is a good sign that I have students that come back year after year, or else it is a terrible dependence and maybe it's not so healthy [*laughs*].

PI: It's like the Woody Allen syndrome where he has been in therapy for forty years.

Exactly, maybe there are some people who feel a little too safe in my workshops and don't want to branch out. But I do see their writing change. When you teach in a university you see the students for a semester or maybe you see them for a couple of years, then they move on.

I can see my students' work develop over five or six years. I can see where they were when they came to me and I can see where they are now. I can see that they have really grown. It gives you more trust that it is a process, that people do get better, that they do develop.

I have students that have gone on to publish books, and that has been a real thrill. I saw many of the poems and worked on them with the workshop group. That feels great. I am so proud of them, they are my little babies going into the world.

PI: Talk about the line in your ad for workshops, "Passion is not enough for writing."

I guess that is where I come from as a poet. e.e. cummings said, "since feeling is first." That is where I come from. I was just reading an article by Paul Hoover about the New York school in *APR*. I am reading their work and I am learning from it, about their strategies, and I am glad that he has written the article. I never have gotten Ashbury and I would like to understand why he is so well-rewarded, why so many people are interested in his work. I have never been able to penetrate it.

What I feel about that type of writing is that it is head games. That is not what poetry is to me. It's not that poetry doesn't have and doesn't need intelligence, but there is a lot of poetry that feels like head games to me, and I am just not interested.

For me it is always about going back to the heart and to the human spirit. That is the source of poetry for me. That is the tradition that I follow and that is the tradition that sustains me as a human being, as interesting as other things can be.

That is what I want to foster in my students. Perhaps that is why students come to me and not some other teacher. That is where I locate poetry, and at the same time I don't believe that poetry is therapy and I am not interested in Vic-lit, feel-my-pain poetry. I think that is a very ego-centered poetry and I don't believe poetry is about the ego either.

For me it goes back to questions of the spirit. I have this weird split personality: I have an intense intellectual side and I have an intense passionate side. I don't think those two sides are at odds. I think those things are trying to be fused. That is what I look for in poems. That is what I try to foster in my students. We can get technical and craft-oriented, delving into those elements, but doing that is in the service of something else. Trying to keep the energy going between the intellectual and passionate poles, not ever losing sight of one for the sake of the other.

PI: Is revision an important part of the workshops?

Yes, it really it. A lot of times people bring in work that they've showed us before. Sometimes people just over-revise. They will bring the same poem back four weeks in a row. I will say, "You have to write something new for next time. It is great that you are working on it, but at this point you are killing it. Go write something new and bring in something really raw."

Revision is definitely a focus because it is crucial to the writing process. It just doesn't come out the first time. I think Ginsberg did a lot of damage with his "first thought, best thought." The truth is, as he admitted later, he did a lot of revision.

PI: Certainly referring to Kerouac's *On the Road* manuscript. The myth that they developed was that he had written it all at once, which became a kind of marketing tool for the book. A romantic version of how the book was written, but it has been proven now that he did a lot of revision and certainly had written sections of the book as letters and journal entries.

I think of it as the difference between an infatuation or a romance and a love affair. The people that are having a romance with writing just want to think of themselves as writers. Their romance is, "Whatever I write is my expression and it is perfect and no one may tread on it."

But the real interest of writing is the love affair, just like with people. It's great to have a fling with somebody, but the real interesting thing is when you start to go deeply into love and discover who the other person is. When you hit your own walls and limitations.

That is the same thing with writing, ultimately you come up against so much in yourself when you go deeply into your writing. You are trying to articulate something in your writing, year after year, and that is where I think the rewards are as a writer.

The process is endless, this process of psychic excavation. At the same time you are learning about language, learning what other people have done, discovering what you can and can't do, getting past your own limits as a writer. That for me is the interesting aspect, the real love affair that engages you on every level. That makes you deal with your shit. Writing makes you deal with your shit if you are serious about it. That is where writing gets interesting for me.

PI: How did you get started in teaching at writers' conferences? Did you apply for positions or at this point in your career are you well enough known that you are just asked to participate?

At this point I am asked, which I feel really fortunate about. I used to wonder if I should send my resumé out to these places to get these gigs. I just never did that because I didn't have the time. I was raising my kid as a single parent. Life in general has taken up too much time to try to promote my career. There are people who do that, but I have been fortunate that people have responded to my work. I have had a couple of writers help me out, but not because they knew me. I know there is politics in po-biz and I know that goes on and I have heard lots of stories.

For me, being asked to these conferences has accelerated since being a National Book Award finalist. That has put a booster rocket on my little sailing ship. That got the book reviewed and brought it to people's attention.

I got an agent because of that. He saw the book, and his dad is a poet. He liked the book a lot and contacted me and said, "Hey do you need an agent? Are you working on any other projects?" As it happened I was, so he took on this tattoo anthology I was co-editing. That book is going to come out this year. It is called *Dorothy Parker's Elbow: Tattoos on Writers, Writers on Tattoos.* We named it that because she had a tattoo on her elbow, ahead of her time.

It is a collection of stories, poems, and essays all about tattoos. Many contemporary writers, but we also have Melville, Plath, Kafka, people like that scattered throughout the book. Melville, besides writing about Queequeg, wrote a book called *Typee* which has some hilarious descriptions of the character almost being forced to undergo tattooing by this tribal guy. Warner is publishing it. That all happened because my book got some attention and somebody saw it. That is the way things have happened for me.

I get a lot of emails from people, which is also really gratifying. High school girls in Japan asking, "Can you tell us please what does woman want?" because they had found my poem "What do Women Want?" They like the poem and want to write about it. It's really fun to find out some girl in Dallas was sitting up late one night Web surfing, found my site, and felt less lonely reading my journal and wrote me.

PI: What is your schedule regarding taking care of poetry business and writing?

I was good for a while. It has disappeared over the past few months as life has intruded with some good and some difficult things.

PI: Didn't you have a message on your answering machine that says, "I will be available to take care of poetry business during these hours?"

That worked well. I gave myself until noon each day to read and write and try to make something happen. Then after twelve I took care of everything else I had to do in my life. But things change. I started working out in the morning. I found I was going to the gym instead of going to my desk. That was important to do at the time. Now everything has shifted, with moving and traveling. Everything is going on now. My mother has Parkinson's. My cat has kidney failure. I am trying to handle it all.

PI: You have started to work out in the mornings. What connection is there between physical fitness and poetry?

I think working out keeps me sane. Writing is so sedentary and solitary. I have always been into sports; I grew up in a sports family. I have always done something. As you get older you have to work out more seriously. The body wants to fall apart. You have to say, "No, I don't want you to fall apart this fast." I find it really helps me to stay more centered and less depressed if I have a regular physical schedule. I have found I enjoy weight lifting. There is only so much time in the day.

I also am playing blues harp now. I am excited about playing blues. Maybe I am just balancing out my life more. Other things are not as important as writing for me, but they are coming close. There are times I feel I need to play music for a few days instead of writing, where once I would have written. I think these other activities feed my writing.

PI: What harmonica players are you listening to?

I am a rabid blues fan: Sonny Boy Williamson, Little Walter, some of those earlier guys. There were two Sonny Boys, one a lot earlier than the other. Sonny Terry and Brownie Magee and the Delta blues. I also love Junior Wells and Kim Wilson from the Fabulous Thunderbirds.

PI: Are we going to hear any blues harp at your poetry readings?

Yes, I have been doing that. When I read from *Jimmy & Rita*, I play blues harmonica in between, doing the poems as a blues suite. I am teaching in a couple of weeks a class on poetry and music, talking about spoken word and integrating music. I did a workshop on poetry and music at Colorado College last year. I put my students in a band on the first day of class. They had to collaborate and come up with a performance that included music.

PI: Did you have instruments for them to play?

I encouraged them to think of music as all kind of things. I showed them the video *Stomp*. They were encouraged to expand their notion of music, from body-slapping to ambient sounds. So being able to play an instrument did not really matter.

They ended up adding theater elements as well. One girl did a piece on how she had always wanted to be a nude dancer. They set up a sheet and used a flashlight behind the sheet to project her shadow. While one read the poem another did an erotic pole dance behind the sheet. You saw her shadow dancing.

PI: Tell me more about using blues harp with your poems from *Jimmy & Rita*. Did you segue between the poems? Did you compose a blues piece or just improvise?

What I did was I picked out the poems in advance. Then I would just launch into the poems and I wouldn't let people know I had a harmonica. I would read a couple or three poems until we were into the story, then I would pull the harp out of my back pocket. I would play a blues riff, then read a couple of more poems, then play some harp that went with the poems.

One poem is about a crazy night that ends with Jimmy driving down a one way street where someone has got knifed in the hand. When I finish that poem I would break into a chicka, chicka riff.

PI: If you did this two different times would the music change? Or had you set the piece so you would play it the same each time?

Well, it is pretty similar, but had some room for improvisation. Then I would end by playing "Amazing Grace." So I think of the suite as, here is where I do a piece that sounds like the Stones song "You Have Got to Move" [*sings riff from song*]. Here I do something fast. There is a quiet piece where Jimmy is in prison that is made up of a series of nouns, after that I would play "Amazing Grace."

PI: Now, of course, people reading this will want to rush out and buy a harmonica, to jam with their poems. So what brand and model do you prefer? What key do you like to work in?

The Hohner Special 20's. I like a C harp, but that is just my way of doing it. Now I have written some poems that are based on jazz tunes. For instance I wrote a sonnet called "Stolen Moments," based on that song. So I play a little riff from the tune before I read the poem. So I will play on the harp [*sings the melody from "Stolen Moments"*]. I will do the first three bars of the songs. I have also written some blues poems. I have written a piece for Robert Johnson. So I am working on an improvisation on "Cross Roads," the Robert Johnson tune. I play the tune. But I am working out my riffs on that tune. Of course, since the harp is a mouth instrument, I can't do both at the same time.

PI: There is a way to do it. Its called the RC-20 Loop Station by Boss. It allows you to capture any music or voice in a loop up to five minutes. These devices have been around for awhile, but what is different about the Loop Station is that it is a pedal that you push down to capture the sounds and you can do it live. So you can play a riff on the harmonica, capture it as a loop, and then recite the poem over it. The other difference is the length of time that the memory holds. Also it has an overdub feature that allows you to build up layers. For instance, you can say a line from a poem, then another line and create a chant-like effect to do the rest of the poem over. The Canadian poet Alexis O'Hara introduced me to it. Are you improvising on the harmonica?

Yes, I mostly take licks from records. I am trying to improvise as much as possible. I improvise on "Stolen Moments." I also do "Round Mid Night" [*sings part of the song*]. "Lush Life" is another one; I have a poem called "Lush Life." That is really a bitch to play on the harmonica, because you have to blend all these notes.

PI: Here is a quotation from Kim's poem "Stolen Moments":

> Now I get to feel his hands again, the kiss
> didn't last, but sent some neural twin
> wildly through the cortex.

PI: When you read a poem, say "Stolen Moments," do you improvise the words at all?

No, I haven't, I just do the poems. I am still working on the tunes and figuring out how to include the music. At this next conference, because it is based on music and poetry, I will perform the jazz poems with the melodies. It is a conference on how to teach poetry for high school teachers. I will talk to them about the program I gave at Colorado College—how I put them into bands, how they collaborated, what they came up with.

I will play them spoken word CDs from Sekou Sundiata to Beth Lisick. Expose them to spoken word and music. For my reading I felt I would be remiss if I don't include some music with my poetry.

I have done poems with music behind me with a band or a bassist. That has been spur of the moment. There is a bassist, Glen Moore, that plays up at Mountain Writers Center in Portland. He plays with poets all the time. I have performed with him. There was a band that performed at a place where I was reading and I got them to stay up on the stage and play with me. I didn't improvise the poems but I was tuned into how they were playing the music. I paced the rhythm so it really fit with what they were playing.

PI: Most people, when you say you are improvising a poem, they think that you mean you are making up new words. When you are playing an instrument and improvising you are not playing the notes for the very first time. You might be making up the sequence you are playing, the rhythm of the notes, but essentially you are trying to relate what you are playing to the melody of the song. When I think of improvising a poem, I might repeat a certain line. Or if the poem has some rhyme scheme I might emphasis that. It is a vocabulary that the poem gives you, and I relate that exactly to a blues scale or a mode that a jazz piece might be in. These are the notes that are in the scale, these are the words that are in the poem, and you can rearrange them in an improvisation.

That is interesting. When I was teaching at Goddard we formed a blues band when I was there. We did a performance there. I did one of my poems, and what I realized from listening and thinking about the oral tradition is the whole idea of repetition that it is built on. When I did that performance I experimented with repeating certain lines or the ends of lines. For instance, "Full moon which goes all over the city, something gets into people." So I would repeat, "All over the city, all over the city, all over the city, SOMETHING gets into people."

There is a lot more that I haven't experimented with that I am interested in. I am trying to integrate more my interest in music and what I am doing on the page. I am not really a performance poet, that is not really my thing. But I am trying to move it in that direction when I get up in front of people, because that is what you are doing, you are performing. If you are reading a poem, it is a performance.

PI: What makes a good poetry reading for you? Obviously the quality of the poems, but I am thinking, how do you prepare for a reading?

I guess the biggest thing for me is just trying to enter the space. Both the performance space and the space of the poems. Sometimes it is hard to do that. The thing about being a performer is—that I have seen over and over in performers that I really admire—is that they create the space for the performance to happen in.

No matter what the environment or the mood of the audience or the character of the space, a good performer will walk into that space and change the energy there through what they do. When they do that I think there is a great connection with the audience.

I remember reading an interview with Patti Smith in the *New Yorker* and she was saying how sometimes she will just stay up there for so long because she is desperate with the audience and she hasn't made that connection yet.

PI: I see you in between academic poetry and spoken word or performance poetry. I wondered how you saw yourself, if it was something that you had thought about? I definitely don't think you are on the Ashberry end of the poetic spectrum.

I do feel like I am neither fish nor fowl. I guess I just align myself with the tradition of poetry. I guess I would situate myself outside of both of those scenes, if that is what you would call them, but still connected.

There are so-called academic poets that I respect and there are spoken word poets I feel the same way about. I just feel like there are a lot of ways to, unfortunately the only metaphor I can think of is skin the cat [*laughs*]. Which is not the one I want to think of. Because my cat is having kidney failure and may not make it. I just think there are so many ways to make poems.

I am not really comfortable in the spoken word scene because I feel like I am not a performer, or not a good enough performer to do that. At the same time I am definitely not comfortable in the academic scene. I would much rather read in a bar than a university auditorium. I am more interested in accessibility and ways of reaching audiences that are not the academic way.

Then again there is plenty of life in academia and a lot of people pass through the university system that are coming from other places and going to other places, to a different kind of community.

I don't want to put that down as a place that is dead, where nothing is happening in poetry. I have just found that not to be true when I have taught in colleges. I also think that a lot of that stuff that goes on in universities ends up trickling down in other ways to people. People go and get their MFA and then maybe they can't be a professor because there aren't many of those jobs around, so what do they do? They go start a poetry group or they go teach at a senior center or find an artist-in-residency somewhere or poets in the schools. I think there are lots of ways poetry ends up infiltrating other areas of life, which is a really good thing.

Beth Lisick: My Votes Had to Have Come From the Schlarman Class of 1955 and the Portuguese Water Dogs Clubs Around the Country

Beth Lisick was a featured performer at the 1994 Lollapalooza Festival, the 1996 and 1997 South By Southwest Music Festivals, the 1998 Lilith Fair show at Shoreline Amphitheater, and has opened for the likes of Jim Carroll, Exene Cervenka, Neil Young, and the late Allen Ginsberg. Lisick has two books: *Monkey Girl* and *This Too Can Be Yours*, which was the winner of the 2002 Firecracker Award for fiction. The Beth Lisick Ordeal released one CD on Du Nord Records. She is currently developing a new and very different musical ensemble called the Gold Dust Twins. She recently co-starred with Tara Jepsen in the short film version of their stage play *Fumbling Toward Rock: The Miriam and Helen Story*. Moreover, she continues to author an informative weekly column for the *San Francisco Gate* called "Buzz Town." And as if that weren't already a full plate, she has now joined the sketch-comedy group White Noise Radio Theater. Her latest book is *Everybody into the Pool*.

Poetry Investigator: Hi Beth, how are you?

I'm doing good. The little guy just woke up from his nap. He's totally cute. He's three months old now so he can smile and stuff.

PI: What is his name?

Gus. So now it's getting really fun. Before it was overwhelming and insane. He was just this little pupa. Now he's totally fucking cute.

PI: Is he talking yet?

He's talking, I just don't know what he is saying.

PI: Tell me about your new book, *This Too Can Be Yours*.

It's so funny—when you come out with a book from a small press nobody knows your book is out—you can just keep reading from it. It won a Firecracker Award at the awards show in New York for small presses. It's one of those funny things. The categories are fiction, poetry, sex, drugs, rock and roll, blah, blah, blah. Tons of different categories.

The winner is determined by internet vote. So it's one of those embarrassing things. I wasn't going to send out emails telling people to vote for me. I would just feel like an ass-clown. But my parents sent out at least twenty emails to the surviving members of my Dad's high school graduation class. In my category there was also Jonathan Lethem and J.T. Leroy who are way too big to have their parents send out fucking emails saying, "Vote for my kid."

PI: So that is your tip on how to win an award?

My votes had to have come from the Schlarman High class of 1955, and my parents' other email list is people who show Portuguese Water Dogs around the country. I am sure that is why I won. It was in the same category as people who are too busy trying to get movie deals to have their parents getting votes for them.

PI: Their parents are probably trying to get them Oscars.

Right, their parents are writing to Harvey Weinstein. It's like the poetry slam of book awards.

PI: What was it like to open for Neil Young?

I thought the booker was playing a joke on me. Neil Young was doing a surprise show at the closing night of the San Francisco Film Festival because there was a film about him. So he decided to play a show for his fans instead of going to the big fancy after-party. It was a last minute decision and they needed an opener. They wanted the opener to be a woman, I don't know why, I guess because Neil is so manly.

They called up the booker from the Hotel Utah who books mostly solo acoustic acts. He booked Jewel her first time through. They thought they were going to get some kind of folkie girl. The booker had seen me read the previous week and just liked my stories. He knew he was doing something that they weren't expecting. He was thinking this would be like a joke on them.

Then I found out they needed someone who just used one mic input because Neil's full electric band was playing the show. So all their available inputs were taken, except for one, which was going to be used for my microphone. That was a key factor in determining my opening for him.

Everybody was drunk and everybody just wanted to see Neil play. Neil was late and so they started chanting. I was supposed to go on and they wanted me to just keep going until Neil got there. I just knew it was going to be total disaster, doing poetry. The lights went down and everyone started chanting, "Neil, Neil! Neil!" I walked out and everyone booed. Really upset and yelling for me to get off the stage. There was a small crowd in front trying to be supportive. So now I can say I opened for Neil Young.

PI: How many poems did you end up doing?

I did twenty minutes. It was a really long time to be up there.

PI: Did they eventually stop chanting for Neil and begin to listen?

Yeah, there was actually a big crowd who came up to the front to listen and I still have, after five years, people come up to me and say, "Oh my God, I saw you with Neil Young."

PI: You really won the crowd over?

If I had come out there and played folk songs I think nobody would have listened. Because I was just standing there with a microphone they did listen and it did end up being a good experience.

PI: Didn't one of the roadies keep asking you about your guitar?

Everybody did, from the door guy to the stage manager to the sound person, they kept wondering where my guitar was. They couldn't figure out why I would be opening and what I could be doing if I didn't have a guitar. The tour manager said, "You can't use one of Neil's guitars!"

People were just there to see Neil, but I think the fact that I wasn't playing the guitar and singing, that I was doing something that a lot of those people hadn't seen before, that the crowd ended up listening. Otherwise it would have been an opening act that people would have been ignoring.

PI: You were working with your band at that time. Tell me about the switch from doing poetry readings to working with a band.

I knew a bunch of musicians and I was always going out to hear their bands play. It seemed to me that it would be really fun and it would be a different way of writing, writing to go with the band.

First, the band composed music around pieces that I had already written. Then they would compose music and I would write to the music thinking of the stories as song lyrics. I had friends that were musicians and I thought it would be a good way to get out and play clubs that were bigger, not just for poetry audiences. I was going to these bands' gigs, having fun and hanging out and listening to incredible people play. I thought, "I want to do that."

They were really excited to work with me because there was no guitar player, so there was no lead instrument. Usually a bass player, drummer, vibe player, or horn player are all performing the music of the lead person, but because I don't write like a lead musician all these talented people who are side guys got to compose music. I think they liked it because of that. It was a good place for the music they had written to get exposure.

PI: How has it worked out? How many years have you been working with the band? Have you changed personnel? [*sound of baby fussing in the background.*]

Just a sec, let me grab the little dude. Come here baby. Hold on, sorry.

PI: That's okay.

Put him on the old boob. I guess we played together for about four years. I recently started a new band that was with the drummer and the bass player and my husband Eli playing guitar. I have been playing a little electric bass.

The other band had samples but there are more samples in this band. It's less of a spoken word band. After a while I got burnt out on talking the whole time. There is only so much I can do with my voice. There is only one timbre that I have when I speak, so I am trying to do different things with my voice, including singing or maybe spoken verses and sung choruses. The new band is called the Gold Dust Twins.

PI: Give us some tips for working with musicians.

Working with musicians who are writing interesting material was important for me. To get people who would compose songs and not just play behind me. I wanted the song to stand on its own, and the musicians did too. The bass player didn't want to be just playing some boom, boom riff behind me. As a listener I wanted to hear something exciting happening with the music as well.

Music can add a lot to a regular poetry reading but it can also get really old. In improvising—how many people do you know that improvise poetry?—it can be a total disaster. Even though the musicians can improvise and they are great improvisers, we wanted to put on a show with finished compositions. Exciting things can happen when you freestyle, but also really terrible things can happen. I didn't want to put on a show were I was freestyling it, and I felt the same way about working with the musicians.

PI: Would you bring a piece to them and have them compose to it?

In the beginning I would bring a piece to them and one of them would work on a four-track recorder coming up with the parts. Then the band would hone that to the final compositions. Toward the end they would come in with a finished piece of music, rehearsing without me, record the new song and I would listen to the song and make up a story to the music. It was really great for me to write that way, as opposed to here's my poem, figure out something to go with it.

PI: Did the pieces feel different when you composed them that way?

Yes, they were more structured. I started writing pieces that had verses and choruses, pieces that went back to themes in the music. Musically there could be themes repeating phrases like a chorus in a song. Whereas in the beginning my spoken word pieces were narrative.

PI: Tell us about playing with your band at the Lilith Fair.

They had a local contest. You sent in a demo, and five hundred demo tapes got scaled down to twenty. Those twenty performed in Union Square and they picked two performers for one day of the show and two for the second day of the show, and we ended up winning that, which is really funny because the other women who won were really good singer/songwriters with guitars. Hey, singer/songwriters with guitars—that's the Lilith Fair. I think I've had a lot of luck with my band just because it's different, as far as getting press or having people come and check it out.

It was a novelty and being different, that helped us get things like the Lilith Fair or getting an article in the paper, because there was a different angle people could focus on. It's funny more poets don't do it. Having a band takes a lot of time—to get people together for rehearsals and to collaborate. I still don't know anyone in San Francisco who is doing a spoken word band. I am sure that there are people, I just don't know them.

PI: How many years have you been doing the "Buzz Town" column?

I have been doing it for about five and a half years. I just got that as part of my day job working as an editor at the *Chronicle*'s website. The week that I started Tom Petty had played five shows at the Warfield. Joel Sullivan was the music critic and that is all they wrote about—dinosaur rock bands. The editor said I could start my own column if I wanted to. I do the column freelance; it's a pretty good job because I can do it from home.

PI: You must have written hundreds of columns by now.

Yeah, I didn't even think of that until recently. I thought, "Damn I have been doing this for so long." In a way it gets tiring because I have to keep up on what's going on. But as far as jobs go it's pretty good.

I was trying to think of some connection between writing poetry and writing the column. The column is a bunch of tiny blurbs, so it's similar to poetry in that way.

The process is similar in trying to consolidate and crystallize your thoughts. Being concise, saying exactly what you want to say because you don't have that many words to say it.

PI: You can describe a party in two lines. The observational skills are similar, being able to pick out somebody's hat or their laugh to describe what a situation was like. I remember the column when Dave Eggers was coming back to San Francisco after his big success in New York and you described him as the Golden Egg. It was perfect short hand for what had happened in his life, with his book sales and the success of *McSweeney's*. It seems like you draw on some of the same skills used in poetry. One last question, what is your favorite color?

My favorite color is Gus.

Andy Clausen: French Fry Shoveler/Poet

Andy Clausen was born Andre Laloux in a Belgian bomb shelter in 1943. He was raised in Oakland, California. He graduated from Bishop O'Dowd High School in 1961 and attended six colleges. He began trying to be a "beat" poet in 1965 after reading Kerouac, Ginsberg, Corso, and others. He has traveled and read his poetry all over North America and the world (New York, California, Alaska, Texas, Prague, Katmandu, Amsterdam, and other places). He has maintained a driven, intrepid lifestyle and aspired to be a champion of the underdog. His chief books have been *The Iron Curtain of Love*, *Without Doubt*, and his selected verse of thirty years, *40th Century Man*. Allen Ginsberg not only called him the "Future of American Poetry" but in the introduction to *Without Doubt*, said he would take a chance on a "President Clausen." Clausen has taught at Naropa Institute and given readings and lectures at many universities. He has worked for poetry in the schools agencies in California, New Jersey, Colorado, and New York. He is now a stonemason, troubadour, and a freelance teacher of creative writing under the auspices of Teachers & Writers in the NYC school system. He is presently working on memoirs of his friendship and adventures with Allen Ginsberg, Gregory Corso, and many others of the Beat Generation. In 1982 he was voted the most exciting poet at the Kerouac Conference in Boulder, Colorado. Clausen is one of the editors of the poetry journal *Long Shot*.

Poetry Investigator: Tell us about editing *Long Shot*.

We get a lot of poems where we say, "We could put this in," but we never have trouble filling up the pages. We do ask people to submit. We do make mistakes. In the early days they turned down Wanda Coleman. It took a long time to get her back and have her in there. Poets don't like to be turned down, and they shouldn't have turned her down. I just hope that it doesn't happen. You know, you are tired and have read forty poems and you put it in the reject pile and it turns out that it actually was very good. People have to realize that editing is not easy: saying yes, saying no.

PI: How long have you been one of the editors at *Long Shot*?

I think for five issues.

PI: That is one a year?

About one a year. There have been twenty-five issues in twenty years. We just had the twentieth year celebration. We had just about everybody who had been published in *Long Shot*.

PI: How did the celebration turn out?

The event at the Bowery Poetry Club was packed.

PI: You raised some money for the magazine?

Yes, our book parties are pretty good; we usually sell about seventy copies. I sold twenty-five at the event here in Woodstock. We sell them for eight dollars in the stores and at the book parties we sell them for six dollars. That is still more than we get from the distributor.

PI: What do you get from the distributor?

We get 45 percent, which is a little less than four dollars per copy. The bookstore takes 40 percent and the distributor takes 15 percent. It is not a moneymaking thing. We break even on most of the issues. We end up selling about one thousand copies.

We have had a couple that have sold over that, which is pretty good for poetry. If you have a poetry book that sells three thousand copies, it is a hit. If Julia Vinograd* could sell them through the bookstores, she would have hits. She is one of the few people I know that can sell that many, but she sells them hand to hand just going up to people and selling them. Most poets are unwilling to do that.

PI: Do you get paid as one of the editors?

No, but I get whatever I want in there. We each get two pushes an issue. If there is someone I present to them and the other editors don't like it, I can override them on

* Longtime Berkeley street poet.

two poems. So I can get two people in that I want. One time it was a prisoner who was in one of my workshops who I thought was a good poet. I get that and I also get input on directing the magazine. What would I say I really get out of it? I would say I get a couple of thousand readers across the country.

PI: You are teaching poetry in prison workshops? What is that like?

It's okay. Most of these guys are interested in saying something. If they are interested in writing while they are in prison it means they have their head together. It is depressing going inside. But it's good work.

PI: You give them a writing exercise?

We read a bunch of poems on the topic or the style or the form. We talk about the topic, then we write. Then if we have time we read and talk about the writing. When you first start the classes, people's egos are a little fragile so you have to respect that. It becomes really important when there is not much happening during your day.

PI: I would imagine that it would be a chance for someone to take them seriously, to be able to express what is going on for them.

I had this one guy who got thrown in the hole, but he got some poems out to me anyway, they were really well-written. They were about the unbelievable grief of being in there, how he hated being there, every single thing about it he hated. He was very eloquent about it. I read it and I loved it for its eloquence and for what he wrote, but what a depressing subject. You would get things about what was going on around them in prison, but a lot of the poems were just about spiritual grief. Why did I wind up in the place were I did that bad thing, which he never tells what it was. I don't ask that. If they volunteer it, fine.

PI: Is it draining for you to teach the workshops? How does it affect you?

Sometimes it uplifts, sometimes it drains. When none of them come to class because they are all watching a basketball game, that is discouraging.

PI: How about your own writing? What are you working on?

I write the occasional poem. Right now I am waiting to hear about my book.

PI: You have a novel out?

It is a memoir concerning the later days of the Beat Generation. The people I knew. It is funny things, not really dirt, more anecdotal stories. The agent says the companies have had it for a long time. I think they will take it, but I think they will make me do a lot more work. Lawyers will have to get involved because I use real names. They may want more pages. I am hoping it will happen and then fuck all the poetry scenes and all that shit.

PI: Is one publisher looking at it?

No, more than one, they don't want to do one because they want the publisher to bid for the book. Me, I could give a shit. I say publish it, put a little money behind it, get me a reading tour to sell the damn thing. See if you can get the book reviewers in the towns where I am touring to write about the book. If the company will do that, then that would be fine. But if they just want to print it and have a nice book and expect me to sell it, I'd rather die with the book. I don't have the infrastructure to do that stuff. Well, we'll see.

PI: What is the book called?

I am not telling you [*laughs*].

PI: It's a good title.

No, that's not it and that's not it either. But I could have a title like that.

PI: Can you tell me who is in it?

Most everybody in the beat generation, Ginsberg, Jan Kerouac, Ken Kesey, Gregory Corso, Ray Bermser, Anne Waldman, Herbert Huncke, and other people appear.

PI: Did you meet them in San Francisco?

No, I have lived all over the country, in Denver, Boulder, Chicago, New York, New Jersey, Katmandu.

PI: When did you live in Katmandu?

In 1990, it is a great place to live, it is exotic. I lived in a section called Genish Town, towards Boda. That is where the largest stupa in the world is.

PI: If I go to read the book, of course I won't know what title to look for.

You'll hear about it if it comes out. There will be controversy.

PI: Any poems in it?

All stories, I tried to stay away from poems.

PI: Any idea when you might find out about it?

No, but the agent keeps saying the longer they have it the better.

PI: Because they are not saying no.

Yes, I don't really know how these things go. I have never had an agent before, because I never had anything that required an agent.

PI: You gave them the manuscript. Did the agent make suggestions or just say yes, let's go with it.

They hung with it, they argued about it, discussed it, and then said let's go with it. One major publisher turned it down, although they said it was good and that they liked it. The young people in the editorial staff wanted it, but the older people on the staff thought it might be a little rowdy and a risk for them. It was a big company.

Also, New Directions turned it down because they don't do memoirs, but I think they also thought it was a little too randy for them. I don't think it is at all, compared to half of what I remember the San Francisco poetry scene to be, it is not randy at all. Not like Danielle Willis* or Bucky Sinister.†

PI: But you have sex and drugs in the book.

Yes, but I try to write about it in a civil, adult way. I'm not trying to titillate anybody or gross anybody out [*laughs*]. I think there are some lower-echelon presses that would do it, but I want somebody who can do something with it. Not somebody who can only sell a thousand copies.

PI: Yes and you have to work your ass off to sell a thousand copies.

I want to sell fifty thousand, one hundred thousand copies.

PI: What are you doing for work? You used to be a hod carrier.

Up here I am a stone mason. But most of my income comes from Teachers & Writers residencies. I teach kindergarten to eighth grade.

PI: How is that going?

I like it. I just did some summer school that was good.

PI: Teachers & Writers is good about getting you work?

Yes, I get really good comments from the teachers in the schools. They keep me working pretty good. The funding is irregular, but at the beginning of last year I had one school I was going to two days a week. I really like to do four days a week if I can.

PI: You stay down in New York when you are doing that?

Yes, I stay at friends' houses. I buy the pizza or whatever. I crash on couches two or three days a week. I have about seven crashes and about three that I use most of the time.

* Willis is known for her vampire poems, dental implant fangs, and blood cutting performances.

† Sinister ran a reading series in San Francisco which featured heckling, fights, and poets getting arrested.

PI: What kind of workshops are you doing with the kids?

I give them a subject then we talk about it. We read poems that kids have written. Then we do a group poem on the blackboard. Next we pick our subject and if we are done early then we have a little reading from what we have done. After ten sessions I take the best one or two poems from each student and make an anthology with illustrations they have done.

PI: That must be exciting to see their poems in a book.

For most of them. Some of them say, "What the fuck is this?" [*laughs*]. So your book is really, "What are the things I have done to keep alive so I can be a poet?"

PI: Yes, tell us about that.

I have done a lot of things. I have cleaned fish. I drove taxi. I was a program director at an alternative culture spa. I have done some funny things. I do stone mason work up here. I guess my strangest job was shoveling french fries at a french fry making factory.

Judith Tannenbaum: Disguised as a Poem

Tannenbaum is a writer and teacher who is particularly interested in community arts and issues of cultural democracy. She has received two California Arts Council Artist-in-Residence grants. The first of these allowed her to teach poetry at San Quentin for three years; the second was for a three-year poetry project at the continuation high school in Albany, California, and at one of the town's primary schools. Each of these grant cycles led to a book. *Disguised as a Poem: My Years Teaching Poetry at San Quentin* is a memoir, and *Teeth, Wiggly as Earthquakes: Writing Poetry in the Primary Grades* is a book for young people. Both books were published in 2000. She currently serves as training coordinator for San Francisco's WritersCorps program, a project of the San Francisco Arts Commission that places writers in community settings to teach creative writing to youth in need.

Poetry Investigator: Let's start with your book. Describe how it came about, the students challenging you to write it. Had you already thought of doing a book?

When I was teaching at San Quentin I wrote poems, as always. Some of that work became a book-length sequence that looked at prison from a variety of points of view. A few of the poems were in my voice, but most were in the voices of imagined people: staff, guards, prisoners, and people on the outside.

As a writer, I felt that I had been given a form true to how I see the world: a whole composed of multiple voices and angles of vision. Discovering the form of that sequence was a huge gift to me as a writer, very freeing. I felt I was the closest I had ever been to being able to write as I saw things.

I made rules for myself such as not to use any details from my students' lives and not to represent any of the actual people I knew. But when I shared the poems with my prisoner students, one or two challenged me. They wanted to know what right I thought I had to write about their world, which was not my world.

The students who challenged me were asking important, intelligent questions. They raised the precise concerns that mattered most to me. I agreed someone—in this case, me—coming in from the outside was responsible in the exact ways they said I was responsible.

My whole teaching life, I'd fought for my students' right to speak from their deepest vision; now I had to decide if I, too, had this right. Asking this question was very big for me as a writer and as a teacher. To be firm about my own right to speak was much harder than to insist on this same right for my students.

I had to fight—within myself—to claim my own voice and vision in writing these poems. Of course, I acknowledged that I was writing "about" prison, but most deeply I felt I was writing "about" wholeness.

These poems are what I wrote. I never thought I would write a book about the experience of being at San Quentin. Though I did take a lot of notes, I don't think I had even an unconscious intention of writing that kind of a book.

PI: Was taking notes a technique you would use to write your poems?

I know many poets who carry notebooks, to jot down an image or a line. Yes, it was that kind of note-taking, or perhaps even more unintentional than that. I didn't think, "Oh I am going to use this information for poems." What I felt was that I was in a world so different from what I'd previously known, and that few people got to see what I was seeing. I felt I had to notice well, remember well, and the note-taking was toward that end.

PI: Even a week later you will filter your writing in a different way than if you are writing it down shortly after it happens.

I think I had many encouragements during those years to pay attention. First of all, I experienced those years at Quentin very intensely. And, as you said, writers write to process what our senses encounter. Also, my nature is to be reflective.

Additionally, I was doing a lot of writing for the Arts in Corrections program. During the last year of my grant, I was hired to write a manual for artists working in prison and to create an Arts in Corrections newsletter.

So I was being asked—by my artistic and emotional nature, as well as by my bosses—to reflect. I was given a variety of opportunities to speak deeply.

PI: They wanted you to document your experience.

They wanted me to document and describe the experience many of us artists had in those years working in California prisons. Those days are so different from these.

PI: It seems like it might be harder to start the programs now.

In January 2003, California's Arts in Corrections was slashed. The program still exists, but in a completely different, and much reduced, form. The experience I describe in my book isn't possible in California prisons any longer. For the decades of its existence, Arts in Corrections was the largest prison art program in the world.

But other states do have prison art classes and programs. There is a really fantastic program in Michigan, for example, called Prison Creative Arts Project (PCAP). It was begun by Buzz Alexander, an English professor at the University of Michigan. He offers a class at the university in which students go into prison and teach, read about prison and community issues, and write and reflect on what they're learning.

One thing I would like to stress, especially for poets in MFA programs, is that there are many ways to make a living as a poet in addition to teaching in college. There's teaching in prisons, old folks' homes, working with youth. The field Bill Cleveland calls "Arts in Other Places," or what's more commonly known as "community arts."

Despite budget cuts and public attitudes about prison, good work is always possible. Tory Sammartino is an incredible young woman who grew up in the Bronx. While still in college, Tory created a non-profit called Voices Unbroken. She is 100 percent committed to erasing the separation between people on the outside and people in prison. Her passion comes from her own life experience growing up seeing someone on the street one day, and the next day they'd be in prison. Then, months or years later, there they'd be, back on the street.

Tory's a powerhouse. She works at Rikers, at other prisons around New York state, in re-entry and community-based programs. She is committed to training people in the community to do what she does, to lessen the separation between prisoner/free person, teacher/student. I'm so grateful to Tory and others like her who are shaping community arts in profound ways.

One question often asked is: when a poet is doing work in the world that is compelling, what does that mean for his or her own writing? In a way, our work in the world always feeds our writing. At the same time, most of the people who "teach" (share the power of writing) with all their heart and soul, often have less left to put into their own work.

PI: It does seems like you have to have a certain drive to accomplish your own work, then there are these other ways of being a poet, bringing poetry into your life and other people's lives, that can be compelling and consuming. The initial drive is loving poetry and wanting to write poetry. Then you have a shift in your focus.

This raises a huge question, one we talked a lot about when I worked at San Quentin. Bottom line, there is no perfect economic choice for an artist in this world. Any choice we make involves some compromise. Artist/facilitators with Arts in Corrections worked a forty-hour week for the Department of Corrections in exchange for earning enough money to raise a family, to buy a house, to count on some degree of job and retirement security. Those of us working as independent contractors never had enough money for anything most of the rest of the world values. Which continues to be true for me. I am fifty-six and don't have any retirement plan; if I'm going to have health insurance, I'm the one who has to pay for it.

These are personal matters that assume greater importance as I get older. But, as training coordinator with WritersCorp, I also wonder how these realities will affect the field. Many young people want to do this work and are really committed; many come themselves—like Tory—from the communities they want to serve, and have no financial resources to fall back on.

My time was different. In the seventies, when my daughter was born, we could live on next to nothing. There was a lot of social support for living on nothing. But it's hard to live on nothing these days. How is the next generation doing this work going to survive?

PI: If you look at the percentage of your income that has to go to rent as opposed to the percentage of income going to rent in the 1960s and 1970s, it is a dramatic change.

Exactly. A few years ago, during the dot com boom, I heard so many young people in San Francisco say something like, "Our friends are making mega bucks, what are we doing making eighteen thousand dollars a year at a non-profit?"

As I say, in the seventies—at least among many middle class whites in northern California!—there was almost a social agreement not to make much money but to be of use in this world. There was a lot more support for that kind of career choice.

Again, that's stating it from a personal point of view. Looking at it from the larger perspective of the work itself, of the field, the question is: will it be possible for people to do this kind of community arts work over the course of a whole life? Or is it going to be work they can only do for a few years before getting a job that will pay more money?

Another important question is the one we were referring to before: what is the cost to one's own writing of doing this work? It is cost and pleasure, both, because the amount of deep creative soul satisfaction there is working in prisons and community settings can, of course, nourish your writing. But it is hard to do both.

In many community arts programs I see, there is a way of perceiving art as what people make together; one's own work isn't separate from what's done with the community. I admire this, and I certainly have devoted most of my work life to community arts, but I hunger for time to write alone at my desk.

PI: Right, let's talk more about your book. You talked about the process of getting to the place of writing the book. Please talk about the writing process and how did you get your publisher. What was that process like for you?

I wrote *Disguised* because of Elmo, one of my San Quentin students. He told me on our last night of class, "Now I'm going to give *you* an assignment. Write about these years from your own point of view."

Elmo's assignment started me thinking about writing a book and when I stopped teaching at Quentin, I began writing. At the same time, I got quite ill and I knew I wouldn't have the energy to both earn a living and write. I thought perhaps I could sell a book proposal and get an advance that would allow me to write.

I put a lot of energy out toward that end, got an enthusiastic agent and had some interest. Ultimately, though, nothing happened.

PI: What year was this?

1991. At that point, both my savings and I were completely depleted. In some way I felt I'd risked everything for this book and all the material I'd amassed seemed negative somehow, tinged with danger. I put the proposal, research, notes, and writing in a box and thought, "That's it!"

I went back to teaching poetry workshops with kids. Slowly, I began to get healthy again. I began to have more energy. In that condition, one day I opened the box. In reading the material, I realized how much I wanted to write about Quentin.

Although I was healthier, I still didn't have enough energy to work and write, so I applied for residencies which would give me free room and board while I wrote. I got two residencies, one after the other, which together gave me almost four consecutive months to work on the book.

PI: So you had time to write and a place. Did they also give you a stipend?

No, but I gave everything up. I gave up my apartment and put my things in storage, so I didn't have many expenses. All I had to do was get myself to the residencies.

PI: That is an interesting thing for people to know, that you didn't have to get money, because you were willing to reduce your actual living expenses to almost zero.

Yes. If you are willing to live on very little, you have more freedom to do what you want to do. The world makes it harder and harder to make that choice, but it is still possible.

PI: It is a strategy in how to use residencies.

It was mostly luck that I got those residencies back-to-back, but I did apply to many residencies hoping for such an outcome. The four months of residency time allowed me to write an entire first draft. Then I stayed with good friends for another two months, which enabled me to finish the book.

Another important aspect of my writing experience is that once I opened that box and realized I really wanted to write this book, I was ready. As soon as I got to the first residency, unpacked my suitcase, and sat down at the typewriter (it was 1996 and I actually was still writing on a manual typewriter!) the story poured out.

So, as is often the case, in retrospect it was good that I wasn't given any money to write the book when I first started to write it in the early nineties. I was too close to the experience at that point, and all the choices I was making about how to write the book were wrong. I can't fathom it now, but then I felt honoring my students required I leave myself out of the book. I don't know how I could have even thought that way, but I did think that way. Obviously, the only story I have to tell is my own. But, apparently, to come to that conclusion required the five years of letting the book sit in the box.

Also, when I wrote in 1990 and 1991, I felt that I had to tell everything exactly the way it happened. By 1996, I realized that in order to make the story work, it was all right to—for example—combine conversations that happened on two different nights into one conversation.

PI: You had to make it work as writing.

Exactly. Part of making it work as writing involved letting the reader know who I was, whose eyes were doing the seeing, whose voice telling the story. I felt I had to convey my values, so the reader could decide if I was a reliable narrator.

At first, I wrote two introductory chapters describing my life before I came to San Quentin. However, one of the writers at my first residency pointed out the obvious: "No one's going to pick up a book about San Quentin wanting to spend two chapters before they walk through the gates!"

One writing joy became finding where the San Quentin story—which I told in a linear fashion—needed to be deepened by more information about me. That layering process was a real pleasure.

In terms of writing process, I made a couple of very useful decisions. The first involved Elmo, the student who gave me the assignment. Elmo is really smart, is a good writer, and was also always very quick to educate me when he felt I needed educating. Before I left for the residencies, I asked Elmo if he would be willing to work with me on the manuscript as I was writing. He agreed, and his help was invaluable. Elmo made sure I got the prison stuff right, and also he found the places where in some way I wasn't going as deep as I needed to be going. Often, his specific suggestions for improvement weren't ones I took, but he consistently pointed out those places where I needed to work harder. Elmo was what I think of as the perfect editor.

Another helpful part of the process occurred toward the end. When I had a penultimate draft, I sent it to ten people to read, three of whom were former prison students. I hadn't wanted much input (other than Elmo's) up until that point, but at that point I was open to everything my wide range of readers had to say.

Then a big New York agent took my book. She called me on a Sunday afternoon and told me how much she loved the manuscript, how it was the best new thing she had read in years, etc., etc. The call was like a dream come true. She was sure she could sell the book in a minute.

But she couldn't sell it, and the process of working together became very complicated. She was a famous agent, after all, and she kept saying the book would sell. But it wasn't selling. But she must know what she was doing, right?

Eventually, I went to New York. I thought if I met with the agent in person, we could figure out what to do. On the same trip, I met with Bruce Franklin* and we had a really nice conversation. He advised me against a mainstream press, recommending instead that I look for a university press. He said mine was the kind of book unlikely to be an overnight success, garnering big attention the first two weeks it was out. Instead, Bruce advised, I should find a publisher who'd keep the book in print a long time.

* Franklin is the editor of *Prison Writings in 20th-Century America* and *Prison Literature in America: The Victim as Criminal and Artist.*

The agent and I agreed that she would continue to approach the big presses and I would start to explore university presses. I wrote query letters to twenty-five different presses.

Bruce Franklin was my most helpful guide. He recommended the presses he thought would be most interested in a book such as mine. And in fact, my book is published by Northeastern, one of the presses Bruce suggested.

PI: That is incredibly important for people to hear. Because when you are first doing a book, the idea is to get a great agent, to sell it to a major press, be sent on a book tour, and to sell hundreds of thousands of copies. Sometimes that happens for people. I interviewed Mary Karr yesterday who wrote *Liars Club*, so it does happen and you should have that dream. But it is important for people to know how in the majority of cases, that is not how books get published. In your case you listened to Franklin, then you wrote twenty-five query letters yourself and made it happen. I think that 95 percent of the time that is the case for how any kind of poetry project gets done.

Yes, I think so, too. Everything about *Disguised*—from writing the book, to finding a publisher, to selling copies—took great perseverance, a quality I hadn't previously applied to marketing my own work.

Also, I think an important part of the story is that on the surface we think a big publisher has to be best. But, I've been learning, maybe best for some things and not best for others. For example, I doubt I'll make more than a penny on this book. But working with Northeastern has been a completely positive experience. The press has a very strong list of prison books, and the editors share my values, and they've given me a kind of support I really appreciate.

Northeastern has a very small staff, so much of the promotion beyond selling to colleges fell to me. This turned out to be fine. I suppose because of the book's subject, I had no trouble setting up bookstore readings. Northeastern was consistently great about following up my phone calls with publicity packets and doing their part.

I have talked to authors who feel resentful about all their small press—and even big presses!—doesn't do, but I haven't felt that way. I just accepted Northeastern's inevitable limitations and what they could, and couldn't, do.

Being my own publicity person has been really interesting. I had never had that experience before: contacting people, getting interviews, setting up readings.

Before the book came out I consulted with a publicist for an hour to get ideas. She asked me a question that surprised me. She said, "Which do you care about most: selling copies of the book or getting to talk about the subject?" I had thought those two things were the same thing, but she said most often they're not.

My getting to speak about prison's issues has just been wonderful and has proved to be the most personally valuable aspect of my published-book experience. I now have conversations about prison issues, not only with people in California, but with people all over the country. I am getting opportunities to speak at colleges and conferences nationally. I meet interesting people and experience different models for working with prisoners.

Best of all, whenever possible, I've gone in to work in prisons in whatever state I'm visiting. I begin by reading poems by my San Quentin students, and then the prisoners share their writing. At this point, when I go into a prison, I have poems by men and women in California, Michigan, Minnesota, Iowa, Kansas, and New York to share.

When you think about how marginalized poets, in general, feel ourselves to be, you can imagine how powerful it is for a prison poet in Kansas to hear what a prison poet from Iowa has to say. So even though my work-life has been based on, and *Disguised* certainly speaks for, the power of poetry, my experiences since the book came out have strengthened my knowledge of this truth. We *are* all part of a community of artists.

Attila the Stockbroker: Yo! I'm the MC of Ranting Rebel Poetry

Rising out of England's punk scene, Attila may be the original rant poet. He has spent the last twenty years performing his work across the world at literary and music festivals, rock venues, arts centers, pubs, universities, schools, folk clubs, and punk squats in the UK, Germany, the Netherlands, Canada, Australia, New Zealand, the U.S., Euskadi, France, Scandinavia, Austria, Switzerland, and Italy—and, more improbably, in Romania, Bulgaria and a hotel basement in Stalinist Albania. He's created his own global network, organizes most of his own gigs (and many for other performers at various one-off events and festivals and at the regular spoken word/music events he runs in his native Southwick), and he's released thirteen music/poetry albums in five countries and four books of poems including *Cautionary Tales for Dead Commuters*, *Scornflakes*, *The Rat-tailed Maggot and Other Poems*, and *Goldstone Ghosts*. He's written for many publications including *The Guardian, Time Out, NME, Sounds Magazine*, and *The Independent*. In 1994 Attila formed his first-ever band, Barnstormer, combining his two great musical loves—medieval music and punk! Attila is very proud to have earned a living as a poet since 1982.

Be kind and tender to the frog

and do not call him names

—Hilaire Belloc

Poetry Investigator: How do you keep your poetry and performances from falling into the dreary boredom of the typical poetry reading?

Energy, stage presence, passion—it's a PERFORMANCE!! I don't stand there apologetically staring at my feet and trembling like a leaf in autumn. I bring the stuff to LIFE! First and foremost of course by having material which is *worth listening to*—not a pile of boring, pseudo-intellectual, whining, self-indulgent, self-pitying dog toffee!! The worst advertisement for poetry is many of the people who call themselves poets!

PI: Here is Attila's signature poem:

My Poetic License (an affirmation)

Yo! I'm the MC of ranting rebel poetry
I know my history and my identity
I'm independent, a red cottage industry
DIY from here to eternity
Now let me tell you what's been going on—
I take my inspiration from centuries long gone
Oral tradition of sedition, that's my position
No court jester with a tame disposition . . .
Poetic license? Twenty years I've had one
and they don't come easy, they're not given out for fun.
You have to earn it, work and sweat and move
not get stuck in a dead poet bore groove . . .
I earned mine in dirty scummy punk clubs
Rock gigs, arts centers, festivals and dodgy pubs
And yes, once or twice I've had to fight—
but when a fascist hits a poet, the poet's doing something right!
So listen up, this MC's here to stay
Wild twenty years ago and still fired up today.
I love words and I've got this message for you:
Poetry's not boring—though some poets bore you
And I have to say that some poets bore me.
They're about as fun as a week on the lavatory!
Dull and pretentious, playing the Art Game—
real problem is they give the rest of us a bad name.
But I'm in the forward line, down there in the scrum.

Tedious whining poets—up your bum!

Now some of the critics think my stuff's no good

but I earn my living at it—those jerks never could

Yes, as you see, I'm a little bit bolshy too

But that's just one of the ways I want to get through

Sometimes it's cerebral, quiet, esoteric wit—

sometimes it's loud and hard and rude as shit!

I love words and I love em in the red and raw

I like to use them in ways they've not been used before

Want you to laugh and want you to think as well

Bollocks to TV—this is live, as live as hell!

Oral tradition—the real origins of poetry.

Attila the Stockbroker—ranting rebel MC.

Dean of the Social Surrealist University.

Welcome to my wild poetic journey!

PI: Please tell us a little about *Bellocose* and Hilaire Belloc. How does your poetry fit into this performance, if at all?

I am inspired to some degree by the work of Mr. Belloc and do a performance which involves his life history as a poet/phenomenon, some of his work and—as an illustration of how he has influenced me—some of mine.

PI: Any tips for incorporating poetry with music?

Write songs—that's what I do. The very best lyrics are precisely that: poetry. Otherwise, don't bother, it won't work. Or become a reggae talk-over DJ or rapper (and find something INTERESTING to say instead of how big your knob is or how many guns you've got.) DON'T create a crap aural soundscape with a computer, end up with something which sounds like Tangerine Dream or Mogadon, and then whine over it!!

PI: Where are the best places to play in England? In Europe?

What a question. The best places for me to play are where I do play—where people ask me to play—arts centers, punk squats, pubs, cafés, rock venues, libraries, literature festivals, schools, you name it. The best places are where people want you. I'd advise all poets to play where people want them (and if nobody wants them, to try and become better at it!!)

PI: When touring Europe, do you make any adjustments when performing in countries where English is not the language?

Well, I speak French and German, so I do my introductions in those languages, which gives the audience a pretty good idea to start off with, and I have a few pieces translated. In countries where there is a total language barrier I stick to playing with my band—and most of my mainland European gigs are with my renaissance punk band Barnstormer.

PI: Attila the Stockbroker is a great name for a poet. It plays against the typical fussy, wimpy image of the poet. Do you see it as a sort of character or, say, mask you use in your performances?

No. It's me. A different side of me from John Baine. But me as much as the other side is.

PI: Any tips for preparing for a performance?

The best way to prepare for a performance is to write some shit hot material, have total self-belief, get a gig in front of people who want to or can be made to listen, have a couple of beers (a couple: no more. Beers: not spirits), and GO FOR IT!

PI: What is the most bizarre thing that has ever happened to you at a poetry reading or while on tour?

Being attacked on stage by twenty Nazi boneheads was quite bizarre. Having someone in the audience starting to shout repeatedly, "I've got some shit!" was weird.

Even weirder when he produced a plastic bag full of his own excrement and started to throw it at the audience, which quickly dispelled my misconception that he was a mere dope casualty.

Then there was the fight between the rugby club and the local boneheads which invaded a performance at a hall in Wales, meaning that I had to transplant myself and the fifty strong audience to the local churchyard and perform standing on a wall (why couldn't the combatants simply have continued to fight in the street where they started rather than invading a poetry gig?)

Once I had maggots tipped over my head onstage. Rival soccer fans have fought in the audience. I have jumped off stage to chase Nazis out of the gig, followed by the entire crowd. A dog tried repeatedly to shag my leg while I was onstage at the Glastonbury Festival. I have performed illegally to a mixture of English soccer fans and secret police in a hotel basement in Albania during the Hoxha regime, to dying cancer patients in a hospital operating room in Bulgaria (they loved it and didn't understand a word). That's just what springs to mind right now. In well over two thousand gigs there have been many more.

PI: Check him out at www.attilathestockbroker.com.

Hettie Jones: All My Jobs and Then Some

Hettie Jones was born Hettie Cohen in Brooklyn, New York, in 1934. She earned a BA in Drama from the University of Virginia and did postgraduate work at Columbia University. Her first collection of poems, *Drive*, was selected by Naomi Shihab Nye to receive the Norma Farber First Book Award from the Poetry Society of America. She is also the author of *How I Became Hettie Jones*, a memoir of the beat scene of the fifties and sixties, as well as of her marriage (1958-1966) to LeRoi Jones/Amiri Baraka; *Big Star Fallin' Mama: Five Women in Black Music*; and many books for children. With LeRoi Jones she established *Yugen* (1957-1963), a magazine that published poetry and writings by William Burroughs, Allen Ginsberg, Jack Kerouac, Philip Whalen, and others. They also launched Totem Press, which published poets such as Ginsberg, Gregory Corso, Frank O'Hara, Edward Dorn, and Gary Snyder. Jones is the former chair of PEN American Center's Prison Writing Committee and from 1989 to 2002 ran a writing workshop at the New York State Correctional Facility for Women at Bedford Hills. She lives in New York City, where she writes and teaches.

Poetry Investigator: So dinner was okay?

Yeah, now I am sort of sitting here stuffed. It was warm, warm, warm in New York and then it got chilly, chilly, chilly. I know you have that sort of changeable weather in New Mexico.

PI: Yeah, it's a little windy but nice, there are some quail and a rabbit outside the window.

Ah, that'll do.

PI: And there are big clouds floating over like animals proud of their pink underbellies.

[*laughs*] Thank you!

PI: Here are a few lines from Jones's poem "Hard Drive."

[. . .] with clouds big and drifting
above the road like animals
proud of their pink underbellies,
in a moment of intense light
I saw an Edward Hopper house
at once so exquisitely light and dark
that I cried, all the way up Route 22
those uncontrollable tears
"as though the body were crying"

PI: I read your poem "Hard Drive" on the internet and saw that you had won a prize for it.

Yes in 1999, the Norma Farber Award that the Poetry Society of America gives. It took a very long time to put out a first book of poetry. It's really my own fault; it's not because I was rejected by other people or any bullshit like that. It's just because I was too lazy. You know I was doing a lot of other things. Which is the subject of this conversation, right?

PI: Yes. I am curious, though: with the award you won, was there any monetary prize?

Oh yes, it was a big five hundred dollars.

PI: Well, that is a couple of dinners in New York.

Yes, it's better than a poke in the eye with a sharp stick.

PI: I wanted to ask you about your poem "Hard Drive." The image "Saturday the stuffed bears were up again"—were they real bears? Or clouds?

They were stuffed animal bears and apparently someone was selling them, and this was their display. Major Deegan is the highway that goes into the New York

Thruway. I can't remember where I was on the way to, some job or another. I am one of the few people in New York who keeps a car. I have always liked to drive, and when my kids were little it really did help to get us out of the house and take us somewhere. Having a car gave us the illusion of freedom, even if we didn't really have freedom.

PI: "Hard Drive" is a wonderful poem, the image of the Edward Hopper house turning into the uncontrollable tears as though the body were crying.

Maybe because I have recited that poem a whole lot and people think of it almost as my signature poem and I am very fond of it—but I can still put myself back on that highway and I'm seeing those amazing clouds that were rolling over and then seeing the house. I must have written the poem early in the seventies, so it's a pretty old poem.

PI: The uncontrollable tears that took over you as though your body were crying.

There are a lot of reasons why people cry. I don't know, maybe I was having PMS or something [*laughs*].

PI: Well you got a great poem out of PMS [*laughs*]. I loved the line at the end: "Woman enough to be moved to tears and man enough to drive my car in any direction."

It is funny because when my younger daughter was in college she told me I shouldn't recite that poem anymore because it was gender-identified, that the roles were gender-identified. But I ignored her advice and I still recite it from time to time.

PI: It's interesting to think of it from that perspective.

That men drive cars and women cry! It's okay. I simply meant that I was all of those things in one body. To me the car and driving represents control over your environment, or that you have control over your life, and the car represents that I'm not held to my place.

PI: I saw the poem as you were striking out. I know for me that is a very common thing, especially when driving, to burst into tears.

One is alone, there's no one to come rushing over and ask what is the matter. There you are: you can laugh, you can cry, you can sing, you can fart, you can do anything you want [*laughs*].

PI: How do you make your living as a poet? Do you identify yourself mostly as a poet? You have written memoirs, run a small press, published other poets.

I published thirteen children's books before I ever published anything else. Now, although occasionally I write a story, for the past couple of years I've been writing poetry. I seem to like that the most, so I guess I'm a poet. But it's hard to stick with one thing and I don't want to put myself in a box and say I am this or I am that. I like to write poetry because it's as close to music as I can get.

I started to play the piano when I was four. Music was my life, my means of expression for about ten years, and I very abruptly stopped in that teenage rebellious way of saying I don't want to do this anymore, it's not satisfying me. I would have gone on had I lived a little closer to the High School of Music and Art in New York, where I passed the test for entry. I was pretty good.

But then I didn't go. I was bored with classical music. I had already heard some jazz and a little Latin. I wanted something more atonal, more unusual, and I would have found it. It's okay. It's the road not taken. I own a piano. I got a piano into my city apartment by having the window taken out. That was when people didn't want a piano and you could get it just for the delivery fee. At least I have one. I do identify as a poet but I always like to leave the door open for doing other things. In fact I have a whole volume of short stories I haven't published yet . . . one of these days.

PI: What was it like to publish *Yugen*?

At first it was a lot of hands-on labor—it was me doing that by hand—typing poems, aligning them, doing paste up. That wasn't hard to do. When the former

LeRoi and I met, I was working at the jazz magazine the *Record Changer*—that was a put-together, hands on job too, so I knew the process. When LeRoi wanted to have a magazine I was really hot for the idea. It was easy enough for the two of us to get it together. Because we were willful and smart and twenty-three and you can do anything when you're that age.

PI: Would you sell them at readings?

I was working at the *Partisan Review*, and the man who distributed most of the serious literary magazines, at least in the East Coast area, like *Dissent*, *Midstream*, and the *Kenyon Review*, liked LeRoi and me. So he took the magazine on, even though normally to find a distributor you had to have a spine on the book and it had to be perfect bound. *Yugen* was stapled at the spine.

Apparently it got to people who knew people and it got to the West Coast, to the Midwest, and to the college libraries. That's how people began to know of us. People we didn't particularly know. Gary Snyder, Philip Whalen, Ferlinghetti, and Ginsberg when he was living out there. They had their finger on whatever was happening. We slid into knowing those people. But insofar as earning a living publishing that, are you kidding? We paid for it. I had a job at the *Partisan Review*, that's what paid for it.

PI: You were really keeping it together?

Yes, LeRoi was an ambitious young man. He was the one who went out and made the contact, who got the work in. He was really the editor. So far as doing the physical work of putting it together, I did that, a lot of it. But we worked together on it, it was a labor of love and we were in love and that's what you did. But it didn't make any money [*laughs*]. No, no.

PI: Now almost fifty years later you are a professor?

I've never really had a real job in a university; I never wanted to belong to anything. I've retained my right to be on the periphery of any establishment, and luckily, I have squeezed through this way. But I'm a teacher, although I adjunct everywhere. I'm sorry for that static on the phone, if it gets to be too bad you hold your ears while I knock the phone on the desk.

PI: Where are you teaching now?

At SUNY Purchase, which is one campus of the State University of New York. I teach a poetry class as well as a class on the personal essay, there and at the Parsons School of Design, which is part of New School University. I've taught at Parsons for quite a long time, it may even be ten years, but as an adjunct. I don't always teach the full year, I often teach one semester at a time. I also teach at the 92nd Street Y Poetry Center in the fall. I have been doing that for a fairly long time, too.

PI: Are you teaching poetry there?

No, I teach memoir there.

PI: How do you see the students you teach now in relation to the poets you knew in the 1950s?

These are kids. I didn't know anybody who was still in school in the New York fifties scene. So I get kids who are nineteen or twenty years old. Parsons is an art school, a design school. They have a liberal studies program, but the students are not writers. A few years ago I taught at a different division of the New School, Eugene Lang College, which is another undergraduate program. That is more a writing program and those kids were more sophisticated. At SUNY Purchase there is actually a writing program and there have been a few good writers in my classes, but not all that many.

PI: Any Ginsbergs or Kerouacs lurking around?

No, there was one good poet in my last class at Parsons; she had been in an NYU writing program. Then she decided she had better find a way to make a living so she switched to Parsons to learn graphic design so she could get a job. She had been studying writing and philosophy. In fact one of my best students at SUNY Purchase was a philosophy major. You can't tell really where a writer is going to come from, not at all.

PI: You were probably in your early twenties when you met Ginsberg and he was maybe just a little older.

Oh yeah, he and Jack, they were all a generation older than we were. We met when we were about twenty-two and Allen must have been almost thirty by then.

PI: He had already written *Howl* when you met him?

Yeah.

PI: So you were quite sure that he was going to be Ginsberg by that time?

Oh, yeah. It was just about that time. I forget the date of *Howl*, 1956 or 1957, and that was just about the time that LeRoi and I met. But Allen was in San Francisco so we didn't meet him until he came back to New York. By that time he was definitely Allen, but that didn't mean anything to anybody.

PI: He was just another poet who was hanging around?

Yeah, people began to notice through certain little magazines that were around, but it wasn't until Grove Press published that Donald Allen anthology, *The New American Poetry*, that everybody started to get a certain amount of notice. Are you familiar with that book?

PI: Yes, when I first started writing poetry that was the book I read the most. I think that's probably true for a lot of people.

There was some ruckus because Allen had been thrown out of Columbia. He got a certain amount of attention, not because of the quality of his writing, but because of the bad boy image of him. Really the same thing was true for Jack, when *On the Road* came out. It also coincided with the increased interest and broader scope of television.

I think young people were ready for something to happen, because it seemed like in a very short time we were the center of attention. It was so bizarre. There was this *Life* magazine article about the Beats. That really upset my mother [*laughs*]. I told her I was not dirty and I did not have a dirty baby.

PI: How did you get involved with doing writing workshops in prisons?

In the search for money. I haven't told you all the funny things I've done for money.

PI: Let's hear about the funny things you've done for money.

After I left *Partisan Review*, I worked freelance for Grove Press, copyediting and proofreading mostly. Grove was at that time publishing the new wave novelists like Alain Robbe-Grillet, Marguerite Duras, all the difficult French people. So I got to do that but my pay was two dollars an hour.

PI: This was in the early 1960s?

Yeah, but I got to stay home and do the work, and that was what I wanted. I just couldn't see myself working uptown. I couldn't lend my skills to those people. That was what I did for the remainder of the time I was married. After LeRoi and I divorced I was penniless. I had to get jobs, very particular kinds of things, doing editing, and I hardly knew what I was doing.

Later I worked in an antipoverty agency during the Johnson administration, helping to write a history of an agency called Mobilization for Youth. They discovered I knew all about child rearing so they put me in charge of an enormous project, an after-school project for second grade underachieving children. It was just amazing that the opportunity arose and I was put in charge of the huge program with eight schools and eight settlement houses.

At least I was earning a living and we weren't worried about the wolf at the door. That ended and I got unemployment. Then I had to have an operation so I got on welfare.

Then I had one of those epiphanies where I realized that if I didn't start writing, I would never write. Because I was thirty-two years old, and that is when it really began to get hard. I got freelance editing jobs so that I wouldn't have to go out to work. But it was touch and go whether I would be able to pay the rent and have us be able to eat at the same time. I did little weird odd jobs because I always managed to keep a car. I got a job driving for NYU, stupid things like that. I was driving some kind of SAT prep test, and I would drive the materials to the different sites. I would get up at 4 a.m. and go driving so these tests could arrive at 7 a.m. Then I would pick them up.

PI: So you were a test courier.

Yes, then I worked in advertising agencies doing proofreading, copyediting. I copyedited romance novels. I was always able to use that skill. I was good at it for some reason.

I began writing children's books. When the first one sold I was still on welfare, but I had to go off because I was afraid they would discover my huge five hundred dollar advance. So I would work on a kid's book for a while, then I would take a copyediting job. I would buy myself some time and then write again. I would get little advances for the kids' books.

Then I was able to sell some stories for textbooks for kids. I remember I got fifty dollars for one story and found out ten years later that it had been in print in a textbook for Macmillan and Company all that time, and I believe it is still in print. The story is called "The Summer House Secrets," the only mystery story I've ever written. I gradually sold things like that and I remember the last kids' books that I did were novelizations of movies that I got through my agent. Those paid really well.

PI: Do you remember the books you worked on?

No, they're on my resume somewhere. But they paid well, especially for the time. I think I got paid five thousand dollars for something that had to be done in six weeks, that was a huge sum of money. The first one was a cowboy story, *Mustang Country*, all about Montana, where I'd never been. I just bought a geography book and looked up the flora and fauna. Every once in a while a friend comes across it in a remainder bin.

Another one was, you know that song "You Light up my Life?" For some stupid reason someone made a movie from the song, and then I was supposed to do a novelization from the movie. They showed the movie in a screening room just for me. Afterwards I was walking up the street and recognized the person who had starred in the movie. I said, "I am writing a novelization of *You Light up my Life*," and he said, "Why would anybody want to read it?" [*laughs*]

I did very well writing those for a while. That's when I started to write poetry seriously and would allow myself to work on it, and had begun to write stories as well. I published some of those stories and poems in a little chapbook called *Having Been Her*. Then I got a different agent who sent around my stories with the idea of generating interest in a memoir, because the stories were autobiographical.

PI: They were the raw material that *How I Became Hettie Jones* came out of?

No, not really. They were other stories about my life. They weren't about that period, they were more about the life I was leading then, after my divorce, when my children were growing up—stories about race, about being the white mother of black children, and other subjects. They have been published in various magazines and they're part of the story collection I mentioned earlier. I'm slow. I managed to get an advance on the memoir, but it took longer to write it than I expected. So I was still doing proofreading and editing jobs.

My kids were in college by that time. When I came home from work at *Partisan Review*, I could work on *Yugen*. I have always worked a lot, days and evenings. But you have to if you want to do everything you hope to do. I remember an interview with Toni Morrison in which she was trying to explain you give up a lot. She said, "I don't go skiing." By the late seventies I started to teach, but you got paid fifty dollars a class, hardly any money. I have taught in a lot of different places.

After the memoir was published, I got more attention, and so I got jobs that paid a little better. Still, it's no joke; I was working in ad agencies the year before last. I have also written reviews for the *Washington Post*. What do I do for money? I have been the visiting writer at the University of Wyoming. I have been the visiting writer at Penn State, to which I drove by the way, five hundred miles a week. That was fun.

PI: How did you like being the visiting writer?

It really wasn't much of an experience, in the sense that I enjoyed meeting different students, but I always meet different students. Being in a different place was relaxing because there wasn't as much temptation. But Wyoming is a weird place for a New Yorker [*laughs*]. The second year I was there was more fun because my friend Dagoberto Gilb was there, and we hung out a lot. I teach one-day workshops from time to time. You asked how I got into the prison stuff. It was because Jeanine Pommy Vega called me one day and said, "Do you want to make fifty dollars?" Of course I wanted to make fifty dollars. This was 1988. It was at a time when the prison system would give you twenty-five dollars and *Poets and Writers* would match it. She asked if I would take her Sing-Sing workshop. She had been teaching poetry there for years and wanted a break. So I went up there to teach prose. As soon as I got there the money dried up, wouldn't you know. Then I was calling all around looking for money and I ran into a woman who asked if I would be interested in teaching women prisoners. Jeanine doesn't mind teaching the guys but I felt a little uncomfortable, somebody was always slightly hitting on me, or threatening to, and the guys wouldn't do their homework. So this woman got me into Bedford Hills and I found that I liked it very much because it was a welcome change from the college students, even though I had to raise my own money to fund the program. It was just another dimension to my life.

PI: How did you raise the funds for the program?

Through the New York State Council on the Arts, through *Poets and Writers*, through the Puffin Foundation. Just little things here and there.

PI: You would write grants to support the program?

Yes, the prison itself never gave me any money.

PI: How was the prison management? Were they happy to have someone running a writing workshop?

Well, I had to go through the security check that everyone goes through, getting fingerprinted, blah, blah, blah. But they didn't seem to have any objection, because at the time, and we are talking about 1989, there hadn't been a creative writing program since the 1970s. There were people there who were very eager to study poetry. It was good; it was good for me and good for them. I did it until this last January; there has been another crackdown in prison life as there is periodically. They told me they didn't have any room for me anymore. Then they wrote me a Dear John letter saying thanks for your years of service. I don't know if I will get to go back there, but I did it for a long enough time.

It was Felding Dawson, who just died, who got me onto the Prison Writing Committee at PEN, which he had just joined. He also taught at prisons. Together we really built the committee up into a very interesting and functioning committee. I have just come off three years of being the chair of that committee. I have taken a leave of absence from everything that I usually do, that I have just finished reciting to you, to write Rita Marley's memoir. Which I'm supposed to begin on June the third if I can ever get my software and hardware together [*laughs*].

PI: Are you working directly with her to write that?

Yes, we actually worked together one weekend about a year ago to do the proposal. The book sold to Hyperion. So we are going to start, but I have one more week of teaching. I am tired of teaching; it's been a long semester.

PI: How did you get hooked up with her?

Through a friend of mine who knew her manager. They brought us together and we liked each other. It was fun hanging out with her. She is a gutsy lady who has a good story to tell that has not been told. One way to reclaim your life, which everybody else has told their version of, is to just do it yourself. That's part of the reason I wanted to write my memoir—to reclaim my own history, to state it as I felt it happened, instead of leaving it to other people who were only surmising. So that's the whole story.

PI: It's a great story.

I am glad you like it.

Craig Arnold: We Are So Practiced in the Art of Talking

Craig Arnold's first book of poems, *Shells*, was selected by W. S. Merwin as the 1998 winner of the Yale Series of Younger Poets (Yale University Press, April 1999). He was awarded the Amy Lowell Poetry Traveling Scholarship in 1996-97, a year he spent mostly in Spain. His poems have appeared in *Best American Poetry 1998*, *Poetry*, *Paris Review*, *Yale Review*, *The New Republic*, *New Letters*, and *Hayden's Ferry Review*. He took his BA at Yale and has a Ph.D. in creative writing at the University of Utah. Arnold was a Visiting Writer in the Department of English at UT Austin in Fall 1999 and was the Thornton Writer-in-Residence at Lynchburg College in Virginia in Spring 2000 and held the John Atherton Fellowship in Poetry at the Bread Loaf Writers' Conference in 1999. He is the singer and songwriter of the band Iris. He was awarded a Hodder Fellowship in the Humanities at Princeton in 2002, where he completed his second book, an erotic/mystic hip-hop anti-narrative entitled *Made Flesh*.

Poetry Investigator: How are you?

I just finished my first week of teaching here for this gig I have for the summer and it's totally exhausting. It doesn't help that it is like an oven here.

PI: What are you teaching?

I'm a TA, assisting for a humanities course, a greatest hits of Western Lit. The professor is cool, one of those old school guys, and I am his second in command. I am grading papers, leading discussion sections. Part of the deal is I get all my meals free. I am reacquainting myself with dining hall food, which I did not miss at all.

PI: How is the food?

It's starchy [*laughs*]. That's about all one can say. It is probably good for dining hall food, but it still makes me sick.

PI: Do you find you eat more when it's free?

Yeah, I do actually. I don't know why. I am stealing stuff for my family as well.

PI: Bringing dinner rolls home?

I am sticking all these chicken breasts in my bag and bringing them home to my starving family. This is the life of a poet. Periods of intense free money, followed by longer periods of complete impoverishment.

PI: Tell us about your family.

There are three of us, my wife and a kid who is eight. We all just came out to Princeton a year ago to do the Hodder Fellowship.

PI: Congratulations on the Hodder Fellowship!

I got my last paycheck on July 1. I will be broke again in a week. I like the question you asked [by email] of how does one fit into the East Coast poetry scene—I thought it was rather richly ironic. I was thinking of hanging out in Princeton, getting all this money and not really having to do anything, except write and be in my office. I was thinking of how much more oppressive that was than just teaching. There wasn't anything expected of me. I think I imagined that there were tacit, unspoken expectations. In some ways it was a lot harder.

PI: Did it affect your writing? Were you able to get writing done during the year?

Yes, it was really good to have this long of a chunk of free time. With having that long of a period, it really encourages me to radically rethink things. I had this big chunk of a book written before I came here. I had written a lot of it the summer before in Texas. With all this time on my hands, in some ways it encourages useless meddling. You take something that isn't broken and fix it.

With that much time and lack of distraction, I was able to come to the root problems of the project I was working on. I don't know if it is entirely successful. The manuscript is being looked at right now. It is a long poem called *Made Flesh*. A single, long dream vision poem. It is partly inspired by reading medieval mystical poets, partly inspired by Garcia

* See Smith's chapter on getting paid to study poetry at the University of Alabama.

Lorca, partly by my dear friend Abraham Smith*, who was a real shot in the arm for me at a very raw moment in my writing career. Running into him was a real wake-up call for me.

PI: As far as his particular style of writing?

Yes, his style of writing, and he is someone with immense imaginative powers, someone I think has really tapped into something, duende, or whatever. He doesn't need to deliberate as much. I don't want to say too much about Abraham's poetry; I think he has his own path to work out.

Just to see someone who could knock off these jagged, sharp-edged, beautiful images at the drop of a hat, string them together, and have them make sense, without having to spend hours and hours poring over it. It made me lose faith for a while in the powers of the intellect. It was good for me because I started out being such an intensely intellectual writer. Very head, brainy writing. To run into him when I did made me say perhaps there is more to it.

PI: I saw him up in Taos this year do a great improvisation with a flautist. It was impressive to see him improvise on the spot those jagged lines and leaps he makes with his images, and have him weave that together extemporaneously.

It is wonderful. If he ever gets his relationship to composition worked out he is going to be the greatest poet of the twenty-first century. At least one of the first ones. He will embarrass us all. He has it where it counts.

PI: Please talk about winning the Yale Younger Poet award and how that has affected your writing specifically, but also how it has affected your ability to get jobs. Has it helped? Has it hurt?

It certainly has helped. I don't know if it has helped get jobs, because I wasn't applying for jobs before. To get a job without a book for the academic world is hard enough. I do have friends who have gotten jobs without books. They do it by being really dedicated, professional teachers. I am more of a free-form, improvisatory, stand-up comedian of a teacher. I like just talking about books, talking about poems, and having free-form floating discussions. There is a really hot groove you can fall into as a teacher in a class where someone has an idea and someone else takes that idea and runs with it. I get off on that. I have learned as much from my students as I have from study.

You could sit in a room for hours with a pad or a computer and you are just talking with yourself. Or you could sit in a room with Dante or Garcia Lorca and you could sort of have a conversation with one of them, but it's one-sided. They are saying things to you but you don't have the opportunity to reply. Of course, people write responses—some people's entire careers are responses to other poets. I don't think any of that comes close to an actual conversation with a living flesh-and-blood human being, who is also talented, imaginative, and knows something about poetry.

Some universities like that style of teaching and some don't. I would say that has been as much of a factor in getting jobs as that book. Obviously, the Yale Younger Poet Award opened a lot doors. They weren't always the doors I wanted to open.

In certain institutions that has a lot of caché. It is a well-respected prize in the academy; it hasn't closed any doors. The book *Shells*, the ethos of that kind of poetry, it is something I love and admire, but there is a lot more that I am interested in. Occasionally I would be going to job interviews where I think they were expecting me to talk about Elizabeth Bishop and the larger modernist tradition and how I fit into that. I talk about Paul Blackburn and the Black Mountain School and Garcia Lorca and all of that.

They say, "Whoa, what planet are you from? We thought you were this nice boy." There is a lot more to talk about than the modernist cannon. Winning the Yale certainly has not been an immediate "let's throw lots of jobs at him" kind of thing. The first two years I went on the job market after the book had been accepted, I didn't get any real tenure track jobs. I got two visiting gigs that may be more a function of me being a lunatic than the book itself. I think the hard and fast rule is having a book makes it easier to get a job, but it is possible to get a job without a book. It is also possible to not be able to get a job while having a book. It is a more case-by-case thing. How it has changed my own writing is a much longer answer. I am not sure I am the best person to answer that.

PI: You had this hit book. Did you feel pressure for your next book coming out to be as good or better?

Yeah, sure, of course. It is mostly internal pressure. I won't let myself do any worse. I can't imagine writing something like *Shells*, but not as good. I am my own most ruthless critic. It may sound arrogant, but it would shame me to no end to try to write another book like *Shells*, another bunch of formal poems tied around a fugue on a central theme. It wouldn't be satisfying; it wouldn't be fun. It would not be a challenge. I feel like I did that. I want to do something else now. This new book is very different. As to pressure from outside, the response has been mixed.

The first set of pressure or weird set of responses I got was when I read the poems to an audience. I do the poems dramatically, I act them and I perform them. Partly the slam influence and partly just the fact that I think poetry is an oral thing. They were expecting the neat tidy poems, given the raw material in them. The fact that I was doing them in a way that they didn't expect was more a source of pressure than anything else.

PI: It was shocking when you would show up at a reading and full-out perform the poems?

Exactly, people did give me that "Wow, we had no idea." That can be a form of pressure. You are not quite what we expected, and often the response was, "And wow, aren't we happy."

PI: It is not necessarily a negative thing.

No, not necessarily a negative thing. I think that was tempting to me. I thought, "Oh, I can write more of these poems, dramatic monologue poems and perform them in an interesting way and I can keep this up indefinitely." But at the same time, I think the reason I started performing them in the way that I did was that I was dissatisfied with the original poems. I didn't think they were voiced enough, I didn't think they had enough of that Blakean fire.

PI: Did you find that you would change them in the performance?

I departed in cases from the text. Mostly I made edits, and the edits were mistakes I made over and over in performance, that I realized were better than the original [*laughter*]. You are doing something from memory and your voice falls into a more comfortable or pleasing rhythm and wants to alter the words of the text to fit that. That is what I realized in some of the poems—there are phrases that are not quite right in the original text. There are rhythms that are not quite on and so I would subconsciously or consciously change them in performance. If I ever did another edition of it, I would probably change the poems. One should write new poems, not try and tweak the old ones. At some point you just have to let them go and write new ones.

PI: I was at a workshop on William Carlos Williams and his quote, "Poetry is a small or large machine made of words" came up, and a woman quoted you as saying, "Poetry is a party where anything can happen." Could you please talk about that?

I don't think poems are machines. They are poems; the machine can only be a metaphor. I think poems work like poems. I think the thing they are closest to is arguments. They are closest to arguments and closest to conversations and therefore I think of the party. Which is not my image incidentally: I believe it is Kenneth Burke's.

I used to rant to my students about this. It was probably in my mind when I was in Santa Fe . . . the idea of the poem being a party invitation. Not that there is necessarily a party going on in the poem, although I have written poems where there is a party going on. There is a long section in the new book that is a cocktail party—a mix of all the different voices weaving in and out of each other. What I would tell my students was I did feel it was more helpful to think of poems as invitations to parties. Because that made it more of a human thing, as the beginning of a dialogue, a dialogue between the writer's voice and the reader's mind.

The point is I don't think poems are things you put together to do things to people with. Which I guess is the importance of the machine analogy. There are poems that are like machines, you turn them on and start them running and the reader puts him or herself through the poem. I tend to resent those [*laughs*] and I think most people do, people who recognize that poetry is a machine acting on them tend to resent it. Just as we tend to resent movies that manipulate our emotions, movies that force us to feel things beyond our better judgement. Obviously, poems have crafted and artistic qualities to them. But so do conversations. The other element of the machine analogy implies that the poem has a life of its own, has its own existence beyond it being read, as if a poem were a sculpture that could be buried in the ruins and could have this ongoing existence. I utterly reject that. Poets who make poems that are little ornate objects that don't expect ever to be read, just an interior perfection of their own, I don't see the point in that. It is a decadence. I am all about decadence, but this is a kind of decadence that does not appeal to me. I think people should write poems so that other people can read them [*laughs*]. Not to have the perfect crafted works in their possession, the whole Emily Dickinson thing.

PI: Talk about winning the Amy Lowell Travel Grant.

The Amy Lowell Traveling Grant is one of the weirder prizes in American poetry. There are a lot of weird prizes in American poetry, but I think the Amy Lowell takes the cake. Amy Lowell, the imagist poet, as a broadening experience, endowed it for American poets. I think she felt American poets in the early nineteen hundreds were a little too parochial. So the idea was to make them leave America and not come back until they had learned something about the world [*laughs*]. When I was awarded that in 1996, I thought, "This is a godsend." One of those things that can change one's life.

We went to Spain for six or seven months, then back to France for a while, then I went back to Spain for a little bit longer. We were in San Lucar de Barrameda, it is one of those wonderful Mediterranean towns where if you don't know anyone, you can't get anything done. But if you know people and they know you, you can lead this wonderful existence.

I went into it without knowing a word of Spanish and had to teach myself the language from the street level up, which was an interesting and painful experience. It wasn't a big city; it wasn't cosmopolitan at all. It was kind of weird to be stuck in this small town in Spain, waiting for our lease to run out. Watching festival succeed festival and party succeed party, realizing we had stumbled into this way of life that had no resemblance to the one we had known in America. Finally I clicked into the Southern Spanish mindset. No pasa nada. Everything is going to be okay.

PI: Were you working on the poems for *Shells* at that time?

Yes, that is when I wrote a huge chunk of the book. There are a couple of poems that are set in that town—the last poem, the snail museum poem, and a couple of explicit references to Spanish flamenco dancers and to Lorca. Then the long poem in the middle of the book, "Transparent," I wrote while there. The mussels poem and a poem that didn't make it into the book were written there. I wrote twenty to thirty pages of the book while in Spain.

That arena, that space that I moved through for six months was central to the entire enterprise. I hadn't thought of the book being organized around shells, for example. Living there is when that occurred to me. Originally it was going to be more about the ocean. The book changed character, and I would not have written *that* book, except for the time in Spain, for which I am eternally grateful.

PI: You are one of the few poets who is active in both the academy and the poetry slam—at least you were active in the slam when you lived in Austin. Talk about the strengths and weaknesses of the poetry slam and the academy.

The problem is, of course, you can speak to the strengths and weaknesses of each camp from the point of view of the other camp, which is easy. I don't even want to bother rehashing those things because everyone knows them or should know them. I have no idea what people are complaining about, or even if they complain about each other. I've heard slam poets complain about the academy. I have heard academics occasionally complain about slam poetry.

One thing I have noticed is that academics tend to be far more interested and excited by the slam than slam poets are by the academy. One could say because the more exciting things are going on in slam and everyone would want to be a part of that. Including people who might not have set up their lives around that.

I think there is an element of truth to that but I don't think that is the full truth. If I had to make a generalization, and I am probably going to make some enemies here, I would say in general people among the academic world are more tolerant and more accepting and more willing to find value in things that don't look like what they do.

This isn't to say I don't know academic poets who don't think the slam is a ridiculous institution. I sometimes myself feel like the slam is a ridiculous institution, for different reasons. Most of the younger poets I know who work in the academy don't have any particular attachment to old school traditional weight or class attached to being in the academy. A lot of them are open to the idea of the slam, open to the idea of performance. Some of the people who are doing more interesting things in performance are in the academy as well, not many it's true.

PI: Can you give some examples?

I am thinking of Elena Davis, who is an amazing poet and an amazing reader, who as far as I know has not been involved in the slam. There are people surrounding the Poetry Project at St. Mark's who have come out of the Bowery slash New York school slash Black Mountain scene—maybe Anne Waldman, Paul Blackburn—who are not active in the academy and have brought that vibe with them. There are a lot of people like that. I think in general there are sections of the academy that are closer to the ethos of the slam than one would imagine.

Here is something I think some academics would advance as a criticism, which I would mean as a compliment: I think that one of the observations that one can make about slam poetry is that it appears to separate itself into one of six or seven readily identified voices. You could give them names. In fact some slam poets have given them names. I am thinking of Big Poppa E and the Wussy Boy School, that is definitely a slam persona. There is what I used to call the Estro Rage poem, which is the angry woman but funny surrealist. That particular variety of rage gets so ingrown on itself it starts knocking off very funny stuff. There is sort of the Maggie Estep school, I don't know if she is a school, and my friend Genevieve Van Cleve in Austin. I love that stuff, I eat that up.

The criticism that some academics would make of the slam is that in any given slam you are going to hear these six or seven distinct voices, people are going to fall into one after the other. Many people would see that as a weakness; in fact I think of that as a strength. It's like Yeats's mask, the essay "Per Amica Silentia Lunae," Yeats talks about the poet finding a mask on a mythological oak tree. He takes down the mask and touches it up a little bit, paints the eyebrows in, adds some blush to the cheek, and puts it on himself. Through that mask he can find his anti-self. By putting on a conventional form, a conventional mask, or a conventional voice you in fact find something new about yourself and your own voice. I totally agree with that. I think it is a fabulous metaphor.

A lot of slam poets, by taking on these fairly conventional personae, have in fact managed to come up with really cool stuff. The reason is—I think a lot of academic modernist poetry is so obsessed with individual voice—is that the poets spend so much time being quirky or idiosyncratic or trying to be original that they forget to say anything [*laughs*].

Sometimes it is so liberating to just say, okay, this is my angry white boy poem or my dirty white boy poem. That is the persona I am going to be taking for this poem and having gotten that out of the way, I don't have to convince you how original I am. I can simply say things that are interesting, useful, engaging, and maybe thought provoking. That to me is the real strength of slam poetry.

I like to think of it as the old Italian commedia dell'arte, where you have these six or seven stock characters. Pierrot, Pierrette, and Pulcinella, the harlequin. It is like superheroes. I am putting this costume on for my poem or I am putting it on for all of my poems. I think that once you have gotten that out of the way, some interesting work can take place.

Now having said that, there are slam poets who think or feel or demonstrate that simply donning the mask is enough. It may be a function of the slam's relative novelty. If the slam continues to go the way it is going, if it continues to strengthen, grow, and develop, then the novelty of simply striking a certain pose will wear off and people will either want to hear more interesting things or they will simply leave. I think that tends to happen in places where the slam is not such a strong force. The slams I have been to in New York and Chicago and Austin, people are less interested in reinforcing their masks. They are comfortable with their masks and they can then go on and do other things.

That is one comment I can make regarding the slam. Now going in the other direction toward the academy, I think one criticism I have heard slam poets make of the academy is that they are too intellectual. I happen to think that there are ways in which you can insult your audience. I think it is insulting to think that the audience can only deal with words of one syllable or very simple parallel constructions, or can't deal with a metaphor being developed over the space of thirty lines. I think that is a form of condescension.

There is a lot in academic poetry that is unnecessarily obscure. A lot of academic poetry is difficult for the sake of being difficult. It could be paraphrased in ways that could make it much clearer. It is unnecessarily busy. I mentioned earlier, a lot of attention goes into constructing an original voice for the poet and less on having something substantial to say. I wouldn't care to speculate why that is the case.

There are a lot of reasons why contemporary poetry has become difficult. Part of it is poetry has become so closely linked to the university. Not only to the university but also to certain literary schools of interpretation that pride themselves on being difficult. I don't think this will be so forever. It's more of a momentary historical brain fart, if you like. I can't see that continuing. The fact is that difficult poetry only rewards a kind of intellectual obsession. Not everybody is possessed of that obsession. I think it will weed itself out sooner or later. I think academic poetry has an awful lot to learn from the slam. The slam has something to learn from the academy, but I don't think it is so much about craft; I think it is more about the way you approach your subject.

PI: In some ways it is a function of having the time to work on your poetry.

It is absolutely a function of time. There are some avenues to support yourself as a slam poet. You can do what Abraham does and drive around the country in a pickup truck, doing slams, and sleeping on people's floors. That is a great existence for a while. I don't envy him, and I have done it myself for a couple of months. There are not that many opportunities to set yourself up on your own feet.

PI: The performance poets or poets from the slam who are really making a lot of money are doing it from appearances at colleges.

So in a way slam poets are living off the academy [*laughs*].

PI: It is an interesting time right now where this crossover is taking place. Although in most cases, the people that are hiring them are not the English or creative writing departments but the student unions.

Which is great, as far as I am concerned, that this grassroots thing is going on, and I applaud it. What really creeps me out are the various corporate sponsorships for slam poetry. That terrifies me. I am glad that people are making money off of it, and I suppose in some ways it can be seen as giving it to the man. These large multinational corporations who are sponsoring slam as a public arts support. It creeps me out. I would rather be supported by the academy [*laughs*]. Obviously the academy is supported by corporate capitalism, as is anything else. We all are. I feel like I have some idea of where the money is coming from. That is not my polemic; it is just a note in passing.

PI: I am interested in that because I have done two tours with corporate sponsorship, one with Grand Marnier and one for Pontiac.

What was that like?

PI: There was very little feedback from them as to what we should actually be doing. Although in the end I think we lost the Grand Marnier sponsorship because of one event where the poets kept talking about being drunk on Grand Marnier. They asked us to say you could get complimentary beverages but they didn't want the poets to dwell on getting drunk on free drinks. That was the thing on the tour

where I can look back and say that really pissed them off, because of how they responded.

That really pissed whom off? The poets or the sponsors?

PI: The sponsors. They were pretty agreeable to whatever the poets were doing in the shows, but in this particular incident the poet kept saying, "Get drunk on free drinks!" and they kept asking him not to say it. On the other hand, we did have a motto that was, "Why not have a pint of Grand Marnier today?"

I also just did a tour for Pontiac, which was very interesting, and there were no restrictions on anything we did. Except that when we performed at GM headquarters they asked us not to do—and this was the tour manager, not the people from corporate—asked that we not do a poem with the word asshole in it.

A lot of the readings on the tour were at Borders and we had no problems with language, until the last reading in San Diego. And there was a woman who got up in San Diego and did a relationship poem where every other word was obscene. So by the middle of the poem, she was into nonstop obscenity, fuckity, fuck, fuck, fuck. The people in Borders were going crazy, and we had a good sound system so everyone could hear.

They had also put us near the children's section of the bookstore. So she got stopped in the middle of her poem, and the Borders people watched us carefully after that. The next poet up was a rapping grandmother who did her rapping-nana poem that had the word ass in it. Of course that got them really upset again.

Pontiac never asked us to do poems about how beautiful chrome was or anything like that. The car was called the Vibe and I developed a bit where I would talk about the car being a vibrator, and I would say in a low sexy voice that you shift, shift. I liked playing with that image. For me the clue is what you said: how different is a university from a corporation that is supported from tax money and money from foundations, donations from alumni who are successful in corporations?

Absolutely.

PI: When you get down to it, if you say, "To be pure I am only going to do readings, and I am only going to make money from the people who pay to go to the readings"—but all of those people have jobs.

Yes, there is no way out of it.

PI: It is controversial within the poetry world, the question of whether you should work with sponsorships.

The fact of the matter is there is no life without sponsorship of some sort. I think it is more nakedly obvious in poetry than other things. Someone is going to be sponsoring you somewhere. If you have a job you are being sponsored. If you own stocks. The difference as far as I can tell is a matter of community standards, what you can do in one arena and not in another. My experience with the academy is not unlike doing readings at radio stations, where I was asked politely, "Please don't use any obscenity because we are broadcasting and we are under FCC regulations."

In other cases at Borders or Barnes and Noble where there were kids present or Mormons present—I won't do those readings anymore. Not because I have a problem with Borders or Barnes and Noble, I just don't think it is the right arena for a poetry reading.

PI: Yeah, they are very dry.

In most cases I don't think bookstores are the right venues for reading; to read in bookstores is really about selling product. We all want to sell books, it's true; at the same time you can sell books without being in a place that is all about book-selling. At least in my experience the atmosphere of reading in bookstores is very oppressive, even in independent bookstores. There are a lot of reasons why. Because they are in the business of selling things, they want to cause as little a stir as possible. It is sort of like piping in the soft music—they want you to be the equivalent of muzak. That is good for some people, but not for me.

The thing about reading at a university is it seems like technically you can get away with everything. But at the same time, what is disconcerting for me is not that they are going to say, "Oh my God, he said motherfucker," it is the fact it will go right past them and they won't give you anything. "Well, he said motherfucker, what sort of person might he be?" Then afterwards they are very polite. There is this overbearing atmosphere of politeness [*laughs*]. People might be offended, or worse yet they might not be offended at all.

The spaces I like to work in now, the spaces I am liking much more these days, are that whole wonderful gray area between the two. I have been near New York for the last year and have been going to all these other readings which are not slams and they are not an academic series either. My favorite is the KGB Bar series in New York, which is amazing. First of all it is at a bar, a place where people go to be social and to engage. People can get drunk. There are lots of conversations before, after, and in the intermission. The readings are good. It is not about propping yourself up behind a pulpit/podium and intoning monotonously, in a preacher-like way or in a singsong way. It is much more exciting and engaging, people read with verve.

At the same time it is not a slam where you have sixteen people going for three minutes, each trying to knock each other off the ladder. They usually have two readers. I think that right now that is my favorite type of reading, this middle space that I don't think would have been possible except for the slam, the Beat stuff, and the Poetry Project at St. Mark's.

I don't think these things would have been possible without the slam—people would not have imagined going to a bar to hear poetry. There is another reading series starting up in the Lower East Side, again at a bar. They have four readers, reading for twenty minutes each, which I think is an exciting format. You get a core regular audience and friends of the poets. So you are guaranteed a pretty big crowd, relatively speaking. You get readers who have some reputation, on the performance circuit or something more academic.

A lot of them are graduate students who are beginning to experiment with their poetry and looking for places to play around with it. I think spaces like that are starting to open up, or maybe they have been there all along and I just never noticed them.

These readings that take the energy of the slam and the engagement of the slam and marry it to a sense of higher calling that I do get from the academy, that sense of dedication and devotion to the craft, to the art. I hope there are more of them.

PI: I think the slam has helped to build an audience. It is certainly a gimmick—the competition part, the judging. It seems once there is an audience you can strip that off and you don't need to do that gimmick over and over. For me the gimmick is a little stale; I like the energy of the performance and having people be able to stretch out in longer formats.

I do have other criticisms of the slam, which are largely to do with the competitive aspect. Also, a lot to do with a real myth, what I see as a self-delusion about the slam. Again this is going to vary from place to place. The idea that the slam builds a sense of community is as far as I can tell completely bogus. Again I don't know Albuquerque, but what I gather is that poets from Albuquerque are respectful of each other's work and that they learn from each other.

The slam that is going on in San Antonio is really hopping; there are some great things going on there. Especially on the national level, the national events I have been to, it seems there is a lot of backslapping going on. Sort of "good job, good job, good job." A lot of congeniality. For my take on things, you build poetic community not by being nice to each other but by being influenced by each other and by arguing with each other.

I love it when slam poets start answering each other, when they start writing poems to each other. I have noticed in the two or three years in which I have been associated with the slam, I have seen the ways in which different poets feed off of each other, learn from each other, and are influenced by each other. I don't see it happening that often. That was in some way what started distressing me about the slam. That a lot of poets were much more committed to sticking with their own voices, finding the thing that works, and doing it over and over again. Maybe it is a matter of ambition but it seems to me that there was not enough of a reward for taking risks.

PI: Sometimes slam poets are responding to the audience with their writing, and

that can be good and bad. You can learn from what people respond to, but you can also fall into the trap of trying to write to that.

Absolutely, the exact same thing is true of the academy. This is true of poets everywhere; it is not specific to the slam. In the academy it is sometimes even more naked. In some ways there is more at stake: what's at stake is not winning the slam that evening but getting a book out or getting a huge fellowship or getting a job—people are even less willing to take risks.

PI: Please talk about making money from poetry.

In terms of dollar amounts and what has really supported me has mostly been fellowships. There is the Hodder $40,000, NEA $20,000, the Amy Lowell $36,000, and a couple of smaller academic grants. There is money from universities as well, especially if you are a grad student. But for me it has mostly been fellowships.

One of the ways I have just stayed alive, and more than that, stayed independent, it is not so much getting the money but getting money that doesn't have any strings attached, so you can just do whatever the hell you want to—it really has been about relentlessly monitoring the fellowships and their deadlines. I am applying for a Guggenheim next year and the Bunting Fellowship as well from Harvard. There is money out there; it is not all for academic poets.

Another thing I don't know if people have talked about is writers' colonies. I just got back from MacDowell. There was one person at MacDowell who had literally been going from writers' colony to writers' colony for the last two years; she has been supported for two years jumping from colony to colony.

PI: Do most of the writers' colonies have a small stipend to help with travel and food?

You might get a tiny stipend; mostly they pay you room and board. Sometimes you get a little money to travel and to cover your bills while you are gone. There are tons of colonies, some of which are more generous with their money than others. That has been a way for people to work it. Especially if you are single [*laughs*].

PI: What was your experience at MacDowell?

It was the most amazing six weeks I have spent in a long time. First of all, because removing the mechanical details of keeping yourself alive is wonderfully liberating . . . simply not having to cook for yourself [*laughs*]. I have resisted that for a long time. I always have to cook for myself, I wouldn't be a responsible human being if I didn't. This was the first time I just kicked back and allowed myself to be fed for six weeks. It removes all the annoying details of living. They serve you breakfast and dinner in the dining room. They deliver your lunch. It creates a little island for you to be on with other artists.

This is especially good for people who are working outside of the academy, who aren't always in contact with other quasi-academic or intellectual types. All of a sudden you are around these people who do the same thing you do and who are dedicated to it in the same way you are. Sometimes the conversations are really dull but often they are amazing and you can really learn from people. It was an eye opener for me because I was spending time with people outside of my discipline. I met some great poets but I was also hanging out with sculptors, avant-garde contemporary composers, visual artists, and filmmakers.

I think I learned more from talking to them, although I certainly learned from talking to poets and writers. In some ways people who are also artists but from other disciplines can give you an amazing perspective on your own work. Because they are not writers, they are not looking at it as writers.

PI: Are you trying to get a full-time teaching position?

My plan is to hold out until I have enough substantial work, enough of an achievement that I am happy with, that the tenure process will not be so challenging, where it won't freak me out [*laughs*]. I have seen a lot of very talented poets go and get their tenure-track job and spend five to ten years to get tenure, which requires of you a certain, shall we say, skill set that has nothing to do with poetry or literature [*laughs*]. That has to do with committee work, making deans happy, making students happy.

To me it is a lot more corporate, with fitting yourself into a certain corporate structure than it has to do with writing. I have seen some people who lost their energy over it. It sucks you dry in some way. There are poets who probably would have been much better off patronized by some rich lord in the seventeenth century, given a little cottage and two pounds a week, and would have been happy.

Some people just need that, but the academy in some ways and some places demands more of you. Sometimes it can demand your soul. I see that happens to teachers who were really hot promising writers, but who for whatever reasons got drained by having to deal with the tenure machine. It is really sad. I hate to see that.

PI: So you feel by building up a track record of publishing, it will make it easier to get to that position?

If I were going to pay my dues, I would rather pay my dues to the house of poetry than to the academy. I would rather live an existence of complete insane uncertainty for five years, going from fellowship to fellowship and job to job, and have some good work to show for it. Then to be able to say, okay, I have done my suffering [*laughs*]. I have suffered on my own terms rather than as an assistant junior level professor, where you don't really get to call the shots.

PI: How about the reading circuit? Are you finding with the success of *Shells*, that you are able to generate income from readings?

Yes. The problem is I have less and less time to travel. One of the things that getting the NEA grant did for me was it freed up an amazing amount of time to do readings. I didn't have to worry about paying the rent and my student loans. I could take time out and do readings. I could travel for three weeks or a month.

I would get one good reading at a college and then set up as many readings as I can, driving there and back. This year it was Boise. I went to Boise to read at a conference, which they invited me to do. They were paying me enough for that so it was worth the while to get a bunch of other readings as well. This a good way to make money doing readings: if you have one reading that is paying well, you can then stack up other readings around it and make it all worth while. A lot of my friends who go on reading tours do readings at colleges and alternate them with readings at bookstores.

The college will pay well and defray some of your expenses, then you can do the readings at bookstores that don't pay anything but you can sell books. I have done that a lot.

Any place I go I try to set up readings, even if it's for a vacation. Of course this gives you a tax write-off. One of the things I have discovered about doing readings in colleges is that a lot of colleges with MFA programs are often the hardest place to get readings. But the smaller state schools or the small private colleges that are off the beaten track are really hungry to have people come and read. Because they don't get anybody, whether it is because the faculty is so small that they just don't have the energy to go out and find people to read or because nobody thinks of them. Some big shot poet is flying into Wichita, Kansas to go read at Wichita University. They are probably not going to think about other places they could read in Kansas. I have had a lot of success reading at the smaller colleges because they are excited about it.

Another trade secret is, and this might not be obvious to people who are outside of the academy, is tenure. Getting the assistant professors that are on the tenure track to sponsor your readings.

One of the things that happens when you are an assistant professor who is going up for tenure is you have to write a report on everything you have done for the department for the last five years. If you have brought a visiting writer in, that is a huge thing you can put down.

One of the things that I do is to go to university web pages and find out who the younger assistant faculty are who might be going up for tenure and write them, rather than writing the head of the English department or the department chair or one of the more senior faculty. Because once you are on the senior faculty you don't really have to do anything. You are set for life. So you engage the younger faculty: they are more likely to be closer to where you are, and they can use it as an argument for tenure.

PI: That is a great tip.

Also, it is their chance to host somebody from out of town and have a party [*laughs*]. Bring some sense of festive occasion to the place.

Larry Goodell: Creeley Took Me By the Ears and Shook Me

Editor of *duende* (and coeditor of *Fervent Valley*), poet, musician, and performer, Larry Goodell is a member of that group of poets defined by *The New American Poetry* in the 1960s and the Vancouver Poetry Festival in 1963. His work has appeared in magazines like *Caterpillar, Conjunctions, Sulfur, Telephone, Puerto del Sol, and Exquisite Corpse*, and he has published four books to date, *Cycles* (*duende* 1966), *Firecracker Soup* (Cinco Puntos 1990), *Out of Secrecy* (Yoo-Hoo 1992) and *Here On Earth, 59 Sonnets* (La Alameda 1996). The following interview was conducted by John Tritica and Bruce Holsapple on two dates, June 9, 2004 at Larry's home in Placitas, New Mexico, and February 12, 2005 in Albuquerque.

John Tritica's work has appeared in *Talisman, Situation, Aerial, First Intensity*, and Central Park. He is the translator of Swedish poet Niklas Törnlund's *All Things Measure Time*. His most recent book is *How Rain Records Its Alphabet*. He lives in Albuquerque, New Mexico.

Bruce Holsapple is a speech-language pathologist working in central New Mexico. He's published critical articles on William Carlos Williams and Philip Whalen, and recently had a long essay on "voice" in *The Fulcrum Annual*. His poetry has appeared in *House Organ, First Intensity, The Poker*, and *Intent*.

Poetry Investigator: I first encountered Larry Goodell at the Jump the Border poetry festival in Bisbee, Arizona in 1990. I came in second in their poetry performance contest. It was the first time I had been paid for my poetry. Goodell was an inspiration, with his masks and the intensity he brought to his recitations. I am happy that John Tritica and Bruce Holsapple allowed me to include their interview with Goodell, which covers some of the most important poetry events of the last forty years and gives a good sense of the development of Goodell's poetry.

Tritica: You studied with Robert Creeley at UNM. What year was that? How would you characterize that experience?

Goodell: '61. I heard Creeley read first, at the Adobe Theater which was in the Old Town, and a very odd experience. I'd never heard anything like that. He kept staring at one person in the audience, Bobbie Creeley. *For Love* had just come out and it was dedicated to her. This entire evening he was directing these poems to her. Meanwhile in the audience, there was some drunk who was a friend of Creeley's—I don't know who it was—saying "Yeah, Yeah, Yeah!" [*laughs*]. So anyways, that was my introduction to Creeley, and then I took this course. It was a small class. What he did was use his Wallensack tape recorder a lot. He played interviews for us. He also had a radio program at KHFM—I think it was called *The Single Ear*—on which he interviewed poets. That experience began to open doors, because the only thing I'd "gotten" prior to this was Dylan Thomas. It was a revelation to hear interviews with Dorn, Ginsberg, McClure, Levertov, Bunting, Zukofsky. That was important for me.

Holsapple: What does an English major do after college in the 1950s?

Goodell: I went to graduate school for one year, then I got a job teaching English at the New Mexico Military Institute. Then I was drafted into the army, and they sent me to Camp Irwin in the Mohave Desert, outside of Barstow which is where I spent my Army years, '59 through '61. Soon as I got out, I got back into trying to finish my master's, and that's when I met Creeley. I had been floundering around. I know in the army I was still interested in Dylan Thomas and more academic types of poetry. When I got back to graduate school, when I met Creeley, I got a job teaching at what was then called the Academy for Boys; now it's the Albuquerque Academy. Then I moved to Placitas. I think Creeley arrived there the same year I did. I saved my money and just stopped working. Since I had the GI Bill, I was working on my master's on and off. But I never got my master's, thanks to my own lack of organization.

Holsapple: The *New American Poetry* comes out in 1960. Was it evident that there were two poetry cultures taking place?

Goodell: Oh definitely. It was so academic back then. There was a post-Eliot "freeze" on—I don't know how many times I had to read *The Waste Land*. Thank God for the San Francisco Renaissance, Allen Ginsberg and the Beats. What Creeley was teaching was part of something that wasn't covered at that time. I learned about William Carlos Williams, whose name I knew. But I didn't understand what was going on in the poetry. There is so much information about all this in Creeley's [own] interviews—I almost had those memorized. I mean, he expresses so well the problems they were facing, the difference between Williams and T.S. Eliot, what that represented, when Eliot was in power, until, finally, the revolution of Williams's way of looking at the language began to take hold. I became aware of all these things by way of Creeley.

Creeley's way of teaching was to have recordings with his poet friends, including Williams. We would listen to those and in every case it was someone who no one knew anything about except Creeley. Not only that. People would visit and he had the radio program, interviews. He used Pound's *ABC of Reading* as a "textbook." It was a breakthrough—certainly a lot more interesting than studying Dylan Thomas. Creeley opened doors, particularly to Charles Olson and the "Projective Verse" essay, which was the most important thing a person could read at that time, covering the differences between closed forms and open forms. I couldn't be academic. I didn't like the stuff. W. D. Snodgrass, Robert Lowell. There were the Academic Poets and the New American Poets. At the time there was camaraderie and interchange of information, a wonderful kind of openness and discovery. And a mission that the New American poets had. So I got to know these people by way of Creeley. He wrote me a note about going to Vancouver. He said Charles Olson alone would be worth the trip. I went to Vancouver in 1963. That was an opportunity to be with all these people.

Tritica: Did that sense of mission give you camaraderie with others?

Goodell: If you had spent two years in the desert in the army trying to write like Dylan Thomas when you were from Roswell, New Mexico and then you took a course from Robert Creeley, you would find it to be an absolute and total revelation. I mean, to be introduced to—my understanding of Ginsberg was what I read in *Time*. To be introduced to interviews with Ginsberg, with Dorn, with Levertov, with Basil Bunting, with Louis Zukofsky, all of these people, was mind-boggling, and it was all new, so my poetry began to change. I began to listen to my own voice, rather than ape somebody I could never become. And that's what Creeley's point of view was—it's a hand to hand operation, where younger poets learn from older poets, period. In the way he learned from Williams, I learned from him.

Holsapple: That must have converted you, I mean, must have swept you up.

Goodell: Yeah, because I was writing a lot, and finally I had something I connected with, Williams's approach to writing, based on American speech patterns. Immediately I started writing my own poetry and was beginning to find sources good for me. To me, a printed poem is like a musical score. It shows the reader how to read the poem—it shows me how to read it, especially when I haven't looked at it in a long time. For instance the end of a line is a breath pause for me. I got that from Creeley. But my lines were longer, and I became aware of pitch in some lines. When you have a long sentence, which is several lines of poetry, it will start up here [*demonstrates*], so the higher the pitch of the line, the farther from the left margin. So I'd start up here and then come down like this as that sentence progressed [*gestures*], until the voice falls at the end. So I used that technique a lot in short and long lines. It can be complicated because sometimes you can use it with both short and long lines. The pitch can drop, but there may be no pause in the line. Often I wanted the line to be longer, and there's a breath pause in the middle of a line. I needed to learn about the line and breath pause and get away from my four-beat stricture.

Holsapple: But you're also saying, aren't you, that use of speech, a speech-based poetic played a big role in what's called the New American Poetry?

Goodell: This gets back to the "Projective Verse" essay (which I wish I had in front of me). I mean, I don't comprehend poetry that is not speech-based. Manipulated, "acanemic" exercises and rehashed and revamped bullshit. Williams's point about the American language is integral; it reaffirms the necessity of using American speech patterns in one's writing if one wants to be honest. And I was terribly dishonest when I was trying to do something else.

Tritica: Could you discuss your Vancouver experience? I know Ginsberg was there, Olson, Whalen, Duncan, Levertov. You mentioned once how exciting it was to meet Ginsberg, who had just come back from India.

Goodell: As usual, there were so many people at his reading, they had to put speakers in the hallway.

Tritica: He was that popular that early? What made Ginsberg that popular?

Goodell: There had been articles in *Life* and *Time*. As I recall, *Time* was following him around. He was very well known—the Beats, that was the biggest literary thing—they could write all kinds of falsehoods about it. And it was outlandish et cetera, and, true to form, the academics despised Jack Kerouac. And could not stand Ginsberg. It's hard to realize that back in those times how revolutionary this was. I mean people starved themselves and with no money hitchhiked to Vancouver to hear those people. It was phenomenal, the energy and interest. And you would hang on every word

The one that I really connected personally with was Philip Whalen. I also got to meet the people I first published: Ron Bayes, who has one of the most wonderful ears in poetry—he was teaching in Oregon in LaGrande, Eastern Oregon College. He's still teaching, in North Carolina. A. Frederick Franklyn from Los Angeles, a film critic and poet. Philip would come over on the way to a lecture. I remember he came to the dorm room where we were staying and started taking things out of this pockets [*gestures*] and stood on his head for a while before we went out. Ward Abbot [of Albuquerque] was at Vancouver with a sidekick; they were getting manuscripts from people for a publication. That's when I saw Whalen's manuscripts, which were eight-and-a-half by fourteen. They were just beautiful on the page, the way the lines were arranged. I fell in love with those, just the look of them. Whalen was very available. At one point we were talking about meaning, and he talked about Gertrude Stein and gave examples of her definitions of literary terms, as in *Lectures in America*.

Tritica: What did you find useful about Whalen's work?

Goodell: Well first of all, those manuscripts, the calligraphy; it's so enjoyable just to look at the presentation on the page, the spontaneity. It reminds me of a quote from Ken Irby: "It is impossible to write of what one has written or lived except as this day is, out the window, new, explicit." And with Whalen's writing you have the feeling that at the moment of writing it's like a jazz musician creating something, there it is. And, when he read, often you didn't know when the poem began and his commentary ends; it's like a wonderful weaving in and out of poetry and talk.

Tritica: George Bowering was there?

Goodell: Yeah, there were a lot of Canadians there, Margaret Avison, Phyllis Hess, Fred Wah. People came from all over the country. There were some there without any money whatsoever. They'd eat what was left in the cafeteria. And Bobbie Creeley was there, Clark Coolidge, David Bromige, Carol Bergé. Then of course there were huge parties. At one session everyone was reading a favorite Williams poem, which was really interesting. This is all on tape, tapes at [SUNY] Buffalo, I've been told. And Carol Bergé did "The Vancouver Report," mimeo, 1964, worth reading if you can find it. Olson was the one who floored you. The leaps. There are ways that university professors lecture, but they don't make jumps that Olson makes from one thing to another. There was a lot of discussion about memory in cells and feelings, Mayan hieroglyphics, Pound, HD. I was trying to take notes. (I still have those, but I can't make much sense of them.) It was mind-boggling to be immersed in those poets and the way they talked, incredible. You had a sense that poetry related somehow to everything, that it "has a sense of everything," as Zukofsky said. The more you learned, the more you could write. When I left Vancouver, I was driving home and I couldn't stop crying. Tears running down my face.

Holsapple: A time of great possibility?

Goodell: I was so overwhelmed with these people, great poets! I was astounded. I visited a college friend in Seattle and I couldn't even talk to the guy. We were in totally different worlds. This was a guy I'd been corresponding with and sending poems to for years. Then I visited Dorn in Pocatello. He was real interested about Vancouver. Then I came home.

Holsapple: Dorn was teaching in Pocatello. How did you come to know Dorn? Did he visit Albuquerque?

Goodell: Oh, of course! Because as usual he was a poet that would often visit Creeley and either I would go over there or hear Dorn at readings at the University of New Mexico.

Holsapple: Do you share Dorn's concern with geography?

Goodell: The importance of it? How could it not be important, especially to someone living in New Mexico who's had any contact whatsoever with Pueblo and Navajo people whose remarkable essence—song and ceremony—is intertwined with the land? And that was something brought out at Vancouver, something I thought a lot about, coming back, going to Mesa Verde National Park—I went to several parks—looking at the artifacts. There was quite a bit of talk about sense of place. To me, a sense of the land.

Holsapple: When did *duende* begin?

Goodell: Soon as I got back from Vancouver. Duncan talked about the 1936 essay on duende by Lorca and we talked about it quite a bit and I read that and found it so intriguing, coming back from Vancouver, so that's where I got the name. I got a mimeograph machine from some nuns. I met Richard Watson in Vancouver in Olson's class. At Vancouver, we were all mimeographing our work, for either Olson or Ginsberg or Creeley, and Watson had a long form he had been working on. I published *History of the Turtle, Book I,* by Ron Bayes, poems of Fred Franklyn [*Virgules* and *Deja Vu*], and this thing by Richard Watson [*Cockcrossing*]. My idea in *duende* was to feature one poet and give them a lot of space. So many magazines would just use three or four poems per poet, if you're lucky; I thought a person needed more space. The issues became like books, really, except it was a magazine, each issue devoted to one person. There were also notes, news about further publications. In fact I stated in the first issue an intent to do long poems; I was writing longer poems and was interested in chance operations. Then I met Ken Irby—I'm not sure when—who was living in Albuquerque, through the Creeleys. He was in the army, originally, now out, working at Sandia Laboratories. I think I went to see Ken at Creeley's suggestion, after Vancouver. That was a major meeting. We became close friends; we corresponded for years and years, although we have not been corresponding for many years now. I published his *Roadrunner Poem*. (It was written in Albuquerque.) Then I published a larger bunch of poems called *Movements/Sequences* in

September 1965. Ken Irby to me was so much like Olson, such a comprehensive mind, an incredible ability to read and remember and to be creative, to have a sense of music in his writing. I think of him as Olson's successor.

Tritica: Were you deliberately blurring the distinction between book and magazine?

Goodell: I just thought that you had to have a larger chunk of a person's work to get an idea of what they were really up to. Simple as that. So that in a lot of anthologies and magazines where they had one or two poems—it wasn't enough to give a sense of the person's creative world. So yes I was blurring, I guess. Also, you know, I had studied Yeats's plays. I was interested in plays, too. I published an Eigner play, *Reception*. And I started writing plays, later on. Those were, in a sense, longer forms.

Holsapple: How about your interest in the long poem, was that from a general interest in developing an inclusiveness in poetry?

Goodell: To paraphrase from Pound, the job of the poet is to build us his [or her] world, the interconnectedness of things . . . . It was a little bit like a piano roll, some of those poems I was writing in the 60s which became cycles. One was in a big loop, for instance, in which I was allowing things to enter the poem by counterpointing what was actually happening in front of me with things I remembered that would surface in my mind. I had showed Duncan poems [at Vancouver] that were dream writings, and he said, why don't you counterpoint this with what's going on around you? So Duncan talking about counterpoint was important. But there's another aspect of the long poem that I got interested in later, which had its germination in Williams's *Kora in Hell* and Jack Spicer's talk of serial poems and dictation. I tried to do that—I mean I wasn't consciously trying, it just began to appear—called *Dried Apricots*. So I've had several phases, first cycles, then "event" poems, then my *Ometeotl Trilogy*, then that phase [*Dried Apricots*], then, more recently, when I was writing sonnets, for two straight years, fourteen-line poems. I had the feeling I was involved with something larger than myself. That was called *All Of Love*, and those sonnets ended up in *Here On Earth*.

Tritica: You published Robert Kelly's *Lectiones* in 1965. In what way were you involved with Kelly and Eshleman?

Goodell: See, again, we're all contemporaries, and Irby knew Kelly and Eshleman and was in contact, so I fell in with that. There were these mimeograph magazines of poetry common back then. The thing is, I got an address list from Amiri Baraka for *Floating Bear* and I sent *duende* to this list. So some of the submissions to *duende* were follow-ups to that. It was great to exchange with other mags, like *Wild Dog* in Idaho.

Holsapple: There is a well-defined community of people who shared the same sensibility?

Goodell: Well, from when the *New American Poetry* came along, you really did feel you were part of that; at least, I did.

Tritica: What drew you to Placitas?

Goodell: A friend of mine, a grad student, rented a place about three doors down from where I live now, and he found out about a house-sitting opportunity. I had free rent. I had saved money from teaching. It was ideal. At one time the owners paid me fifty dollars a month to do routine things, water the plants, etc. Basically I lived in a little rural casita adjoining the large adobe house. The owners came out on weekends to stay. So that's how I got to Placitas. Then I met [my wife] Lenore, who as a sculptor-photographer from New York City had come out to New Mexico to get her master's. We had our son, Joel, in 1969. It was eleven years in that place. Then we had this place built and moved here in '75. During the time I was there, I was often visiting the Creeleys at their house in the village. That was an amazing experience also. I met Stan Brackage, Ed Sanders, Max Finstein, and Jonathan Williams, who had a wonderful tape of Basil Bunting's.

Holsapple: These people were traveling around, visiting each other?

Goodell: Visiting Creeley, yes. I can't think of anything comparable except with Gertrude Stein in Paris. That's the place where all the writers came. There was this camaraderie, cross-fertilization. People would stay there, then move on.

Holsapple: Ekbert Faas interviewed you in 1993 for his biography of Creeley. Have you read that? No? The book offers a somewhat flat view of Creeley. You don't get much sense of his presence. But you're presenting a pretty dynamic version of Creeley.

Goodell: I owe my existence as a poet to Robert Creeley. I mean, all the things he's had to say about the poetry of others, his generosity in opening his home to people, to help other poets, suggesting things to do, places to publish; writing helpful notes for people's books. I don't know how anybody can give a flat presentation of Robert Creeley!

Tritica: In "The House That Makes It So" you talk about that atmosphere, ". . . as":

Back to the kitchen, the slow night weaved on
and alternative worlds to where I was born
Played over the cassette player or hi-fi out to space
and Max, or John, I never saw, or
Stan & Jane & Ed & Tuli & Jonathan & Ronald & Ann & George
& on & on came through (I forgot Allen & Lawrence),
To meet like Gertrude Stein's patio in their adobe hacienda
where children pulled apart & adults prospered
and friends analyzed until the dawn trailed off
the always fresh love of poetry that was life, life blood.
If apprenticeship is anything, or hand to hand, a better poem
commands itself to be written in the house that makes it so.

Goodell: There was a lot of white wine, marijuana. I basically didn't partake much in the discussion. I think I've always been a kind of outsider. At Vancouver I was overwhelmed. It was good that I managed to become friends with Ron and Fred and got to know Phil Whalen. Bobbie and I got to be pretty close. Bob and I had many conversations, a lot of which I don't remember, because I was drunk. I remember him looking at me and me nodding my head as though I understood every word.

Tritica: You were at the Berkeley Poetry Festival [in 1965]. Who impressed you there?

Goodell: Drummond Hadley, Ed Sanders, Jim Koller, John Wieners, of course Duncan, McClure. There were a lot of people who impressed me. Ed Dorn of course. But also that's when Olson's drunken lecture was—have you read that? That was a monumental event! A lot of people walked out and you could hardly understand what he was saying. But it was like Olson running for president, was what it was! It was just such a bizarre thing, and to me that's exactly what academia needs. People didn't know what to do, walk out, stay, and it's—you know, there's a lot there in what he had to say.

And it was an amazing experience to encounter Jack Spicer. I didn't know anything about Jack Spicer. I thought he was a young poet. This old guy comes in and tells people not to worry about publication. He was involved with *Open Space*. I liked the idea that there was a publication, perhaps modest, right there in San Francisco. I liked the modesty of his approach. But more than that, his concern with dictation seemed to fit for me and help with my own writing. The way he describes what happens to him when he writes a poem. I discovered that was the way I worked in my poems, in that I would not write something down that I was consciously manipulating or adding too much to from my brain—that, if it was truly dictation, then I was writing something that was coming to me. There was a faithfulness to the innovation of new sentences arriving in my brain. I don't know how else to express it. He says that you might want to write a poem about Vietnam, but when you sit down, the poem might be about skating in Vermont. Intention has nothing to do with it as far as I'm concerned. I have his "Vancouver Lecture," where he talks about ghosts and Martians playing with blocks to try to communicate with us.

Holsapple: I've heard of Drummond Hadley, but don't know anything about him . . .

Goodell: I forgot to mention him being at Vancouver. The thing that was impressive was that he had a lot of his poems memorized. He worked as a rancher. He has the animals, livestock. A very connected person. And he's incredibly good looking. His delivery—he stares right at you, you know, and here come the poems. He plays the guitar with some poems. That impressed me. I have a book of his called *Strands of Rawhide*. It's a wonderful book of poems.

Holsapple: Poets tend to create their own traditions from within the larger cultural nexus. I would guess Stein is part of yours.

Goodell: Especially the Caedmon recording. It's tragic that there aren't more recordings of Stein. To hear her read makes understanding Stein easier. I'm not as good at reading the difficult stuff. As an exercise, I open *How To Write* and read. It's amazing how much music there is in her writing. I can't take very much, because it is daunting. I can't give up reference, whatever the referent is. I don't like secondary stuff and I don't like use of metaphors and language that are separate from what is right there before you in writing. I like to be able to come up with references, some sense of what a poem is stating.

When you participate in a lot of readings, the viability of hearing poetry read out loud becomes essential to the poems. I don't know if you've heard of this one recording of Whitman on a wax cylinder? I find that incredible. I'd give anything to hear Shakespeare read, or Emily Dickinson. I just can't think of poetry as separate from performance.

Tritica: What comes first in your experience, page or performance?

Goodell: Page. What comes first is usually a line. To see something different, sometimes in the middle of the night, usually, just a line, and if I'm doing my duty, I get up and write it down. Generally, that's how a poem starts. I try to be subservient to the form, so I don't know if it's guiding me or I'm guiding it, but that's a precious moment, and when it comes to an end, it comes to an end, and I don't revise it, because there's no way I can get back to that incredibly distinct moment. It's a little like a jazz performance: you record it, and it's frozen in time. The musician doesn't go back and change it.

Tritica: When did you first begin giving performances of your work? Who were the people who informed or inspired you?

Goodell: Once I started putting out *duende*, there were readings. I guess it was after '64. I remember reading in the Thunderbird Bar in Placitas; they were having major musical groups coming through (Sonny Terry, Brownie McGhee, Asleep at the Wheel) and they asked me to do readings. That was when I did some of the early theatrical pieces.

Tritica: Were there masks and other props?

Goodell: Yeah, sometimes with Lenore's help.

Holsapple: You're a little uncomfortable, I take it, with people classifying you as a "performance poet"?

Goodell: Yeah, because it puts me in some other category, when all I am is a poet. See, the only people—any time I experienced anything other than someone reading from their poetry to you at a reading, it was startling, when someone had something memorized, like Drum Hadley. See, it dates back to this. Look. I thought I wanted to be a composer, and I found out I'm not that good, and I started writing poems that kind of related to music. But also in college I took a lot of courses in art and got involved in painting and sculpture, so that I was interested in music, writing, the visual arts, and was terribly interested in opera. I was kind of brought up on Hollywood musicals.

So being a New Mexican and going to Native American dances, to me that's an indication of where poetry possibly comes from. It's not someone reading from a page to other people. Here were people chanting poetry, there were dancers involved and meaningful dress—I don't want to use the word "costume." So the important aspect of seasonal change and the rites that occur meaningfully from the land, from working the land, from living on the land, are evident in the ceremonies. And yet, being Anglo, I couldn't use that consciously in my own work. But it revealed to me that poetry is not necessarily what you study in school. It's again "a sense of everything," as Zukofsky says. So when I started, interested a little bit in John Cage and Jackson Mac Low, in chance, in using cards, in writing things on cards, the idea was to have a room, so that in a bag you had six cards, and you put one on the ceiling, one on the floor, one on each wall, arranged in the six directions, and to read that, you have to walk around. That's a sort of borrowing from Native Americans.

And then we did a play out on Fourth Street, *Wherever She Blows*. We did a mock poetry reading and whenever they would shine a spotlight on one of us, we had to read a poem, and progressively we start making things up as the spotlight hit, and towards the end, I would be reading something and tearing it up or making something up or . . . . So the idea of having happenings began to emerge. I wrote several happenings, one called *The President*—there are about four of those—events—take twenty to thirty minutes to put on.

Holsapple: Was there a regular New Mexico poetry scene at this time, what with Keith Wilson, Margaret Randall, Bobby Byrd, and Gene Frumkin around? Was there a poetry circuit so that poets were talking with one another?

Goodell: Gene Frumkin has been around all this time. Margaret off and on. Keith Wilson and Joseph Somoza down in Las Cruces. There were several important poetry festivals, the Southwest Poetry Conference, organized by Randall Ackley. There was one in Durango, and one in Santa Fe that Drummond Hadley organized. One in Albuquerque. A really good one in Colorado College. These were good because, for the first time, there were Hispanics, Native Americans, and Anglos involved. It was varied and fresh. I miss them.

I worked in the Living Batch Bookstore with Jeff Bryan [of La Alameda Press] and others, for Gus Blaisdell, and there was an opportunity to have lots of readings there. Then there was an effort to revive the downtown area. All the storefronts were closed. It looked like a ghost town. Lots of artists started moving in. We had "Downtown Saturday Nights." Gene Frumkin was involved with this, Keith Wilson, and Rudy and Patricia Anaya. They organized the Rio Grande Writers Association, which set up a "coffee house" in an old vacant shoe store, summer of 1978. There would be a throng of people and it would have different ethnic emphasis week to week. That was exciting! We had about fifty poets read that summer. We made money selling beer and paid the poets.

Holsapple: You published Margaret Randall's *Some Small Sounds From the Bass Fiddle*. Can you tell us how you met her?

Goodell: Well, my world began to open when I began sending out *duende*. It got beyond New Mexico because we exchanged magazines, and I got *El Corno Emplumado* faithfully from Margaret Randall, down in Mexico. Again, she was another contemporary, so when Lenore and I went to Mexico, we visited her. She fixed this huge wonderful salad for us! Always felt very close to what she was doing. I thought *El Corno Emplumado* was one of the most important publications in America. Getting these people translated, bringing together these two worlds. Plus you know we'd been studying the PreColumbian. So it was a great series of publications. I've seen her several times since then, but not recently. She liked *duende* and wrote me about it, so I did a little book of hers.

Tritica: Did you work with Joy Harjo?

Goodell: Joy? A long time ago, KUNM would have readings on Saturday night and bring poets in, and Joy and I were reading together. I think that's where I met Joy. That's when she was married to Simon [Ortiz], and I knew Simon much better than I did Joy. As far as I'm concerned, he's the number one Native American poet in America.

Holsapple: Anyone else?

Goodell: I haven't mentioned Keith Wilson. I didn't like his poetry at first. I thought it was plain old regional poetry. But the more I got to know him and his wife, Heloise, the more I became aware of the different facets of his work. Slowly I began to realize he is a fine poet and that no one can write like him. The more you read, the more you can hear his voice. When he's gone—and his health is not good—no one can ever do what he has done. He has the essence of place more honestly than any other writer. It's amazing how he can capture it.

Tritica: Joe Somoza is also a New Mexican poet.

Goodell: We became good friends. He's retired now, but I used to go down there to visit when he was teaching. You sit in his backyard and it's like you're sitting in one of his poems. It's the same thing I got from the New American Poets, Irby and others, Creeley too. There's something specific, no bullshit. That's what you need. It has strength. It doesn't matter where you are or what you're doing. Other people will relate to it, when you're really being specific. Duncan says it: "Every particular is an immediate happening of meaning at large."

Holsapple: In 1984, Whalen came to Santa Fe to work with Richard Baker. Were you able to reestablish contact with him? He read at the Living Batch, for instance.

Goodell: Oh yeah. He was a monk then, and he and Robert Winson used to come into the bookstore, and Whalen read there. When I gave a reading at St. Francis Auditorium in Santa Fe—it was video-taped—there were three people in the audience, Phil Whalen, Drum Hadley, and a friend of mine who had helped me load and unload the car! Oh, and my wife—maybe there were five there. He really liked my "Shaman Song," which is a spoof of the poet as shaman and I hold a staff with a shoe on top of it and wear bells. I didn't spend a lot of time with him, but I saw him many times in the bookstore and we talked.

Holsapple: In 1972 you began *Fervent Valley*. Can you talk about your involvement with that group—you, Bill Pearlman, Charlie Vermont, Stephen Rodefer?

Goodell: Bill Pearlman named it; *Fervent Valley* referred to Placitas. There were four editors, fighting all the time. But each issue was a little different. Lenore was the art editor. Pat Bolles [of Grasshopper Press] sold me his Davidson offset press for a dollar, and we moved it to an off-room of the Thunderbird Bar and I printed there. Stephen Rodefer did one [issue] primarily on his own. Then he started doing the Pick Pocket series. Steve was teaching at UNM.

About this time [1974], Steve and I went on tour. I took my medicine bag—my circus trunk—and we went off in a Datsun station wagon, Steve and Lenore and my four-year-old son, Joel. We had a National Rifle Association credit card. We went all over the country, even Canada, thanks to Steve's organization. We read in Chicago. We went to

Connecticut where the Olson archives are now. We read at St. Mark's in New York. We went to Buffalo and Toronto. Each place I'd do a rather elaborate set up of the Ometeotl poems.

Holsapple: There was, I take it, an active poetry scene at the national level, so you could set up readings?

Goodell: Yeah, again, this is by way of friends. Steve knew a lot of people. He went to graduate school at Buffalo and we visited friends of his there who were involved with Olson.

Holsapple: What are you up to these days? What are your interests?

Goodell: I'm involved in looking back over my creations, activities, and archiving, actually. Sounds dreadful, but I'm trying to make sense of all this. My study is a small room added to our house, built right to the property line (at the time), and I have everything in that room, all my records, a huge number of tapes, especially tapes done at the Living Batch from years of readings, plus ancient videotapes of my performances. I've got some sixty notebooks. I'm trying to get stuff onto the computer and get it published. I've worked back through about eight years. All my boxes of quasi-ceremonial reading paraphernalia are there. Since I can now use the computer to transfer cassettes, I can make recordings of piano songs I wrote and put them on CD. I now have a Roland Keyboard. Lyrics are extremely hard—I may never get around to more lyrics, but I do have an idea for a musical. I continue to write in my notebooks and type things up and give readings. I irrigate Lenore's organic vegetable garden and help maintain our fruit trees. We're on the acequia system here in the village. And I do just about all the cooking. So that's about what I'm doing.

Eleni Sikelianos: There Better Be Sex in Heaven

Eleni Sikelianos was raised in California. She received an MFA in Writing & Poetics from the Naropa Institute. She is the author of *The California Poem*, *The Book of Jon*, *Earliest Worlds*, *The Book of Tendons*, and *To Speak While Dreaming*. She is also the author of a number of chapbooks, including *From Blue Guide*, *The Lover's Numbers*, and *Poetics of the X*. She has received numerous honors and awards including a National Endowment for the Arts Fellowship, a Fulbright Fellowship, a New York Foundation for the Arts Award for Non-Fiction Literature, and two Gertrude Stein Awards for Innovative American Writing. She has been writer-in-residence at Princeton University, poet-in-residence for Teachers & Writers Collaborative in New York City, and taught Literature and Thinking and Writing for Bard College's Clemente Program. Sikelianos ran the Wednesday Night Readings at the St. Mark's Poetry Project in St. Mark's Church. She currently lives in Colorado with her husband, the fiction writer Laird Hunt, and teaches in the MFA program at Naropa in Boulder, and in the Creative Ph.D. program at the University of Denver.

Poetry Investigator: Receiving all the awards comes from writing great poetry, there is no getting around that. I want to look at some of your poems in *Earliest Worlds*, your new book from Coffee House which is actually two books put together. In the second book, *Of Sun, Of History, Of Seeing*, you used an interesting idea for the titles, designating different poems: "Essays," "Origins," "My Love," "Notes," "Study," "Artifact," "Histories," "Film," "Sound," and "Reprisal," among others. Could you please say something about that?

I partly think of them as a series, a connected series, rather than just discrete poems. Also, that I was bringing different kinds of diction into the poems. I was interested in layers of diction, not just poem-like language. A lot of it is kind of thick and maybe even a little bit dry [*laughs*].

PI: Something that is dry might be an artifact.

The artifacts are often found text that is rewritten. The artifact, "When Out of Delight," is from Abbé Suger. He was responsible for some of the beautiful French architecture.

PI: In that particular poem, had you visited a site he had designed? Where did you get the text from?

A lot of these poems were started in France when I got the NEA and had the year off. I was reading a lot of text about Abbé Suger. Many of these poems are influenced by Proust.

PI: Here are the opening lines from "When Out of Delight":

ARTIFACT: When—out of...delight

When—out of my *d* in the *b* of the house of *G*—the loveliness of the many-

colored stones.................,and.................,transferring that which..........

PI: For instance in this particular poem, where you have the ellipsis in between the words, that is that where you have just taken out his text?

Yes.

PI: So in a sense you took his text and crossed out the words you didn't need for your poem.

Exactly. Some of the places I took out whole sections of words and just left the letters. Like "the house of G—" is the house of God. Then the other poem, "ARTIFACT: Two Ink on Pottery Fragments (7th–8th c. AD)," I used the same technique except here I changed some of the words.

PI: So you give yourself freedom to add what you need?

[*laughs*] Yes, I don't think it was, "Tell these matters to all the peas." *Ostracon* is a word for fragments of pottery. It is where we get the word ostracized from, because they would write someone's name on the fragments who they thought should be kicked out.

PI: After they were broken they would write the names on the fragments?

Yes, it was recycling [*laughs*].

PI: So they used an *ostracon* to do that, and they were being ostracized?

Exactly. So some of them still have fragments of writing on them. Then I would add my own things like, "the radishes lit up like minor fireworks out on the river." That wasn't on a fragment.

PI: Talk about that line, what is happening when the radishes light up?

[*laughs*] I don't know, Gary. What is happening?

PI: In some cases, for instance with this line, are you going more for the sounds of the words and the ways the words are playing together, or is there a concrete image in your mind that you are bringing up?

There are all kinds of things. One is a layer of historical artifact and some message that someone wrote on a pottery fragment.

PI: It is a metaphorical representation of that?

Yeah, I guess. I don't know if I would use the word metaphorical, but it is a layer. I think that is one thing with the different headings for the poems, that they are layers of things. Some kind of compendium of various cultural markers. These provide for me a layer of history. I think one thing that happened in seeing some of the fragments—for instance, in this poem the beginning is ". . . Behold, another 4 carrots," which refers of karats to gold or jewels. So I started playing with that, all the vegetables. It is also playing with subverting these kinds of prayers into something more mundane.

PI: Of course one hopes people bring something of their own to the poems—it doesn't have to be exactly what the poet was thinking when they were writing. Your poems are certainly open and allow people to enter them in that way.

[*laughs*] I hope, unless it makes them crazy.

PI: Just to go back to this last line. I could read it as . . . not really an explanation but as an image of what is happening in the poem. Ceramics with something written on them could be seen as minor fireworks.

For me that is a beautiful image. I think I may have had birds light up like minor fireworks and then the radishes came in because of sound and wanting to play with the vegetable image, or continuity with the vegetable theme.

Certainly, in terms of what I had in mind for any of these, I had a very clear idea of where they came from. But I am also in the same boat as the reader. They always mean something new to me. One's poems are often smarter than oneself. They are making more connections than one is capable of in your conscious life.

PI: In order to get to that state, what is the structure you set up for yourself? You have gotten awards that allow you to have long stretches to write. Please talk about your writing routine.

It is interesting. Because I had this year off, I really felt an incredible difference—how far my mind was able to go not having to be concerned with any sort of daily things.

PI: Tied in with a teaching schedule, grading papers, that kind of thing?

Exactly. So I was really able to go pretty far, and it kept accruing in a way so that the more months I had off the further I was able to go, until I just ended up crying every day. For a while anyway.

PI: All day long or just at certain points?

Just certain times; it was just so intense.

PI: So at some point each day you would be emotionally overwhelmed and would break down and cry?

Yeah.

PI: Was this after you had written?

Yes, often. It was after about four months. It was also in France, so I was also culturally cut off. A further voyage in a way. The first book in *Earliest Worlds* was written in Paris. I was also reading a ton of prose in French. I was reading Flaubert, Proust and Genet, which I think comes into influence in the second book, where I was working with the sentence more. I think the first book is more lyric. I was probably writing about six hours a day. I would write at home, starting at about noon, and then I would write until about four or five and go out for a walk for an hour. I was close to Bois de Boulogne. Then I would come home and write for another two to four hours.

PI: You are writing longhand?

I would take my notebook everywhere. I almost always write longhand first, especially for poems. Then I would type them up and work on them. There are two other manuscripts that I wrote that year that I have abandoned.

PI: Do you think you will go back to them?

I am not sure. I have cannibalized one of them. I have taken about eight pages out of seventy-five and used them. Then in the second book, we moved to New York, so that saturation of information, noises, and people influences it.

PI: Let's talk about your poem, "FILM: How to Exploit an Egg." Could you walk us through the poem, talk about the lines, tell us what you were aiming for, if anything?

I am never aiming for . . . I guess I often start with a phrase I want to use or a word or an image, so the poems always start off with a small fragment that I want to make a poem out of. When I start aiming for ideas I almost never keep those poems, because they tend to be too closed for me.

PI: Do you remember in this poem what the inspiration was?

Sometimes there will be a few of those juxtaposed. Clytemnestra is this very negative figure, and I was interested in how she might be a positive figure or a generative figure. The other thing that is in here is some footage from my great-grandparents' first Delphic Festival from 1927—there was a seventy-year anniversary celebration at Delphi in 1997; someone had footage from 1927. It was this beautiful dream-like, ghostly, greenish footage, so that is in the poem, also.

PI: That is the line:

> **a woman**
> **back in the sky, a woman**
> **dancing in a mask made by Eleni**
> **on a screen of gray which is a blue.**

Yes, and of course there are all these masks . . . I think the play was *Prometheus*. My great-grandmother made all these masks and you could see them on the screen. The lines:

> cubits
> of microspace
> which make up the rocks

. . . having been a biology major and wanting a biological background in the poem. "Wherefore speak you so, Stranger?" I think is from *Prometheus Unbound*, and it is the Oracle speaking to somebody. It turns into myself speaking to my own voice. Then it gets back to this generative thing, how things are made from eggs, earth, moon, materials—either made in real ways or made to resemble other things. The phrase, "cigars sent by lords," is from one of the Mayan gods.

PI: Not Wallace Stevens?

Is there a Wallace Stevens poem with cigars?

PI: "The Emperor of Ice Cream."

Right, right. No this refers to one of the Mayan gods who gets cigars sent to him.

PI: Will you read the last section of the poem?

[*reads*]

Moon, O moon, harken
& reflect: this egg-house made to birth surfaces liquid & curved

Said egg, come, mock rock & bone
come, skull, shell, formed inside
come, ship, brains, & beans
o, come, paw, dabble & dangle in sugar pools
Said curved egg, come, claw
come, cigars sent by lords
come, liver, come fur, be birthed
& bent space itself will truly think in every limb & velocity of stars

PI: Amazing.

A lot of connections there for me—basic matter, how we come into being. I always ask my husband Laird, "It's clear what I mean here isn't it?" And he says, "Ah, no."

PI: Speaking of being clear, I find it interesting that, with take for instance Gertrude Stein's work, which for me is difficult reading, but that after hearing a recording of her reading, her work became much clearer to me. I wondered if you felt that? When you are reading your poems, when you read the line, "Said egg, come, mock rock & bone," to me it is very clear that the egg is talking, and I don't know if I was so aware of that when I was reading the poem to myself this afternoon. Do you find that with people, either hearing them read or when you give readings?

Definitely. There is that story that Kenneth Koch told about hearing Ashbery read: for the first time he understood the poems in a whole new way. I think that's true; poetry is an oral tradition. I still feel that strongly. However abstract it gets it is still oral. Language is a sound.

PI: When you are writing do you say the lines aloud when you are honing them?

Definitely. Yes all the time, over and over. My first impulse in poetry was music, but I came to a place where I felt the music was overpowering the poem. I was attached to beautiful music or pretty music, so one of the things I worked with here was awkwardness, more thickness, and even derailing the line.

PI: The fourth stanza seems to fit that description. It is musical but it has awkwardness to it.

[*reads*]

whites and in the
patates of patates in the
myth of the rape
of potatoes I would put

Even just saying *patates* which means french fry in Greek [*laughs*]. I am trying to remake myths. I wrote the whole poem while I was watching the film in Delphi. It took a long time to decipher what I had written because I had written it in the dark.

PI: Maybe it's not even what you wrote?

[*laughs*] I do rely on misreadings.

PI: That's a good technique to have—surprise words come in.

The binding element in the poem is birth.

PI: Okay, moving on to the next poem. Everyone turn to page 203. See, this is a great way to sell books: to really follow along with the interview you have to have the book. (Pssssst, buy her book.) This poem is: "ESSAY: When I Think of Sex, a Moist Fig." Take us through the poem.

The first thing that made me want to write this poem is one of Leslie Scalapino's lines about sex, how the male lover is a seal barking. So that is what started the poem.

[*reads*]

When I think of sex, some people
think of seals barking
but I think of shrimp and bleach.

Shrimp and bleach odors associated with sex [*laughs*].

When I think of sex with some people
I think of cones and rods, but they
think of flywheels.

Cones and rods. I was thinking of shapes, but also the cones and rods in the eye. I was just in Slovenia for a poetry festival and they translated this poem into Slovenian. "Cones and rods" is pretty common knowledge in the States right?

PI: Any kid you say "cones and rods" to knows you are talking about the eyes.

The Slovenians do not know this.

PI: The poor Slovenians.

So that was interesting.

PI: You would think that of any knowledge, that scientific knowledge would translate across borders, but in the case of the Slovenians and eye science it doesn't.

[*laughs*] It is one of those things that for whatever reason, American schools have decided it is important to teach. Maybe the Slovenians know something else about eyes that we don't know.

PI: It is interesting to think there is a direct correlation. That there is some other knowledge that we would be shocked to learn.

That was the thing they had the hardest time with.

PI: Right, if they translate it directly they would think of ice cream and fishing. Maybe they don't even think of those.

Flywheels—just the generation of energy and that kind of frenetic activity. Plastic and rubber. Rubbers, which got me to Frisbees, which got me to International Ultimate Championships.

PI: Note: if you are Slovenian, Ultimate is the game that people play with Frisbees.

They had a little bit of trouble with that but not as much. Which brought me to grass stains on the knees from playing Ultimate Frisbee. Which got me to . . .

PI: The most interesting part of the whole poem.

Somehow the zippers got me to the cartoon image of x over eyes. This was another place they had trouble with. The Slovenians do not do x over the eyes of their cartoons, they put pluses. So they changed it to pluses.

PI: So that is a cartoon image.

Yeah, and that is where the whole poem does a shift.

[*reads*]

of them and sex I think I do not
want to have sex with a dead
person until I am dead.

PI: So talk about . . . I love this because I get to say in interviews, talk about for a moment why you only want to have sex with dead people only after you are dead.

Wouldn't anyone? [*laughs*] Why in the world would you want to have sex with dead people unless you are a necrophiliac?

PI: I was just going to say, are you not afraid of offending the necrophiliac poetry fans?

I think they get plenty of opportunity to get included.

PI: In Bukowski poems?

Yes, exactly. I guess it is this idea that we do get to have sex after we are dead.

PI: See, that gets to the crux of the poem. Is that the ultimate insider information we get from talking to you?

Yes, there better be sex in heaven.

PI: I think I just got the title for your interview.

There better be sex in heaven.

Liz Belile: Gynomite: Fearless, Feminist Porn

Gynomite isn't just a reading series, a CD compilation, a Web site, and a book. It's a forum and a mission for freedom from anxiety about sex. Not just how anxious we get when we actually have sex, but how we get when we—oh . . . my . . . god—talk about having sex. Liz Belile created her first pornography in the fifth grade when she drew naked lady magazines—"miniature *Playboys*"—and sold them to the boys for a quarter. Since then, she has earned an MFA in Poetics from the Naropa Institute, has performed and published widely, has a book out, *Polishing the Bayonet*, and a CD, *Your Only Other Option is Surgery*. She has focused mostly on *Gynomite* and on her lit art site, www.bodyofwords.com, both paying bills and getting her thrills by editing and creating interesting content for the web—since 1995. She lives in Texas and teaches yoga as well as workshops for women who want to write and perform their own pornographic texts.

Poetry Investigator: Tell me how got started doing *Gynomite*.

It was 1994, in Los Angeles. I was working with these amazing women writers. I was also meeting a lot of women who worked in the sex industry. People behind the cameras or people who owned the companies, dancers, and dominatrixes. I don't know if it was just my age or just living in L.A., something about being there at that time changed my definition of feminism. All these women I was meeting considered themselves feminists, and some kind of change took place in me. I opened up.

I started thinking that these women who felt empowered working in the sex industry, who didn't feel exploited, opened my eyes and made me realize how repressed I was. My writing has always been graphic and sexually explicit. It seemed to me there weren't enough women creating erotica for women that was really nasty and hot.

So it was a combination of all those things and also doing grassroots political work, hosting poetry readings where people came and paid money and we were able to use those readings as fundraisers. That was the milieu in which I came up with the idea that I wanted to have a reading series for women writers writing very, very hot erotica. I knew the women would come up with a wide variety of whatever porn meant to them.

PI: You have come up with the term "Feminist Porn" to define what you are doing.

I thought I created that. I guess I did a bit, but it was collective consciousness because Susie Bright also calls her work feminist porn and Candida Royalle makes films she calls feminist porn. I felt a bit isolated from them as they were mostly in New York and San Francisco. Carol Queen, Annie Sprinkle, and other women performers were also working in that area.

PI: It seems like that happens with an idea, or in this case a phrase, to describe a way people are working or a movement pops out in different places.

I love it when that happens. I also like the juxtaposition of feminist and porn. *Gynomite* was also a direct response to Andrea Dworkin and Catherine MacKinnon and passing legislation and writing legislation that would outlaw pornography. I thought, "That is not the solution at all, and that would just lead to more repression." It came about for me as a real transformation. Up until then I was very opposed to pornography, but I realized, "I am opposed to this but I haven't explored it at all." I realized I was repressing myself. It came as an awakening and I thought that to create porn would put the means of production in the worker's hands.

PI: Literally in their hands.

[*laughs*] In their hand.

PI: So it started out as a reading series in L.A. and the series was called *Gynomite*. How did it go from there to creating the anthology and then doing the workshops?

The readings were very popular. I made it a point to charge more than was usually charged at readings—we charged ten bucks. That was so I could pay myself for producing the event and pay the writers something. Part of it was I wanted to see women making money off their own porn writing. I don't remember how much the writers made at first, twenty-five or fifty bucks depending on how many writers there were. I also think that charging that much money for a reading gave the audience anticipation that they would be seeing something good.

PI: It also set yourselves apart from the other readings because you were saying, "This is professional."

Exactly, I would pay that much to go see a band, so why not pay that much to hear something really mind-blowing. I realized I could make money doing this. Especially calling it porn—porn is always going to make money. At one point I had one of the writers accusing me of using the word porn as a marketing tool and I just looked at her and said, "So be it if that is what I am doing."

Not only is using the word porn asking the writers to go out further than they might if they were writing erotica, but it also drew curious audience members. I had a lot of help with the series in L.A. DuVergne Gaines and Weba Garretson were my co-producers; I could never have done it without their help. We did the PR with all our contacts.

PI: Talk about that please. What would you do to get people out to the readings?

Now I have email, which is great. First we would tap our collective producer contact list. We would approach a venue and nail down a date. Weba is a musician so she had some contacts with clubs that do music.

We would get the date first, try to get a Saturday night. Then we would start calling our list of writers, starting with the big name writers, people who we thought would be a draw. We would get them secured, see who would fit with the schedule. Sometimes, if you had a real strong headliner, we would change the club date to fit their schedule. We did try to bring in well-known writers to help build the audience and expose them to the lesser-known writers.

Then we each had contacts at the different press outlets. We would go on public radio. Most public radio has a place were we would fit in—spoken word, women's issues, or even just supportive DJs.

We would try to go on a week in advance. Sometimes we would give away tickets to the show. You have to get your PR out according to the deadlines of the publications. We would contact all the papers, the daily, alternative weekly, and student papers. The weekly papers were the best outlets for us. The daily papers rarely run articles on feminist porn. We made sure that there was a fun, provocative publicity photo. I can't stress that enough for people trying to do their own PR. I know that as a person who edited for an alternative weekly, if there was a funny photo that caught my eye, I was much more likely to run it.

We collectively wrote the press release. We would send it out to every radio station. We try to get contact names whenever possible. This is true of all the readings I do for *Gynomite*, not just the series in L.A. I try to have a contact list of the five or so people at papers that I target to run a story on the event. You follow up; you just explicitly ask them to run something. Will you give us a pick, will you write a blurb, will you run our photo? Sometimes they would say yes. We would try three or four different people at the paper.

PI: In sending publicity to *LA Weekly* for instance, you would send the info to three or four people who were working there?

Right. Since I lived in L.A. and knew some of the people at the paper and knew the sections of the paper where they might write something, I would contact the music writer because I would have musicians in the roster of writers. Sometimes I would contact feature writers who were sympathetic to women's issues. That is the beauty of *Gynomite*. It is such a diverse group we could pitch from many different angles: minority, cultural, spoken word. I would reach out to writers who had interest in those areas.

PI: So you would pay attention to who was writing about what and pitch it accordingly.

Yes, who writes about sex, who writes about performance. For touring I always try to get a contact name. Sometimes I just cold call and say, "This is what the show is about, is there anyone at the paper who writes about these issues?" Always try to familiarize yourself with who writes about what. Now I do all that with email and at the readings I collect email addresses. People forward emails, so that can help too.

PI: Do you also send the provocative photo to the papers electronically?

I say send hard copy photos along with your digital press release. You want to contact the calendar person at the paper or whoever you are sending your press release to and ask them specifically what resolution you need for the tiff or jpeg. But I would say back it up with a hard copy.

PI: You may be able to get someone's attention with a photo they see rather than have to download and open a file.

Right, it is important to have a good publicity photo. A lot of times the calendar editor, even if it is a big city like Houston or L.A., they will have a lot of stuff but no great photos.

PI: When did you realize you should do an anthology out of the series?

I guess it was in the back of my mind the whole time. There is the *Herotica* series. I still am more interested in the live performances and the workshops. The guys from New Mouth from the Dirty South approached me wanting to publish it. They said they were looking for their next book project. I think it killed them, though, because they are not publishing books anymore.

PI: Had they come to one of your performances?

Yes, they came to one of the performances. So for people who might be interested in attracting publishers, keep doing readings, keep the publicity cranking. What happens when you do performance is other writers come and you never know who will show up, who will see it in the paper. My first book happened because Gary Hust, the head of Incommunicado Press, saw me read. That, also, is how the *Gynomite Anthology* happened.

I am not sure what is going to happen with the book. It might go out of print. I think if I had to do it over again with the book I would seek an agent to represent it to larger publishers. That is another discussion, whether to go with a small press or a large press. The benefits of going with a small press are that you can have a lot of creative control. I felt with these guys that they had toured a lot and could help set up a tour, and they did that. They knew the whole independent feminist network and that was good. A big publisher would offer wider distribution.

PI: Talk about the process of editing the book. How did you choose the pieces?

That was a bit of give and take with the publishers. We set up a production schedule that I knew from the beginning was going to be deadly. I think we had six months to put the book together. If anyone is reading this and thinking of doing an anthology, give yourself a year.

You want to have the energy and excitement behind what you are doing, but six months is a short time to do rewrites, to do the book cover, to do all the things you need to do.

I got laid off from my job so I had a bunch of free time to work on the book. I had done a workshop in Houston, and I realized I could make money from that. So that supplemented my income, and it was a great way to get material. It was the first workshop reading that we did in Houston that the publishers saw and thought, "This is amazing, we should do a book."

I already had some ready-made material. The initial vision of the book was to get ten writers to do twenty-page stories, long juicy stories. It sounded good but most of the writers I wanted to use were not writing twenty page pieces of erotica. That is a long time to keep it up. You have to get to the action quicker than that. I decided it would be better to chop up the format, to put a poem after a long piece, then an experimental piece, and have more variety.

I knew that I wanted to have as much diversity as I could get. I just hounded specific writers. At first I wasn't sure about my ability as an editor. What I decided I needed to do with this particular book was to push people to write and to go into the scenes. Some of the stories that came in were perfect and didn't need editing, but some needed real nuts and bolts editing.

I cast my net as wide as I could. Some pieces I knew right away they would go into the book. The work had to be exciting to me. Over the course of six months I was able to see what wasn't being written about. I wanted to have sadism. I needed lesbians, I needed bisexual, black, brown, white—I wanted to present as much of the female sexual experience as I could. The big surprise was that so much of the material was funny. I don't know if it is because sex is so funny. The editing process was fun. I also battled with the publishers over pieces going into the book.

PI: What was the percentage of material you used compared to the percentage of material you rejected?

I would say I was able to use about 85 percent of the material. I didn't turn a lot away.

PI: You were going after specific writers. It wasn't an open call, so you knew who you wanted to work with.

Exactly. When I was editing the website for the *Houston Press*, it was an open call and the percentage was more like 10 percent useable. It had to be good writing and have something unusual about it.

PI: Do all the pieces in the book turn you on or can they affect you in other ways and still be effective?

You would be surprised at which pieces turn me on, as I was surprised. Which is of course the nature of feminist porn. We really don't know what exactly turns women on—it is a big still mystery. That was always fun to be reading something and go, "Oh, that makes me feel funny" [*laughs*].

There are pieces in the book that weren't explicit that still turn me on; they had to have some quality. That is what Susie Bright says when she is editing *Best American Erotica*, that the pieces that she uses all turn her on in some way or another. I would say that is true for me also, or that they had to present sexuality in a way that I hadn't thought of yet.

There are a couple of pieces that do that in the book. There has to be energy, that it has some kind of life. There is so much porn that is pure formula, which has no sense of quirkiness. I try to look for quirkiness.

PI: Talk about the *Gynomite* workshop and how you see writing porn in people's lives. How does it affect them? Is it important?

Gynomite satisfies me on every single level—as a writer, as a performer, having this weird desire to teach, shepherding people through some kind of healing transformation in their own lives, as creative people and as writers.

How the workshop works is I will have six to ten students at a time. It is an eight-week process. I have had a range of students from teenagers to women in their sixties. The highest hope I have for anyone that comes into my workshop, just like in teaching yoga, is that I can somehow ignite within my students the desire to rise to their highest potential or highest self.

I am kind of rambling. In these workshops what I start with is the body. I start with doing some yoga and breath work. I get my students centered in their body.

A lot of the exercises I give are timed writing exercises. So what happens is the students come in with all the shit, all the damage, all the hurt, all the shame that they have ever had around not just their sexuality, but their creativity and having their own voice.

I think that many writers, men and women, come to writing as adults with all this damage. Thinking they have to sound a certain way or that they have to write about certain things. I don't know if creativity gets smashed in us when we are kids.

Something I learned at Naropa was to honor my own voice, allow that I have a unique voice that has every right to be heard. People in my class and across the board don't believe they have a unique voice.

They try to develop their version of Kerouac's voice or Bukowski's voice or Joyce Carol Oates. So that is my first goal, to get the writers in touch with their body and voice, then come to the understanding that there is not a technique, not a system. All they need to do is tune into their own voice and write it.

So in the timed writing exercises I will say, "Okay, describe the first orgasm that you had and you have three minutes." Then the timer will go off and they will sigh and say, "We need more than three minutes to write about orgasms." What happens with the timed writing exercises is that the self-censor has no time to come in, the editor that we all have inside us that keeps us from ever expressing ourselves.

This is a technique from Natalie Goldberg's *Writing Down the Bones*. Just to abandon all preconceived notions and jump in and write. I think it is exciting to do this with sex in particular. Most of the people who come to my class have never written about sex at all. The stories that come out are true and buried very deep. Often it is a big surprise and fun. People have told me it gives them courage and it has changed their lives.

Michelle Tea: You Always Need a Little Extra Cash in Case the Van Poops Out

Michelle Tea's first novel, *The Passionate Mistakes and Intricate Corruption of One Girl in America*, was published on the tiny, cult-hero press Semiotext(e). Her second, *Valencia*, won a Lambda Literary Award for Best Lesbian Fiction, and was selected by *The Village Voice* as one of the top twenty-five books of 2000. Her third book is *The Chelsea Whistle*. With performance poet Sini Anderson she created the legendary Sister Spit tours. She is the producer of Strombolli's Island of Donkeys and Dolls, a transgender, lesbian, straight boy, hip-hop tour. In 2000 she worked with author/filmmaker Shar Rednour to bring The Wasted Motel Tour across America. Michelle writes for the *San Francisco Bay Guardian*, *Girlfriends Magazine*, *On Our Back*, and *Nerve.com*. She was an honorary Grand Marshall for San Francisco's 2002 Pride celebrations. That's how gay she is.

Poetry Investigator: How did the name Sister Spit come about?

Sini Anderson thought up that name. It is really funny for me and Sini and I think for the crowds who came to Sister Spit. I think that we all possessed a certain queer sensibility that laughs at that kind of lesbian sister thing—it seems a little hokey, a little Birkenstocky. But it kind of pokes a little fun at that. For some reason it seemed kind of hard and good, when Sini came up with it, and it has such a ring to it. I did the flyers. I would write Sister Spit in whiteout, so it looked like there was spit on the flyer [*laughs*].

PI: Take us back to the early days of Sister Spit. What were the readings like?

We started Sister Spit in 1994, Sini and me. The two of us had been going to the open mics around San Francisco and having a really good time at them. We loved them but also realized that they were totally male-dominated and you had to have a certain type of steely nature to get up and read your stuff.

We recognized it was an environment that not a lot of girls were going to feel comfortable in. Sometimes we didn't have the energy to go and fight to be heard. So we started an all-girl open mic just to provide an alternative and to get some of the females in the city who were out there writing great stuff who weren't going to the open mics, because it didn't feel like a cool place to be. So that is how it started and it really took off. As we suspected there were tons of girls in San Francisco who were writing really great stuff and once they were given a good stage to show it off on they came out and they kept coming.

It worked to foster a writing community. It kept people writing because you knew at the end of the week there was a place for you to bring whatever you had worked on that week. Everyone kind of fed off of each other and inspired each other. We did that for two years and then we got burnt out and took a break for a year.

Then we came back and decided we wanted to go on tour. Because we had been seeing our friends that were in punk bands or rock bands touring and they were marginally successful undertakings, but they managed to do it. We thought we quite possibly had an even larger potential audience than a rock band, because everybody likes to have a story told to them and to hear about other people's experiences. It didn't matter if you liked punk rock or hip-hop, there was something for you at our shows.

So we gathered up eight girls that we had featured at Sister Spit at the open mic and took them across the country, and it was really exciting. As we suspected, there was an audience. We did three cross-country tours and many regional tours.

PI: Tell us how you selected the girls to go on the tour.

We put the names in the hat of people we would like to take with us and our criteria for that was: people who were serious about their writing, people's writing we really enjoyed, also people who we thought it wouldn't be a nightmare to be in a van with for two months [*laughs*]. We considered dedication, their talent, and their personalities. They were so many, we couldn't take them all with us, so we put the names in a hat and picked them at random.

PI: Do you make that a public event?

[*laughs*] No, that would be really funny, do it in the town square. We had to have some really frank talks about who we wanted to come on tour and who we didn't.

There were times when someone was in the hat and when we picked their name we both realized we didn't want them to come. The dark side. I hope that we served our community.

That is what we wanted to do but it was not a 100 percent egalitarian community process—we had standards that we wanted. Also, for our own sanity, some people you just know they are going to be very difficult to travel with and the tours were always very difficult to begin with. So we needed to have any personality glitches to be at the absolute minimum.

We were always really excited about it and we had to start doing our fundraising for the tour immediately, to get the funds up to make the tour happen. We would do benefit after benefit and include one or two of the people who were coming on the tour in the benefits. Sometimes those people didn't live in San Francisco so they couldn't be part of the fundraising throughout the year. We encouraged people to do their own fundraising in their own towns but nobody ever really did that [*laughs*].

PI: You bought vans for the tours?

We bought two vans [*laughs*]. We had a hard time with the vans. When our final van got taken away, I knew I would do no more Sister Spit tours. I didn't have it in my heart to do fundraising for another van, and I just didn't like the idea of rental vans. It is such a huge waste of money and they just don't have any personality.

PI: How much money did you raise for the vans and how long would they last?

They cost about fifteen hundred dollars each. Of course we had to put a lot of work into both vans. The cost of registering them, tune-ups, new tires, as well as making them look pretty, getting leopard seat covers and stuff like that. It is hard to say how much we actually made. I think that if Sini and me had sat down and budgeted things out we never would have done Sister Spit. We did kind of have to do that towards the end for some grants that Sini was trying to get for us. Once we saw how much money we were actually raising at the shows, I was shocked; it was thousands of dollars.

We would start fundraising about six months before we would go on tour. We would raise at least three thousand dollars for the van, and we would always take a thousand dollars with us as emergency money. I think we would fundraise about six thousand dollars, which is a lot for me. It still sounds like a lot.

How much we made on tour we never really kept track of. We just knew we had enough money to put gas in the van. We would travel with two vans. All three years we were lucky enough to have someone that had their own van. We were gassing two vans, we were feeding twelve girls.

We were being thrifty, but we would also treat everyone to lobster when we hit Provincetown and things like that. I think we were making a good amount of money. Towards the end Sini and I realized that if we felt like staying on the road forever, like some bands do, we could make a living on the road that we would never be able to make staying at home.

PI: Did you have an experience with the product Febreze in the vans? Did you approach them to try to get sponsorship? Tell us about Febreze.

That was not done in any kind of seriousness. We would have loved to get a sponsorship from Febreze, don't get me wrong. Febreze is a really weird product. It is a cleaning product. It doesn't actually clean anything; it just makes it smell like it has been cleaned.

The reason we got attached to it is on our second tour in our second van there was a really bad problem with the cooling system in the van. So whoever was driving the van, their foot would start burning. It was really bad. We would have to keep a towel in the front, which we would dunk in the cooler where there was melting ice. Then the person would have to wrap their foot in it to be able to drive. We called it the foot towel. Then it evolved into Fa-towel, because it sounded more French and glamorous, instead of a skanky towel that had been wrapped around everyone's sweaty foot.

So we were calling it Fa-towel. Then we started using Fa, tacking it onto all kinds of words to mean gross. It became the Fa-van or your Fa-underwear. Then we realized there was a product that was designed to get the funk out of things that was called

Febreze. We thought that was hilarious and it had been made especially for us. It became a big joke, to the point where I called the Febreze 800-number and told them about our tour, asked them if they would be willing to sponsor us. They sent me a ten-dollar Febreze phone card.

PI: So they did sponsor you?

[*laughs*] Right, they sponsored ten minutes of the Sister Spit phone calling.

PI: What was the response of the person on the 800-number?

I think she just thought we were crazy or possibly crank calling them. I don't know how much experience she had with performance art. I don't know if she knew what we were talking about. We would get delirious, being sleep-deprived and hungry, so things would get wildly funny.

PI: The tours would run about two months?

Yeah, that is kind of how long it takes to get you across the country if you are doing shows. It was worth our while to stop every night and perform in the city we were in because even if we didn't get a ton of money, we would at least get gas money. It was always better to stop and pass the hat than to keep going and then have to get a hotel room.

PI: Did you stay multiple days in any cities?

In some cities, Chicago, New York City, we would do more than one show. In some cities we would incorporate an open mic, where we knew they had a strong writing community. Generally we would do one show a night in each city.

PI: Describe the shows. How would you program them?

It would be eight performers plus Sini and me. Sini and me would host the shows. We have always had a special banter between us that is 100 percent unrehearsed. We have good chemistry together as hosts. So we would get up there and banter with the audience, tell stories and make fun of ourselves, be scandalous and obnoxious, gossip about what had happened in the van. Then one by one bring up the performers. They would do their acts; they would read their poetry or do a performance piece. Once we traveled with some girls who were trapeze artists, they were really great.

PI: They had a mobile trapeze set?

They did and in many of the places we performed at it worked out they could rig their trapeze set into the beams in the ceiling. We were at Beyond Baroque in L.A. and they rigged it from the tree outside. So we started the show outside under the tree, then everyone did a procession inside for the rest of the show.

Another time in a warehouse space in Providence, Rhode Island they were able to rig it from a streetlight in the parking lot outside.

PI: Did they read poems while they were on the trapeze?

Sometimes they would read before or after. Two of the girls in the three-girl trapeze act are also poets. There was a lot of text in their performance which drew us to them. Sini always wanted there to be more visual performance to offset how heavily spoken-word it was.

PI: Financially did you need to do the fundraising before you left? Or were you making enough on the road to support the tour?

We needed to do the fundraising. There were so many expenses in planning the tours. The first two years buying the vans; the third year one van had gotten seized by the city for parking tickets before we left town. We had to borrow money to get it out. There were always expenses that were van-related.

There was also the cost of flyers to promote the benefits and the tour. There was also the cost of sending press kits, photographs, all kinds of support material. Long distance bills, website bills, so we needed to fundraise straight through.

The emergency money we brought with us came in really handy, because while some shows were really great, some shows really stank. We always had van trouble on all three tours—you always need a little extra cash in case the van poops out.

I am booking a tour for this fall. Even though Sister Spit has not toured since 1999. I have booked two other nationwide tours since then, this being the second one. The more that I continue doing it, keeping those contacts, keeping the audience bases that we started with Sister Spit, the less fundraising at home, which is really cool.

This tour I haven't done any fundraising. I think that the city of San Francisco is really pooped out on my fundraising. I don't think they want to give me any more money. The few shows I have done have been really small and I haven't been doing a ton of them.

Because this is the fifth cross-country tour I have booked and organized, I have better contacts and I have more college contacts, which is great because then you get guaranteed money and you get better money than if you were playing at a bar or community space. Hopefully this next tour we will get money immediately on leaving town and it won't be a problem that we aren't leaving town with a lot of money.

PI: You are bringing a smaller group of people also?

Yeah, just one van. We have crammed seven people into it. It is a lot, but Sister Spit traveled with twelve. So it is less poets and we are gassing just one vehicle so it will make a big difference.

PI: With this tour you are doing more college shows. What is the percentage of college shows to bars and cafés?

We are probably doing 20 percent college shows. Still, the vast majority of the shows are bars and community spaces.

PI: What is this tour called? How is this tour different from the Sister Spit tours?

Strombolli's Island of Donkeys and Dolls. It is from Pinocchio. The way that it is most immediately and radically different is that there is boys on it [*laughs*]. This tour is me and two other dykes, two straight boys, and two transgender boys. It is a wider mix of people's genders; it is also a wider mix of what people are doing. We still have primarily spoken word, but we also have somebody who has been a clown with Circus Ridiculous and he is going to be doing clown stuff as well as reading his writing, and we have a hip-hop band that ends our show.

PI: Was it a conscious decision to bring boys on the tour?

Definitely, I wanted it to be really different from Sister Spit, because Sister Spit was amazing and fantastic; it had its moment, and for me that moment is past. I don't want to be bringing a kind of cut-rate Sister Spit tour into the world [*laughs*]. That would be sad for me and sad for the audience.

I wanted to make this tour as different as possible, so that people don't feel like, "That was no Sister Spit." All these years I have been the curator of these all-girl tours. I have a lot of friends who are boys who are great poets too, who have always supported Sister Spit, read at benefits, and I have always wanted to tour with them, but because of the rules we imposed on ourselves, we never could. So it is cool to be able to tour with different performers that I have always admired.

PI: Is it affecting the venues you book?

Most of my contacts are in the queer community, so that is still where it is happening, kind of post-Riot Grrl scenes or queer scenes. It says in the wording of our press releases that it is a mixed group, that there is something for everyone [*laughs*]. Straight boys, tranny boys, and gay girls, I think everyone will be fine with that.

At certain Sister Spit shows we would bring local boys up on stage and nobody ever had a problem with that. People just want to see really good performances and that is what they are going to see. Of course, it might be a little weird for the straight boys to be performing for lesbians every day for two months [*laughs*]. We'll see how they feel about it. We are bringing Bucky Sinister.*

* Author of *King of the Roadkill* (Manic D Press) and host of the imfamous Chameleon readings in San Francisco.

PI: Does the response change across the country?

Yes, those shows that aren't in cities that have larger queer communities—the shows are always smaller, that is true, but folks are really appreciative. I did a tour called The Wasted Motel Tour, and we did a show in Salt Lake City, at a lesbian bar there. People were so appreciative. They said, "Nobody ever comes to Salt Lake City, thank you so much."

It was a small show, and it's true the audience reacts differently because there is a chance they have never really seen what you are doing before. They might not have had a lot of exposure to spoken word and they might not have had a lot of experience with people being so blatant about being out and being queer, with people talking so frankly about sex. Being in San Francisco that is so run-of-the-mill, you have to remember places where that is still radical. When you go out on the road you see places where that is still radical.

Patricia Smith: That Word Felt So Good on my Tongue

Patricia Smith is a four-time National Poetry Slam champ. Her books include *Life According to Motown*, *Big Towns, Big Talk*, and *Close to Death*. In the early days of the poetry slam, Smith developed a style of performance poetry that defined slam. More than any poet, she set the standard for combining writing and performance. She is perhaps even better known as a former columnist for the *Boston Globe*, where she worked from 1994 to 1998. In the spring of 1998, Smith was nominated for a Pulitzer Prize for her newspaper work. Later the *Globe* withdrew her from consideration when it was rumored that some of her *Globe* column's stories contained fabrications. Smith admitted to the fabrications and lost her job at the paper. The loss of her job and the break-up of her marriage happened simultaneously, and the resulting stress almost ruined her health. *MS* magazine later hired her as a columnist.

Poetry Investigator: What do you see as the poet's job?

I think that the poet's job is to show everyone that poetry is something that we all own. I can't tell you how many times I have gone into a class or onto a stage and felt this real division that you are poet and they are the audience. No one feels that you are about to do anything that is accessible to them or that is relevant to their lives.

I see my job as helping people to realize that poetry is something that is accessible to all of us. The only difference between me and someone who doesn't live and breathe poetry is that something happened in my life to click that lock loose. A door opened and poetry came spilling out. I said, "Wow, this was here the whole time." I like to see that look in people's faces when they realize that poetry is another option to express yourself, in terms of what the world can do.

PI: What was the trigger in your life that led you to write poetry?

I won't say that I started to write poetry right away after this, but it was something that made the possibilities intriguing. I was about nine years old. The teacher wrote a word on the board, a word that she didn't expect any of us to know. She asked if anyone wanted to take a stab at pronouncing this. The word was anomie.*

I can't remember if I pronounced that word right the first time, but eventually I did. I didn't know what it meant. That word felt so good on my tongue, I must have said it over a hundred times that day, before I even knew what it meant. If the mechanics of a single word can change the way you feel, I wondered what other power words have.

That feeling led me to concentrate on the music of words as much as their meaning, and led me to look into poetry. It also led me to joys of reading everything I read out loud. That was my opening to poetry. Saying I can't wait to find more of these words and I can't wait to see what they do, and if they do this to me, what will they do to other people?

It didn't turn into poetry right away. I started writing these endless, painful, what I called short stories, where I was the star. Once I figured out that words could do that, then poetry wasn't so far behind.

PI: How did what happened at the *Boston Globe* affect your poetry?

I don't think it changed anything. I think it gave me another reason to call upon poetry. By that time I was already used to using poetry to make sense of the world. Writing personal poems for myself. Just to get past something in my life.

The one thing that it did do was root me more deeply in the community of poets. I cut myself off from everything—the only group that really reached out and said, "Oh, come on now," were poets. Nobody I worked with, nobody I grew up with, nobody in my family, but poets reached out. It was right before the National Poetry Slam in Austin, and I was not going to go. I wasn't going to go anywhere.

I kept getting these weird notes from Wammo and Mike Henry (two of the Austin poets who organized the National Poetry Slam in 1998). They sent me this group picture where they were all wearing Mexican wrestling masks. I hadn't laughed at all and I started laughing. They said, "Come on, get back into this, there are poems to be done."

* An anxious awareness that the prevailing values of society have little or no personal relevance to one's condition; also, a condition of society characterized by the relative absence of norms or moral standards.

I realized that poetry was my safety net. If I was going to step back into the world, that was going to be how I did it. I wouldn't say it changed my poetry at all; it did give me more introspective things to write about. It changed the way I felt about the community. Even though the community was always very important to me, it was a social, recreational community. It was like, okay, I have done my work, now I have to go play with the poets. It proved to me that the community was so much more than that, and it was even more important to me than I initially thought it was.

PI: Talk about some of the poems that came out of that time.

I wrote a whole piece, which I did around Boston mostly. Then took it to the O'Neill playwriting conference. I was a writer-in-residence there. There were actors, actresses, and playwrights around so I could see what they thought of the material. I did a reading there and they said, "We've discovered a new school." You know how it is when you are around theater people, you read one poem and they freak out. I was talking to them about, not particularly those poems, but just the idea of putting poems together in a theatrical setting.

Since then I have gotten interest from a director in New York about putting those poems together to make a show. Which a year or two ago I probably would not have done, but it is fine with me now. The poems are chronicles; I realized that I was being unfair to people by shutting myself off. There were people who were looking for me, who wanted to talk to me, and I was making that difficult for them. I thought that the best way to bring them up to speed was to show them what I was writing while this was going on. There are poems for every stage, the worst stage, the recovering stage, and the back-at-the-world stage. It was a journal, except the journal took the form of poems.

PI: What do you call the piece?

Professional Suicide.

PI: Will you perform in the piece?

Yes, I was going to tell them that I did not feel comfortable handing it over to someone else. The producers came to a couple of readings in the city and they also thought that I should be the one to perform the poems. Which is both good and bad. It's going to be a shitload of work. But that's okay, it is one piece I have written. I keep saying "piece," but it is a bunch of separate poems. Right now we are trying to figure out the best way to link them. It is the one thing I have written that I think was really life-saving. I couldn't have handed it over to someone else.

PI: Right now it is in the shape of a one-woman show?

Yes, I did some more work on it recently. I hadn't touched it in a couple of years. I was not really thinking of it for the stage; I had done some shows with a band. So I had to do some fiddling with it to help it fit into a theatrical setting. The producers are thinking about visuals and backdrops. Deciding if they want to have the band with me or not. I am kind of staying out of that part of it. It is funny—I was telling someone last summer that every year when it would get to the time I got fired, I would get sick, my stomach would hurt. This year it just passed and I didn't even know it. Now is the time I can objectively look at this piece and turn it into something lasting and something that will say something to someone outside of my immediate circle.

Before, I was too much in the middle of it. Now I can see it as a piece of work. I can see it as a piece that addresses issues that I have not seen addressed anywhere else, at least not from that perspective. I can see perhaps the value it will have to people outside of myself. I can talk to people very openly about this and it does not affect me in the same way it once did.

PI: How do you see poetry and journalism affecting each other? There was a thesis where the student talked about your poetic techniques and journalistic techniques. This was written previous to your being fired. Creating characters and dialogue is such a part of poetry and writing stories, how do you see those working together?

What you have to understand is what I did was a choice that I made. The part of it that was the most troubling to the sacred journalist circle was the creation of character that popped in at the end to pull the story together. They weren't populating the whole column, but that was a choice I made.

The other thing, which is the poetic element of journalism, I have no problem with and they obviously have no problem with because that is how I got the job in the first place. Honestly, there was no way—I had no straight news experience. I had been writing features my entire life, basically with no college training in journalism. The only thing that brought my journalism to the attention of people was the poetic element. The fact that I would spend a lot of time trying to find an unexpected entry point to my story.

My companion right now is an editor at the Associated Press where the department he heads is called news features. They are basically the storytellers. His reporters can go out and spend three weeks on a story and turn it into a serial narrative. That is something that probably will stay there—the only thing is some journalists are against it and some journalists aren't. It is attention getting, it is what makes you read one story as opposed to another.

Because it is drawing you into the experience, instead of saying, "We are the voice of the news, and this what you should listen to." Instead it is saying, "We are the voice of everybody, and you too are part of it," and that is the difference. I would never downplay or speak out against the role that poetry played in my getting as far in journalism as I got. I think there are still people doing it.

There never was that heavy line for me between journalism and poetry. I couldn't do that because I was too much of a poet. It was impossible for me to draw that line. Sometimes I would have parties at my house, and the poets would be on one side and journalists on the other. They would be glaring at each other, like they didn't both use language. There was so much that the two camps could learn from each other. I think that the reason that so many of my poems are based on convicts, police, and things like that was that I learned so much about them, being a journalist.

The two things fed each other very well. I wasn't afraid of the language—I didn't think there was a certain language that always had to be used in journalism. There was nothing that I was afraid to write a poem about. I had seen very pretty and very ugly things in journalism, and I knew that they all had a side that wasn't being written about. I was allowed to write about those sides in my poetry.

PI: That makes me think especially of your poems "Undertaker" and "Skinhead."

Those poems came directly from news stories. How many of us have read news stories and then been bothered by them a week later? If you are poet, you can figure out what bothers you about that story and address it in your poetry. It keeps us from shooting up post offices.

PI: How do you prepare for a poetry reading? Is it different than preparing for a poetry slam?

In the early days, when I was enamored of the Green Mill and my life was going to the poetry slam, that was my social circle. Those were the most important people in my life. I couldn't believe what I was learning, what people were teaching me. That was the center of everything. When I was going to the Mill I would think that there were things you must do for the slam.

When the poem started to feel a little worn at the edges, or I was in the middle of the poem and I didn't remember starting it . . . I felt the mechanics of it carrying me away; it is very easy, no matter what you are talking about, whether it is poetry or hitting a baseball. It is easy to learn the mechanics of something or to strategize and let that take over. I had to force myself to remember why I was writing poetry in the first place.

After that, preparing for the slam and preparing for a reading were not that different. Preparing for a reading depends on who I am going to be in front of. I used to think I needed a set list and to have practiced the poems. Now I feel better waiting to get to the reading and see who is coming into the room, what the age mix is, what the race and gender mix is, what people are buzzing about when they walk in, what part of the country I am in, what the news is there, what they are concerned about. I like to choose the poems after I have been there awhile. Which is why I hate coming in at the last minute. I like to get there as early as possible.

One of the advantages of having a large body of poems is you can say, "This is what I feel tonight." One of the things that does happen is people say, "Oh, we have the slam champion coming in." You have to get past feeling that you have to perform, that you have to be a slammer, and that all your poems have to be off page, that you have to walk around in the audience. It is a quest of mine to get people to realize that there should be a solid poem beneath anything I do, beneath any theatrics, beneath any slam scoring or anything else.

Too often you are walking away from a reading, and you are saying, "Wow I never knew poetry could be performed like that." And someone says, "Can you tell me about any of the poems," and you can't. You can't quote any of the lines. You don't leave with an impression that the words made on you. That has been increasingly important to me, so I spend more time thinking about the people I am reading for than I think about what poems I am going to do. The poem choice comes last.

The audience is a way that I revise. If I am writing new poems, I like to say to the audience, "Come up to me after and tell me what worked and what didn't work and why." I don't want that line drawn where you feel like there is somebody up there who is supposed to entertain and teach you and your job is just to sit back and take it all. I want the reading to be an interactive experience.

In that I have begun to think of the slam as not so much of a competition but as an interactive experience between poet and audience. Where they can come back at you and say, "Oh, no," or "Oh, yes." You can either strengthen your poetry or be adamant about it and leave it the way it is, according to what they say. It used to be very different. I used to prepare in different ways. But then again you have to keep in mind that I am not slamming anymore. Not for any conscious reason, more geographical than anything else, I got away from places where I could walk out of my house and half an hour later be at a slam.

I guess you are expected at some point to say, "It is time to move on, move on to this book or move on to this or that." I have never really looked at slamming like that. It has never been a stepping stone for me. If there was a slam that was close enough to me and I didn't have family obligations that keep me from going, I would be there.

PI: You used to practice your poems until you could do them ten times in a row without making a mistake, do you still do that?

When memorization was really important to me, I would see myself on a tape and know that I wasn't really there. There is a way of learning too well. You can get away from the spirit of the poem and into the spirit of performing the poem. I can remember going into the bathroom at the Green Mill and not feeling confident unless I had done the poem ten times over in my head without a mistake.

That was fun then, we all had our little quirks and things that we did. A constantly shifting idea of what was important. It was a really addictive community at the time. It was important for me to be a part of it. I shifted during that time of what was important for me, at that time perfection was important. The more you did it the more important it became, because people expected you not to make mistakes. I felt like I had to live up to that, now I don't feel that so much.

The good thing about having done that is now I have a body of work, an old body of work. I can now go into schools and concentrate on analyzing pieces and just going in and doing them. It is nice to have that groundwork established. But then I have new poems that I can talk about in a different way. Honestly, I have pieces that are two or three years old and I could not get up in front of an audience and do them without reading them. But that is okay, I don't see that as some sort of failure. I am thankful for what I learned early on, and that strength that knowing those pieces gives me—when I don't want to have paper in front of me or I want to walk around and perform the poem—it is good to have that, but it is less and less important to me as time goes on.

PI: What are you working on now?

I go to Northeastern College in Boston every summer and give a workshop. This year we are doing a poetry choir. It is an idea I came up with last summer, to write a collective piece, a long poem in three parts. We are going to orchestrate it like a symphony, with kids changing places, voices dropping in and out.

PI: How many kids will you work with?

There will probably be about fifteen. What they do is they come in and take dance classes from a dancer, they take instrumentation classes, and they take a poetry class. At the end of the session they do a big show. The poetry choir will be our part of the show. We are just going to score it like a piece of music.

PI: Are you going to use sheet music and block the piece off in bars?

That is the way I was thinking of doing it. I have been working with a couple of bands. So I have gotten used to thinking about poems that way. One of the bands is kind of a blues band. I discovered them in Boston. They first started playing with me because I wanted to use music with the *Professional Suicide* piece. The vocalist is a really good blues singer. We just did a CD and we are thinking of what we want to do with it, how we want to market it. After years of not having an official name, we just picked a name for ourselves. I am leaving all the PR and marketing to them. The name is Bop Thunderous. The people who are producing the play are deciding whether to use them as the house band. We have a gig coming up in Atlanta next year that Stephen Dobins has asked us to do.

PI: Are you singing your poems as well as reading them?

A little bit, not because I said I must sing, but the band is so good they pull me into it. I'll be in the middle of a performance and find myself singing. Then there is a jazz group that I performed with a bunch of times. I perform with them when they call me. We have done the Knitting Factory and a couple of other places. They are called Paradigm Shift. I am also doing some work with the Tempered Ensemble, led by an old-time jazz musician, Bill Cole. They are doing a program in October at Carnegie Hall.

PI: Are you still writing for *MS* magazine?

MS magazine has moved to the west coast and I did not want to move. They said when they revamped and got the column straight they would call me, but I don't know if they will or not.

Right now I don't even know if I would be able to do it. I am writing a biography of Harriet Tubman. Which is an all-encompassing project. It bothered me when this play came along, because I don't know if I can do both things. When you called, I was at my computer, just buried in Harriet Tubman. She is on the floor, on all the shelves; there are pictures of her on the walls. She is everywhere. It will take me two or three years, but I like it.

PI: Have you written any poems in her voice?

Yeah, because she talks to me when I want to go away: "You know you should be in here doing this." The book itself is going to have poetry in its opening chapters. It will be poetry I write in her voice about some incident in the upcoming chapter.

PI: That was my last question—where poetry is taking you now, so I guess we know the answer.

Yes, to Harriet Tubman.

Quincy Troupe: Transcircularities: On Putting Together a Poetry Book

Quincy Troupe was a featured poet on Bill Moyer's PBS series, *The Power of the Word*. Troupe is the author of nine books including *Choruses: Poems*; *Avalanche*; *Weather Reports: New and Selected Poems*; *Skulls Along the River*; *Snake-Back Solos: Selected Poems*; and *Embryo Poems*, which received an American Book Award and is a two-time winner of the World Poetry Bout. He is also the author of *Miles: The Autobiography*, which received an American Book Award; *James Baldwin: The Legacy*; and the memoir *Miles and Me: A Memoir of Miles Davis*. Troupe edited the anthology *Giant Talk: An Anthology of Third World Writing* and is a founding editor of *Confrontation: A Journal of Third World Literature* and *American Rag*. In 1991, he received the Peabody Award for co-producing and writing the radio show *The Miles Davis Radio Project*. Among his honors and awards are fellowships from the National Foundation for the Arts, the New York Foundation for the Arts, and a grant from the New York State Council on the Arts.

Poetry Investigator: Let's talk about your new book on Coffee House Press.

The book is called *Transcircularites*. That is a word I made up.

PI: What does it mean?

For me it means circular moving across everywhere. The title poem is "Transcircularites"; the book is *Transcircularites: New and Selected Poems*. It goes from 1968 to 2001. For me the poem is trying to deal with the way that human beings just continuously make the same stupid mistakes from time immemorial, all over the world.

I'm not just talking about the United States or the Middle East: it is everywhere. We don't seem to learn from history, we don't seem to learn from our mistakes. We just continuously make the same mistakes over and over again. It is dealing with that but not directly. In many instances I see religions that are supposed to save man—it is driven by religious fervor. You look at the Middle East. You look at Northern Ireland.

PI: It seems like you can say any war has a religious component.

Yes, a religious component, or it is color, or it is ethnic, but a lot of times it is driven by religion. People are constantly trying to make people over into their own idea of what they should be and if they don't, then they fight. So that is what that poem is trying to deal with, those kinds of issues. Not directly, it doesn't name anybody, it just talks about it in a way. Hopefully, in a meaningful way.

PI: It is an interesting concept.

Yes, an interesting concept, for me it is. Then when we get to a brink—when we go to the graveyard, the only thing there is are tombstones and the owl looking down on us—then we realize what mistakes we have made and look up again to heaven for our savior to come save us from our own stupidity. When actually we could do it ourselves. It brings to a close a certain kind of poem that I have been writing for a long time.

PI: Talk about how your use of forms, because you write villanelles, poems like "Song," and the great Michael Jordan poem, "41 Seconds."

When I first started writing poems I didn't know anything about poetry and I found out I really loved it. I wanted to find out as much as I could about it, so I went back and taught myself how to write sonnets, sestinas, villanelles, haiku, tanka, and ballads. I used to do it just to see if I could do it. Then I discovered the poet Ojenke, who is still around but doesn't write as much as he used to. He is probably one of the most influential poets on the West Coast, in Los Angeles. Had a big influence on Jayne Cortez, myself, on Stanley Crouch when he was writing poetry, Kamau Daáood, Wanda Coleman, just a whole bunch of people. He became a Rastafarian. He doesn't write much now; he is more of an oral poet.

When I first heard him read his style was coming out of the church. I said, "Oh that is what I should do; I should be doing that instead of writing these forms." Just by listening to his work I decided I was going to because I grew up in St. Louis, I grew up in the Baptist church, and I grew up in an African American neighborhood.

Listening to all that music, and I decided after listening to Ojenke a couple of times that from that point on I was going to try to create a form or forms that came out of the African American experience. Not so much the blues form, which had already been done by Jean Toomer, Langston Hughes, and others, but to try to fuse the blues, the sermons, and jazz with speech.

Perhaps come up with something new. I didn't know what it was, but I was always in pursuit of it. Ultimately, it became a pursuit not only of the African American form but the American form. I guess you might say that I got on the road that Whitman was on. People like Langston Hughes and others are on that road. To write in this great American language that we all speak.

PI: This is a simple question. When you are putting the books together, how do you decide the order of the poems?

A lot of people put the new poems first. I don't like that, because I like to read up to new poems. In this particular instance, since it was going to be a new and selected poems, I went chronologically from the oldest poem to the newest poem.

"Transcircularites" happens to be the newest poem, so it is the last poem in the book. So you go from a very early poem to that poem. It kind of laid itself out.

The problem for me was in editing the book. When I first turned it in, the publisher told me to send in whatever I wanted. It was about four hundred pages. We decided we would cut fifty pages, and that is what we did. That was kind of difficult. Some things had to come out that I really wanted to stay in, and they were hard cuts.

Other books like, for example, let's talk about the other two books that proceeded *Transcircularites*. I will start with the oldest one, *Avalanche*. It was set up in the way that an avalanche works. I went to a geologist and asked about how avalanches work. He told me that if you were up on the mountain you would hear this crack. Then the earth would start to give away. The ground, rocks, and trees would start to come down at unbelievable speed. You hear this crack and this speed coming at you. The second part is when it hits bottom. It takes maybe a day or so for it to settle. Then, the third part of it is, if you were to fly over the site a week or so later after everything had settled, it would look like a still life, like it had always been that way.

So that was three different kinds of movements. I had a poem, "Avalanche," and I decided this would be the title of a book. The poem is not even about avalanches. It is about an avalanche of language.

All those poems that came in that year, I broke them down. First I wrote the poem about the sound breaking loose. In the first part, the poems reflect the speed of the avalanche, images coming at you. The second part slows down and is about the shifting fragmented kind of movement in the poetry, and it stops. Then the last part of the book is about still lifes. I tried to create this new form called the terzatina, which is a twenty-one-line poem with a terza rima rhyme scheme. It means a dance. I felt I had to write something new, to create a new form in a way.

Because of the fact that after an avalanche, what is there is a new form: it is a transformation. That is the way that book operated. First the crack, then the speed, the shifting around, the unevenness of language, and last, the still life. I wrote about nine poems in there that all had seven stanzas with three lines apiece with no rhyme scheme. The last one of the poems in that section had that terza rima rhyme scheme on it.

Choruses was a different kind of book. It was moving from form to freedom. The last poem written for that book was the first poem in the book, entitled "Song." I had written the poem for Allen Ginsberg entitled "Choruses." The publisher liked the poem and he liked the title, so we determined that would that be the title of the book. Since it was going to be called *Choruses*, it suggested to me the whole idea of song and singing, and that it should have that kind of feeling. Therefore, I thought, "Let me figure out how to do this." At one point the last poem in the book was that poem "Words and Sounds that Build Bridges towards a New Tongue." But I thought it would be good if I wrote a villanelle, which is songlike, along with the sestinas and the villanelle you mentioned about Michael Jordan. I already had some haiku and tanka written for that book. I had also written an extended blues form about this guy going downriver.

I realized I needed a poem, something that would suggest song at the beginning of the book, and I specifically wrote the poem to be the first poem in the book. The idea was that you move from form, the whole idea of whether it is a haiku, tanka, ballad, or an ode—you move from there to freedom.

The poem that suggested that for me is "Words and Sounds that Build Bridges towards a New Tongue." That poem is a fusion of jazz, rock and roll, rap rhythms—all kinds of Americana is thrown into that poem. You move from song through all kinds of different rhythms to a freeing-up of the verse. So that is what that book is about. I am always trying to play with concepts in books.

PI: This line is catching my eye, "in the backyard of a favorite uncle waxing real with his sho-nuff-to-god, hope-to-die-ace-boon-coon-throw-downs."

[*laughs*]

PI: That is certainly a great line, a very free line.

That is free. If you read the last part of that poem, I created a rap. It is a rap rhythm. The poem moves from rock-n-roll to, beedle-loo, beedle-loo, beeboli bop, which is Charlie Parker, which is Dizzy Gillispie. That's what that is. In the beginning of the poem you have all of it thrown together, smashed together. That was one of the most fun poems I have ever written.

PI: Tell us about how you got your relationship with Coffee House Press.

Well, I was writer-in-residence at The Loft in Minneapolis. I knew Coffee House Press, but I had never met Alan Kornblum. I had two readings at the Loft, one by myself and one with Hamiet Bluitt, the great baritone saxophone player. I noticed this guy sitting in the front row, and when I read alone—later I had this big reading for The Loft—he was sitting in the back. I notice people. He came up to me and said, "My name is Alan Kornblum, I am the publisher of Coffee House Press." I said, "Oh, how you doing? I really like your books." He said, "Well, that is what I am here to ask you, if I can publish your work." Just like that, point blank.

PI: The new book is your third book with Coffee House?

Yes, the third book. He calls me up and says, "I think it is time for another book." I did *Choruses*, and he called up and said, "I think it's about time we did a selected poems."

PI: Please talk about the Wastewater Treatment Plant project at Point Loma, California.* How did you get involved? Did you write the poems out at the site or just visit the site and then write them? Because they seem like such a good match to that specific place.

First, Mathew Gregoire, the guy who those poems are dedicated to, called me up and said he wanted to talk to me about something. He is a great sculptor. He said, "Listen, I have been chosen to do this project at Wastewater Treatment Plant. I am going to make some sculpture, bring in other artists, musicians, architects, landscape engineers, and it would be good if I had a poet."

At first I didn't know what he was talking about. He looked at me and said, "You want to ride out and see it?" I said, "That would be good." So we looked at it and I took my notebook with me—I always take my notebook because I used to be a journalist. I took notes on everything as we walked around. He showed me where he wanted the poems. When we went underground, I thought, "They probably are not going to want a long poem under here. I could write a haiku, tanka, or haiku-like piece, that would be quick to read." Some of the longer poems face the ocean. Some of the poems meander around this trail in the back of the place. One of them is in a parking lot where you can park at either end of the lot, so I made the poem so you can read it coming from either way. They are sandblasting the poems into the walls and up stairs. The workers who work out there love the poems.

* To visit the project call the Waste Management public relations office at 858-292-6414.

Tom Mayo: Their Human Connection to the World

Tom Mayo, an associate professor of law at Southern Methodist University, teaches "Law, Literature & Medicine" at the law school and at the University of Texas Southwestern Medical School at Dallas. The course is an examination of professionalism and its implications for and applications to a wide variety of patient and client encounters. The materials are almost exclusively literary—novels, poems, plays, and short stories. He is the regular poetry columnist for the *Dallas Morning News*. His column appears monthly in the "Sunday Reader" section.

Poetry Investigator: Please talk about the class for the law and medical students you teach.

It is a class that meets in the final semester of the third year for the law students and the fourth year for the medical students, so they are all about to finish up their graduate studies and head off into their early professional training.

I typically have ten students from each school; it is a self-selected group. It is not a required course and it does not satisfy any graduation requirements for the law students. It does for the medical students, but they have a million ways to satisfy that requirement for an elective in their fourth year. It is the only humanities elective in the upper level at the medical school, so it is somewhat unique, and it is pretty unique on the law school side as well.

We don't read cases or statutes or law review articles. The upshot of that is that it is a very self-selected group, and a very motivated group, looking for something different in their professional training. They want to be there. They are either searching for something new or in some cases trying to regain something old; a connection to literature they may have had before they got started in law school or medical school.

I had one student who was an English major at Yale, got a master's degree in English at Columbia, and had a strong literary background. I have had other students with similar backgrounds. I think that law school and medical school both, whether they try to or not, manage to squeeze any humanities approach to the world out of people.

We pride ourselves at law school in training our students to think like lawyers, and I have been doing this for eighteen years and I am still not persuaded that there is anything helpful to that. It is like boot camp in the first year and then just a lot of learning about the law in the second and third year.

This course is a way for both groups of students to bring themselves back to their beginning, to reclaim to a certain extent their human connection to the world. If, for a couple of years or more, they have been putting one side of their personality on hold and pursuing a kind of analytical and professional identity, this is a way to start harmonizing those different directions.

There are conflicts between personal beliefs and professional duty that arise in both professions. There are times when you question if what you are doing is the right thing, even if your mentors or the law is saying that you should do it. Those kinds of points of conflict, more than just irritations, are a serious questioning of what you are doing and why you might require some ability to distance yourself from the situations.

This course provides a student with a way to view problems in literary terms, to use literature as a tool to help explore some of those conflicts and work towards a resolution. This sounds kind of touchy-feely but I really have quite a few specific teaching goals, and students are able to use the literature to achieve them. The poetry is about half the reading, maybe more than half in terms of discussion.

With the exception of the occasional master's degree English student who has studied poetry, most of these students gave up on poetry in high school. Like most people, they don't trust their poetic instincts, if you will. They don't think they know much about poetry, and they probably don't. They don't think they know much about how to read or enjoy poetry.

That is exactly where I want them to be. It strips away their professional learning, their arsenal of professional skills, and their armor of professional identity and returns them to a very undisguised state. They have to encounter these poems as human beings because nothing they have done at law school or medical school prepares them for it. It is as constructive and healthy a seminar experience as I have ever seen, thanks to the poetry.

People are open to other interpretations. They try them on, they test them, and they challenge them. Nobody is able to trump anybody else by saying, "That is just wrong," or, "Laboratory tests prove," or, "the Supreme Court has held." There are no final authorities for them. Now, some of their readings are really bad. Some of their readings are off the wall, but usually they are brought back into the fold a little bit, and I'm not big on the "correct interpretation" of any poem. But I do think you have to be attentive to the words the poet is using and to the structure and direction of the poem. Over time they get it. This class is just a real useful medium for getting them to a point of vulnerability, of openness, and of sharing in a way that they probably have not done in all their years of professional training.

PI: I was struck by your comments on your use of narrative and how a patient or a client might describe their legal or health problem and how that related to literature.

I think that unbeknownst to most of the law and medical students, many of the skills that they have been slowly acquiring are a kind of narrative skills. You deal with patient narratives, with client narratives, you construct narratives with them. The editorial decision of what to include and what not to include, what to emphasize and what not to emphasize, comes from years of professional training. There are clinical storytellers who are unbelievably good at building those narratives and then shaping them and passing them on. To be able to stack those different cases up, compare them, contrast them, to learn from them—that is a narrative skill.

Obviously you need to know a lot of law or of medicine to figure out how to do that. But you can't do it without being able to deal with the stories your clients or patients bring to you. I also think it is a way of being an effective professional in dealing with other professionals.

It is the old, "I had a patient once who . . ." sort of thing. Searching back through your memory banks, pulling out the analogous patient experience, comparing and contrasting, differentiating what it is that made that patient different or the same for purposes of treatment.

For a client, it might be writing their story down in such a way that it is compelling for a judge. I am convinced that judges rule based on characterizations that are essentially narrative characterizations. A construct for a story, a way of regarding that story in terms of who is the victim and who is innocent, who tried hard and who didn't try at all to fulfill their obligations.

You write those stories in narrative terms that pull the judge in and lead the judge to a set of labels and a set of conclusions that flow from those. It is all about storytelling. It is about being persuasive and using narrative in a particular professional way.

PI: You have been teaching for eighteen years. What was the inspiration for the class? Did it come out of your love of literature?

It actually came out of something very much more specific. After my first year of teaching here, I had two students in my civil procedure class who came back to law school for their second year after the summer and were just despondent. They had no enthusiasm for finishing. In separate conversations with each one of them I tried to find out what the problem was, if there was something missing, what had we done, what were they doing or not doing.

It turned out they both had been English majors as undergrads. Both of them had not done any of that kind of reading during law school so far. I got the feeling that this is what it would be like if you were an athlete who was used to working out three days a week and then for a year didn't run, or sprint, or stretch, and felt kind of slow and fat. You think, this was who you were and what you were and now all of a sudden you are not doing something basic to your nature. It is not good for you.

I started talking to them about reading, and as I did, I remembered a law and literature course I took in law school. I said, "If you want to get serious about this, there is a lot of great writing out there that we could package into a reading course.

We could read the stuff every week, we could talk about it, you could write a paper, and you can do it for credit." One of those papers won the prize that year for best student paper.

That encouraged me. They stayed in law school, they continued to thrive, they did well, they graduated. I replaced those two students with a couple more the next year. Soon I was doing it with eight or nine students as solo directed research, independent study.

For economy's sake, we would all get together on a Friday afternoon and have a seminar, even though it wasn't recognized as a seminar in our curriculum. After doing that for a few years, I started getting medical faculty sitting in, and my interest started heading off toward bioethics.

I started to shape the readings to cover issues in law and medical ethics looking at the same set of problems from two different perspectives, in literary terms. Eventually the class got approved at the medical school and at the law school as a course and reached the point where I could offer it for credit under its own name as a freestanding, recognized part of the upper level curriculum at both schools. I thought it was quite a leap for the faculties to recognize and adopt what is for them a really strange methodology.

PI: Do you know of other programs like this?

No, but medical humanities is growing, and law and literature has been around as a course offering at law schools for twenty-five years or more. I don't know of another course where the law and medical students are thrown together and where the readings are selected to teach them about each other's sense of what it means to be a professional.

PI: Please talk about how the *Dallas Morning News* column came about.

I used to be a newspaper columnist when I was in high school and college. I did a weekly column for seven years. It does not seem possible now. It was two thousand words a week for three hundred and sixty weeks. It was a kind of writing that I enjoyed. I hadn't really thought about it for a long time. I graduated from college in 1971, so it had been thirty-one years.

Then all of a sudden I am teaching this course. There is a ton of poetry in it, I am studying poetry, reading everything I can get my hands on to be a better teacher in this class. Then it dawned on me that I couldn't remember reading a single poetry review in the *Dallas Morning News* in all the time I had been here. I am sure there had been a few and I just missed them.

I thought in my sort of teacher's way that there really needs to be coverage of poetry in a major city paper. I contacted the then book editor of the *Dallas Morning News*, and he said, "We never publish poetry reviews. Every time I publish a poetry review I get in trouble with local poets, so it's just not worth the hassle."

Instead, what I proposed to him was for National Poetry Month, in April of about four years ago, was a column of a bunch of reviews or mini-reviews all strung together. Darned if he didn't get back to me in late March and say, "Okay I can run them this Sunday. Do you have the reviews?" I didn't because I had not heard from him. But I holed myself up for a day and had five or six books I really liked at the time and cranked out the reviews.

That was his last year as book review editor. He retired and was succeeded by an editor who I then contacted and said, "I really enjoyed doing that, and if you think there is some value here, would you like to get some reviews from me?" She said, "No, I inherited eighty or eighty-five reviews from my predecessor. I am booked for the next year, but what I really need is a column. Would you do a monthly poetry column?"

She has been very supportive of the column. It is a good relationship. Because they are available online and because *Poetry Daily* has been very good about putting my column out on their news page, I have gotten comments about the column from people around the world. It has been a fabulous experience for me. English teachers or poetry fans from all over the country have written.

I think Dallas is the eighth largest city, but not one that is known for being literary readers. I don't know if people read poetry, but they like to buy poetry books, and they like to give them. I am positive that we have tapped into—it may not be huge, but there is a kind of underground level of support for poetry. People don't talk about it a lot, but I think there are a lot of fans of poetry.

PI: How do you choose the subject matter for the column? Is it just whatever is hot for you? You seem to have a really wide range of interests. Is that a conscious decision to choose new subject areas?

Yes, whatever is hot for me. I just think there is so much good poetry out there it would be a shame not to promote it. There also are some good small independent presses out there, and it would be a shame not to highlight some of the things they are doing, which can be a little more experimental or a little more ethnically or culturally centered. Those are themes that keep me going.

I am working on a column on Persian poetry. It just occurred to me that getting a lot of books for review from publishers can give a seemingly random sample, but it seems like last year was a big year for sonnets. I will do a column on modern sonnets. Last year was also a big year for haiku, and I really like some of the experimental haiku that people have done.

The one limitation that I put on myself is I want to write about stuff I like that I think other people will like. So I don't write a lot of columns where I am bashing someone's poetry about not being up to snuff by whatever standard there might be. It is more important to me to find books that have genuine moments of pleasure to offer people who like to read poetry. If the book does that well, I am going to try to think of a way to package that with something else—an idea, another book, or something to let people know about it.

A lot of folks seem to use the column as a source of recommendation, so when they walk into a bookstore with a stack of poetry books, they start picking titles to buy. If I have really raved about something, I hear from folks that they have picked up the book and read it, and they will write to me and say, "That was a great pick, I really enjoyed that." I have not heard from too many who say, "Such and such a title was really terrible." It is a way to help people cut through the welter of new titles. There are thousands of new poetry books a year.

PI: How many books do you receive from publishers? Is your house getting full?

If there are one thousand a year, I probably get seven or eight hundred. I am running out of space. Let me tell you! It is exciting, too. When you see so many books of poetry and you know you can't read them all. I do try to get into every book that comes across the desk. It is a great time to be reading poetry.

Dayvid Figler: Las Vegas Judge/Poet/Radio/ Fiction Guy

Dayvid Figler's humor commentaries have been featured on NPR's *All Things Considered*. His work has appeared in *McSweeney's* (online), *Uber*, *Exquisite Corpse*, *Time Out*, and in the Las Vegas anthology *In the Shadow of the Strip* (University of Nevada Press). Dayvid is the youngest retired municipal court judge in Las Vegas history. The former capital murder defense attorney has been a featured reader at many national festivals including South by Southwest and Lollapalooza. In 1998, he was awarded an artist fellowship from the Nevada State Arts Council and was named a Nevada Tumblewords Poet. His one-man show, *Dayvid Figler is Jim Morrison in Hello, I Love You (Where You Folks From?)*, sponsored by the City of Las Vegas, was selected as a feature on the literary stage at the 1999 Bumbershoot in Seattle, Washington. He once was the opening act for the Beastie Boys—it didn't go well.

Poetry Investigator: What was it like to open for the Beastie Boys and read from the stage of Sam Boyd Stadium at the opening concert of the Lollapalooza tour in 1994? Wasn't that the stadium that was also the site of your high school graduation?

The Las Vegas shirtless boys, in the middle of summer, had little use for anybody being anything other than a Beastie Boy or a Smashing Pumpkin. I faired well for the first forty-five seconds. It was quite a rush having my words being heard by ten thousand youngsters at that stadium of my past and to hear them all laugh at one point, or at least enough of them to get a wave of laughter to hit me. But then the wave of water bottles that followed it was not as rewarding. It's all on videotape and I love how on the videotape my friend says after my introduction by Mud Barron—Mud came out in the old-time preacher outfit and was getting universally booed upon his appearance. Every time he emerged from backstage the crowd knew that it was not time for one of the bands they wanted to see. He was doing this old-time preacher brimstone and fire routine and the Vegas crowd did not want that on any level. I think the fact that he was wearing this head-to-toe all black outfit in the middle of summer made everyone in the hundred-plus temperature even hotter than they already were.

PI: Didn't he also tell the audience they were stupid and that the poets were there to educate them?

To make them smarter and that they would be cast into the lake of fire if they didn't pay attention. I was initially supposed to go out in front of one of the earlier bands, like the Breeders, which might have been a little friendlier audience. It just kept getting pushed back. I had spent the earlier part of the day in the poetry tent, then got whisked backstage and didn't get to see much of the show and was sitting backstage forever. Then I was told I was going to go out in front of the Beastie Boys, and I know that crowd and didn't want to go out in front of them.

So Mud comes out and they are booing him, and he says, "What is it that I can do for you to make you happy." The boos get louder and he says, "I have a notion, it's the Beastie Boys that you want." Suddenly the crowd turns in his favor and starts yelling, "Yes." Then Mud says, "Well, I've got the Beastie Boys for you in thirty minutes, but first a poet." That was my introduction, so my friend Doug, who is videotaping, turns and says, "Figler is going to get killed." So I came out and I did my song and dance, telling this story about graduating there. They were with me for a little bit. Then the first kid throws a water bottle, then the avalanche of water bottles, the stage manager yanking the microphone out of my hands, proclaiming, "There will be no more reading of anything for the rest of the tour." They took me backstage and put me in a trailer, where I thought I was going to be whipped by Perry Farrell, but they gave me a hundred bucks and sent me home.

The actual reward out of the experience was I got to meet a great group of writers, Pleasant Gamin, Bucky Sinister, Juliette Torrez, yourself included, who I don't think I would have met, and there was a certain connection right away, maybe born out of sympathy.

I was already a lawyer at that point, and meeting all those writers gave me the encouragement to pursue writing more and led to going to the National Poetry Slam held in 1995 in Ann Arbor and meeting Justin Chin, Beth Lisick, and the other Manic D Press writers and meeting Kevin Sampsell, who has published my short stories.

PI: Talk about your connection between your training as a lawyer and your writing. Is there any connection? Is there any crossover in the skills you use?

I used to have a different answer than what I am going to say now. When I went into law school, I had a desire to maintain a creativity in anything I did. As an undergraduate, I was a political science major, studying cold and dry political systems, which is about as far away from creativity as possible. I was doing sketch comedy writing, with this troop. That was the balance for me, keep the creative side over here and keep the dull school shit over here, just to get my degree. When I got out of college, I didn't want to go to law school. It would just be more of the same and going more to the side I didn't like as much.

When I wasn't discovered in my underwear, sitting in my bed, staring forward, as a comedy writer, I went to law school. I immediately learned they don't want you to be creative. That's how I used to answer that question. I think the goal of law school is to train your mind to just be logical. To be detached, to not look at the colors, to compartmentalize every color of the rainbow. It's flow-chart thinking.

They teach you to break down your thinking, to figure out what area of law you are in, what area of precedent applies. That is the mindset they give you as a lawyer. At that same time I was trying to do readings, which I described to my friends as my way to blow off the stress of the legal training. It wasn't poems, it was just terse commentary, with odd line breaks.

After I passed the bar and I came back to Vegas, I was struggling to get law work. I continued to do readings, and by 1994, I had become a cog lawyer. I worked for a small law firm, working for unions, fighting unfair labor practices, kind of heavy stuff. My creativity has always been linked to humor, and there is nothing funny about unfair labor practices. There is not even a lot of room for parody.

I have never really thought about it this way, but after Lalapalooza, I started to transition into a trial attorney, getting more involved in the courtroom, presenting cases to juries. By 1997, my writing is really improving and my lawyering is not what I was taught in law school. I think that the way I approach writing and communicating through my writing made me more suited than some of my colleagues to be a trial attorney. Presenting cases to little audiences of twelve, who hopefully wouldn't be pelting me with water bottles when I tried to convince them that this really ugly guy standing next to me didn't commit murder with a screwdriver and a knife and a gun and a blowtorch. At the time I was working for the public defender, so you are presenting these loser cases.

I wound up doing exclusively murder and death penalty cases. You have to work through these scenarios, or if you want to call them plots, and find out what makes sense and where it doesn't make sense and develop a line of reasoning. Still using all the tools they taught you in law school, the way of logically flow-charting things, but also communicating, as a human, the story that occurred that either limits your client's culpability or convinces a jury that there is not enough evidence, based on the way the plot has been laid out, to hold the man accountable at all.

I have gotten acquittals, reversals, and dismissals on murder cases through my career—that came with more experience. But at points along my law career, some of my closing arguments tended to a strange hybrid of the creative process and the logical process.

The very long answer to your short question is, while I didn't use to think they were not the same, in fact I thought one was an antidote for the other. I now think the two serve each other. While I don't write about the law yet, in any significant way, I think that being in that creative space requires my mind to seek out other ways to look at things, and when I am in lawyer mode, the way that I look at things creatively maybe gives me an edge in how I fashion things, how I present things through a creative filter.

PI: Does the presentation in front of the jury play into the presentation of your fiction in front of an audience? Do they complement each other? In the way that you noticed your development in being able to tell the plot or the story, did you also notice that your presentation skills were growing?

Yes, I think that is true. I am sort of audience-driven, and you have to be, in front of juries. If you see your audience nodding off, you can have the best presentation crafted, but if you are losing them, you have to make adjustments. It might not be just in tone, you might have to on the fly alter where you are going with things. It's a gut instinct, it's a judgment call, and you might not be right on it. You are constantly scanning your audience. For better or worse, that is what I do as performer.

I don't always stick to the script. In fiction it's a little harder. When I was doing the commentaries, I would always leave room for cream. I don't read pieces the same way twice very often. If I get a good reaction, I bump it up, sort of milk it. I tend to comment on my own work as I read it. Say a line goes well and gets a laugh, I try to rephrase it and get another laugh. Just sort of blurt out what comes to mind. That's how juries are too. I write out my summation, to a certain extent, in much the same way I used to do the slammy poems. I have different cues along the way to help remember parts, but I wouldn't be stuck on page. It's not good to be stuck on page in front of juries.

Juries are probably as unforgiving as slam judges. They want you to live it for them. Of course the stakes are different, entertaining a group of one hundred people at a bar, or a bookstore, and communicating to twelve people. My goal is not entertainment with the jury. Getting them to understand where I am going from, educating them, maybe even a little manipulation. Some of those things cross over into audience.

There was one case where I had this kid, who was up for an attempted murder. He probably did it, but the penalties were just out of line with how it went down. I really got into it in a way that I became more entertaining than I should have. I was presenting this closing to the jury where I was getting very animated, where I was becoming one of those kind of lawyers. It was under control, but I was taking a risk. I felt that the facts were so bad in this particular case: the kid was shot point blank in the neck and my client basically admitted that he was the shooter.

It made it difficult to not get an attempted murder. I figured there was less to lose than if I just went in there dry. It was very much like a performance piece: it was about me at that point. People were coming in from other courtrooms to see what was going on. I got very loud. I had that jury riveted. They were following my every move, and they acquitted my client. I broke down afterwards. That was not right. While I felt the circumstances warranted it, I also felt I should not have done it, and I didn't feel good about how I had performed in front of the jury, that I had let too much creativity seep into my closing. Since then I have learned to keep it under control. I can still bring on a very compelling argument, I can still be interesting to the jury, I can still use all the skills I have acquired as a performer, but I think I can keep the priorities straight.

PI: How has your life changed, being a judge?

I did the judge thing for about two years. Here in Nevada we have appointed judges, and then one has to run for election. I don't want to get into my reasons for not running. So I am getting back to being a lawyer.

I was in the lower courts, misdemeanor charges, what I like to call the sex, drugs, and rock and roll offenses. Crack pipe but no crack, stereo too loud, prostitution, nothing too bad. We did have some serious cases that would come before us—domestic violence, DUI—but a lot of the cases were like, homeless running afoul of the various laws that fall under being out in the street a lot, falling asleep on a bench, jaywalking. I had just come out of this world of murder, so I probably had a different perspective than my fellow judges. I felt that I had the ability to be a congenial character on the bench, who could get to the heart of things and put things in perspective. I am never going to throw someone in jail for jaywalking, which my colleagues would. If someone was a habitual offender and chronic homeless who would jaywalk every day, they felt there was no other way to teach these people a lesson than to throw them in jail for sixty days, or one hundred and eighty days. The district attorney filed a motion against me when I was first appointed a judge, that I was not to have cases involving the homeless come before me, because I was predisposed to not give them jail time.

There are two great things about being a judge. One is that you are always right, even when you are wrong. There is no one in the room who is going to tell you otherwise, because you have the power to throw people in jail. Two, they have to laugh at all your jokes, for the same reason.

I had a guy in front of me who got busted for low-level pot, less than an ounce, which is a misdemeanor. I gave him a three hundred dollar fine, which is the standard fine. He said, "Can I have a year to pay it?" I said, "A year is a little rough. You had enough money to buy the pot. I'll give you four months." He said, "Can I have more time? I don't really have a good job." I said, "What's your job?" He said, "Have you ever been to this one restaurant in town?" I said, "Yes, I go there all the time." He said, "Have you ever noticed the guy in the chicken suit who stands out in front?" I said, "Yes." He said, "I'm that guy." It was summer, and I said, "You have to wear that suit in July in Las Vegas?" He said, "Yes." I said, "Were you busted in the suit?" He said, "Yes." I said, "All right, credit for the time served. Case closed." I thought the man had suffered enough. He was driving to work and they pulled him over, because he didn't just smell of chicken.

The weird thing was I was still doing the radio commentaries while I was still on the bench. The lawyers who were before me would say, "Your honor, can I approach the bench on an unrelated matter." They would say, "Hey man, that thing you did on the radio today was incredible." They always were positive, nobody said, "You really sucked," because you were the judge. I like to think that they enjoyed the pieces, but in the back of my mind I thought they were just trying to kiss my ass. In all the commentaries, they would refer to me as a poet. I hate that because I feel it is an offense to actual poets, who are skilled and craft their work, as opposed to the little throw-offs that I do. The worst was when a lawyer would come up to me and say, "Your honor, can I talk to you about something?" I would say, "Is there a concern?" They would say, "No, no, I have a bunch of poetry, and I have wanted to get it published. Can you help get me published? Can we talk about my poetry?" This would happen in the middle of court.

PI: It speaks to the harsh reality to trying to get published.

Yeah: "He ruled in my favor, maybe he'll like my poetry." I haven't really written about the judge experience. I might write about the judge experience, I was fairly young when I was appointed. Ira Glass was in town, and I had recently had a couple of pieces on *All Things Considered*. I started to tell him about the pieces, and he just stopped me and said, "I have plenty of funny white guys. If you want to write about some of your law experiences, I would be more than happy to look at them."

PI: You started doing radio on your local station and then got picked up on NPR. Talk about what makes a good piece for you. How do you put together a commentary?

It's funny: I didn't realize I was pretty much doing commentaries throughout my writing career. I was doing a reading with a couple of friends—one is a journalist, the other is a poet. We had done an annual reading that took place the Saturday before Christmas, and we called it "The Three Wise Guys." The general manager for the public radio station in Nevada was in the audience. He came up to me after the show and said, "I hate poetry, as far as something people are always asking me to put on radio. I don't think poetry in most mouths works on the radio. But I don't think what you are doing is poetry." I said, "Finally, someone gets it."

He asked me to write a piece for a segment they do about what it means to be from Nevada. That led to us having lunch and talking about doing a regular commentary. He wanted to get more local voices on the station.

I wrote a piece about why my family came to Nevada. It was an epic trip in the family station wagon that included losing me in the snow in Chicago. The car broke down as we hit the border. We had it towed to my uncle's house, and my dad went in the backyard and shot the car. The shoot station wagons, don't they?

They really liked the piece, and the station manager asked if I could crank something like that out every week. I was just starting a death penalty trial. He asked if I would write about the trial and I said, "I don't really want to write about that, it might be exploitive to my client." I didn't want to tap into the emotions of being a lawyer because you do have to stay a little detached. The trial went well, and the producer called and said, "We really want you to submit more pieces."

What was on my mind was the weirdness of juries. So I came up with a topic I want to talk about, in this case jury selection. Because I write humor commentaries, I look for what is ridiculous in this subject, or what needs to be exposed? Then I start to think about the subject in those terms. I am not here to be the town explainer. I am not going to talk about how juries are selected to talk about the process. I just think, "What is weird about this, or odd, or inconsistent?" Inconsistency is an aspect of how I decide what to write. Then I take it to its illogical extremes, which is where I find a lot of the humor. Eventually, lines start to rise to the surface. Those little lines become the anchor for the piece. The topic causes the thought process, looking for the humor in the subject. You have to contextualize it, giving enough information so that the audience knows what you are talking about. Then you go into the studio, and I was blessed to have great producers who were very good at coaching line reads.

I didn't want to be pigeonholed into doing just law stuff. I just started to talk about Las Vegas a lot, because it was something I felt needed exploring. Then I would talk about current events, pop trends, and all these other things. Then I was dating a girl who was kind of a hippie writer who said, "You know, you're really funny, but don't you think you should have some meaning in your stuff too?" So that ruined my commentaries for about a year. I started getting a little more message-oriented.

It was funny: she was right on one level, in that I was getting way more attention, way more letters from people as I would strike a chord or discord with people. I was getting enough hate mail to realize I was making some impression. But that was my philosophy for a while: make sure you throw in the meaning. It's fun to be frivolous, but make sure you throw in the meaning. She had my mind racked for that year. That my obligation as a person that was communicating to so many people, that I wasn't just a clown, but perhaps the court jester that was pointing out certain things in ways that would cause reform. That was like a virus.

Finally I was able to get rid a little bit of that, though the scars still remain. Right around that same time, there was this very lovely woman working for NPR, lower on the totem pole. What she was doing in her very industrious way was going around the websites of all the NPR affiliates, looking for voices that she thought she could present to her bosses at NPR as discoveries of hers, to make regular commentators on the national broadcasts. She contacted me and said she liked a few pieces, because they are listed on the web. She said, "I think you'd have a good shot at being on *All Things Considered*." She didn't really explain to me her low status at NPR, so it became a little bit of an adventure, and then the burden became mine to keep trying.

Then 9/11 happened in the middle of all this stuff, and eventually perseverance paid off. I got a producer who had the authority to pieces on the air, who really liked my stuff. That's the way that worked. They had a more stringent time requirement than the local station because they pay fifty dollars to one hundred dollars a minute. So you can't ramble—they don't have the budget for ramble. They also don't have the time for ramble. *All Things Considered* is an extremely tight ship.

The other requirement is that it have a more universal appeal, though they like the local angle that has universal appeal: "Yes, you are coming from Las Vegas and talking about your pear trees blooming, but that could be anyone who is triggered by a blossom on a tree to react the way that you did." They were really nice and that led to a couple NPR writing things. I did a piece for *Wait, Wait Don't Tell Me*, and I did a piece for *Living on Earth*. They pay really well, and people tend to give you a little more attention when you have "NPR commentator" on your bio. I heard from old high school chums who were living in Maine. But then I started to get more involved in the law stuff, and this has always been the struggle: when one heats up, the other takes a little bit of a hit.

PI: Let's close with a bit of Figler's "70s Music Is Stupid."*

"Time in a Bottle" by Jim Croce

First of all, you can't. Time is a concept. But you knew that, you're just getting all literary. Cool. No problem. Still, the first thing you'd do is "save every day till eternity passes away"? Okay, since by "saving time in a bottle" you mean suspending time for everyone except you and the object of your affections, there would be no eternity—time would just stand still in your fucking bottle. It would be like that episode of *The Twilight Zone* with the librarian who breaks his glasses. Creepy silence in a world

* You can read the whole piece at www.yankeepotroast.org.

without time. (Have fun making out.) Also, you never mention if you'd ever let the time out of the bottle and what the repercussions of suddenly unleashing bottled-up time would be. You just want to take all time from everyone else in the universe for some selfish little dream and completely ignore the consequences. If you indeed had the technology to save time in a bottle, don't you think you should use it more wisely—like, say, stopping a plane from crashing right before it hits the ground. (What? Too soon?) And by the way, how big would the time-saving bottle have to be? And why a bottle? Why not a Mason jar or a glass bong?

Abraham Smith: Living the MFA Life: Shouting at Raccoons

Smith was born in Madison, Wisconsin, and has lived in Texas, Scotland, and Spain. He was a featured performance artist at the 2000 South by Southwest Music and Film Festival, at the 2000 National Poetry Slam, and at the 2002 Taos Poetry Circus. His poems have appeared in *CrossConnect*, *Poetry Motel*, and *New Orleans Review*. He received an MFA from the University of Alabama.

Poetry Investigator: Tell us about the fellowship program at Alabama.

I am working in the University of Alabama, which is located in Tuscaloosa, Alabama. It is just like any other MFA program. You submit your poems, typically a ten to twenty page manuscript, and hope that they accept you. I was accepted into this program.

It is unusual from other programs in one way: you can stay for up to four years. Most programs are for two years. To be there up to four years is nice; it gives you more time to write.

The main reason to be in an MFA program is to get a book together and make a few contacts so you can get a few poems published hither, thither, and yon. To get a book out through one of these big university publishers, it helps to be in an MFA program. My fellowship means that I am given a stipend each month, my tuition is waived, and I am asked to teach two classes, basic English composition and literature classes.

PI: How much time do you get to spend writing?

Nearly all my time I get to spend writing. It is low-stress teaching. In fact, often we will team-teach the courses so there will be a second teacher in the room. In terms of my duties, they are very slim. I have to take courses as well, but they are mostly geared to the writing we are doing. Or they might be a survey course where you read a variety of contemporary poets. This last semester I read a lot of Wordsworth and Coleridge. It is really geared to you doing writing.

PI: Do you have a particular teacher you study with throughout the four years?

You kind of change off with different members of the faculty. As you near the completion of your book, you pick a thesis committee. You work with all the poets equally and then in the end you choose a smaller thesis committee. So I work with all the poets on the staff. If I am struggling with a poem or if I really like a poem and want their feedback, I can walk in at any moment and seek their feedback.

PI: How are the teachers that are in the program?

Robin Behn, she is a very good poet, has a lot of books out. She also teaches at Vermont College.

PI: Didn't she do the book, *The Practice of Poetry*?

Yes, she did indeed. We have a new hire, Joel Brouwer, who is also an excellent poet. Amongst the university poets, and there seems to be millions of them, it is hard to know them all. We are hiring another poet in the fall, so that will mean we have three poets and three fiction writers as well. It is very fluid. For example, last semester I took a nonfiction writing class. The degree is very fluid in that way; we can dip into other areas of writing we are interested in. Many of the poets are also working on screenplays. Every kind of writing you can imagine, you are encouraged to explore.

PI: Give me an example of advice or a tip with your writing that has helped you.

It is a funny thing because while you are in these classes and workshops if you regard yourself as a strong artist you think, "These guys don't know what they are talking about. This poem is great, screw them." So you don't hear, in a certain sense, their feedback or advice. Maybe six months later in a quiet room you think, "They were right about that."

There are all kinds of things that come up like that. You think, "I know that metaphor makes no sense. I know the whole poem is going 'you, you, you' and then it goes 'I,' but I want 'I' there, I don't care if it makes no sense." Six months later it comes back to you. The best thing I heard lately is, we bring in a lot of visiting writers, and we brought in this guy named—maybe I shouldn't say his name, he is not a very pleasant man.

PI: He's not?

He just annihilates all students in the programs he visits. One of the great stories about him is there was a student at Syracuse, was weeping. He was just grilling her, saying this poem is a bad poem, and he said, "That's all right honey, I cry when I write bad poems too."

He said to me he hated my poems. A few of the poets in the class who I regard as boring, he loved their poems, but he hated mine. He said, "Your poems are the poems of a mentally sick person." He said to me, "You should be reading the poems of people who you write like. There are poets who write like you, and I'm going to figure out who they are."

My style on the page is fairly uncommon: it is all lower case and there is no punctuation. It is rare—I think you see it more in slam poems, but you don't ever see it in academic writing. So he found all these Polish poets from the late sixties and early seventies, and it looks as though I was living in Poland in the late sixties. They are writing on the same themes, using the same style in lower case with no punctuation. That was very helpful, to find poets that were my blood, my path, my tribe, my little pack.

PI: Do you remember any of the poets? Wislawa Szymborska?*

No, there is this anthology of Polish poets from the early seventies. Zbigniew Herbert is one. I think I found a sort of echo of what I am doing in his poetry.

PI: Was it clarifying for you to see other poets writing in that style?

Yes, it is good especially as a younger poet. I think that is one problem a lot of young poets have: they don't read a great deal, so they get this idea that they are doing something unique, and the more you read . . . I think it is a great comfort to find your community. As good as you might think you are becoming, there is a larger community and to find them . . . . At first you say, "Oh, I am not unique and the wonderful shining star I thought I was." Then it is good to know that there is a whole big house of poets speaking your language.

* She won the Noble Prize of literature in 1996.

PI: You recently got an award from the university and you now get free housing along with your stipend.

Yes, this is another reason to come to Alabama. First, they are well regarded and their stock continues to rise. The Yale Younger Poet winner last year was from Alabama. They have this free-rent cabin that most people don't want to stay in because it is a little bit from the university. It's not bad though, maybe a seven minute drive.

PI: People want to be on campus?

Yes, they want to be on campus, and they also have a lot of stuff, all these poets have a lot of stuff. They need at least a two-bedroom place. Another thing about Alabama is the rent is very cheap. I was living in a massive duplex for three hundred and forty dollars a month. But what is even better is this free-rent cabin. Nobody really applies for it; there are just a few names that go into a hat and they draw your name out, and you stay in the cabin until you leave the program. I will stay there for two more years, in this little cabin in the woods and shout to the raccoons and shout to the owls.

PI: The program is focused on making you a better writer, but do they give you career advice? Do they talk about ways for you to make your living as a poet once you leave the program?

Yes, that certainly comes up. As you near the completion of your book, you spend a lot of time working one-on-one with the faculty, whittling the poems into shape. During those conferences, from what I have been able to glean from other people in the program, they talk about where you might latch onto a teaching job. It is a slim road to hoe. There is not that much going on in academia and to get one of these upscale university gigs is pretty hard. You have to have a couple of books and schmooze, but if you write good poems and get some books published, there is a place for you in the world.

Those one-on-one readings of your poems as you finish your degree with the faculty are giving you ideas of where you might go. The thing is in academy, just like in the rest of the world, it is who you know, so if you have faculty who are connected, they can dial someone up or write you a letter, and that can help you to find a position somewhere.

PI: Szymborska has a great line in a poem called "How to Write a Resume." She says, "Who knows you matters more than whom you know."

Indeed.

Taylor Mali: Don't Move Unless you Know Why You're Moving

For the better part of ten years, Taylor Mali taught during the day, wrote poetry at night, and competed in poetry slams on the weekends. This formula produced two spoken word CDs, several books, and four National Slam Poetry Championships, not to mention one professional performance poet. His voiceover work includes Burger King and the audio version of *Shipwreck at the Bottom of the World: The Extraordinary True Story of Shackleton and the Endurance School*. *Library Journal* said, "Taylor Mali's narration of the book . . . is riveting, and his shifts from one accent to the next are effective." Mali's newest book of poetry is *What Learning Leaves*. He studied acting with members of the Royal Shakespeare Company at Oxford University. Mali received a 2001 Artist Fellowship from the New York Foundation for the Arts to develop a one-man show based on his experiences as a poet and teacher. One of the original poets to appear on the HBO series *Russell Simmons Presents Def Poetry*, Mali was also the villain of Paul Devlin's 1997 documentary *SlamNation*. For the last five years, NASA has invited Mali to speak at their conference for the nation's top educators. His perks include a space suit and experiencing weightlessness. Mali was a long-time teacher in New York schools. He is now a full-time poet.

Poetry Investigator: How did you develop your performance skills? Did you study?

I did go to drama school. Ultimately I decided I did not want to be an actor. Certainly a lot of those skills in terms of diction and movement are applicable to being a spoken word poet. Then I really honed my craft at the slam. There's nothing like getting booed and heckled to help hone your craft. I practice a lot in front of a mirror. You run through your poems while you're walking down the street. You do yoga. Fifty push-ups every day. There is no reason not to do push-ups.

PI: Where did you study acting?

Oxford. It was a program to get American actors over there, closer to the birthplace of Shakespeare, to study with members of the Royal Shakespeare Company, to try to give them a better feel for Shakespeare.

PI: Is there anything out of those studies as far as techniques that they taught you that you still bring to a poem today?

Yes, don't move unless you know why you're moving.

PI: That's a great tip, because a lot of times in slams you will see poets kind of rove around the stage.

And that is nervousness, isn't it? Everybody knows it is nervousness.

PI: Give us an example from one of your poems.

Here is a slightly different example. There is a line in "Playing Scrabble with Eddie" about a dyslexic kid playing scrabble. I am talking about how great he is at finding words, using combinations of letters on his rack. But when it comes time to spelling the words he can't always get all the letters in the right order. Although I don't spell it out that clearly. The line says, "Ask him to spell these ten words and he may dare to read dear when the word reads dread." And all of those words, except for dread, are anagrams of *r*, *e*, *a*, and *d*. They are all rearranged. Which is a neat line because that's what is going on in his head. The audience wasn't getting it. So I thought, "What can I do, performance-wise, that will help the audience understand this line?"

I developed something I do with my hands, where I show my palm, flip it and show the back. I am constantly flipping my hand in a kind of performance semaphore, inviting the audience to do with my words what they see me doing with my hand, see me flipping my hand. Every since I have started to do that, I can hear that wonderful sound you sometimes hear in the audience, people going, "Ahhhhh." It was a physical gesture that made it possible for people to understand what I was saying.

PI: Talk about being a full-time poet. How many years have you been doing it?

I think it gets harder and harder to chuck everything, try to make it as a professional poet the older you get. There is a poet that said, "With time things take on weight." You get more to lose. I am living my dream; you cannot put a price tag on that.

What do I have to do today? Got to get to a yoga class. Got to do my fifty push-ups. My only gig today is reading at this old folks' home, which I do once a month. I bring two different poets with me every month. The audience has been slowly growing. It's about fifteen ladies in their nineties, and they love it. So I bring two poets from the New York scene, or maybe someone from out of town who is here to feature at Urbana or Bar 13. Their only payment is I take them out to lunch beforehand.

If I were teaching, I'd be in school now instead of wandering around wearing my toga and drinking coffee. I mark my years as a professional poet by the academic calendar, so with school winding down in a couple of weeks, I feel like this is the end of a second year off. Two years is going to turn into three. I think this fall is going to be my busiest couple of months ever.

PI: You're working though the Global Talent agency. How many gigs do you have this fall? How much are you getting per gig?

About two thousand. I think October has about fifteen gigs and November about the same.

PI: Wow, so you'll make almost sixty thousand in two months. Does that cover your expenses, too? Or do you get expenses above the two thousand?

The school covers the expenses. Occasionally there might be something like a taxi to the airport that I cover and then I just get a receipt, take a deduction on my taxes. There is a lot of record-keeping involved.

PI: So you have a big shoebox?

Shoebox I have found is a bad idea. Because then tax time comes and you have a shitload of work at tax time.

PI: How do you do it?

I use Quicken to balance my checkbook. So any time there is a poetry-related expense, it has a category. You also have to log in any money coming in. There are two types of ways money can come in: either it's honoraria or it's product sales, and it's good to be able to split those two up. So I get a check from PSI, Poet CD.com, or Amazon, or I come home from a gig and a bunch of people have written me personal checks, I deposit that stuff, make sure it gets logged in as product sales. When I get a check from Global Talent—"This is payment for three gigs, Alaska, University of Wisconsin, and the gig you did in Delaware"—those get logged in as honorarium. Obviously receipts for taxis and stuff get logged in as expenses. I spend a lot of money eating on the road.

PI: You do this monthly? Or each time you get back from the road?

I need to do it monthly as I balance my checkbook. So it all works out. Including the cash receipts. That makes the end of the year easy: I print out a report. I can see exactly how much I made as a poet and how much I spent.

But the difficult part, the more important part, is what to do with the receipts so they link up with the report you create on Quicken, so they don't pile up in a shoebox. I have a binder with blank pieces of paper in it. As I log in the receipts, I tape the receipts into the binder. That is where any kind of explanation goes. The receipts that have to do with one trip are all going to be together. That's where I tape them in and say, "This was the trip out to Los Angeles." I'll even put in the plane ticket, even if I didn't pay for it.

Then the last thing is I have a self-inking stamp that provides each receipt with a number. I put a number on the receipt, and when I log in the computer, I put that same number. That's what I call a ledger number. So when I'm looking at the itemized report at the end of the year, or God forbid the IRS is, they can say, "Wait a second, wait a second, what is this fifteen hundred dollars you're deducting, the CD duplication place, ledger number 272?" I go to the book and actually that's a check that I wrote to the CD duplication place that makes my CDs. That is the best tip that I can pass on. I've tried to get Mums the Schemer to adopt my system, but I'm afraid he's addicted to his shoebox.

This is the second year I have been doing the binder system. Then if he ever loses it you say, "You bad, bad man. Okay, here is another copy." Taping the stuff into the binder is only an extra half-hour a month.

* Mums played the role of "Poet" on the HBO series "OZ."

PI: Talk a little about going from being a teacher to working with Global Talent.

Right. During my six years as an independent schoolteacher, less so during my three years of graduate school, I would periodically get invitations to go read at various schools. I would have to make this work into my schedule. After I won the Poetry Slam national competition for the second time, those invitations started coming more frequently.

I would say the gig that made me finally say that maybe I should try doing this for a living was the University of North Dakota at Fargo. Rob Thibault, who was on the Fargo team who took on the Nuyorican Slam Team on the CNN special in 1998, he said, "We'd love to get you out here, what's it gonna take?" I said, "Hold on a second. Let me talk to my headmaster." The headmaster said, "You have already taken two days off this year for poetry-related things. That's too much," and I kind of agreed with him. So what do I do? I thought, "I am going to try to price myself out of their league."

I went back to Thibault, I said, "All right, it's going to have to be . . . " and I thought of the biggest number I could possibly think of. It was fifteen hundred dollars. He said, "Done, that's easy." "And the airfare." "Of course," he said. "That's expected." "And a hotel." "Of course." Then I said, "I still can't do it." I realized, how often am I going to be able to turn down fifteen hundred-dollar gigs? If these are coming in, maybe I should see if I could do this for a living.

That was about the same time that Global Talent said, "We'd love to work with you." Global Talent submitted my stuff to the National Association of College Activities (NACA) showcase. I got into two of them that first year. That's how Global Talent works: they come from the speaking circuit, they book people on college speaking tours. They were smart enough to say, "This spoken word thing is smart. Let's become the agency that deals with spoken word." They just plugged their spoken word talent into the college speaking circuit. Now there are a couple of people who are making a living at it.

PI: You've taken your experience teaching and turned it into a one-man show. Talk about that, how you got hooked up with NBC and how far it went and what your experience was.

I always thought that the primary reason I was taking a year off of teaching was to write a one-man show about teaching and poetry. Since even before I took the year off, so much of my work was about being a teacher and a poet. I went around telling people I thought I had about 90 percent of the show already written. Which turned out to be ridiculous. There is a lot more to doing a one-man show that incorporates poetry than just stringing your poems together with just an interstitial word here and there.

The show took longer to write. In the meantime I applied for a New York Foundation for the Arts grant. That was going to cover October to April. The grant said, if you give me this grant, I will write this show. You submit that and then you're not going to hear for six months. What, are you not going to work on the show?

So you bang away on the show, you figure if you get the grant that will be a nice confirmation, a validation of what you've been doing. Two days before I go to do the show for the first time, I find out I got the grant. Just enough time to go to Kinkos and say, "This performance made possible in part by a grant from the New York State Foundation for the Arts." So they got all the credit for the hard work I did without their money.

That was when *Def Poetry Jam* came to me and said, "We are thinking about trying to sell this show to HBO. A variety show of poets—we got some important people coming into the house at these gigs in New York." There were two or three shows in New York where the folks from *Def Poetry Jam* were trying to sell the show to HBO.

At one of them Stew Smiley was there. He's the executive producer of *Everybody Loves Raymond*. He is also the founder and director of US Comedy Arts Club. He said, "Hey, the Comedy Arts Club is sponsored by HBO. Why don't you bring your *Def Poetry Jam* show out to Aspen? We'll pay you this, this, and this and do it out there for my festival." They said, "We like that." That was the show that made HBO sit up and pay attention. That was the year *Def Poetry Jam* went to Aspen, and there was a bunch of people watching.

Somebody who saw the show in Aspen runs a venue here in New York called PS NBC. It's a small wing of NBC. His job is to find talent, book them into his theater. The performers can do whatever they want for an hour. They get paid nothing, but they can invite anyone, the show gets taped, and the tape gets sent out to L.A. It's the new way that a bunch of the networks in L.A. are doing casting and finding writers: they get sent these tapes of people doing their one-man shows. When he invited me to come and do whatever I wanted, I said, "I have this one-man show, it's almost done. I think it is ready for a performance. I'll do that there."

That was how *Teacher, Teacher* made it to the stage the first time. Even though I had taken a year off to write the show—here it was April—I had just barely completed my first draft. If it hadn't've been for that, I don't know how long it would have taken to finish the first draft.

That got sent out to L.A.; I got some fans at NBC. Stew Smiley said, "Do you think you could write a TV show about being a teacher?" I said, "I've never written a TV show. I would like to work with somebody." He said, "Well fine. Let's work on this together." We developed a holding deal that said I would not accept any parts on any other major networks. That was fine because that was not what I was going to do anyway. They would pay me not to do anything with anybody else.

Then I went out to L.A. and met with writers. We banged out a draft about the story of a guy who fancies himself a poet and ends up teaching, learns to love teaching, and his attitude toward poetry goes from academic to spoken word. It was a heartwarming story. In retrospect, it wasn't all that it could have been. We made it pretty far. They choose about thirty scripts every year, and we were one of the thirty. From the thirty scripts they ask about ten of them to make pilots, from the ten they choose anywhere from two to eight. If it's a bad year for television and they are canceling a lot of their shows, they might take all eight. If it's a good year for television, they might only take on two.

We made it to the thirty and they said, "No thanks, no reason for you to go ahead and make a pilot." There are things I'll do differently. I still have some die-hard fans high up at NBC. They want me to do something for them. We may start back at square one. Now I have to look at my one-man show, which went to the Aspen Comedy Festival this year and won the jury prize for best one-man show.

PI: Who inspires you in regard to one-man shows?

Eric Bogosian, Spalding Gray are my heroes. I saw Al Letson's one-man show and that inspired me, made me think I could do this. I saw Staceyann Chin's one-woman show and that made me think I can do this.

PI: Any last advice?

I have one other tip. So many of the gigs, not the ones Global Talent books, the ones I book myself, are done through email. What I did was to create a little contract. Not to be signed. I call them confirmation contracts.

If you were to invite me to a gig, I would then email you back and say, "Okay. What are the terms? What would you pay me?" You email me back saying, "I would want you to read for this long, and here's what I would pay me." I would write you back saying, "Yes, I would like to do it. We are not confirmed yet until you send me one more email spelling out everything I need to know about that show in one email. That is: where's the gig, what are the directions to the gig, what's the phone number at the gig, what's every conceivable cell phone number I could need on the day of the gig. In case I get a flat tire on the way to the gig and I'm just going to be a little bit late. Spell out how much you're going to pay me. What's the format of the evening?" Someone even suggested I want to be able to dictate that I don't want to get there at seven o'clock and have you spend four hours telling everyone, "At the end of the show we have Taylor Mali," when everybody has gone home.

It's a way of getting you and the promoter on the same page. When I hear poets saying, "I thought I was getting one hundred and fifty dollars for this gig, I thought that there was going to be a break after my feature set to sell my product," I think, "This all could have been taken care of, you weren't on the same page, there was a misunderstanding, don't you have a piece of paper that you can show the person?"

PI: Here is Taylor Mali's simple confirmation contract for your amusement and profit:

Dear Poetry Promoter:

First of all, I thank you for your persistence in trying to book me. Send me an email with everything I need to know. And everything I already do know just so I'll have everything in one place:

The venue name and address.
What time you want me there.
How long you want me to read for.
How much you're paying me.
Whether you'll have a merch table with a bank.
And every conceivable phone number I might need on the day of the gig.

If it all looks good, then I will then send you an email back. THEN we will be confirmed.

Now for something I've never requested before. Could you arrange the evening so that there is a break right after I read? That's the best time to push merch, as I'm sure you know. And lastly, borrowing a page from Galway Kinnell, I'll have about three hours to spare that night, so tell me when you want me to show up, keeping in mind I'll have to leave three hours later. Do I sound like a prima donna? Too many gigs where I stuck around for five hours and read at a time when I couldn't sell merch, I guess.

Hope this is cool.

Taylor Mali

Al Letson: Poeticals, Hip-Hop Theater, and Bringing Slam to the Stage

Poet, actor, and playwright Al Letson has become nationally recognized for his soul-stirring, multidisciplinary work. In 2005 Letson was awarded the Individual Artist Fellowship by the State of Florida in conjunction with the NEA. *Griot: He who Speaks the Sweet Word*, a ninety-minute ensemble piece commissioned by the Baltimore Theatre Project, enjoyed its premiere in 2004. Letson's teen drama *Chalk*, which was commissioned by the Baltimore School of the Arts, also premiered in 2004. He has appeared on *Russell Simmon's Def Poetry* on HBO. In 2004, Al received the opportunity to perform a promotional spot for CBS that aired before the NCAA Final Four tip off, and was seen by over 45 million viewers. His poem "Stoplights" was adapted into a critically acclaimed short film that was an official selection of the 2001 Urban World Film Festival.

Poetry Investigator: Please describe your play *Chalk*.

Chalk is a play that is the first in what I hope will catch on as a new genre of theater. I call the genre a "poetical." A poetical works just like a musical but instead of the characters breaking out into song, they perform poetry. The type of poetry they perform is more like slam poetry than the literary form. The poetry is used to push the story forward. Sometimes with simple musical accompaniment, and then other times, it's just the words.

PI: What were you hoping to accomplish by writing the play?

I wanted to bridge the gap between spoken word and theater. I started seriously doing theater five years ago with a one-man show I wrote. That show, *Essential Personnel*, had a lot of poetry, and I was always surprised at how many traditional theater lovers had never seen "slam-like" poetry. So I thought the poetical would energize current theater lovers and bring new people into the theater that normally would not go. Additionally, *Chalk* is about relational aggression, which simply is "girl aggression." Bullying is a huge problem for young people. I wanted to write something that spoke to this generation currently going through the transition of child to young adult and at the same time remind the older generations of their past.

PI: Has *Chalk* been effective in working with young people?

Extremely. Young people dig *Chalk* primarily because it talks about their lives in a realistic way. But secondly, the newness of the genre attracts them. They've never seen anything like it, and they latch onto it.

PI: How do you see *Chalk* fitting into the hip-hop theater movement?

I think it is totally a part of the hip-hop theater movement. I believe hip-hop theater has a lot to do with where the playwright is coming from. I come from the generation that created hip-hop. I was raised with it; it informs my view of the world and the way I create art. So hip-hop is an integral part of how I think and how I approach writing. So the rhythms and cadences of the poems are definitely hip-hop inspired.

PI: What was your process in going from writing poems to writing hip-hop plays?

Writing poems is a simple concept. I get the concept, then write. Maybe a little research if necessary. With theater, there is a simple concept at the heart of it all, but subplots and characters complicate it. I spend a large amount of time researching, creating an outline, and then finally start writing. Writing the poems for a poetical is more akin to songwriting for a musical because each piece has a goal it needs to accomplish to help it move the story forward.

PI: Talk about your other projects in bringing poetry to theater.

With my play *Griot: He Who Speaks the Sweet Word*, is a, what I call a choreopoematic play. The choreo-poem (a theatrical event that mixes poetry and movement) was created by Ntozake Shange. With *Griot*, we (I wrote the play with additional collaboration from Larry Knight and David Pugh) expanded on the idea and added dramatic scenes. So the piece flows in and out of poetry.

PI: What is next for you?

I've been commissioned again by the Theatre Project in Baltimore to create a new piece entitled *Julius X*. *Julius X* will be a poetical that is a re-envisioning of Shakespeare's *Julius Caesar*. Set in the 60s in the civil rights movement, the play mixes Julius Caesar's and Malcolm X's assassination to tell a new story about a deposed leader and those who conspired against him.

Mike Henry: Slam Planet: War of the Words

Mike Henry is the co-director of the National Poetry Slam, 2006 and 2007. He has served as Austin's Slammaster since 1998 and as executive director of Austin Poetry Slam. Henry is a past president of Poetry Slam, Inc. In 2004, he became co-director for *Slam Planet: War of the Words*, a feature-length documentary film about slam, focused on the 2004 National Poetry Slam, currently in postproduction. His work has been published in *Poetry Slam: the Art of Competitive Poetry, Worcester Review, Borderlands: Texas Poetry Review, The Austin Chronicle, The Austin American-Statesman*, and in a chapbook, *It's Times Like These*. He served as curator for the SXSW spoken word showcases for six years. His one-man show, *Bar Fight*, was named "Best of Festival" at the 2003 FronteraFest at Austin's Hyde Park Theater, and the 1999 *Austin Chronicle* named Henry's performance "Best Local Show" in its annual music critic's poll, marking the first time in the publication's twenty-plus year history that a spoken word performance had been recognized in the poll. Henry also toured the US and Europe for two years as a member of Austin's infamous Asylum Street Spankers, 1999-2001. He is happily married to a slam poet named Sonya Feher who is much smarter and more talented than he is.

Poetry Investigator: What is your new film called?

It's a feature-length documentary called *Slam Planet: War of the Words*.

PI: How long have you been working on it?

About two years, including the preproduction and fundraising phases.

PI: What do you hope to accomplish with the film?

My hope is that *Slam Planet* will introduce many thousands of people to poetry slam who have never seen it before. I hope to tell an honest, genuine story that presents the poets as they truly are and links their compelling back stories to the competition and the poetry that they rock on stage.

PI: How does the film work with your website SlamChannel?

We see *Slam Planet* and www.slamchannel.com as two parts of a wheel. One of the things that the film will do is serve as a tremendous marketing campaign for the website. The website, in turn, will provide filmgoers with a more interactive experience and give them much deeper access to the characters in the film and to the slam movement that they represent. SlamChannel also gives the audience member the opportunity to go home after the movie and download poems by the poets that they most loved in the film. It's all part of a broader business model. We look at ourselves as digital content providers, and I believe that poetry slam, as an explosive, entertaining, three-minute form, is perfect content for the new digital media marketplace and for modern media users who have grown up on MTV and have the ability to take in a lot of information quickly.

PI: You had an interesting experience in putting together the funding for the film. Could you talk about that?

Fundraising for a project is always an interesting experience. We were able to fund our film via private investors, mostly from our local community. It got even more interesting when the building that housed our edit suite burned down. We had to struggle back through a three-month delay. It's a good thing we were making a movie about poetry. The power of the work that I knew was contained in our footage was what kept me going from day to day. If we would have been making a movie about, like, stockbrokers, I think I would have just fled the country.

PI: How did you come to get the ad agency GSD&M* as a partner on the film?

Our executive producer, Tim McClure, is one of the founders of GSD&M, which is one of the top ad agencies in America. Over the past few years, Tim had also founded Mythos Studios, a new film studio dedicated to making affordable, commercially viable movies here in Austin. He became interested in our project pretty much in the same way that anyone becomes a fan of poetry slam: he came to a show.

* This is the ad agency that, among other projects, created the "Don't Mess with Texas" anti-litter campaign.

PI: What are your goals with SlamChannel?

Part of the reason I wanted to create SlamChannel was because, as a poet, I was tired of there not being a badass, media-rich, powerful web presence for Slam. The site has been a bit on the back burner while we worked on the movie, but my goal for the site is to evolve into the top destination for slam on the internet.

PI: What do you look for when selecting a poem to be animated?

Good question. I guess I just look for pieces that I think would appeal to our market, and I look for performers who are pretty much "animated" already. Slammers whose performance vocabulary lends itself to the flash animation medium, as far as how they move, their facial expressions, etc.

PI: Talk about the profiles you use to showcase poets on the website. How did you come up with the questions? [See example below]

I wrote a set of questions that I personally wanted to know the answers to and tried to give the poets a lot of room to express themselves in whatever way they wanted. They can write about themselves better than I can. That's what slammers do, in general. Like Uncle Walt said, "Sing of yourself." We try to do that through a website.

PI: Has working on the film helped you as a poet? As a performer?

For me, the creative process is always the same and is related and interwoven through all sorts of genres. Writing a poem is directing a movie is painting a picture is crafting an innovative new business plan is doing a dance. I think it's all about seeing the world, pulling together the pieces that are related but perhaps not obviously so, and presenting it in the best way possible. Getting paid to do it is a dream come true.

PI: What do you look for in selecting poems for the film?

It's one of the most difficult parts of making the movie. Because there are so many incredible poems to choose from. We look for the moments that are best captured in terms of narrative and image, so there's that, but most of all we have to feature the poems that best fit the particular storyline we're telling. What serves the movie as a whole and is also a mind-blowing window into a character? Making this movie is like scripting a two-hour group piece.

PI: What tips can you give poets who would like to have their poems in films, on television, or made into animation?

I'd say the same thing I'd say to a poet who wants to do well at a slam. Write without ceasing, every day, and learn to edit. Know the power of performance and own the fact that it's what we do. It's a tool that you must master, just like any poetic device from alliteration to slant rhyme to metaphor. Rock the mic, and rock it like you rock it, not like anyone else you've seen.

PI: Anything else you want to say about the film or the website?

I guess the biggest myth that I hope to dispel is the idea that the live experience of slam doesn't translate to video or electronic media. I think that's ridiculous.

PI: Let's end the interview with an example of a slamchannel.com profile featuring one of Austin's most loved poets:

NAME: Matthew John Conley

REPRESENTING: Austin frickin' Texas baby! A little spot rightfully named Ego's

HOMETOWN: Woodbury New Jersey (suburb of Philth-a-delphia)

BIO: Born & raised in southern New Jersey, educated in Albuquerque New Mexico, cleansed by fire in Minneapolis & delivered to Austin Texas. Toured with Lollapalooza, created Drive-By Poetry, South by Southwest Slam Champion 2000, Austin City Champion 2002, member of eight Slam teams from three cities including Coach of the Team Austin 2003 which recently claimed Third in the Nation at the National Championships in Chicago Illinois. Seven chapbooks, one CD, published in numerous anthologies such as *Revival* (Manic D), *Poetry Slam* (Manic D) & *Freedom to Speak* (the Wordsmith Press), co-founder of Broken Word touring over the past year from Rutgers (Camden, NJ) to the University of Alaska (Juneau, AK).

TEAMS AT NATIONAL POETRY SLAM: Albuquerque 1995-98, Minneapolis 1999 & 2000, Austin 2002, 2003 & beyond . . .

SELECTED PUBLICATIONS/DISCOGRAPHY: Chapbooks: *My Foot Bone's Connected to your Ass Bone, The Gin Talking, Storm Going Past, My Friend Billy* (Kapow! Press). Periodicals: *The Word* (Dallas), *Poetry Motel* (Duluth), CD: *When I Talk to You* (Dental Records).

ANYTHING ELSE YOU'D LIKE TO SAY? I believe that it has not all been said before, & that words are adequate to express how we really feel. Maybe I'm wrong, but don't defeat me before I have stopped trying.

TELL US ABOUT THE FIRST TIME YOU PERFORMED YOUR POETRY. I got published in *Conceptions Southwest*, the art & literary journal for the University of New Mexico. On the phone a "yeah, do ya wanna share your work at the opening slash reading?" "Yeah, what the hay." I'd never done it before (except for a few times at churches unexpectedly) but had been contemplating it. Invited like a vampire, I agreed to attend. I had a mohawk, wore a Cleveland Browns t-shirt (don't hate me 'cause I'm beautiful) and announced to the audience "folks I write short poems, I believe that the silence in between words where they mingle is important" (or some crap like that), "and I'm gonna read one & then let you hear it for a minute or so before I read the next." Then I say, "blah blah blah" for five lines, finish, and stand there. Take a sip of water. Wait. Another sip. And then I'd read the next one. It was terrible.

Last book you read? Just about finished with *A Natural History of the Senses* by Diane Ackerman next is either *The Avengers: A Jewish War Story* by Rich Cohen or *Cartucho/My Mother's Hands* by Nellie Campobello.

Besides performing poetry, what are your other interests? Cooking, Quakerism, huge sports fan of all teams Philadelphia, thrift stores, modern (& matador) art, crossword puzzles, the Weather Channel, moving the sofa, playing Dress Up, old suitcases, Philip Seymour Hoffman, Etel Adnan (the greatest writer you never heard of in your life), Dr. Seuss, Muddy Waters, Francis Bacon (the painter not the philosopher), honey, stickers.

Who is the person you'd most like to have lunch with (living or dead)? My nephew

If you were a super hero/heroine, what would your superpower be? Did you say "If"?

NUTS/BOLTS/RANTS/MANIFESTOS

I like it when you're silent because it's like you're not there.
—Pablo Neruda

Taking a Rock for Poetry

If I feel physically as if the top of my head were taken off, I know that is poetry.

—Emily Dickinson

The rock hit the back of my head. I turned and saw a blur of kids careening away. Not Palestinians with their furious windups challenging tanks, but American kids unable to pass a class, with the stuck-in-summer-school blues again. What was I to these kids? Obviously, I was an authority figure with a bull's-eye saying, "School me." Their weapon of choice went thump; I thought, "White flag. Cock-a-doodle-doo. My, these stars are pretty."

I wanted to be a superhero poet. Yes, I fantasized about helping these underserved, at-risk cherub monsters we call kids. Racing to the rescue with rhythm and rhyme. Cape flapping, leaping tall metaphors with a single bound. The poet who reached these seventh and eighth graders, who had all flunked at least two classes. The poet who put his hand on their gelled heads and raised their reading level, shouting, "Can you feel the power of poetry, child?" "Hey mister, save us. Please use your super powers for the good of all humans. Teach us to spell and how to pronounce 'alliteration' and 'hyperbole,' what they mean, and how they will lead to good jobs with white picket fence pensions and that sweet old American dream. Right all wrongs, Man of P, PoetMan!"

The thump hurt but was too quick to be scary. I flashed back to the day before and the student sitting at his desk, shaking with rage—a little hormonal earthquake. When I asked him why he was fuming, he rumbled, face hot, unable to speak, as if he might explode and shoot around the room like a popped balloon. "Take a walk, go get a drink," I said. He seemed better when he came back to class, no longer shaking uncontrollably. What was scary was that as the class ended, one of the students (the angry kid? I couldn't be sure) said, "You are looking for Columbine." I brushed it off, until the morning when I sprung up in bed, thinking, "Alarm bell. Danger, danger. Columbine. I should tell somebody."

I woke up the whole school with my crowing, and soon I was sitting in a conference room with the principle, the school therapist, and the student. We talked about his rage—a girl had spit water in his face. We talked about dealing with anger. We only had to go back to the previous Friday to find an example of a kid shooting his family to death, in a rage over being abused. The principle said, "Gary, tell us what you heard." "'You are looking for Columbine,'" I said. "I think I heard you say that as you were leaving." "What?" he said. "I never said that. I don't even know what Columbine is. What's Columbine?" The therapist said, "You have never heard of Columbine?" "No," he said. "You have never seen the movie, Bowling for Columbine?" "No." "You don't know about the students who shot other students and then killed themselves?" "No, I would never shoot anybody."

Later it came out that the boy's father had been reported to the state Youth and Family services for beating him and that the father had an extensive gun collection. "GUN NUT DAD BEATS BOY" is what I was thinking of when I saw the rock settling—his blank face, his flat voice denying having heard the buzzword for school violence, how chilling the denial.

Now all I wanted to do was get out of there before they hurt me or I hurt them. It was the last day of summer school, no one had been kicked out, they would not have to repeat a grade. There is some small victory in that, something worth a three-hour headache and being forever known as "Poet Rock-Noggin."

One of the things we love about poets is their tragic deaths. This wasn't Lorca and a fascist firing squad, not Plath's easy bake oven or Hart Crane swan-diving off an ocean liner. This was just a double flunker with a good arm and eye teaching me the lesson of my life: "Don't think for a moment your fancy pants poetry can do us any good. What we want most is for you to feel the sting of how smart we are and to go—now."

I give myself an F. I figured out why those kids acted out, refused to read aloud or write on the board. They are embarrassed by not reading and writing well. Their brilliant strategy: a constant whirl of clowning, fighting, and sullen whining keep the teacher and the other students from knowing how poorly skilled they are. They were furious when I made them read *Green Eggs and Ham*. "That is for little kids," they said. But the Spanish-speaking students loved translating it into Spanish: *Verde Huevos y Jamon*. In the end, I, like all their other teachers, passed them and their problems on; an assembly line of semi-blank minds speeding out of control.

If it had been a bullet, people would have said, "He died for his art." Other people might have said, "Perhaps the kids were right. I never liked studying poetry either." What a great poet's death it would have been: "MAN MURDERED BY POETRY-HATING MOB." Instead, only my pride died, and the headline reads, "POET PUNKED BY ROCK."

Giving Birth to Bards

I never kept sheep,

But it's as if I'd done so.

—Fernando Pessoa

This interview was conducted with Bob Holman's mother, Sally. Among the many hats Bob Holman wears is owner/operator of the Bowery Poetry Club (bowerypoetry.com).

Poetry Investigator: Please tell us what Bob was like as a child.

He was kind of an intense little boy. He did a lot of things that were a little different from his friends. He had a lot of little records, of music and stories. He was crazy about them, and he lugged it around. He wasn't more than two or two-and-a-half. I had a big basket to hold the records, and he lugged that around. He played them on a phonograph that he knew how to work. That kind that you put the needle in, those old-fashioned things. It was for a child. That is when I first began to notice that he was intense about his records. He loved them, and if he had a little friend over and the child wanted to play a record, Robert wouldn't let him touch the machine. He put the record on. When it was over, the other child would take it off, and Robert would say, "No, no, you have to listen to the other side, you have to listen to both sides." He did things like that. He was kind of a different child, very interesting. He was a good little boy.

PI: Do you remember what type of music he liked?

They were called *Little Golden Records*, and they were children's songs. Some of them were stories, and they would have a book for him to follow along as the record played. Those were called *Bozo*, I remember that. Bozo was traveling around, and he went to New York on one of his trips. Robert said to me, "I would like to see the Fliberty." I said, "What's the Fliberty?" He said, "You know, in New York. The

Statue of Fliberty." He picked up on everything, whether he got it right or not. He was very kind to Stuart, his little brother, his baby. If I got mad at Stuart, he got mad at me.

PI: What is their age difference?

Two and a half years. In the meantime their father died, and he became even more protective.

PI: I bet that was hard for you too.

Yes, it was very hard, yes.

PI: Do you remember when Bob started to write poetry?

About third grade. He wrote a little play, and they produced it in his third grade class. His teacher told me she just thought it was wonderful. She said, "I never had a student do that before, and I have been teaching a long time." That was the first thing that I remember that he wrote.

Then he began to write poetry, especially when he got into high school, he became very interested in poetry. It just sort of snowballed. I didn't pay much attention to it at first, because we all thought he would be a lawyer, he expressed himself so well. His grandfather said, "I know he's going to be a lawyer." He could take his part with words, when other children would hit.

PI: Was this in Kentucky?

Yes, that was in Kentucky. Then we moved to Cincinnati. It was 1951, he was just three.

PI: Bob tells a story about writing a poem called, "George Washington Followed Indian Trails," and that when he gave it to his teacher she thought it was too good to have been written by a kid and that he must have copied it from somewhere.

I do sort of remember that. I'm eighty-one and a whole lot of this escapes me. And I have four children, so I get them mixed up sometimes. He was an excellent student from the very beginning. He always loved books, he had such a love of reading, which pleased me because I was that kind of a kid.

PI: You taught school didn't you?

I taught when I was very young, starting at nineteen. It was during World War Two, and they had a teacher shortage. I had two years of college, and they hired me to teach. I taught in a one-room class, with three grades in it. That was way out in the hills of Kentucky.

PI: Were you born in Kentucky?

I was born in the hills of Kentucky. Robert was the most intense of my children.

PI: How old were you when you had him?

Let's see, I was twenty-four.

PI: What was his favorite food?

I don't remember much about that. I know he didn't like tomatoes when he was little, but he learned to eat them. He liked most everything. He was a good eater and he still is.

PI: Do you remember his first date?

I remember a little girl that he liked and I took them in the car—we were living in New Richmond, Ohio, then, out in the country, in a house that was built in 1813, and it was a fabulous place to live, we lived right in the middle of sixteen acres. Her name ... oh gosh, I have forgotten her name ... Evelyn Funk! That was her name. They were in junior high and he wanted to take Evelyn to the movies, so I had to take Stuart with me, I didn't have any place to leave him. Stuart was in the back seat and I was driving and Robert was up front and we were going to pick up Evelyn Funk, to drive into New Richmond to the movies, and Robert said, "I feel just like a boob." You can hear him saying that. We picked up Evelyn and went to the movies and Stuart went to the movies too, and I said, "Don't you sit with them, you sit someplace else." He had a number of girlfriends. He was such a different kind of kid, I was surprised when he liked girls as much as he did, because he always had his head in a book.

PI: What was it like for you raising your family?

It was crazy and wonderful. I thought we were having a good time. When I remarried, that was kind of intense, but we made the best of it and then I had two more children. Robert adored them and they adored him. His brother Lewis lives in Brooklyn, Amy lives in Richmond, and Stuart lives in Cincinnati. Stuart and Robert were pretty close growing up. It was fun to raise Robert because he was a different kind of child.

PI: Tell me about your job as a teacher and if that played into at all in Bob's education as a poet.

Well, as I told you, I taught school way out in the hills of Kentucky. I loved teaching and I loved the children—I still keep up with one of my students, she is sixty-seven. We had nothing to work with—we didn't even have electricity in the school. In the wintertime we had to wait until it got light to be able to read, because we had no lights. We had a big old stove in the middle of the room, and one of the boys, who was fifteen in the third grade [laughs], would light the stove and get the room warm before I got there in the mornings. It was a good year. Later, I taught kindergarten in Ohio for twenty years. That was wonderful job.

PI: Did Bob have any pets?

We had just one dog when the children were little. Her name was Sukey. They loved that little dog. She was a wiener dog, a miniature dachshund. I remember when Robert went away to college and was coming home, she had a little sick spell and I took her to the veterinarian. He said, "She's not got a good heart." I said, "I'll hate to tell Robert. She carries on so, when he comes home." He said, "That won't be good for her. You should put her away somewhere, so she can hear his voice and get used to him being there." She really did carry on when he would come home from school.

PI: What was his schooling like?

He was a good student. He was valedictorian of his high school class, student council president of his high school, was on the greater Cincinnati Student Council and the State of Ohio Student Council.

PI: What advice would you give to other mothers who want to raise poets, if you would give them any advice?

I would give them advice. I would tell them to take it seriously, to encourage it because it is their very soul. The poet's soul is in his writing. I wasn't surprised he choose that profession, because I could see it early on. He was gifted with words.

Alzheimer's Heckler Project

I ask if she remembers

when she thought nuns never died.

I haven't seen a dead one yet,

she replies.

—Thylias Moss

I have been working with Alzheimer's patients since 1997, when I received a small grant from *Poets and Writers* magazine. When I received the call from the woman administering the grant, she told me I had not been their first choice. Now, the facility was about a mile from the flower shop that I owned and had worked at for almost two decades. I had grown up in the town and had graduated from high school there. I belonged to the Kiwanis club. I am not sure why she felt the need to tell me I was not their first choice, but it dawned on me that if I couldn't get a grant in my hometown—being an upstanding member of the business community who gave away ten times more in goods and services to local charities than the amount of the grant—that I may not ever get a grant again.

There was no instruction from *Poets and Writers* on what to do with the Alzheimer's patients—just to use poetry with them in some way. I hit on the idea of using classic poems that they might have learned as children, and this turned out to work very well. They would remember lines and words from the poems, and that would lead to spirited discussions. Here is the story I always tell to explain how I got hooked on working with Alzheimer's patients.

One of the men in the group had his head down and was not able to participate. I recited the first line from the Longfellow poem "The Arrow and the Song": "I shot an arrow into the air." The man's eyes popped open and he said, "It fell to earth, I knew not where." It was a breakthrough, and now, years later, I have worked with thousands of patients in seven different states and this summer started the project in Wellington, New Zealand.

Like many things in life, events do not always go as planned and the Alzheimer's Poetry Project sometimes offers surprises. For the most part, the people are wonderful to work with and much of their sense of humor remains intact even in the late stages of the disease.

One of the women I work with calls me a blowhard and blows me a Bronx cheer or "raspberry." I will be reading a soft love poem, saying, "How do I love thee? Let me count the ways," and she will say, "You blowhard, Brööötttttt," kicking me in the butt as I pass her. Another woman that I have worked with was a poet, who had been published by *The New Yorker* and *Poetry* magazine. She had a great knowledge of poetry, and when I was reciting Blake's "The Tyger," using the opening couplet as a kind of a chant, reciting, "Tyger, Tyger burning bright,/ In the forests of the night," to each of the residents and holding their hands, letting them feel the rhythm of the poem, she would say, "You know, that poem has more than two lines." So I recited the whole poem to her and she said, "Oh, so you do know it."

At one session in Georgia, I was reciting "The Tyger," and when I got to one woman she looked up at me reaching out for her hand and said, "Does the monkey want a peanut?" Now I am a poet in an old folks' home, dancing around, reciting a two hundred year old poem. I do want a peanut. She kept getting louder, saying it over and over until she finally shouted, "Somebody get this goddamn MONKEY a peanut!" The nurses started laughing and even I had to laugh and start calling myself the director of the Alzheimer's Heckler Project.

Here is a sample brochure from the Alzheimer's Poetry Project.

The Alzheimer's Poetry Project is a simple idea: read classic poems to the patients that they might have learned as children.

This activity helps to stimulate memories and provides enjoyment for the patients.
APP can help to reduce stress in both caregivers and patients.
Communities benefit from the APP by providing an enjoyable activity to an under-served segment of their population.

For more information contact:
Gary Mex Glazner
Director, APP
12 Highview Lane
Santa Fe, NM 87508
505-438-6607
poetmex@aol.com

Photo credit: Reid Yalom

The Alzheimer's Poetry Project has been covered by NBC's "Today" show. NPR's "Weekend Edition," the Voice of America and New Zealand National Radio.

A tax deductible donation will help to continue the poetry sessions at local assisted living centers. Please consider helping to fund this worthwhile project.
Please make check out to:
New Mexico Literary Arts
C/O:
Gary Mex Glazner
Director, APP
12 Highview Lane
Santa Fe, NM 87508

Photo credit: Daniel Barsotti

Caregivers at Sierra Vista
Assisted Living Center

This project is made possible in part by New Mexico Arts, a division of the Department of Cultural Affairs, and the National Endowment for the Arts. APP is partially funded by the City of Santa Fe Arts Commission, New Mexico Arts, McCune Foundation, Beim Foundation, Puffin Foundation and Bread for the Journey.

Alzheimer's Poetry Project

I shot an arrow into the air.
It fell to earth
I knew not where.
-Longfellow

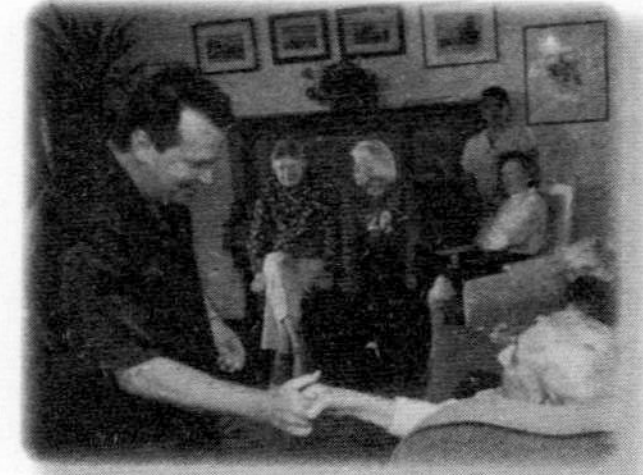

Photo credit: Daniel Barsotti

As seen on NBC's "Today" show.

Partially funded by the National Endowment for the Arts.

Sponsored by
New Mexico Literary Arts
A non-profit 501(3)(c)

APP OFFERS:

- Staff Training on using poetry with Alzheimer patients.
- Workshops for family members.
- Finding poets in your area to work with facility.

Photo credit: Daniel Barsotti

APP is happy to announce Bread for the Journey will fund a Spanish language edition of our Anthology entitled, ***Memorias Que Chispean: Poemas, Dichos, y Cuentos Populares,***

ALZHEIMER'S POETRY PROJECT

Background and Experience

In 1997, Gary Mex Glazner received a grant from "Poets and Writers," magazine to fund an eight-week residency at a senior center in Northern California to work with Alzheimer's patients using poetry.

I believe the follow example shows the effectiveness of the program. I was reading Longfellow's poem "The Arrow and the Song." As I spoke the first line,

"I shot an arrow into the air,"

a man who had spent most of the class with his head down seeming to be asleep, looked up and responded,

"It fell to earth,
I knew not where."

The smile on his face and that moment when he was able to reach back into some part of his psyche, not damaged by the disease, was a wonderful breakthrough; one of the many we experienced during the residency.

APP is not the type of poetry reading that takes place from a podium. The APP is about making contact with people who may have very little physical contact in their lives. We recite the poems directly to the folks, even holding their hands.

Photo credit: Daniel Barsotti

The people we serve are often in late stages of Alzheimer's and can have a hard time holding a conversation, or in some cases even speaking; when you see and hear them respond to the poems by saying words and lines along with the poet, it can be quite moving. Often a mother in late stage Alzheimer's will not recognize family members. For a daughter to read poems to her mother and have the mother respond emotionally can offer the daughter a connection she needs and craves.

For more on the Alzhiemer's Poetry Project, check out Alzpoety.com. Let me close with my poem "Imogen":

Imogen

Imogen wears silver shoes,
with which she kicks me
in the butt.
She's an explosion
of sound
reaching for words
she cannot find.
Mememememememe.
She's a Bronx cheer.
Calls me "blowhard."
A compus spinning
with no north.
She cheers me on
Brööötttttt!
Wants me to stop,
won't let go of my hand.
She has a shiny bead bracelet
that rattles when she shakes.
Smiles, wrinkes up her nose.

She is hahahahahahaha.
Imogen wear silver shoes,
reaching for words,
spinning,
never letting gogogogogo.

Imogen
is tongue
and lips
flapping,
loose in the air.
She is silver shoes,
and shiny beads
lost inside
her rattle—
find her there.
Trumpet
and silver air
she won't let go
your hand.

Having Sex with Poets: A Manifesto

When power narrows the areas of man's concern, poetry reminds him of the richness and diversity of his existence. When power corrupts, poetry cleanses.

—John F. Kennedy

Whether "wandering lonely as a cloud," or "decreeing stately pleasure-domes in Xanadu," poets get it on; poets do the deed. Of course other people get it on too—that's how you get poets. Sex is everywhere, not just the prerogative of poets. But what do regular people and poets have in common? Poets *are* regular people! So get over yourself, poet: once you start thinking of yourself as no different from the plumber next door, your hourly rate will soar. Plumbers get laid too! That's a metaphor and a fact. The point is—this does have a point—seduce life. Get out there and make things happen.

Don't sit on the barstool and wonder what it would be like to talk to that cootie with tattoos and piercings. Talk to the circus freak! How else are you ever going to know if you are trapeze artist material? Don't just sit there, dance! See, now you're wiggling your butt: poets put the giggle in wiggle. Poets are lap dancers. That's not a metaphor: lots of poets are sex workers. Come on baby, pitch some woo! Okay, where was I? Oh yes, poet as sex machine, poet as raving, tree-hugging world-licker: "I think that I shall never see / A poem as lovely as a tree." Want to Funk and Wagnall? Want to poetry boogaloo? Want to do the nasty haiku? Want to pitch a little po? Want to go up to my place and see my sonnets? If size doesn't matter, why are epic poems so Homer erotic? Is Homer our homeboy?

I'm talking oral tradition. I'm talking what's going on down there is connected to what's going on up here. Poems are sexy. Poems are romance. Remember the film *The Postman*? How the local loser goes to Neruda to get lessons on writing lover-boy poems? Remember *The Owl and the Pussycat*? "O lovely Pussy, O Pussy, my love, / What a beautiful pussy you are, / You are, / You are! / What a beautiful pussy you are!" Here's clue: Edward Lear did not own a cat. Lear was a dog person. I'm talking oral rendition. I'm talking deep sea fishing. I'm talking the inner meaning of your creative position. Are you on top? Are you in control, or are you tied up and loving it? Either way poetry will get you there. Poetry will find that missed connection.

You, blond in line at the fancy-pants coffee shop. Me, bald, staring in the window, drooling, creating smudges. You looked, then looked away. Do you love me? If so, or if just into casual fling, call 6969-spank-me-pinch-me-love-nest! Your mouth is the sexiest thing in the whole poetry business. Not just for the words, fish and flossing. But all that chewing that scoots out of thick fleshy slabs. Dribble, dribble dollhouse. It reminds me of dragons and daisies and Catherine Deneuve . . . The backs of your knees are perfume factories. Grinding away the kisses into something useful. Like a grant to study free love of the 1960s in Prague.

I burp you. You spit up on my shoulder. What's all this talk of stinking ships? You old sailor gal. You next year's calendar. You crease my Dockers. I mix up a special lip-gloss of old *Playboy* pages, wrap it inside a stuffed animal named Bunny Bun. Here, he's yours. Come on, let's make a porn flick. Are you winking a pass at me? Nibble, panties, shower, pole, raunchy, really, really, ready or not, here I come. My cock is smarter than me, I don't know why he speaks in a whisper. I wish he would shut up, or just say what's on his mind clearly and plainly, so everyone can understand. Your lips red as any siren, soothing as help on the way. Soft as arrested. Whirling, spinning, the sound flashing warning into air.

With poetry you will wear the pants in the family and the panties. With poetry you will give birth to words that don't reach the outer margin of the page. With poetry it will be Valentine's Day, every day. Poetry is Cupid and you are the arrow, flying through the air, poking the curvy rump of life. With poetry you'll never be lonely, except when you are around other poets. Forget about other poets, you're the pun baby. Don't forget to compare people to "a summer's day." Don't forget "How do I love thee," and to "count the ways." Don't forget your "love is like a red, red rose," and don't forget to take off your clothes.

Naked poets on parade. Naked horny poets. Talk to a naked poet for a buck. Poets doing thinking-cap dances. Stuff a buck in my po-thong and ask me to recite something slow and wrong, "and then my heart with pleasure fills, and dances with the daffodils." Yeah, little kitty nip, yeah, little rough-textured kitty tongue, that's what I'm talking about. Lap it up.

Poets are people just like you, only they've got a mouth full of words and aren't sure if they should swallow. Swallow poets, swallow. It's the essence of life and makes your coat shiny and puts the bounce in your tight little hiney. That's a simile; what I am saying is mind is sexy, brain is sex organ, poetry is exercise for the gray matter-chatter, and more poetry will help you find that perfect mate, and when you do, don't forget to sigh softly and whisper sweet Stanyan Street into her ear hole. O, Poetry, I'm so lonely.

The Slam Poem as Poetry Form

The poets have been mysteriously silent on the subject of cheese.

—Gilbert K. Chesterton

Written by Logan Phillips and Suzy La Follette

Logan Phillips was born in Tombstone, Arizona and spend his first eighteen years living near the Mexican border. He recently graduated from Northern Arizona University with a degree in Spanglish and splits his time between Flagstaff, Arizona and Querétaro, Mexico, among other places. In Flagstaff he's called Dirtyverbs and in Mexico he's called Timoteo. He earns money through teaching and working unmentionable day jobs; he makes his living as a poet and organizer. He is a three-time member of the Northern Arizona slam team. His chapbooks include *Sun Said Shine* and *This Line Drawn Across Footprints*. He has had several pieces of writing published, including a review of Tony Hoagland's latest book of poetry in the *Review Revue*. More can be found at dirtyverbs.com.

Suzy La Follette received her BA in English at Northern Arizona University. She is a powerful performer and dedicated student to the art of poetry. She has been featured on ABC, NPR, *The Best of Urbana 2004* CD, and is published in *Big Text, Texas A&M Literary Journal*. She has toured the country performing at universities, Take Back the Night, LadyFest, Prides, smoky bars, and poetry slams and has shared the stage with the likes of Diane Di Prima and Billy Collins. She placed sixth in the nation at the National Poetry Slam in Chicago, 2003. She has graced the stage from coast to coast, including The Bowery Poetry Club, The Bezerkely Slam, The Green Mill, The Nuyorican, and countless others. She lives in Austin, Texas with her partner and her cat.

Poetry Investigator: I had the good fortune to meet Logan Phillips and Suzy La Follette when I was giving a reading in Sedona, Arizona a few years ago. I was impressed with their writing and performance skills and intrigued by Phillips's travels in Mexico. This summer, while on tour, Phillips made time to come by for an interview on my radio show, *Poetry Talk*. He read some of his poems, which are set on the Mexican border. In the course of talking about poetry, he told me about the piece he and Suzy La Follette had written on slam poetry as form. I loved the idea and thought it pushed the discussion about the poetry slam in the right direction, and I was happy when they agreed to let me include the piece in this book.

Go to enough poetry slams and you'll surely laugh, cry and then, suddenly, you just might get a feeling that starts in the back of your throat or in the seat of your pants—

many of these poems sound alike! The near-unvarying three minute length! The bombastic, repeating finish! It could of course be that poets, well, enjoy poetry slams and attend them often, maybe too often. The words and styles get swirled around like a latté or a mai thai, depending on the venue. Then, the poets return home after too much of said drink, sit down to write and are subconsciously influenced by the work of their peers. Of course. But there is something more to why these poems sound alike: many poems performed at slams belong to a just-emerging form of poetry, as valid as a villanelle or a sonnet: the slam poem. The poems we hear at poetry slams, despite their wit, finesse, energy and creativity, use many of the same techniques and have carved out a new form of poetry, right under the nose of the establishment.

This idea—that both an Italian villanelle and a Nuyorican slam poem are both equally poetic and valid—just doesn't always strike people as true. In fact, cultural critic Harold Bloom called slam "the death of art" in an interview with *The Paris Review*. This "page vs. stage" confrontation is something that slam poets are challenged with on a regular basis. Slam poet Big Poppa E has much to say when told that slam poetry isn't real poetry. "That is such a meaningless statement to me. You might as well say that slam poetry is not a potato. It's also not a skyscraper or a dentist's drill or a handful of pennies either. But whatever it is, it is exciting a whole hell of a lot of people and serving as the impetus for a lot of people to express themselves in ways they never thought were possible." We are too accustomed to hearing "page vs. stage" arguments in universities or coffee shops and have begun to see things in such a two-tone hue. "Spoken word is a mutated hybrid of hip-hop, stand-up blitzkrieg comedy, performance art, and fucked-up theater," says Jamie Kennedy, the host of the poetry show *Tourettes Without Regrets*, in Oakland. This hybrid is creating a new form of poetry, a form that is meant to be spoken and heard. As the cliché goes, poetry is a tree with many branches, which is the sort of thinking that makes me want to "give it a ten!"

* Dury, John. *The Poetry Dictionary*.

First, we have to draw some quick lines: a poetry slam is the event we're all familiar with, a public competition of performed poems, with judges selected from the audience. That one's easy and probably inspires no book burning. From here on out, though, we'll be defining slam poetry, which is a term that belongs, we argue, along with pantoum and haiku in the definitions of formal poetry. And of course, a slam poet, as many are fond of saying, is just a poet who competes in poetry slams. And keep in mind, all you slam poets out there, this chapter, like the rest of this book, isn't a strict "how-to." Many successful poems heard at poetry slams contain the features discussed here, but many don't, and no great poem has ever been written by just following a checklist of features.

The first aspect of any form of poetry that is discussed is the form's origin. The sestina originally comes from the troubadours of twelfth century Italy, the villanelle was originally a French adaptation of Italian folk songs about rural life, slam poetry was created by an American construction worker at the Get Me High Lounge in Chicago in 1986. Now we're talkin'. But that construction worker can't take all the credit for the idea of competitive poetry readings: it might be the Ancient Greeks saying so what! to Marc Smith. After all, they had their eclogues, which were "a pastoral poem, or one dealing with rural life, especially a dialogue;"—and get this—"a singing contest between two shepherds."*

Every environment influences the art born of it, yet the setting and rules of a poetry slam are especially critical to understanding the form birthed of it, slam poetry. The most visible difference between a poetry slam and any other poetry reading is the judges. They, of course, make it a competition. Marc Smith saw the addition of judges from the audience as a way of democratizing a poetry reading and holding the poets accountable to their audience. "Marc Smith never claimed to have invented a new kind of poetry, 'slam poetry'; he invented a new way of enjoying it (the poetry slam)," says past Poetry Slam Inc. President Taylor Mali. Smith created the game, the competition, the entertainment, and a new animal of poetry evolved on its own.

Many veteran slam poets, such as champion Buddy Wakefield, have good perspective on the competition. As he and others are fond of saying, "The scores are just a gimmick to get people interested in the poetry." The second largest difference is the time limit. In a poetry slam, each poet has three minutes to deliver each poem. Third, poetry slams are most commonly held in bars or cafés, which can be rather rowdy even before the poetry starts. Over time, the style of the venue can begin to rub off on the poetry that takes place there, but we'll get to that a bit later. Now let's get into the metaphoric meat of the thing—the features of a slam poem.

Three minutes of bliss

All forms of poetry have something to say about their length. A traditional sestina is either thirty-six or thirty-nine lines long, a haiku, three. And since slam poetry is primarily an oral form, it makes sense that its length be measured by number of minutes rather than number of lines.

Thanks to the time limit, there happens to be a very definite standard length for a slam poem. Of course it's not required that a poem be three minutes long, but in practice the time limit seems to create a void that should be filled by the poet in order to impress the judges as much as possible. Though it's not often talked about, it is obvious from watching judges in action that there's a certain feeling of them being cheated by a poet who uses only thirty seconds of the time given to them on stage, no matter how amazing. Sure, that was an amazing half minute, but what could that poet have done with a full three minutes? Many poets find it harder to write a killer ten line poem than a rocking four minute roller coaster. But it's important to remember, quality and quantity come under the judges' scrutiny as the host shouts with a smile on his/her face, "Okay judges, assign that poet's outpouring of soul a numerical value!"

But why three minutes? Why not five or twenty? Slam lore has it that the only timepiece that could be found in the aforementioned Get Me High Lounge the night of the first slam only ran up to three minutes. Go figure. The sports correlation has also

* I first heard this from the wise Flagstaff poet and professor Jim Simmerman.

† Drury, 120.

been suggested by some—namely that boxing has compacted its own grisly art into rounds of three minutes for decades.* But it's something a little more banal than either of those that really seems most likely: would you want to sit through twenty minutes of an ass-scrapingly bad poem? Would a modern audience even tolerate a long work of quality? Sure, there are prose readings at universities that can push the hour mark, but how about the Get Me High Lounge sitting through a reincarnated Homer going on in epic style for days on end? I imagine things—big, heavy, breakable things—being thrown just about the time in Day One when the inebriated crowd realizes that this Ithaca business is going to go on for a while. It has a little to do with a lot of things: television episodes, music videos, the creation and rise of ADD—our attention spans have shrunk to the lowest levels that any of us can barely remember. Specifically it means that we have become accustomed to consuming arts and culture in bite-sized bits. It is a fact that one is hard-pressed to find a top-forty pop song that clocks in at over 3:10. Like it or not, this is the context in which all art finds itself in the mainstream, slam poetry being no exception.

Politics, Pop, and Sex, Oh My!

All forms of poetry have their traditional subject matter. The Middle Eastern ghazel, whose name means either "the cry of a gazelle when it is hunted down and trapped" or "to make love; lovers' exchange,"† depending on the mood you're in, was originally conceived as an erotic love poem written to God. Needless to say at this point, not all poems written in a particular form will have traditional subjects, especially ghazels. Keep this in mind as we take a look at "traditional" subjects of slam poems. As in all poetry, the subjects of slam poems run the gamut. However, there are some major trends in slam poetry that do deserve being mentioned.

Political and protest poetry is particularly popular in slam, for a number of reasons. Again due to its oral nature, slam is well-suited to deal with the immediacy of social issues. Rather than a poet writing a poem and having to wait for it to be published or wondering if it will ever be published due to its revolutionary content, the poet can go out to a slam within the next week and perform the poem to a crowd. After that the revolution is in the judges' hands. Audiences have always appreciated immediacy, a poem that is being read because it must be rather than because the poet wants to smell his/her own breath behind a microphone. It follows that judges will appreciate immediacy and weight as well. There is the long history of poetry's place in political movements, a history probably as long as that of poetry itself. Within our own time, it's important to acknowledge the poetry of Amiri Baraka, Gil Scott Heron, The Last Poets, Audre Lorde, and Rodolfo Corky Gonzales within their own respective political movements. What is traditionally considered by established institutions to be the "minority voice" is wonderfully well-represented in slam poetry. The openness of poetry slams—allowing anyone to sign up and be heard—has allowed formerly marginalized groups to share their work in front of large, usually receptive audiences, thus allowing the slam to act as a much-needed megaphone for social issues. One thing is beyond argument and politics: it is hard to find a more diverse group of people than a group of poets at a poetry slam.

And then there's the blissfully inane. Who wants to be forever serious anyway? Audiences like to laugh! Pop culture is often referenced, critiqued, put on high and shot down low in slam poetry. Many times this is done with a slice of that other slam poetry influence: stand up comedy. "I believe comedy is integral to successful and accessible spoken word performance. Even the most serious poems need a laugh line here and there. It makes the truths sink in deeper," says Taylor Mali. Look no farther than Austin poet Andy Buck's brilliant attack on The Establishment, placing the blame for all modern social ill squarely on what deserves it the most: "Janet Jackson's Titty". (If you don't follow me here, it means you've probably forgotten the 2004 Super Bowl Halftime Show. More power to you, really. This also illustrates one feature of pop culture references in poetry: they tend to age more like whole milk than fine wine.)

While we're on the subject, we might as well point out that sex and eroticism is a staple of slam poetry. It's probably popular for the same reason as laughter. Something to do with biology that is (just barely) out of the scope of this book.

There is also a wider relationship between the venue and the subject matter of the slam poetry that takes place there. As Flagstaff, Arizona poet and university professor Jim Simmerman points out, the three subjects we mentioned above—politics, comedy, and sex—are all staples of bar and coffee shop talk regardless if there is a slam that night or not. Much depends on the venue. A poetry slam at a youth center at two o'clock on a Thursday afternoon is going to be just a bit different beast than Jamie Kennedy's infamous *Tourettes Without Regrets* poetry slam in Oakland on any night of the week. This is all thanks to that original democratizing idea of poetry slam: giving the audience the score cards.

Repetition. Repeat-ition. Repeat-a-thon.

We've said something like this at the beginning of every other section and we'll repeat it now. Many forms of poetry have rules regarding the use of repetition. The sestina calls for one of six repeating words to be used in each of the six lines in each stanza, for a total of six stanzas. No wonder it's called a "song of sixes." One reason that slam poetry uses repetition is the same reason that sestinas and other forms of poetry do: they're all rooted in the oral tradition, which employs repetition to help storytellers and poets remember long pieces while reciting them from memory.

Then there again is the attention span problem we mentioned before, remember it? Repetition helps beat home an important image, central idea, or enjoyable piece of wordplay so that it sticks in the judges' minds after the three minutes are up and the crowd (hopefully) begins screaming like a gaggle of monkeys lounging in a lake of banana pudding. Regrettably, within a dense and lyrical three minute poem, it is not uncommon for the audience to become lost, especially since said poem is still competing with MTV, which has now even begun to fade songs out after a minute and half. Repetition is a straightforward and easily overused method of maintaining audience interest during the performance of a slam poem.

The next three features of slam poetry we'll mention—rhythm, rhyme, and meter—are really just variations on repetition: rhythm being repetition of timing, rhyme of sound, and meter of syllabic emphasis. Good rhythm is just plain pleasurable to listen to, bad rhythm (think limerick) is hardly tolerated by an audience at a poetry slam. Likewise with rhyme: it's said that at the famous Green Mill Tavern slam in Chicago, if an audience can guess the end-rhyme of a slammer's next line by shouting it out before the poet gets to it, well, that's a cue for the poet to wrap it up quick. If not, he/she will be snapped and then stomped off stage by the audience. Again: the crowd rules, and internal rhyme is usually the way to go, adding a good subliminal musicality to the language.

In the meter of slam poems, as well as rhyme and rhythm, it's common to notice a strong hip-hop influence. Both hip-hop and slam originated around the same time—late seventies/early eighties for hip-hop and mid-eighties for slam—and in some of the same big cities—New York and Chicago—so it makes sense that they have much to do with each other. Rappers such as Providence's Sage Francis also participate in poetry slams, and it's common for poets such as Sekou (tha Misfit) from Los Angeles to record their poetry over breakbeats for release on CD. The hip-hop/slam connection runs deeply intertwined but is not universal. As influential as hip-hop rhythms may be, it's good to keep in mind that there are poets who do not rhyme at all and many poets like Taylor Mali, who claims not to be influenced by hip-hop at all. As stated previously, the styles of slam poetry run the gamut and the hip-hop influence is no exception.

The Same Line Three Times

Ah, here we are, the big finish. There are often set ways in which a form wraps itself up. The sestina calls its last stanza the envoi or tornada and requires the poet to use all six repeating words in three short lines. Not an easy finish. But then again, neither is ending a slam poem. The lines spit by the poet in the last ten to twenty seconds are going to be the lines ringing in the ears of the judges as they hold up their score cards moments later. Who has time to quietly consider the poem in all of its intricacies and nuances? This is a rowdy poetry slam, for chrissakes! The host is already back on stage calling for the numbers, and the audience has (hopefully) transmogrified into monkeys again, this time chanting, "Ten! Ten! Ten!"

So what does a slam poem offer up last? Affirmation, consolidation, and recap. It generally doesn't work very well to throw the crowd a new, complex revelation or big idea that tweaks the meaning of the entire previous three minutes right at the end. There's no time (or attention span) for the audience to mentally "reread" the entire poem with the new information in mind like there would be if they were reading the poem on page.

For the hilarious spoof on a typical overused ending, look no further than NYC-Urbana's master slam poet, strategist, and past PSI President Taylor Mali in his meta-poem "How to Write a Political Poem." And why not end this chapter with the end of Mali's poem:

and maybe it's true that they're still counting votes in Florida
but when you get to the end of a political poem
that shit just doesn't matter anymore
because all you gotta do to end a political poem is say
the same line three times
the same line three times
the same line
three
times!

Insurance for Poets and Writers

You don't have to suffer to be a poet. Adolescence is enough suffering for anyone.

—John Ciardi

PEN American Center

(212) 334-1660

An association of more than 2,700 poets, playwrights, essayists, editors, and novelists as well as literary translators and agents "who have made a substantial contribution to the literary community." Benefits of membership include access to group health insurance. Call membership information at (212) 334-1660 extension 101 for more information about insurance plans currently being offered.

National Writers Union UAW Local 1981 AFL-CIO

(212) 254-0279

The NWU health plan is available only to members and associates living in the state of New York. The dental plan is available nationwide. The plan is administered by Alicare. Call (800) 725-9213 for information.

Writers' Guild of America East

(212) 767-7800

In addition to the Guild's health plan, members have access to health insurance throught TEIGIT (go to www.teigit.com). Writers Guild East members also have detailed health and pension information available at a members-only website.

Authors' Guild, Inc.

(212) 563-5904

Members can obtain health, hospitalization, dental and life insurance from a number of insurers-including CIGNA, Oxford, and GHI-under several different Authors' Guild plans. Plans vary by state. Call the Membership Coordinator at (212) 563-5904 or email staff@authorsguild.org for details.

American Society of Journalists and Authors

(212) 997-0947

A national non-fiction writers' organization that also offers choices of several health insurance group plans for members. Site includes excellent article explaining health insurance deductions for freelancers.

IWWG: International Women's Writing Guild

(212) 737-7536

A worldwide non-profit organization open to all women writers. Site states on 6/24/02 "group insurance plan to be announced." Check for updates. http://www.fracturedatlas.org/site/services/healthcare/

ACKNOWLEDGMENTS

To the poets who spoke openly for this book about their lives I offer my thanks. In the bios of the various poets interviewed, many of their books are listed in the hope that you, the reader, will buy some if not all of those books. This is the secret agenda of *How to Make a Life as a Poet*: to help sell poetry books. To Margaret Victor, my wife, for her help in writing this book and the constant help she offers this dyslexic, word-challenged poet. Thanks to Bob Holman and Elizabeth Murray for their secret recipe for life and grilled sausage. Many thanks for the support from all the people at Soft Skull, big shouts to Anne Horowitz, Kristin Pulkkinen, and Richard Nash.

Photo by Reid Yalom

Gary Mex Glazner makes his living as a poet. HarperCollins, W.W. Norton and Salon.com have published his work. He is the author of *Ears on Fire: Snapshot Essays in a World of Poets,* published by La Alameda Press. The book chronicles a year spent abroad in Asia and Europe meeting poets, working on translations and writing poems. Glazner is the author of *How to Make a Living as a Poet*, published by Soft Skull Press in March of 2005. The book features essays on creative poetry programming and interviews with leading poets including, among others, Mary Karr, Naomi Shihab Nye, the Taco Shop Poets and Sherman Alexie. That book along with the one in your hands is part of a three-book series, with the third to be entitled, *Still Not Making a Living as a Poet?*

Glazner is the director of the Alzheimer's Poetry Project (APP). NBC's *Today* show, NPR's *Weekend Edition*, and Voice of America have featured segments on the APP. The broadcasts reached over twenty million people. The APP is a simple idea: to read classic poems to the patients that they might have learned as children. Even in the late stages of the disease, this helps to spark memories, and the patients can often say words and lines along with the poems. Glazner is the editor of *Sparking Memories: The Alzheimer's Poetry Project Anthology*, and he recently started the APP in Wellington, New Zealand, where he was featured on New Zealand National Radio. For more information, please visit alzpoetry.com.

Glazner's student group, the Precision Poetry Drill Team, was featured on NPR's *All Things Considered*. He has worked in poet-in-the-schools projects since 1990 and was poet-in-residence at Desert Academy in Santa Fe from 2004 to 2006. He is the editor of the Word Art: Poetry Broadside series at the Palace of the Governors Museum, where he sets type and runs the old printing presses. Glazner was commissioned by the Santa Fe Opera to create a performance based on the work of the Spanish poet Federico García Lorca, for their festival on Lorca. Glazner, along with co-producer Don McIver, was the winner of the 2004 Special Merit Award from the National Federation of Community Broadcasters, for "The Poetry of Vietnam," which was broadcast on KUNM in Albuquerque. He is the host of *Poetry Talk*, a bimonthly radio show on KSFR in Santa Fe.

To my father, Edward Marquise,
who taught me the power of hope and positive thinking,
and to my mother, Eva Klein Marquise,
for giving me my first journal,
which laid the foundation for my life as a writer

Oh, the joy of writing, a joy so intense
so pure, so all-absorbing and free and all-
encompassing, flooding the soul in mystical
ecstasy, elevating and sanctifying, infusing
beauty in the humblest subjects and a purpose
in the most wayward life.

—Anaïs Nin (*Volume Two*, pg. 8)

Foreword

Diana Raab's *Writing for Bliss* is so many things: a meditation on, and paean to, writing and the writing life; a reflective and deeply felt guide for those wishing to speak their minds and hearts, whether silently or aloud; and, not least, a valuable how-to book, the how-to in question being less about this or that writing technique or strategy and more about life and what we might do to live it more fully and with more sense of its great abundance. Perhaps more than anything, though, Raab's book is about the profound ways in which we may be transformed in and through the act of writing.

In reading some of her lovely introductory words about this process, I was reminded of a phrase attributed to the French philosopher Jules Lequier: "To create, and in creating be created." In some ways the idea is a simple one, but its significance cannot be overestimated. For what it ultimately suggests is that writing—meaningful writing, issuing from the heart and soul of the writer—is a vehicle of *change*, of moving from one state of knowing and feeling and being to another, one that is deeper, more real, more true. In carrying out the research on which this book is based, Raab "found that the act or experience of writing results in a heightened sense of awareness and an identity that becomes transformed, in addition to a deeper understanding of one's place in the world" (p. 5). This may be so whatever genre one chooses, but it is especially so when writing about one's own life. "By documenting the story of your life," Raab adds, "you have the chance to relive, examine, and reconstruct your lived experiences in a way that can be empowering." What's more, "By working through your life, you are able to draw a certain amount of energy from what you have been through, reconcile yourself with your experiences, and then move forward" (p. 6).

As Raab well knows, this process doesn't always work neatly. In fact, there are times when it doesn't appear to work at all. For some, telling the story of their lives can be anything but empowering; suddenly seeing what they either couldn't see or wouldn't see earlier on can be draining and demoralizing—at least for a time. There may be no reconciliation, either, and no moving forward; one's now-open wounds may be too fresh and too paralyzing. If Raab is right, however, there still remains room for growth, painful and difficult though it may be, and writing can play a vitally important role in the process. This is because what may have heretofore been inchoate and obscure or even utterly opaque has at least risen into the light of consciousness. And for all the pain that may be involved in this rising, it is the pain of birth and growth. Something has become available that wasn't before, and coming face to face with that something is the requisite condition for moving beyond it.

By her own account, Raab's intention in creating this book "is to share my passion for writing and how it has helped me heal over the course of six decades" (p. 7). This healing has surely been suffused with the pain that has preceded it and required it. How fortunate we are to have the gift of writing to deliver and redeem us! How fortunate we are to have the opportunity to "follow our bliss," wherever it may lead. Doing so is not always blissful, though. It can't be. That's part of its beauty.

On my reading, there are three ideas that aptly characterize what is most fundamental about Raab's book: *reflection*, *truth*, and *freedom*. Indeed, these three ideas are intimately connected with one another. "Reflective writing," Raab suggests, "is about digging deep down into your emotional truth... digging into your heart's center to write about what you are *really* feeling, rather than about what you *think* other want to hear" (p. 87). Reflection, therefore, entails stepping out of the flow of unconscious being and seeing things anew. And writing, as an act of reflection *par excellence*, allows this seeing-anew to take center stage. Whether the resultant work is fiction or nonfiction is largely secondary; what matters most is that reflection has been employed in the service of fashioning a more capacious and indeed truthful version of experience. As for how freedom enters the picture, it has to do precisely with liberating ourselves from those coercive holds on our experience, both other-imposed and self-imposed, that frequently find their way into our lives. Writing is about fashioning alternatives, ones that can allow us to see things in a different light. It's about remaking the world, both outer and inner, and in so doing remaking ourselves.

Diana Raab's *Writing for Bliss* is an excellent sourcebook for engaging in the arduous, sometimes painful, often glorious process of writing. I am grateful to her for sharing it, and I trust that you will feel the same as you read on. May you savor the journey.

—Mark Freeman, PhD, Distinguished Professor of Ethics and Society at the College of the Holy Cross, author of *Hindsight* and *The Priority of the Other*

Acknowledgments

Writing for Bliss has been inspired by my many years as a writer, observer of life, and writing teacher. Writing has brought me so much joy that I realized I wanted to share my passion with others. I am blessed to have had many people in my life whose teachings and inspirations have informed my own work. I have benefited tremendously from all their insights, priceless gifts of wisdom, and friendships. I am also thankful to all my journals and computers for being the container for my musings.

The seed for this book was planted during my doctoral work when I was studying the healing and transformative powers of writing a memoir. I will be forever grateful for the participants of my study, including Maxine Hong Kingston, Kim Stafford, Mark Matousek, Monica Wesolowska, and Alexandra Styron for their willingness to share their stories, their candor, and their generosity of spirit. A huge thanks to the members of my dissertation team, who have all become dear friends and colleagues—Jay Dufrechou, Tristine Rainer, and Dorit Netzer—for their support and enthusiasm during my two-year research. I am grateful for all our wonderful conversations and brainstorming sessions.

Every writer needs a great book editor. I could not have had a better one than Sharron Dorr, who has been instrumental in bringing this manuscript to fruition. I am appreciative for her enthusiasm, attentiveness, creativity, integrity, keen eye, and professionalism while working on this book. She has been a sheer delight. Deep gratitude to my publicist, Carina Sammartino for her efficiency, creativity and most ambitious pursuits. Deep gratitude to others who have also been instrumental in bringing this book to fruition including Jill Kramer, Melissa Esposito, Beth Brody, and Kathleen Lynch.

A deep bow to my publisher, Victor R. Volkman, for once again believing in me and my work, and whom I applaud for his vision and generosity of spirit.

Thank you to all my friends and colleagues who have enriched my life through conversation, spirits, laughter, and creative exchanges. My having been a writer for more than four decades, this list tends to be very long; but there are certain people whose names rise to the surface and who deserve my deepest gratitude. They include Tristine Rainer, Robert Bosnak, Jeanna Zelin, Perie Longo, Nancy Leffert, Linda Gray Sexton, Susan Wooldridge, Gail Kearns, Gail Steinbeck, David Starkey, Susan Wyler, Brenda Stockdale, Bernie Siegel, Connie May Fowler, Richard Goodman, Sena Jeta Naslund, Karen Mann, Philip Lopate, James Brown, Stephen Jay Schwartz, Darlyn Finch, Michael Steinberg, Mark Freeman, Dinty Moore, Elizabeth Lesser, Jina Carvahlo, Mary Francis Hoffman, Melinda Palacio, Steven Beisner, Jim Alexander, Marcia Meier, Laure-Anne Bosselaur, Mary Francis Hoffman, Julie Gohman, Pat Aptaker, Susan Chiavelli, Julie Montgomery, Rose and Jack Herschorn and last but definitely not least, Lei'ohu Ryder. Deep gratitude to my two physicians who have kept me healthy over the years, Soram Khalsa, MD and Keith Stewart, MD. I will be forever grateful. If your name is not listed here and we've had substantial interactions, please forgive me, as, finally, I am feeling the effects of being a sexagenarian.

A special tribute of thanks to my late friend Thomas Steinbeck for more than a decade of literary discussions over tequilas and for his friendship, inspiration, compelling stories, and adoration. Thomas, I will forever feel your presence in my heart.

Most of all, I want to thank my family, from my husband, Simon, for his relentless enthusiasm for all my endeavors and who encouraged me to reach for the stars every step of the way; to my loving children, Rachel, Regine, Joshua, Daniel and Richard for their ongoing interest and support of my creative life. Also, I want to thank the inspiration of my two grandchildren, Jaxson Alexander Bassett and Lila Augusta Mae del Valle. You are all the light in my life, especially during my darker moments. You are the ones who make everything worthwhile.

Preface

> *If you follow your bliss, you put yourself on a kind of track that has been there all the while, waiting for you, and the life that you ought to be living is the one you are living. Wherever you are—if you are following your bliss, you are enjoying that refreshment, that life within you, all the time.*
>
> —Joseph Campbell

Most writers will confess that they write because they have to write, not necessarily because they want to write. They write out of necessity because either it makes them feel better or they want to share their story with the world. I fall into both these categories: writing makes me feel good; when I don't write, I feel as if something's missing from my life, plus I also yearn to share my stories with others in the hope that they will resonate in a way that brings healing and a deeper way of knowing and understanding.

My beginnings as a writer began when I was ten years old, writing in my journal to help me cope and heal from the suicide of my grandmother, who had also been my caretaker and had lived with us in my childhood home. I was the only child of immigrant parents who worked all day tending their retail dry-goods store in Brooklyn, New York. On Labor Day in 1964, I was at home with my grandmother. In many immigrant families of the post-World War II era, children were reared by their extended families, particularly grandparents. My grandparents lived with us, and while my grandfather spent much of his time in New York City becoming culturally acclimated, my maternal grandmother, Regina, stayed home to take care of me.

It was a hot Indian summer day common to the season. We lived in a suburban community along with other immigrant families, and I had many playmates in the neighborhood. I was excited when a friend invited me to go swimming in her pool. With a child's enthusiasm, I knocked on my grandmother's door to ask for permission.

There was no answer. I tried several times, but still no answer. I called to her, but there was only silence. Trembling with fear, I phoned my parents at their store. I sat with my nose pressed to the front bay window until they drove up the driveway in Dad's pink car that matched the house's shingles—the color he had painted them the day I was born. My parents dashed out of the car and up to Grandma's room. Before I knew what was going on, my beloved grandmother was being carried down our creaky wooden stairs on a stretcher and put into an ambulance. I never saw her again.

Like most children, I took the experience in stride and did not think too much about it. There was no doubt that I missed my grandmother, Regina, the only grandmother I ever knew. My father's parents had perished in the Holocaust. I was lonely for my grandmother's company and her love. After all, she had been the one who had taught me how to type short stories on the Remington typewriter perched on the vanity table in her room. Her loving attention was something my mother was unable to provide in a meaningful way. Now in addition my mother, who had also been an only child, was dealing with her own grief over losing her mother.

My mother knew I was grieving and wanted to help me through the trauma of having lost my grandmother. Reaching out to therapists was not done in those days; and even if it had been, we would not have had the money for it. Others might have seen therapists, but it was certainly not something anyone ever talked about. My grandmother had been a journal keeper. After some contemplation on how to help me cope with the loss of this important person in my life who had also been my caretaker, my mother went to the nearest stationery store and bought me a blank, red leather journal with a saying by Kahlil Gibran on the top of each page. I had many favorites, but in coping with the loss of my grandmother, this is the one that helped me: "If you love somebody, let them go, for if they return, they were always yours. And if they don't, they never were."

One thing I learned from my grandmother was the importance of having love in my life. At the top of one page in my red-leather journal was Gibran's saying, "Life without love is like a tree without blossoms or fruit." In this page I wrote about how much my grandmother's love meant to me and how, after losing her, my life felt so empty.

For many months after my grandmother's suicide, my mother continued to encourage me to write down my feelings about my grandmother. Having been an English major in college, my mother thought this was the best way for me to deal with my grief.

In those days, children were unwelcome at funerals, so I was shipped off with my journal to my aunt's and uncle's apartment in New York City. I guess everyone thought that the funeral experience would be too traumatic an experience for me. Certainly things would be different today, at a time when kids are exposed to a lot more than funerals. For days on end after my grandmother died, I sat at my small birch desk or in my walk-in closet under the hanging clothes, writing about my grandmother and how I missed her.

Little did I realize that my mother's seemingly mild gesture of buying me a journal would set the stage for my lifelong passion for writing. As I grew into adulthood, each time I encountered difficult times—including my turbulent adolescence in the 1960s, my daughter's drug addiction, and my battles with cancer—I wrote about what I was going through. Not only did I explain my lived experience, but I also wrote about how the experience made me feel.

It was more than four decades after my grandmother died, when I was forty-seven years old, that I received my first cancer diagnosis (about which I wrote in *Healing with Words: A Writer's Cancer Journey*). After healing from the physical and emotional trauma of that experience, and of course chronicling my journey in my journal, I decided to follow my dream of returning to graduate school. I pursued my MFA in writing, and when the time came to consider a subject for my thesis, the story of my grandmother's life occurred to me.

Coincidentally, around that time my mother gave me my grandmother's hand-typed journal telling of her early life as an orphan in Poland during and after World War I. When Mother handed me the journal, I felt as if I had been given the biggest gift a granddaughter could ever receive. I devoured every word and realized that my grandmother had shared my passion for journaling. My MFA thesis, which involved studying her life, turned into my first published memoir, *Regina's Closet: Finding My Grandmother's Secret Journal.*

In this memoir, I dealt with the two major turning points in my life: losing my grandmother—whose loss had been all the more traumatic because she had also been my caretaker—and then discovering her sacred journal. The journal was sacred because of its role in my understanding of my grandmother and why she might have committed suicide. It was also sacred because it was another chance for me to get close to her intimate and private thoughts. I realized that writing about my grandmother was healing, as it allowed me to honor her and keep her alive, and it was also a way to come to some resolution about her suicide.

I had always been a seeker, but the experience of reflecting upon my grandmother's life and then finding her journal led me on a path of discovery and further transformation as I tried to understand why she had taken her life at the age of sixty-one—the age, in fact, that I am now as I write this book.

Studying my grandmother's life leading up to her suicide helped me to understand, grow, and become empowered by her experience to take on the role of a woman warrior. I realized that she had been a survivor for most of her life. She had survived the trauma of being orphaned, she survived two world wars, she survived an emotionally abusive relationship, and she survived long enough to see me go to school. I learned from my grandmother that no matter what happened, I too wanted to be a survivor and a fighter. I wanted to become empowered by my experiences and also to help others become empowered by theirs. Thus, my grandmother had left me with a huge gift.

My MFA was not to be the end of my pursuit of education. It seemed as if whenever a life-changing event occurred in my life, I returned to school for another degree. My MFA was initiated as a result of my breast cancer diagnosis; and six years later, after being diagnosed with smoldering multiple myeloma, a cancer of the bone marrow, I returned for my doctorate in psychology. About that time, I was approaching the age of sixty-one—again, my grandmother's age when she took her life—and had begun reflecting on my own life and on how I felt there was so much more I wanted to accomplish. Having had *two* cancer diagnoses and dealt as well with numerous losses of loved ones, I fully realized the fragility of life. By returning to school, I hoped to merge my passion for understanding the psyche with my great passion for writing. Thus, the subject of my dissertation research was the healing and transformative powers of personal narrative, which became the impetus for writing this book.

Basically, my research examined how life-changing experiences have inspired some well-published authors to write the narratives of their lives. I interviewed writers such as Maxine Kong Kingston, Alexandra Styron, Kim Stafford, Monika Wesloweska, and Mark Matousek. During the course of my research and while compiling the results, I discovered the healing and transformative power of personal writing. Writing one's story is a way to reclaim your voice, to share a family secret, or simply to share a story with others. In my study, I found that the act or experience of writing results in a heightened sense of awareness and an identity that becomes transformed, in addition to a deeper understanding of one's place in the world. Most of those who participated in my study had been exposed either to early-life trauma and significant loss or to addiction, either their own or that of a loved one.

The actual decision to write a memoir depends on both intrinsic and extrinsic factors. The intrinsic factors may be related to the individual's emotions, and the extrinsic factors may pertain to what occurs in his or her world. Writing about certain experiences helps provide an understanding of one's unique self, as well as of one's relationship with others and the world at large.

My research incorporated the work of one of my favorite humanistic psychologists, Abraham Maslow, who, as you might recall from one of your psychology courses, coined the term "the hierarchy of needs" that identifies basic human needs such as security, love, and shelter. He illustrated this hierarchy in the form of a pyramid, at the top of which he spoke about the self-actualization of people who are motivated by higher means or higher truths. These self-actualized or highly motivated individuals are those who are extremely dedicated to some task that results in the higher good of others.

You might know someone who is self-actualized in this way; it might even be you. Such people feel an urgent or deep need to make a change in the world or to serve humanity. It might be something that possesses you. There are different terms to explain the idea of your calling in life. The Romans called it your *genius*, the Greeks called it your *daimon,* and the Christians call it your *guardian angel.* James Hillman used even more words to describe one's sense of calling, such as, *fate*, *character*, *image*, *soul*, and *destiny*, depending upon context. If you know someone who has this kind of passion for doing something, you will recognize that they might feel an obligation and deep connection to their work and are driven by a great need to make some contribution to society at large. These people become one with their work and are inspired by both internal and external drives.

My research interest was based on the fourth and newest branch of psychology, *transpersonal psychology*, which is concerned with the study of optimum psychological health and well-being and with the idea of reaching your highest potential. *Transpersonal* means "beyond the ego" or "beyond the personal." It has to do with the exploration of the unconscious as a way to tap into the higher self, personally and in terms of the collective. This new psychology grew out of the mid-twentieth century humanistic psychology movement and the study of alternative states of consciousness. It was originally founded and introduced by Abraham Maslow in the 1960s at Esalen Institute in California. Transpersonal psychology encompasses all other types of psychology, such as psychoanalytic, Jungian, and behavioristic, as well as humanistic. It also incorporates the spiritual aspects of the human experience. When studying this newest branch of psychology, I incorporated transpersonal experiences, which are experiences that extend beyond the ordinary and usual ways of knowing and doing.

Transpersonal psychology also accentuates various ways of healing, and writing is considered a transpersonal practice in that it encourages self-expression and self-discovery; it helps you identify your strengths and weaknesses and how you can achieve your potential and lead a happier life. By documenting the story of your life, you have the chance to relive, examine, and reconstruct your lived experiences in a way that can be empowering. By working through your life, you are able to draw a certain amount of energy from what you have been through, reconcile yourself with your experiences, and then move forward.

Other practices that are highlighted in transpersonal psychology are geared toward helping an individual reach their highest potential. Many of these practices will be discussed in greater detail later in this book and include setting intentions, mindfulness training, meditation, yoga, psychotherapy, creative visualization, and hypnosis, as well as journaling.

During my research, I learned that I was not alone in my pursuit to write to heal from pivotal or life-changing events in my life such as my grandmother's suicide and a cancer diagnosis. Such experience sometimes serves as a stepping stone for a writing project.

I wrote and published my first memoir, not only to help me accept and understand losing my grandmother but also to help others who might have faced similar losses. My intention in creating this present book, *Writing for Bliss*, is to share my passion for writing and how it has helped me heal over the course of six decades. I hope it will help you transcend what immediately meets your eyes by digging deeper into your psyche and hearing the voice of your true, authentic self, while listening to the messages of your heart rather than suppressing them. I want to share the different ways of reflecting and self-discovery I have learned as a way to bring a sense of wholeness and, ultimately, a sense of bliss. My hope is that readers will become inspired to write during their joyous and difficult times, while also experimenting with different genres and ways of writing and being.

Introduction
Writing for Change

The pen is mightier than the sword.
—Edward George Bulwer-Lytton

When considering any kind of change or incorporating a new practice into your life, whether it is writing for bliss, writing for therapy, or writing for transformation, I like to mention what Zen master Shunryu Suziki referred to in his book, *Zen Mind, Beginner's Mind* (1976), as maintaining the sensibility of the "beginner's mind." The idea is that the beginner's mind tends to be open to many possibilities, unlike the expert's mind, which only sees few. Remaining open-minded and available for new ideas is important, in the same way that we might witness in young children, who are like sponges for learning. Having a beginner's mind is also about suspending your disbelief and going with the flow of your experience, as discussed in more depth in step 1 of this book, "Preparing to Write."

Hopefully, when you have made the decision to engage in personal writing you've given yourself permission to take yourself on a voyage of self-discovery. This entails reviewing your life with a child's curiosity, awe, and simplicity. In so doing, there is a good chance that significant revelations will begin emerging from your subconscious mind. Writing with the magic mindset of a child can be a fun and poignant way to write and to unleash deep, dark, and surprising secrets. Throughout this book I offer writing prompts as a springboard for your writing. Their intention is to whet your writing appetite. It is not necessary to do all the prompts, unless you feel particularly compelled to do so. You might find some resonate more with you than others. Perhaps some relate to a particular life situation at a particular time.

When my three children were young, we sometimes took family vacations to places I had already visited earlier in life. I was often fascinated about how those places seemed so newly unique and different when I returned to them with the children. They viewed those experiences with new and curious eyes, as opposed to my older jaded ones. They made observations and noticed things that I either took for granted or simply never acknowledged. For the first ten years of each of my children's lives, I kept individual journals for them in which I accumulated all their questions and answers, vowing to share each one's journal with them on their wedding day. This was a gift I would have loved to receive from my own mother.

After my grandmother died, and as the only daughter of two hard-working immigrants in the 1950s and 1960s, I was often left to my own devices, in the sense that I was often left home alone to entertain myself. My mother did not allow me to watch television, advising me that it was bubble gum for my mind; however, she was a big believer in books and journals, thus setting my platform as a writer. Because I was alone much of the time, I was forced to pose many questions to my journal, but many of my questions remained unanswered. Therefore, when I had children of my own, I encouraged them to ask questions out loud, both at school and at home. I often reminded them that there is no such thing as a stupid question. Admittedly, as a result I sometimes felt less than smart, because there were times when I was unable to answer their brilliant questions without the help of my support system at the time—the World Book Encyclopedia.

One of the best questions posed by my son, Josh, was, "Daddy, why doesn't the ceiling fall?" My husband, a scientist, was able to provide a decent answer, as I sat in amazement of my son's question and of how sometimes the simplest of inquiries require the most complex answers. When posing the more personal questions about our lives, sometimes it can take years to come up with the answers.

One of my favorite poets, Rainer Maria Rilke, has this to say of the beginner's mind:

> Be patient to all that is unsolved in your heart and try to cherish the questions themselves like locked rooms and like books that are written in a foreign tongue. Do

> not be focused on the answers, which sometimes cannot be given because you would not be able to live them. The point is, to live everything. Love the questions now. Perhaps you will then gradually without noticing it, live along some distant day into the answer (Rilke, 2000, p. 10).

Patience is important to remember when you are engaged in writing about your emotions and experiences. It is also a good idea to view your experiences with both narrow and wide-angled lenses. Viewing your life with a wide-angle lens allows you to see the big picture of your life in a universal context and see the patterns. Viewing with a narrow angle lens allows you to view the specific details of your own life and your own particular patterns. Doing so will bring a renewed perspective to your experiences—a new viewpoint, a sense of inquisitiveness and curiosity—which will give your writing more poignancy and depth.

The art of writing for change is about setting out on a journey. Imagine yourself packing to visit a new land—one you've never visited before or one you have not visited in a long time. Be alert and mindful of the details of your landscape. Document them in your journal or on your computer. Don't worry about the direction of your musings; for the moment, simply accumulate them. You can decide later whether your writing will be for you alone, for prosperity, or for public sharing.

Writing Prompt i:1 – Observing with Fresh Eyes

Go for a walk with your journal and pen and stop at a convenient place to write about an observation that captures you. Write about it using a beginner's mind, as if you are visiting our planet and viewing it for the first time.

Sufi poet Jelaluddin Rumi spoke about the phenomenon of the "Open Secret." The idea is that we all hold a secret—not necessarily a large secret, but a secret nevertheless. Whether our secret is a subtle one or a larger one, we know that we are not being entirely transparent. For example, when meeting you for the first time someone may ask the pat question, "How are you?" You might answer, "Fine," but you know in your heart of hearts that things are really not fine. Perhaps a parent just died or your dog is in the hospital; perhaps you just lost your job, your spouse is cheating on you, or your garden hasn't been tended in weeks. Perhaps you have a great deal on your plate and you're really not fine, but you use a certain discernment and choose not to share your problems at that time. This is perfectly okay. We all play the same game in covering up what we are not ready to share; that's why Rumi calls this sort of choice the "Open Secret."

While it is fine not to share your secret with whomever you don't care to share, sometimes it can be healing to share your secret by writing about it in your journal—your special confidant. Writing can unleash the secret inside of you as a way to tap into your shadow. The *shadow* is a term introduced by depth psychologist C. G. Jung as it pertains to the unconscious or less-liked part of us. He said that even though we might not want to acknowledge our shadow, if we confront it in an honest manner, it can prove to be pure gold for us. This will be discussed in greater detail in step 2, "Cultivating Self-Awareness."

As you write about your secret, continue to use a beginner's mind. Do it slowly. Be patient with yourself; you will see the results.

Writing and Bliss

Bliss may be defined as a natural direction to take to maximize your sense of joy and sense of fulfillment and performance. It is a more powerful word than *happiness*. Sometimes people equate bliss with being in a state of euphoria, but in reality it is about learning what brings you joy, which is often connected to what you were meant to do with your life—your calling. Mythologist and writer Joseph Campbell coined the phrase, "Follow your bliss," which is another way of saying to follow your heart or to listen to your authentic inner voice, as further discussed in step 3, "Speaking Your Truth."

To find bliss, we get rid of habits, ways, situations and relationships that no longer serve us in a good way by replacing with ones that do. Finding your bliss is about bringing into your life all those things that bring out your potential and help you live your life to its fullest. Once you open your eyes and are aware of your bliss, opportunities begin to come your way. For years I've known that my bliss revolves around writing. I knew that because whenever people ask me when I feel best, I respond by saying, "When I'm writing." This can be true whether I'm writing poems, blogs, essays, or books. I also know that I am blissful when studying, which is one reason why I returned to school for two advanced degrees during my middle age.

Another aspect of following your bliss concerns young adults when they are contemplating a career path. Most of us have an innate desire to please our parents. Sometimes this means following the desires and expectations of others while pushing aside our own dreams or the messages of our inner voice or heart. While this behavior might be subconscious, many young people might consider pursuing the career paths of one of their parents or what they think their parents would like for them to pursue. They may continue down that path until they come to the realization that another path would bring greater joy.

My story is an illustration: My grandmother always wanted to be a doctor, but her dreams were shattered as a result of wartime. My mother was a medical receptionist. Thus, I began my journey as a registered nurse and nursing administrator, and while I enjoyed working in the hospital with patients, I came to realize that what really made my heart purr was writing. Sometimes life flows in a way that dreams easily become realized, whereas at other times, pursuing them is a more conscious decision. For me, it was the former, because the timing was perfect as I had to resign as a hospital administrator and submit to bed rest when I approached my third month of my first pregnancy. This confinement lead me to do a great deal of writing, thus returning me to the bliss of my childhood. I ended up extending that bliss by availing myself of my medical background to become a medical journalist, reporting on the latest medical research and findings.

As my experience shows, following your bliss usually entails connecting to your life theme. This subject will be discussed in greater detail in step 4, "Examining Your Life." Following your bliss is also a key component to achieving happiness. Bernie Siegel in his book, *Love, Medicine, and Miracles* (1986) says that if people manage their anger and despair, they typically do not get sick. He believes that those who are happy, in general, do not get sick. "One's attitude toward oneself is the single most important factor in healing and staying well. Those who are at peace with themselves and their immediate surroundings have far fewer serious illnesses than those who are not" (p. 76).

Happiness is a function of our genetics, personality, and life experiences. Further, there are many factors that make us happy, but the key ones include having meaning, hope, and purpose in your life. Writing can help identify what fulfills these factors for you, whether you're writing about a recent event or one that happened a while ago.

Writing Prompt i:2 – Imagining Dreams Fulfilled

Find a quiet and private writing place. Write about what you imagined your life would look like when you were just beginning it. Imagine that all has gone extremely well in your life and that all of your dreams have come true. Refrain from simply doing a recap of your accomplishments. Write instead about how you arrived at the point of fulfilling all your goals in the life of your dreams and what you were feeling along the way. Write from your heart.

Humanistic psychologist Abraham Maslow believed that mental health professionals place too much emphasis on disease, so he devised a pyramid called the *Hierarchy of Needs*. On the bottom of the pyramid he placed our basic human needs and at the very top of the pyramid, what he called "self-actualization," or the point where we have found our true meaning and purpose in life and, ultimately, our bliss. For the most part, we all strive toward self-actualization, which essentially leads to a deep sense of satisfaction and bliss. Maslow identified peak experiences or life-changing circumstances as powerful moments accompanied by a sense of euphoria or pleasure or a deep sense of harmony that could lead to the individual's self-actualization and subsequent movement in the direction of bliss. He also believed that those who are highly evolved, such as mystics, are those who have experienced these peak moments that could result in a state of bliss.

Figuring out what your bliss is can occur through the writing process, because when you write you set out on a journey of self-discovery, and during this journey you learn about all those things that you were meant to do to bring you joy. By writing about what makes you happy or sad or what are your triggers, etc., you can be guided to your bliss. There is always something to learn from our lived experiences. An essential part of acknowledging or honoring those experiences is to document them in our journals. Writing can also serve as a baseline for us to look back at in the future. That's why it is important to date your writing, so that you can return to it at a later time and compare your feelings then and now, while at the same time observing the evolution of your musings. Bathing in our joy brings feelings of bliss, and it can also permeate to those with whom you come into contact, offering a positive shift in perspective.

Finding bliss through writing involves a sacrifice. You need to be alert and mindful of all the things, situations, and people that make you happy. These are markers or life-enhancing moments that you can keep track of in your journal. By writing down your feelings, you are led to self-discovery and more easily able to ascertain what brings you joy and bliss.

Elizabeth Lesser (1999) talks about how in her classes she has students create what she calls an "autobiography of joy," which encourages them to remember and document the happy moments in their lives. She found this to be a positive exercise in that each anecdote or story can become like a shiny fishing lure that can be saved and used during darker times when we might need a reminder of the way toward the light. In a sense, this process is similar to keeping a gratitude journal in which you daily record what you are thankful for. Gratitude journals will be discussed in greater detail in step 1 and again in step 5, "Finding Your Form."

Lesser also claims that by creating grief stories we can see the ebbs and flows of our lives and identify the triggers and patterns that move us from one point to the next. This process can help us better understand ourselves and gain wisdom from the knowledge.

Ralph Keyes (1995) writes about the connection between writing and the state of euphoria, which to my mind is akin to the state of bliss. He suggests that when you take a risk with your writing, the reward is often a sense of euphoria or bliss or exhilaration. The state of bliss can be identified as a trance-like state that Mihaly Csikszentmihalyi (2008) describes as the feeling of "flow," which will be discussed in step 4. The sense of flow has been shown to be connected to the release of a flood of endorphins that can lead to an intense state of concentration during writing. I have often experienced this state when working on long book projects. When my writing is going well, it seems as if I am in a trance. In fact, sometimes I have no idea where the time goes, but I look up and realize that all I've done all day is sit and write at my computer. One symptom of being in the flow is losing track of time.

Timothy Wilson (2011) believes that while writing doesn't solve every problem, it can definitely help people cope. He says that the writing process encourages people to recreate or reconstruct the story of what has been bothering them, and that in doing so they are able to discover new meaning or explanations for it. Ultimately, this process leads to a sense of calm, happiness, and bliss.

Writing Prompt i:3 – Conjuring Bliss

Find a quiet and safe place to write. Write about a time or times when you felt joy, elation, and wonder. Then write about a time when you truly felt light-hearted and your life was filled with light.

Writing as Therapy

Today, many therapists use writing to augment talk therapy. In fact, sometimes writing is a vital part of many psychological interventions. Usually, writing is a solitary activity that can be done before or after a therapy session. Sometimes practitioners ask their clients to share their writings as a springboard for beginning the discussion.

Writing is also one way you can communicate with yourself. It provides a container for your feelings and emotions. Sometimes such writing might feel good in the beginning, but if you write about painful subjects, the process can become too painful for you. This would probably a good time to take a break and do something else. In other words, write until it hurts, then stop. Chances are that you will have already achieved the therapeutic results of writing for healing.

While a lot of therapeutic writing often falls into the genres of nonfiction or poetry, there are those who choose fiction as a therapeutic form. Margaret Atwood's novel *Cat's Eye* has been called a fictional autobiography and is one example of a fictional exploration of a traumatic experience in that the protagonist tries to maintain a sense of control over her identity and memory. Christa Schönfelder (2013) in her analysis of this book she shares that many trauma psychologists encourage this sort of self-narration as a way for people to integrate their trauma into the story of their lives and come to terms with their past. She uses Atwood's narrative as an example of how the act of writing can work as self-therapy for those who are recovering from either a recent or a distant trauma.

One of the most amazing and magical aspects of writing for healing is that, once you make the decision to put your pen to the page, you have no idea what will emerge from your subconscious mind. For example, a friend of mine had gone into counseling as a result of childhood abuse, and the therapist gave her some writing prompts to get her creative juices flowing. The narrative writing helped her revisit her childhood trauma, which had resulted in post-traumatic stress disorder (PTSD). The writing process helped to dissipate some of her overwhelming emotions about the trauma by providing a safe container for them. Her therapist also suggested writing a dialogue between herself and her perpetrator, and the writing that emerged revealed essential information that resulted in transforming her outlook on her life. For example, she realized that much of the dialogue that emerged was similar to the dialogue she had in her adult relationships. She acknowledged that she frequently repeated the patterns of her childhood. Her therapist tried to help her break those patterns and move forward with her life as a way to become whole and have a sense of well-being. In addition to have stimulated her imagination, this exercise helped her to identify different points of view about her past,

Surely, you have met people who express themselves with more ease verbally and others who find writing easier. Those who opt out of writing may not be big readers, or they may have had a bad experience in school where they were told they were poor writers. When doing therapeutic writing, it is important to remember that grammar and syntax do not matter. Writing about feelings is simply a way to document or chronicle life issues or experiences. In a sense, you are having a dialogue with yourself. Writing down your feelings can be liberating because you are not sitting face to face with someone, sharing deep and intimate secrets and living with the fear of being judged. Indeed, you don't have to share your writing with anyone at all, if you don't want to.

Sometimes people have expressed to me that they are afraid of what their subconscious minds might bring forth during the writing process. But if you think of such writing as a self-discovery exercise rather than a painful rehashing, then the benefits can be enormous. Writing that taps into the subconscious mind is writing that originates in your body and has been coined by Rosemarie Anderson (2011) as *embodied writing*. This type of writing will be discussed in more detail in step 3.

In my writing workshops, when I help participants tap into their subconscious minds they are often amazed and fascinated at what emerges. They may begin writing about one subject and then take off on a tangent and write about something completely different, which often leads to a deeper sense of self-discovery. In the end, they find themselves writing about what it seems they were meant to write about, rather than what they *thought* they should write about. In doing so, they learn that they have a container for their true feelings, which can be very empowering.

One thing I have noticed—and a word of caution I'd like to share—is that too much of therapeutic writing can sometimes lead to what is frequently been called "navel-gazing" or ruminating. When that happens, you can become stuck in the drama of your past without examining ways of healing and moving forward through the pain and trauma. The best way to avoid navel-gazing is to merge or weave your story with a universal truth or sentiment. For example, if you are depressed about your youngest child leaving for college, think about the havoc happening in war-torn countries and how many children there will never have the chance to step foot into college. This puts your life in a larger context.

Ever since my childhood when my mother gave me my first Kahlil Gibran journal to help me cope with the loss of my grandmother, I have often used writing as a way of healing. Serving as my best friend and confident, my journal held all my deepest and most heartfelt secrets and contained all the sentiments and feelings that were most important to me. What I loved most about journaling is that I had a friend—a friend who was not judgmental or opinionated, a friend who *listened*.

Sometimes all we want is someone to listen to us. My journal was wonderful because it did not talk back to me. Writing was my way of being heard, given that my parents held the old-fashioned tenet that children should be "seen and not heard."

My colleagues and I would not be the first writers who have reported that we write to dissipate pain. Fiction writer D. H. Lawrence use to sit at his mother's bedside while she was dying and write poems about her. He also began an early draft of *Sons and Lovers*, his novel that explored their complicated, loving, painful, and close relationship. Marcel Proust wrote *Remembrance of Things Past* while sick in bed with asthma. Flannery O'Connor wrote some of her best stories during her bout with lupus, from which she ultimately died.

Writers May Sarton and Anaïs Nin wrote in their diaries to pull them through their difficult times. Nin's writings deeply resonated with me, and she played an important role in inspiring my own writing. Also, we both began journaling at the age of eleven—I in response to my grandmother's suicide, Nin as a letter to her father after he had left the family for a younger woman. We both began writing as a result of losses in our lives. As I did, Nin transformed her traumatic experiences into art. Her journal entries amounted to more than thirty-five thousand pages, which eventually were excerpted and put into seven published books. In her own book, *Recovering* (1980), May Sarton chronicles her battles with depression and cancer.

Journaling is a cathartic and safe way to spill out your feelings. It is important to note that, in journaling, you are not necessarily chronicling the events of your day; rather, you are documenting and getting in touch with your feelings and thoughts as you write. My attitude is to "direct your rage to the page." I have a writing colleague who says, "If it hurts, write harder," and for years those words were posted above my computer until they simply became a part of my literary life.

In his book, *Writing to Heal* (2004), James Pennebaker says that the art of writing has the ability to break down some of the barriers between you and others, and that sometimes writing to other people is an easier way to communicate rather than looking at them in the eyes. Pennebaker believes that a certain type of writing erupts when we are faced with loss, death, abuse, depression, and trauma. He does have one rule, however, that he calls "the flip-out rule," which proclaims that if you get too upset when writing, then it's probably best to stop and take a break.

Basically, therapeutic writing can help you understand yourself better and deal with various obstacles in your life that could include depression, anxiety, addiction, loss of loved ones, diseases, and life transitions. As writer Graham Greene deftly said, "Writing is a form of therapy; sometimes I wonder how all those who do not write, compose, or paint can manage to escape the madness, melancholia, the panic fear which is inherent in a human condition" (1980, p. 10).

Writing Prompt i:4 – Reflecting on Joy and Sorrow

There is something to learn when you merge the strong emotions of your joys and sorrows. Write about what brings you joy or what makes your heart sing. Now write about what makes you sad or angry or brings tears to your eyes. Now go back and write about the origin of these feelings and why you might feel this way.

Your writing response to this prompt can provide useful information and be a good guideline for you when you are trying to make a decision about something.

Writing for Healing

We are all storytellers. Stories help us understand and make sense of our lived experiences, the lessons we've learned, and our dreams for the future. The stories of difficult life situations or experiences are often complicated, but they are stories that must be told. In fact, there is nothing much more important than acknowledging and writing our own personal narratives as a way to examine our lives, in terms of what happened, what it was like, and where we are now. Studies have shown that such writing allow us to change our perspective, which in the end leads to more self-awareness through deeper insights and thus to recovery. Writing for healing is very useful when recovering from trauma such as PTSD and certain illnesses. It is also helpful when in recovery from addictions. Sometime memories from our past experiences become blurred, and writing can help us organize our thoughts.

In his book *On Writing* (2000), Stephen King says, "Writing isn't about making money, getting famous, getting dates, getting laid, or making friends. In the end, it's about enriching lives of those who will read your work, and enriching your own life, as well. It's about getting up, getting well, and getting over."

Arthur Frank (1995) talks about how writing can help physically and psychologically wounded individuals find their voice, basically because stories help us heal. His premise is that the wounded healer and the wounded storyteller are one and the same, but different aspects of the same figure. In other words, those who are wounded are wounded, not just in body and mind, but also in voice. Writing can help reclaim the voice after it has been taken away or silenced by a difficult circumstance or trauma. Finding one's voice as a way to healing can lead to huge leaps in transformation.

Some people find it useful to write as they move through a chaotic or difficult time; but, more often than not, a certain distance from the event offers a better perspective needed for healing and transformation. It took me more than forty-five years to write about the trauma of finding my grandmother dead from suicide. The distance provided the perspective I needed to understand why she chose to depart from this life in such a way.

If you write about something you are presently going through, you will more than likely be writing an account of the experience and chronicling the facts, whereas if you allow some distance from the experience before you write about it, you will have gained perspective and will more easily be able to incorporate reflections. The distance also allows you to have some control over the experience, rather than having the experience control you.

James Pennebaker was one of the earliest pioneers to have researched the therapeutic power of writing. He did a number of studies, but the most quoted one is that in which he asked some of his college students to write for fifteen minutes a day about an important issue in their lives. He found that, after doing this exercise, the students who wrote about personal issues had fewer illnesses and visits to the student health center. This is just one of many examples of studies that show the healing benefits of writing.

Other studies of Pennebaker's found that when writing expressively about upsetting experiences, people don't always initially write in a coherent way; but as they deepen the writing process, their story becomes more cohesive and understandable. In fact, what happens is that the narrative begins to hold together as a story that actually makes sense.

Since an early age, I have been using writing as a form of healing. After my grandmother committed suicide, my mother gave me my first journal saying, "This journal will help you move through the chaos of the moment and move forward into healing." I have carried that message with me for more than five decades. At various stages in my life, my journal writing has also been complemented by writing letters, poetry, and short stories.

Learning to open up about issues and traumatic experiences, even when you are writing only for yourself, does not happen overnight; but it is all part of the healing process. Author Louise DeSalvo, an advocate of writing for healing, began crafting her own memoirs, *Vertigo* (2002) and *Breathless* (1998), as a way of coming to terms with her own pain. Her book *Writing as a Way of Healing* (2000) embraces all the basic concepts about using a passion for writing to help cope with life. In a section called, "Why Write?" she concludes that writing is cheap, writing doesn't need to take much time, writing is self-initiated; writing is flexible, writing is private or you can share it, writing is portable, writing can be done whether we're well or ill, and writing to heal requires no innate talent.

Whether you are affected by change, loss, or pain, finding the time and courage to write can support the healing process. Some people prefer to write nonfiction, while others may choose the modalities of fiction or poetry to help them express their thoughts and feelings. My advice is to choose the genre most compatible with your story, your sensibility, and your personality. In the end, this is what healing is all about. See step 5 for more on experimenting with other genres.

A few years ago, a writer friend forwarded me an article from the *New York Times Magazine* (March 23, 2012) called, "Why Talk Therapy is on the Wane and Writing Workshops Are on the Rise," by Steve Almond. Coincidentally, I met Steve at a writer's conference a number of years ago, where he served on a writing panel. I remember his compelling story and that, after the panel when everyone approached the other panelists with questions, he stood at the side of the podium giving away copies of his newly released book—a beautifully generous gesture by an emerging writer.

As the son of two therapists, Steve clearly understood his proposed premise. In his article, he defends writing as a cure, particularly in this boom of memoir and biography and the idea. He says, and I agree, that writers and artists should be forged by the fires they experience in their real lives. Steve Almond taught a workshop for baby boomers in their fifties and sixties and advised that it did not really matter whether they become published writers or not. The important thing was that they found a way to face some tough truths within themselves and begin to make sense of them.

Speaking your emotional truth is something you can do quite easily when writing poetry. Chances are that those poets whom you enjoy reading are those who are in touch with their emotional and authentic truths. Poetry is the voice of the soul, and writing and reading poetry can help us tap into emotions and feelings of which we might not have been aware. Because every word counts in a poem, poetry quickly delivers the message meant to be delivered. See step 6, "Unleashing with Poetry," to learn how to find the dormant poet inside you.

Whatever genre you decide to write in, whether or not to try to publish your work is obviously up to you. Sometimes the things we choose to write are best kept locked inside our private journals; and other times, we might feel compelled to share our stories sand experiences with others. See step 8, "Sharing Your Writing," on guidelines and suggestions for how to go about making your work public.

Writing for Transformation

Transformation may be defined as a dramatic change in an individual's physical or psychological well-being. Basically, the path of personal transformation is a process of becoming aware of, facing, and becoming responsible for one's thoughts and feelings. This process can lead to self-realization, which can occur over a long or a short period of time, but most often it is initiated by a pivotal event that can be easily identified. If you choose to write about the event, you can be transformed during the process, and that is when important revelations can be made. When thinking of writing in this way, we can say that writing can be considered a spiritual practice. In doing so, you are freeing yourself from your story or the story that might have trapped you.

In general, spirituality may be seen as the search for truth in one's life in the interest of being happy. Writing as a spiritual practice can connect you to what seems most right for you both personally and professionally. It can help you determine your mission and reason for being, which will aid you immeasurably with the goal of how you could be happiest. Writing can help you tap into some of the answers to your deepest questions and move forward in a positive and productive direction. As a result, this process leads to a sense of well-being, a sense of balance, and feelings of elation that could lead to a personal transformation.

When considering writing as a transformative and spiritual exercise, it is important to know that, to receive the best benefits, it must be developed and practiced on a regular basis. Also, the deeper you go into your thoughts, the more transformative the exercise will be. Like everything else, you get out of it what you put into it. Comparing your current work with previous writings helps you gain an additional perspective.

Writing provides a great way to work through your feelings. It also can help you figure something out about a lived experience. The art of writing helps your thoughts become more concrete, putting them in a form that shows you what your inner or authentic self is trying to articulate. Writing encourages you to reflect on your feelings, thus helping to create a deeper harmony and peace of mind.

You might begin with chronicling about one event and somehow the trajectory of the writing ends up somewhere else. For example, perhaps you begin to write about the time your sister fell off her bicycle and got a concussion and ended up in the hospital for a long period of time; and then, before you know it, you are writing about a family secret that you hadn't thought about in years. Maybe that secret is about a parent or loved one who battled addictions, and you were told not to tell anyone; or maybe it was about an abusive relationship. If you are spiritually inclined, sometimes during the writing process you may find that you attain a form of redemption.

The actual pivotal or life-changing experience you write about may be one that confirms your identity or who you have become in the years following the experience. Maslow talks about peak experiences as valuable life-changing revelations. He claims that many writers "describe these experiences not only as valuable intrinsically, but also as *so* valuable that they make life worthwhile by their occasional occurrence" (2011, p. 67).

When I look back at my own life experiences and reflect on which ones have truly transformed me, challenged me, or made me feel more aware or more alive, I must say that they were pivotal events involving the death of loved ones, the forming or evolution of relationships, becoming a parent, sexual encounters, and conversations with others. These have all been subjects of exploration in my journal writing that has led to some form of change.

When writing for change, it is important that you are alert for the messages of the universe and also for messages or clues of synchronicity or groupings of coincidences that seem to pile up upon one another. These can be diverse things such as experiences, elements, or sightings that might bring light or inquiry to a situation.

Writing Prompt i:5 – On Meaningful Coincidences

When we are mindful, we are more likely to notice synchronicities or meaningful coincidences in our lives. Think of a time when you felt a sense of synchronicity. How did the experience unfold for you, and what was your understanding of all the events that occurred?

Writing Prompt i:6 – On Decisions and Consequences

Think of a time when you made a decision about which you were unsure of the consequences, but they turned out better than you could have anticipated. Write about the circumstances of the decision. Feel into the decision. How did your body, mind, and spirit feel at the time?

How to Use This Book

Writing for Bliss will inspire and teach you to learn more about yourself, tap into your emotional truth, find your authentic voice, and write about your own losses, challenges, and joys. In doing so, you will be directed to a life characterized by joy, fulfillment, and purpose. By using these simple prompts and other writing techniques and tools that I suggest throughout the book, you will empower yourself; and you will be led to remember that it is when we connect with who we truly are that happiness ensues.

This book shares my psychospiritual and creative journey as a way to show and guide you on your own journey. I write not only as a teacher, but as a fellow traveler interested in the transformation through the writing process. The important thing is to keep an open mind and an open heart.

This book is geared toward the emerging writer, the seasoned writer, and those in academia. I suggest that readers read through the book first and then return to do the writing prompts scattered throughout. During both passes, I recommend always having a journal and pen beside you, keeping in mind that we never know when inspiration may come and when we will be overwhelmed with inspiring ideas.

The most important thing to remember during self-discovery through writing is to enjoy the journey, which is rather like the spiraling journey of a labyrinth. A labyrinth is a wonderful metaphor for life, given that, in it, we follow the path inward and then return back out, using a circular repeating pattern. Inside the labyrinth, as in life, there are times when we might feel lost and other times when our path flows more easily. We feel free. We feel blissful. We feel as if we are headed toward enlightenment—which, according to Bernie Siegel (2013), means that you understand the power of love. When you understand the power of love, you open your heart to an enormous amount of compassion and wisdom.

Just as life itself, the art of writing as I teach it here is also like walking a labyrinth. As you follow the directions in this book, you might be on the path to step 7, when suddenly you are diverted or side-tracked into another writing project. And that's okay, because creativity is not a linear process. It is a process that beats to its own drum and is done in its own time. It can be thought of as always cyclical and meandering.

For example, when doing stream-of-consciousness writing or automatic writing (discussed in step 5), you will have no idea what will be released on the page. You will simply be going with the flow. Sometimes you might be amazed at how well your words flow, while at other times you might feel frustration and a sense of feeling "stuck." This stuck feeling means that it is time to take a break—always keeping in mind, though, that you will return to your writing, because in the end it is the writing path that can help you attain a sense of bliss and wholeness. As the old adage says, "Patience is indeed a virtue."

Step One
Preparing to Write

The job of a writer is not to judge, but to seek to understand.
—Ernest Hemingway

One rule about writing is that if you want to be a writer, you need to be a reader. If you want to write in a particular genre, such as nonfiction, it is a good idea to read more in that genre. If you want to write poetry, then crack open some poetry books. Reading helps you to examine how others write, while helping you to explore your own creative self. Reading also helps to fill up your tank with ideas, stories, images, and words that fuel your own creative writing and help to inspire you.

In many ways, I believe that we are our childhoods and whatever books we enjoyed or were exposed to as children will be what inspires us as we move forward through life. I have always been drawn to biographies. I think my mother read a lot of them, and the biography section was the first place I dashed to when she took me on my weekly visits to the library. As a child, I loved reading stories about real people doing and feeling real things. The fantasy world never fascinated me and still doesn't, but this does not mean that I don't admire those who can bring that world to us. While I occasionally read fiction (especially if written by a colleague), biographies and memoirs continue to be my genre of choice.

When you read only like a reader, then you pay more attention to what is being said, but when you read like a writer, then you should be more attentive to the way the author is expressing him- or herself. I think that the best writers read as both readers and writers, striking a balance between the two.

When learning how to read like a writer, it is a good idea to read the works of those writers whom you admire and want to emulate. Sometimes the mere act of reading their works serves as a form of osmosis to their style. When you read like a writer, you are observing how the author pulls you into his or her story and holds your interest. While reading, consider the authors' writing techniques. Examine the style and sentence structure. If it is their voices that you like, think about what is compelling about them. Did they use first or third person? Was their voice playful, authoritative, inquisitive, or telling? Do you like how the writers share visuals or images? Can you visualize what they are saying? Do you like the settings they created? Another helpful tip while reading is to highlight your favorite passages for future reference. This practice will inspire you and give you a style to emulate.

If you are studying to be a writer, I suggest reading your favorite books at least twice. The first time, read for information and content, and then reread for style or to learn how the writer said what he or she said.

In my writing workshops, when students are working on an essay or a full-length book I suggest that they choose a writer they want to emulate and read that book over and over again. When I was working on my first memoir, *Regina's Closet: Finding My Grandmother's Secret Journal,* I was inspired by Tobias Wolff's classic memoir, *This Boy's Life* (2000). I just loved Wolff's voice in that book. In a sense, he became my writing mentor, and I was so delighted to have once had the chance to sit next to him on a plane across the country. Our conversation changed my life and inspired my writing even more. Basically, it was hearing about his process and his interest in my own work that inspired me.

Many people ask me whether I think the ability to write is innate or if it can be taught. I think that some people are born with the talent and others have to work harder at it. While taking writing classes and reading numerous "how to" books on writing can help, the best way to learn how to write is by example—by reading the books of writers you enjoy. Becoming a writer and a better writer is like anything else: it involves practice, which always involves failures and successes.

Being a published writer presents even more challenges, because rejection is a huge part of the profession. Many writers, myself included, have made comments about decorating our walls with rejection letters. It is just a part of the game and something you get used to. You need just to believe in yourself and continue to send your work out. More on publishing will be discussed in step 7.

Becoming a Seeker

Spiritual seekers are those who follow the path of self-discovery. One way to navigate self-discovery is through the process of writing. Being a seeker might be a lifelong path or one sought as a result of a life-changing event, such as trauma. I have been a seeker my entire life, and when I stop to think about it, it was probably initiated during my childhood when my voice was silenced and I had to seek peace and answers from within, from my readings and from the jottings in my journal. My seeking might also be traced to my fascination as a young girl with reading biographies and magazines that featured true stories about real people. Real-life stories provide a deep connection to the kinds of experiences that offer answers for seekers posing questions. We want to learn how to navigate our paths and often do so by reading and hearing about how others have found their own way. Those lessons are consciously or subconsciously incorporated into our own lives.

Some years ago, I facilitated a workshop called "Writing with Lust" at The Open Center in New York City. Regardless of the specific reasons why people enrolled in the workshop, there was one common thread—each person in the room said they were a seeker. They had questions for which they sought answers. They were on a journey of self-discovery, and writing is a great way to take that journey.

Spiritual seekers are not necessarily religious. Most often, they have little interest in organized religious practice. In fact, studies have shown that 33 percent of Americans are spiritual and not religious in the more traditional sense of organized religion.

Christina Grof, a psychotherapist and co-creator of Holotrophic Breathwork (see step 2), was often called a spiritual seeker, pioneer, teacher, and humanitarian. Like many spiritual seekers, Grof came from a dysfunctional family in which she had been abused by her stepfather. She also had medical issues such as lupus, chronic back pain, and a painful autoimmune disease that severely interfered with her everyday life. Trauma often leads people to become seekers as a way to come to an understanding about themselves and the world in which they live. During the process of helping themselves, they are often compelled to share their findings, thus helping others. Christina's journey led her and her husband, Stan Grof, to create Holotrophic Breathwork in addition to the Spiritual Emergence Network, two powerful modalities to encourage transformation.

Many writers, especially poets, are seekers of transformation. While a poet might write a poem to look for answers to a question or to tap into a deeper sense of knowing, sometimes the poet's specific intention is unclear at the outset. However, during the process of writing the poet might find him- or herself transformed. In fact, poems often contain underlying meanings or messages that can move or change us and/or offer hope to our situation. I wrote one of my first poems as an adult just after an elderly gentleman sitting on a bench near my parking spot watched me parallel park. It was one of those moments about which I was compelled to write, which is one good reason always to have writing material available. What compelled me to reflect on in my poem was how often men mock female drivers. The expression on the old man's face told me that he was sure I would smash my car into the car parked in the space behind—which of course I did not do. The poem ends with my saying that I'm a great parallel parker. When I started to write the poem, I had no idea where I was going with it, but by the time I reached the end I knew exactly why I was writing it, and that was to crush men's stereotypes about women's driving skills.

In *Letters to a Young Poet,* Rilke summarizes the essence and importance of being a seeker as it pertains to writing poetry:

> Be patient toward all that is unsolved in your heart and to try to love the questions themselves, like locked rooms and like books that are written in a very foreign tongue. Do not now seek the answers, which cannot be given you because you would not be able to live them. And the point is, to live everything. Live the questions now. Perhaps you will then gradually, without noticing it, live along some distant day into the answer (p. 35).

To some degree, we are all seekers, and if we care to share our learnings with others, then we also offer them the opportunity to learn from our experiences while examining their own.

In preparing to write, consider having an open mind to new experiences and thoughts and ways of doing and being. Opening your mind means that you examine who you are, where you have come from, and what your belief systems are. Opening your mind also means pushing yourself to go places and do things that you might not ordinarily do. It is about letting go of fear. As Eleanor Roosevelt suggested, "Do one thing every day that scares you." This means facing your fears head on. Sometimes writing your deepest feelings can be scary, but the results are often worth the risk. No risk, no reward. Writing from your deep, authentic self leads to healing, growth, and transformation.

Rituals for Writing

When writers talk about their writing process, they often refer to details about where they write, the time of day they write, what they wear when they write, the music they listen to, their inspiration, their attitude, the tools of the trade, and how they go about revision. All such factors are ritualistic elements that can enhance the writing experience.

Creating a Sacred Space

Writers need privacy and solitude to tap into their creative selves. Writing is not easy, but it can be even more difficult if is done in an uninspiring environment or surrounded by unwanted people and noise. Before you begin your writing practice, find a time and place when you can be by yourself uninterrupted for at least half an hour, keeping in mind that where you write can influence your writing. Virginia Woolf stated the importance of having "a room of one's own" in her book by that title. She was referring to a figurative room, which can be a deeper concept than what might be an actual physical space. She believed that women (and all writers) should have a place where they can go to write and feel safe and comfortable—a place that offers a blanket of support, while also being inspiring.

Your writing area can be a room in your home or even a *part* of a room there; it can also be in a public place where you feel comfortable. If you choose to make it a sacred space in your home, you may want to consider including special items that inspire you and make you smile. Perhaps they are artifacts from memorable travels or family heirlooms that jog your memory about certain times in your life.

My writing space has candles, essential oils, prayer beads, and photos of my family. I am also surrounded by my collection of typewriters, as a reminder that my first book written in the 1980s, *Getting Pregnant and Staying Pregnant: Overcoming Infertility and Managing your High-Risk Pregnancy*, was written on a Smith Corona. In the corner of my desk sits a Buddha holding a stone that says "serenity." Seeing his face grounds me. Years ago, I read that some major corporations placed coffee-scented candles in their offices as a way to increase productivity. So now I have one of those burning on my desk. I find that it alerts my senses and keeps me motivated, perhaps in the same way as drinking a cup of coffee would. Behind my desk is a bookcase holding all my favorite reference books, and nearby is my altar and a chair for my daily meditation practice. My room also has a reading chair and an ottoman facing my garden.

There have been times when I was not blessed with such a special sacred place, because either I was traveling or my living quarters weren't amenable to one. Nevertheless, I was able to create a special space wherever I was. Here's a good way to do it:

- Make yourself comfortable.
- Close your eyes, uncross your legs, and take some deep breaths. Breathe in through your nose and out through your mouth. Listen to your breath and concentrate on it.
- Imagine visiting a room of great importance in your life. If you don't have one or want to create an imaginary one, that's okay.
- Use your third eye (the space between your eyes) as a movie camera, and try to visualize the room. Capture all its details. When you are ready, open your eyes.
- Now pick up your pen and write about the space, describing it in great detail. Stay in the moment and

write without lifting your pen off the page. What do you see in your space? What are you feeling in your body when you are in your space? What is your heart feeling while in your space?

Campbell (1988) also spoke about the importance of having a sacred space as being necessary for everyone—a place without human or world contact, a place where you can simply be with yourself and be with who you are and who you might want to be. He viewed this place as a place of creative incubation. He said that, even though creativity might not happen right away when you are in this special space, just having it tends to ignite the muse in each of us.

Sometimes it is a good idea to vary your writing location. Working or writing in a different place brings an altered perspective to your creativity. When there was an abundance of chain bookstores, I spent a lot of time in their coffee shops. I did some of my best writing there—perhaps as a combined result of the ambient noise, the smell of coffee, and being surrounded by books. At home, sometimes classical or spiritual music helps me concentrate. However, listening to music with lyrics can be difficult while writing, although the lyrics of some musicians, such as Leonard Cohen or Bob Dylan, are very inspiring for some people.

During my teens, my grandfather introduced me to the fine art of people watching in Parisian cafes. We'd sit for hours observing people and talking about them. I am still inspired by the white noise of cafes. After my grandfather passed away, I continued the practice and then expanded to bookstore coffee shops. When not working on my projects, I would write in my journal about what I saw. I wrote about the people passing by, wondering what they were doing when not in the book store. I also sometimes documented conversations. It was a fun exercise that I sometimes suggest to my workshop participants. For another change of venue, on a nice day I like to write sitting in a park—another great place to people watch.

Grounding

Grounding is a useful tool that creates a solid foundation of support between you and your surroundings. It puts your mind, body, and spirit in the present moment. It is best done first thing in the morning or right before writing. You can also practice grounding during the course of your day while you are sitting, walking, or driving. It is a way to check in with yourself. Grounding serves as a container for your thoughts and creativity, but it is also a way to find relaxation during tough times. Grounding yourself is a way of bringing yourself literally back to earth.

Perhaps you've heard someone suggest that you ground yourself, but you are unsure what that means and how to do it. One of the easiest ways to ground yourself is to bring attention to your breath as it enters and leaves your body.

How to Ground Yourself

- Begin by placing your feet comfortably on the ground.
- Take three deep breaths, and with each breath release any negative energy.
- Put your attention on the soles of your feet, and imagine big roots from them planted going down about six or eight feet into the earth.
- Place your awareness in the base of your spine, sometimes called the first chakra, or "energy point," in the body.
- Imagine your spine going deep into the earth.
- Feel the magnetic pull of gravity coming from the earth's core.
- Breathe in for three counts. Hold your breath. Now exhale for four counts.

By the end of this exercise, you will probably feel much more connected to your physical self. You might then bring awareness to the sensations in your body, moving from your head down to your feet, exploring and inquiring as you move along. Just a few minutes of this practice may bring you home to your body and to the earth. This is what it means to ground yourself.

We receive powerful energy from the earth just as we do from the forms of energy we associate with the sky, and our body is a tool that brings these two energies together in a sacred union.

Grounding can be done while seated or moving about. Fortunately, bringing your conscious awareness into your body and the earth beneath your feet is as simple as it is to walk. Sometimes we need only remind ourselves to do it. I vividly recall what one of my meditation teachers taught while I was living in Montreal when my children were young. At the time, the provincial license plates read, *Je me souviens*, which means, "I remember." The teacher told us that whenever we saw that license plate we should be reminded to take some deep breaths and ground ourselves. Like New York, Montreal is a walking city, so I saw those license plates wherever I was and they were a constant reminder. For me, this worked very well.

The Buddhist monk Thich Nhat Hanh has a great little poem that he recites to ground himself whenever and wherever he is, whether it is while walking, in the kitchen, in the city, or in the garden. It goes like this:

> I have arrived, I am home,
> In the here and in the now.
> I am solid, I am free,
> In the ultimate I dwell.
>
> —Thich Nhat Hanh (2001, p. 39)

Feeling Gratitude

Gratitude is about feeling love and appreciation for the self and others. As poet Pablo Neruda says, "You can pick all the flowers, but you can't stop the spring." Many of us take our lives for granted and do not express gratitude often enough. In addition to keeping a gratitude journal, which will be discussed later, it is important to permeate each day with gratitude and marvel at the life we are living. This is one of the many reasons that Thanksgiving is one of my favorite holidays. More often than not, I think gratitude should be a built-in part of our everyday life and journey. Expressing it is like keeping a tuning fork alive and vibrating the joy throughout the universe.

Janice Kaplan (2015) says that, in addition to the feeling of gratitude being fun, looking for the positive in her lived experiences has alone changed her attitude toward life. She has realized that it has not so much been her experiences that have affected her happiness as it has been how she chose to frame them and thus how they affected her. "I could decide to feel annoyance and torment—or I could decide to feel joy. It still required some conscious effort, but gratitude was helping me to feel the joy" (p. 90).

One of the reasons to keep a gratitude journal is to document all that you have to be thankful for. You can keep the list for future reference when you are not having such a great day. Studies have shown that those who are more grateful and express it more readily are more likely to be happy. Writer Oliver Sacks (2015), who suffered from pancreatic cancer, said that having gratitude was responsible for keeping him alive. Even though he knew his life was coming to an end (he died in 2015), he was grateful for the opportunity to look back and to see his last days in the context of his entire life with a deep sense of connection. He said that, while he was afraid of dying, his predominant emotion at the end of his life was gratitude. Knowing that he was dying made him feel even more alive. He was able to do all the things he wanted to do before his transition—such as deepen his friendships, say good-bye to loved ones, travel, achieve new levels of insight, and write. For those at the end of life, writing can be very cathartic and healing. In addition, it is a memorable gift to leave behind for loved ones.

Writing prompt 1:1 – Expressing Gratitude for Gifts

Write a gratitude letter to someone in your life who has given you something special, taught you something special, or inspired you in some way. Explain what their gift has meant to you, how you felt when you received it, and how you feel now.

The Mind, Body, Spirit Connection and Writing

To maximize the quality of the writing you do, it is important to have a balanced body, mind, and spirit. But what does this mean? The body, mind, and spirit are forces of energy that work together and react to one another in either a positive or a negative way. Connecting the body, mind, and spirit is a way to keep the energy flowing in your body. When your energy flow is in balance, your state of being is altered, and your state of being affects your overall physical and psychological health.

With your body, mind, and spirit in balance, you also feel joy more easily. You are respectful of yourself and others, and you have a sense of life purpose. This balance or sense of harmony can also lead to feelings of euphoria or bliss. This message comes through in the below excerpt of Rumi's poem, "Chinese Art and Greek Art."

> Drumsound rise on the air,
> its throb, my heart.
>
> A voice inside the beat says,
> "I know you're tired,
> but come. This is the way.
>
> —Rumi, translation by
> Coleman Barks (1995, p. 122)

Most good writing begins with the body, because the way we experience and describe our experiences or feelings is with our senses—seeing, touching, tasting, smelling, and hearing. Writing begets writing, and the more you write, the more you get in touch with your senses. A good way to get into the flow of your body is to begin your writing with breathing exercises (see step 2).

Writing from your heart is important, because our hearts are usually truth holders. It is hoped that your writing will allow you to speak from your heart because, in speaking from your heart, it opens up and expands. This expansion can lead to a sense of freedom and bliss.

When we talk about the mind, we are usually referring to the self or the person whom we consciously perceive ourselves to be. Some people might call this entity the *ego*. In thinking of going below the level of ego consciousness, I am reminded of the elevator metaphor. Imagine yourself lying down and remaining perfectly still in a moving elevator. Your eyes may be open or closed. As you begin to relax, imagine the elevator doors opening slowly on each floor, allowing people (or secrets) out that have been patiently waiting to leave. Then, figuratively push the button to descend, imagining yourself going even deeper into your mind—each floor bringing you deeper—as the doors continue to open and close on each floor.

If the elevator doors remain closed for too long in your life, your mind becomes cramped and unhappy. This exercise is a good one for helping to release the resulting negative energy. Writing is another good way to bring about such release.

The mind plays a vital role in both physical and psychological health. Bernie Siegel, a pioneer in the discussion of the body-mind connection, said that the mind's effect on our health is both direct and conscious, and that the communication between the two is continuous. He uses the example that we can determine how much we love ourselves by how well we take care of ourselves—whether we eat right, exercise enough, sleep enough, and wear our seat belts when we are in the car. In other words, "The body responds to the mind's messages, whether conscious or unconscious" (Siegel, 1986, p. 66).

When opening yourself to spirit, you are opening and connecting yourself to the world beyond the mind. Spirituality means different things to different people. I view it as an understanding and recognition of a certain sense of interconnectedness among people. It's a reminder that we are not alone and that everything we do has the potential to affect others. Spirituality is also about relaxing into our own sense of being. And it is about finding our bliss, which is often a life-long journey during which we search for meanings and definitions. Elizabeth Lesser (1999) concludes that some of the larger issues that people seek to understand are those of life purpose, love, human suffering, higher consciousness, and death and what lies beyond.

Even in the midst of this searching for spirit, we may be touched by darkness—whether that be through a loss or a physical or psychological health problem or addiction. In discussing recovery from addiction, "What we most fear," says Levine (2014), "is not darkness—we know the darkness all too well; what we are most afraid of is the light (p. 102). Crises such as addiction are often the catalyst for leading us to understand the deep connection among the body, mind, and spirit. Writing is one way to bring the light back into your life, facilitate healing, and begin thinking positive thoughts.

Writing Prompt 1:2 – Autobiography in Brief

Write a one-page autobiography. Go back and highlight one poignant sentence. Use that sentence to start your second page of writing. Then go back and highlight a sentence on your second page. Do this four times (or as many times as you like). You will notice how it opens your mind and expands the stories you want to tell.

Calming Your Mind

One of the important aspects of calming the mind is that it reminds us to be in the here and now. Being present in the here and now is called *mindfulness*. It is essential for the best writing, because it taps into the messages of your heart and soul. Being mindful entails awareness and interconnectedness between your inner and outer worlds. If we are more awake and alert, we can more easily receive the messages from within us and from the universe. Natalie Goldberg (2013) reminds us of the importance of mindfulness as we move about our day, whether we are writing, doing errands, or engaging in interpersonal relationships. Some of the characteristics of mindfulness also include being nonjudgmental, being patient, being accepting, trusting, maintaining the beginner's mind, and letting go.

When considering how to quiet your mind, try to sit for a minute and think about what calms you and contemplate how you can incorporate those things into your daily life. Even just a few minutes of walking meditation or mindful breathing can bring you into the present moment. In addition to incorporating mindfulness into your day, such as when standing in line at a store, it is good to practice it before sitting down to write. My day always begins with a meditation, sometimes even before my coffee. Sometimes I do a shorter meditation later in the afternoon to give me a boost of energy.

Goldberg (2013) in her Zen writing retreats reminds her students to anchor their mind to their breath by using paper and pen to write. This helps you stay in the moment, as does the mantra, "Sit. Walk. Write."—which she calls the "true secret."

"Creativity needs space," says Buddhist teacher Kimberley Snow (2014, p. 20). The only way creativity can be released is if the doors are swung open, and this openness is easily achieved by those with a regular meditation practice. The silence inherent to meditation encourages and inspires deep listening within, which is the cornerstone of writing. If you are connected to your inner self, you will more easily be able to connect and understand the external world and thus bring about the interconnection of the inner and outer realms.

Even though the mind is a wonderful thing, it can sometimes get in the way of creativity, mainly because the voice in our head can get in the way of what our heart wants to say. Sometimes the voice in our head turns to the dark part of ourselves. This voice can point to feelings of fear, guilt, anger, sadness, envy, and resentment, instead of a sense of lightness of being. It might seem like a nagging parent or spouse.

The ego has the ability to create false thoughts, which is the inner chatter we hear most often. In fact, it is the voice in our heads that we sometimes try to tell to "shut up." Otherwise, we can become overwhelmed by these thoughts and lose touch with reality. This is one reason why during meditation it is a good idea to let thoughts come and go, rather than becoming obsessed by them or focusing on any one in particular. If you focus too intensely on your thoughts, the chance is greater for you to lose touch with the here and now. On a recent trip to Maui, I attended a retreat led by Ram Dass, one of the most influential spiritual teachers of the past few decades. Even though he had a stroke a few years back, he still continues to relay his very important message of "be here now," the simplest and best advice for being mindful. His book, *Be Here Now* (1971) was like the Bible to many hippies like myself in the 1960s.

Those who live in the present moment, often come across as being more grounded. As Ram Dass says, "When you meet a being who is centered you always know it. You always feel a kind of calm, emanation. It always touches you in that place where you feel calm" (1971, p. 46a). The more we bring our focus into the present moment, the more we experience the bliss and joy of that moment and what our true essence is.

Writing Prompt 1:3 – Being in the Here and Now

Practice focusing on the here and now. Take a few slow, deep breaths and focus on your belly. What are you seeing, sensing, hearing, or intuiting at this moment? Ask inside your body what you are feeling. Do you feel discomfort anywhere? Does an image pop into your mind? This is body intelligence.

Writing Prompt 1:4 – Differences in Perception

Describe the person your mind thinks you are. What do you look like? What do you believe? What is your connection with the universe or loved ones? Have someone else write about you. Is how they perceive you the same as how you perceive yourself?

Being Fearless and Courageous

Being fearless and able to take risks is essential for being a good writer. When you release your fears, you accept what happens in your life, and a sense of wonder follows. When writers encounter writer's block, typically it means that fear is showing its ugly face and the unconscious mind is trying to get in control. Writing entails having a huge amount of audacity.

Fear can actually be a showstopper. I heard through my late friend Thomas Steinbeck that his father's manuscript, *Of Mice and Men,* was partly chewed by his dog, Toby. While John Steinbeck might have been traumatized, he went on to continue the book and eventually got it published. One of the first things my beloved father-in-law, Alexander, told me just after my breast cancer diagnosis in 2001 was "Diana, have no fear." Most of us offer words of wisdom based on our own experiences, and as someone who escaped the Nazis of World War II and immigrated to Canada to start a new life, Alexander could have definitely been called a fearless man. Therefore, I took his advice seriously, and it has served me well in many realms of experience.

Writing takes a huge amount of courage, but submitting your work for publication takes even more. As Ernest Hemingway once said, "There is nothing to writing. All you have to do is sit down at a typewriter and bleed." When I was a medical journalist reporting on medical innovations, it took courage to go out and interview doctors about their work. That was a different kind of courage than it took to write my two memoirs, *Regina's Closet: Finding My Grandmother's Secret Journal* and *Healing with Words: A Writer's Cancer Journey*, the latter of which focused on my personal life story. In this situation, I had completely to expose my inner self, the voices of my heart, and the feelings of my soul.

Exposing my raw self to the page led to my experiencing a number of breakdowns in the process. Similar to other writers writing about difficult subjects, I had to have numerous therapy sessions to give me the courage and emotional support needed for completing my project. Memoir writing (discussed more in step 5) takes a great deal of self-reflection, which can be daunting to those who have not done a lot of it in their lifetime.

As I mentioned in an earlier section, the reward from taking risks and being courageous is having others read and enjoy your work. Some writers would say that if you are not afraid while writing, then you are not telling the story you need to tell. This type of writing has been called "writing close to the bone."

It is interesting that we often hear people complaining about their chosen career path, but it is quite unusual for writers to say that they do not like what they do. They might complain about their writing and how it is not progressing, or they might suggest that others not become a writer, but they rarely say that they do not like being a writer. More often than not, the writing profession chooses them. They write because they have to write. Writing is where they find their bliss. Sometimes, people might start out wanting to be a writer but then choose another path for increased financial gains and living a more luxurious life, only to return to their passion for writing in later years.

When you are fearful about writing about a particular aspect of your life, it might be a good idea to stop and think about the reason why. Sometimes we may not be fearful until something happens to trigger our fears. When writer Mary Karr visited my hometown last year, someone asked her how she knew she was feeling bad, sad, or depressed. Karr replied that when she felt any of those emotions it was as if she was falling from a plane—like having a crash landing. Personally, when I am fearful, it feels as if I have butterflies in my stomach, and my hands begin to tremor. Everyone embodies fear differently. Karr, for example explained that she felt fear carnally.

John Steinbeck said that he was often overcome by terror and shyness and suffered from the fear of writing down his first line. Many writers fear the first sentence—something to which I actually look forward. My first lines are launching pads for the rest of my essay or book. They almost direct my way of thinking and the trajectory of my writing. The pages of my journal have many first lines that I use in future work, whether poems, articles, or books. Some people say that the best time for writing is before the words have been put onto the page or the computer. Some writers, in fact, walk around with the entire book in their heads before they put one word on the page.

Sometimes it is a matter of just sitting down and beginning to write. During this process, there might be a major shift in your attitude as you uncover a profound insight or make a deep revelation. It will take courage to notice and honor this insight.

There is no doubt that writing takes a huge amount of courage, especially if you have decided to write about your personal life. One of my favorite books is *The Courage to Create*, by humanist psychologist Rollo May (1975). He said that courage is not a virtue but the foundation needed for all other virtues. He says that courage makes *being* and *becoming* possible. To be courageous, you must make choices that ultimately lead to transformation and bliss. In order for transformation to occur, you must allow your inner self to become exposed. As May says, it is much easier to be naked physically than it is to become naked psychologically or spiritually, but the latter is necessary in order for your deep emotional truth to be revealed in the course of your writing.

Fear can be immobilizing and limit your joy and bliss. If you are fearful, then you are not living in the moment. Living fearlessly can transform your feelings to a more peaceful and grounding place. When thinking about your fear, think about whether it is based on fact or something you've imagined. Sometimes our minds can be very powerful in choosing our direction or lack of it.

Tips for Being Fearless and Gaining Courage

- Choose the time of day to write when you're most productive.
- Establish calming prewriting rituals.
- Speak and spend time with other writers.
- Take a writing workshop.
- Journal fifteen to twenty minutes a day.
- Write letters.
- Read the work of writers with courage, such as Marcel Rita Dove, and Edmund White.

Writing Prompt 1:5 – Embodying Fear

Write about a time or situation when you were fearful. Embody the feeling of fear and try to recreate the emotions you were feeling. Write a page about that fear in a way that if someone else was reading it, they would also feel fear.

Writing Prompt 1:6 – Challenging Fear

Think about a small fear in your life, perhaps of spiders, rats, parallel parking. Imagine it vividly in your mind. Feel into the fear, realizing that you are actually safe and that the fear may be based only on your memory of a fear. Write about the fear and whether it is true and how you might conquer or deal with it.

Nurturing Creativity, Inspiration, and Flow

The act of creating something begins with the need or desire to express yourself. Inspiration originates from a burning desire to create something. Perhaps there is a subject you want to write about or a story you are yearning to tell. Much of my own inspiration comes from my lived experiences and also from reading the works of other writers whom I admire. I become inspired when I read the works of great writers whom I want to emulate. I know when I am inspired because, after I read their work, all I want to do is sit down and write. Most of us have favorite writers; personally, when I need to be inspired, I read the works of Anaïs Nin. She's my muse, and she fills me with ideas and wonderful rhythms of writing.

On some days these writers nurture my creativity, but on other days I might need a walk in nature to feel nurtured. Being in nature also tends to clear our minds of the cobwebs in a way that allows our thoughts to become clear. In addition to being nurturing, nature, according to Jay Dufrechou, (2015), can encourage psychological healing and growth. In fact, in addition to writing therapy, wilderness therapy is considered invaluable for women, the youth, and those who have survived abuse. What inspires you, who inspires you or where you get inspired, depends on your mood and upon or the day. The important thing is to keep your energy flowing while giving voice to your feelings and experiences.

Whether you are a fledging, an emerging, or a seasoned or published writer, and whether your medium is poetry or prose, you will have constantly to nurture your creativity and find ways to remain inspired. For some people this is an easy task, while other must daily feed their muse. Such muses can be real or imaginary people who inspire you and help you create.

Mihaly Csikszentmihalyi (1996), who has done extensive research on creativity, defines creativity as any act, idea, or product that has the ability to transform an existing domain or situation. A creative person is someone whose thoughts or actions change or establish a new domain. Creativity of course does not only apply to writers, who are only one type of creative individual.

For creative writers, it is common to feel inspiration and flow one day and then wake up the next day to find that the words are not flowing. Every creative person has experienced this problem. At the same time, we just never know when inspiration strikes and what it is we can do to remain inspired. It is a magic that has been studied for years. To minimize the difficulty of facing the blank page, novelist Ernest Hemingway made a point of finishing his work for the day midsentence, so that it would be easier to pick up the following day. I have adapted this practice in my own writing process and find that it truly helps prevent me from becoming blocked.

When you are in the flow of your work, you will not feel time slip away; you will go into a sort of trance-like state. It is a blissful state. It is a state of ecstasy. Those who have experienced it say that it is a high like no other. Even when you achieve this wonderful state, there will be times when you feel stuck and words do not flow easily. You might want to try the Proust approach. This approach involves engaging in stream-of-consciousness writing to release unconscious ideas and fresh ideas from your mind. This type of writing will be discussed later, but basically it allows you to reconnect with your inner psyche and allows the thoughts and words to flow as they want to flow—in no particular pattern. It might feel as if you are simply "dumping on the page." You never know where the dumping leads, and if it never leads anywhere, that's okay too!

Step Two
Cultivating Self-Awareness

What lies behind us and what lies before us are
tiny matters compared to what lies within us.
—Ralph Waldo Emerson

Self-awareness may be thought of as having knowledge, understanding, and recognition of who you are. Knowing who you are means that you are mindful of your personality, your character, your motives, your strengths, your weaknesses, your passions, and your desires. Being self-aware means being able to identify what makes you unique, in terms of your thoughts and actions. Having all this information can be empowering because, when you know yourself, you are more likely to be introspective, which is an important element of healing and transformation. It could also be the springboard for deep, personal writing.

Transpersonal Psychology

As I say in the introduction, transpersonal psychology is the newest and fifth branch of psychology concerned with achieving your highest human potential. It encompasses all the other branches of psychology, including, psychoanalytic, Jungian, behavioristic, and humanistic. In general, transpersonal psychology emphasizes the positive experiences of transformation. Transpersonal psychology draws viewpoints from both Eastern and Western paradigms and also includes the spiritual aspects of the human experience.

From a clinical standpoint, the main difference between the transpersonal approach and other psychological approaches is that transpersonal psychologists focus on fostering and developing self-awareness by using some of the methods discussed in this step. Increasing your self-awareness is also a good way to prepare for your writing practice, as it encourages you to dig deeper into your psyche.

The goal of transpersonal psychology is to transcend or to go beyond the physical realm. In other words, instead of the focus of healing being on your body and mind—which is usually the focus of other forms of therapy—transpersonal psychology emphasizes the importance of integrating spirituality into your life. It also taps into areas such as psychological health and well-being, altered states of consciousness, self-realization, peak experiences, and other ways that we can transcend the human psyche. As the Buddha (Hindu Prince Gautama Siddhartha) said:

> We are what we think
> All that we are arises with our thoughts.
> With our thoughts we create the world.
> —Buddha (Byron, Trans, 1976, p. 3)

Transpersonal Techniques

Certain techniques are used to support transformation using the transpersonal psychology paradigm. If you are facing life challenges, chances are that you are seeking the guidance and assistance of a qualified therapist. If you decide to seek the support of a transpersonal psychologist to help you navigate your journey, he or she will introduce you to a new belief system. While the beliefs might vary from therapist to therapist, here for the most part is a summary of some of the general goals of transpersonal psychology:

- You will increase your self-awareness and broaden your world view.
- You will live more passionately and authentically.
- You will become more deeply connected to your spiritual side.
- You will use your talents and resources to heal.
- You will self-actualize or aim to reach your full potential.

All these goals, which can be brought out during your writing, will help to balance your body, mind, and spirit and create a sense of well-being. The remainder of this chapter will discuss the various techniques you can incorporate into your life to cultivate your own sense of self-awareness. They can be used prior to sitting down to write or at any other convenient time during your day.

The transpersonal techniques discussed below include setting intentions, mindfulness meditation, guided creative visualization, hypnosis, breathing/breathwork, dreamwork, and accessing your shadow. The most important thing to remember is to choose the technique that feels most right for you. After a while, you might find that you have favorite techniques that you use on a regular basis, while you feel less comfortable with others.

Setting Intentions

Setting an intention involves focusing your thoughts in the particular direction of what you want to bring about or manifest in your life. The first step is to decide that you want to do something or—more importantly—to make a change. I once heard an addiction therapist use the example of fishing as an analogy to setting an intention. You make the decision to take the day off and go fishing. You are focused on catching a fish and make all the preparations to do so. You prepare all your equipment, you find a place to fish, you prepare your fishing rod. And then you cast your line. All your thought processes are geared toward catching that fish. The task becomes your focus. If you had not made the choice or had the intention to go fishing, you would never even have had the chance to catch a fish. This is what setting an intention is all about.

The second step in setting an intention is to decide to surrender to and manifest it. For example, you continue to focus on going fishing, even if you are distracted by other opportunities claiming your attention on that day. Maybe a friend asked you to go shopping with her, but you decline because you have made the intention to go fishing. You suggest that the two of you go shopping on another day.

One thing to remember is that, even before you set an intention, you need to make sure that you believe in it, that your heart is in it, and that you cannot be swayed. Also, your intention should be in line with your life purpose, meaning the real direction you want your life to take.

Intentions may be set on a daily basis first thing in the morning or just before sitting down to write. You can think of an intention as having a plan or focus for your day. On a broader scale, setting intentions can also be a way to navigate through difficult times. They are a way to break down the task of handling troublesome situations, encounters, or events that might emerge in your life.

Setting an intention is different from setting a goal. A goal, for the most part, is a valuable aim that you work hard at achieving, but it is more long term than an intention. For example, in the Buddhist tradition, an intention is not orientated toward any future outcome; rather, it is a path that you follow for that day or another designated time period. In the practice or path of Buddhism there are three treasures or paths—awakening (Buddha/Bodhi), Dharma (truths/teachings, and Sangha (a sense of the community). If you want to write more intensely, you can set an intention. Doing so will put you in the right mindset and inspire you to be more aware of what you write about. When you hold the intention to write, then you are more motivated to do so.

You might want your intentions to be more specific. For example, you might say, "Today I am going to recount the story of the day my sister was born," or, "Today I'm going to write about the trauma my father caused me." Intentions are useful in changing behavior, as in the case of addictive behaviors. (But it is important to keep in mind that you can only make intentions for yourself; you can offer *hope* to other people, but you cannot make intentions for them.)

There are many different ways to set an intention. For example, perhaps you are feeling stressed because you will be having dinner with a difficult family member. Perhaps you have had a pattern of being reactive this person's hurtful comments to you. On the morning of your dinner, you might decide to set the intention that you won't be reactive but instead will take on a different stance—you will become an observer to the circumstances in which you find yourself.

Another way to set an intention is to write it, as in, "My intention for today is aimed at what my best interest is, and this is directed at my highest good. My intention will unfold or manifest in the best possible way. My intention is to..."

Another method of setting intentions is to use intention cards to gain ideas. Some people use tarot cards for this purpose. In the writing workshops I facilitate, I share intention cards with the participants. I walk around the room with a fanned deck of cards and ask each person to pick one. The card's message is to be their intention for the day. I ask that at the top of their journal page, right beneath the date, they write down exactly what the intention card says. It is interesting to note that when they glance at the words on the card, more often than not they are surprised to have chosen a card that resonates with their particular state of mind at that time. Sometimes it is uncanny, and I see people shaking their heads in awe. Similarly, drawing an intention card can offer you your first prompt to jumpstart your writing.

Setting an intention in the morning is also a good way to set the tone for your day. If you wake up in a bad mood, for example, setting your intention is one way to change the day's trajectory. It is like waking up again on the right side of the bed instead of the wrong side. In other words, you can choose to turn a bad mood into a good mood. To set an intention is empowering. It provides you with the choice to make a change where change is needed.

Like the choice of picking an intention card, we all have choices in most realms of our lives. Years ago when my eldest daughter was in rehab, one of the books she was given to read was Viktor Frankl's *Man's Search for Meaning* (1984). This poignant book is really about how one choice can affect the trajectory of the rest of your life. If you haven't read the book, I highly recommend it. Frankl, a Holocaust survivor, made the choice to remain behind and care for the patients in the concentration camp. He made this decision based on an intention he had set for himself and on what he saw as his life purpose. He intuited that offering love and care to those in need would lead to his own bliss. As he wisely said, "I understood how a man who has nothing left in this world still may know bliss, be it only for a brief moment, in the contemplation of his beloved" (p. 49). Frankl understood his place in the world and what it meant for him to be a human being, a friend, and a physician.

Recently, I had a powerful experience with intention-setting when I ventured on a spiritual quest to Maui to meet with my spiritual guide. I brought along my Hawaiian healing cards that I use as intention cards, and every morning I chose one before leaving my hotel to meet my guide in the day's designated spiritual spot. How those cards helped to set the tone and focus for us was amazing.

I continue to hear my spiritual guide's words of wisdom echoing in my mind: "You know, we all have choices." Her words emphasize the importance of always setting our own intentions about what is good for us, as opposed to what others may want for us. Her words both empower and liberate me as I move forward through my day, always keeping in mind that we make millions of choices during the course of our lives. By the time you reach the end of this book, you will have to make another choice—deciding whether to write for publication. Whatever choices you have and decisions you make, always remember to follow your bliss; write what is in your heart and be true to yourself.

While intentions focus more on the short term, it is always a good idea also to set long-term goals. This is important, for example, in the case of healing from addictions. However, sometimes due to daily obstacles and/or "triggers" (meaning anything that brings back thoughts, memories, or feelings related to addictive behaviors), setting daily intentions might be more realistic, less daunting and intimidating. The intention you set for yourself is highly personal, but I would like to share examples of some of the participants in my writing workshops:

- "Today, I choose recovery."
- "My intention is to reach out to those who can support my growth and transformation."
- "My intention is to reach out to those who need love."
- "One day at a time."
- "My intention is to not be concerned about what others think."
- "My intention is to speak my truth whenever possible."
- "My intention is to be authentic verbally and when writing."

- "My intention is not to judge myself or others."
- "My intention is to take wise risks, but to do things differently."
- "My intention is to be light-hearted and look at life with a sense of humor."
- "I intend to focus more on just being, rather than focus on doing all the time."
- "My intention is to have a daily intention."

Writing Prompt 2:1 – Intention Setting

Begin to incorporate intention setting into your day. Take your journal and your pen and jot down a couple of intentions that immediately pop into your head. You may borrow from the list above or you can create your own personal intentions. Keep writing until you cannot think of any more intentions.

Mindfulness Meditation

Mindfulness meditation, which originated in Buddhist circles, encourages you to focus on feelings, experiences, and internal and external processes in a nonjudgmental manner. It is about being fully present in the moment, thus making you more aware of yourself, others, and your environment. Mindfulness meditation is about paying attention to the thoughts racing through your mind, without obsessing about them or trying to fix them in any particular way. Meditation is one of the best ways to increase self-awareness, calm your mind and your body, and connect with what is happening in the present moment.

Many studies have shown the benefits of mindfulness meditation. Some institutions, such as the Mayo Clinic, have already integrated mindfulness meditation into many of their programs to foster healing in those dealing with mental and physical illnesses. When mindfulness meditation is used to help addicts in recovery, studies have shown that it minimizes the stress caused by the trigger to use alcohol or drugs. The results can be very effective when used in conjunction with other modalities, such as psychotherapy.

Mindfulness meditation forces you to sit with yourself and to accept and tolerate your feelings rather than medicating them. Sitting with your problems and recognizing them with curiosity and acceptance helps you better to diffuse any triggers that you may regularly encounter. One of the many wonderful aspects of mindfulness meditation is that you can do it alone and anywhere. You don't need props, mentors, or facilitators. It only takes a few minutes, and the results are effective, long acting, and empowering.

Meditation may be practiced either while sitting still or, for those who have difficulty sitting, while walking. Other practices such as Qigong and Tai Chi are also good options. In mindfulness meditation, the idea is to sit still and focus on the breath—breathing in and pausing, breathing out and pausing. Full awareness is kept during the breathing process, even when there are outside noises—such as cars honking, dogs barking, trains passing, or people engaged in conversation. You will notice that, even while focusing on your breath, your thoughts might interrupt you, but your attention should quickly return to the breath.

Before beginning your meditation practice, it is important to sit still on a chair or cushion with your back straight. I like the metaphor one meditation teacher taught me of imagining your head being a helium balloon floating through the roof into the atmosphere. Then, as a grounding force, think of your spine sinking into the floor. This prepares you to anchor yourself in your meditation experience (for how to ground yourself, see step 2).

When I was recovering from breast cancer surgery, my meditation instructor taught me to imagine a ball of white light above my head permeating into the crown of my head and moving down through my body. The idea was to purify any negative energy or thoughts. I had to remind my body to relax. I dropped my shoulders, the part of my body where I hold a lot of my tension. Then, I focused on my breath and said, "Breathe in, breathe out." I repeated this until I felt a deep sense of peace. Sometimes I even drifted off, but paying attention to the breath is important as a mindset.

For those who have struggled with addiction, mindfulness meditation is an important part of recovery. Noah Levine in his book, *Dharma Punx,* says that prayer and meditation became an integral part of his life and that it helped him find a sense of purpose in his life. "Being an addictive type, when I find something that makes me feel good I want to do it all the time, so I did, I turned my life toward recovery and spiritual practice" (2003, p. 84).

One way to achieve bliss through writing is before writing to engage in what Levine calls, "Appreciative Joy Meditation," where after settling the body, you focus on breathing into the heart center. With each breath concentrate on appreciating all the joyfulness and happiness you've experienced in your life. This might be a good time to wear a slight smile on your face. Now offer some intentions to encourage your deep gratefulness.

The intentions you set can be ones you create for yourself or you may use the suggested ones provided by Levine, such as:

> May I learn to appreciate the happiness and joy I experience.
> May the joy I experience continue and grow.
> May I be filled with gratitude.
>
> (2007, p 150)

Writing Prompt 2:2 – Giving Thanks

After doing" Appreciative Joy Meditation," consider writing a few pages on what you are thankful for, presently and in the past. What you are thankful for can pertain to certain individuals who have been in your life, belongings, experiences, feeling, and/or ways of being.

Hanh, a mindfulness advocate, wisely says that the breath is the bridge connecting our life to consciousness. It also unites our bodies to our thoughts. When your mind becomes scattered, focus on your breath to get hold of your mind once again. In Hanh's tradition, *zazen*, or seated meditation, is a part of everyday life. In Western living, meditating for fifteen or twenty minutes might be all that is needed to calm you, but of course you may do so for as long as you like.

I like Siegel's (1986) definition of meditation as a way to focus the mind into a state of relaxed awareness. Relaxation is the key here because, even though the mind tends to be less responsive to distraction during meditation, it can be more focused on certain images or feelings. These images are usually important to us, whether they are connected to healing or peace.

Writing Prompt 2:3 – Meditation Review: Mood Shifts

After your meditation, write in your journal about your experience. Did you notice any mood shifts or subjects that kept popping into your mind?

What thoughts kept interrupting your attention to your breathing? How did those interruptions make you feel?

Writing Prompt 2:4 – Meditation Review: Triggers

Write about any triggers that arose during your meditation and your response to them.

What might you be able to do to divert the feelings that the trigger elicits?

Kimberly Snow (2014) discusses the importance of combining meditation with writing. After being a meditation teacher for many years, she has found that the more she meditates, the more insight and creativity she brings to her writing. Writing and meditation work well together, because both practices lead to a deeper sense of self-discovery and seeking of what is most authentic in your life. Writing helps you to "get real" and face situations that might have been bothering you. Whether writing fiction, nonfiction, or poetry, sometimes you need just to get out of your own way and write.

A Simple Meditation Exercise

Sit comfortably in a chair with your feet flat on the ground. Sit as if you are a puppet and there is a string attached to the top of your head. Gently let your eyes close. Allow your body to become relaxed and quiet. Take a deep breath through your nose and let it out through your mouth. Repeat this a few times. Allow your mind to become peaceful and quiet. Let go of the emotional and mental chatter. Expand your awareness. Feel the silence within. Keep your eyes closed for about fifteen minutes; then pick up your pen to write about your experience.

Lovingkindness Meditation

Lovingkindness meditation cultivates feelings of kindness in you and in others. It can be especially helpful in circumstances when kindness might not be your first reaction. It can help you get through difficult times. There are many variations of lovingkindness meditation. One is to begin thinking of yourself and your small world and then extend out to the universe. Another is to start with the universe and then return to yourself. The method I like best incorporates both and is done in three parts. The first part extends lovingkindness to a living benefactor, the second part to someone deceased, and the third part to yourself.

Begin this meditation in the same way you begin the simple seated meditation above. Sit comfortably and allow your mind to become peaceful and quiet. First, think of someone who at some point in your life helped you, and allow the memory of their help to warm your heart. Visualize this person looking at you with love and warmth. Now, with a pause and a breath between each phrase, recite each line below. Repeat a few times, if you like:

> I would like for you to be safe.
> I would like for you to be healthy.
> I would like for you to be happy.
> I would like for you to be at ease in the world.

Second, think of someone who is no longer alive. Perhaps it was someone who helped you or continues to inspire you in some way. Repeat the below phrases, replacing the pronouns *her/his* with the person's name. Repeat a few times, if you like:

> I remember her/his kindness.
> I remember her/his love.

Third, extend lovingkindness to yourself. There may be certain times in your life when you feel unable to love yourself. It is a good idea to inspire yourself by thinking that it is only by loving ourselves that we are truly able to love others. So keeping yourself in mind, take some deep breaths and say the following lines. Repeat a few times, if you like:

> I would like to be safe.
> I would like to be healthy.
> I would like to be happy.
> I would like to be at ease in the world.

The fourth part of the meditation is optional and involves offering lovingkindness to someone about whom you feel neutral or do not think about very much. Sit quietly and visualize this person as best you can. Again, replace the pronoun—in this case, *you*—with the person's name. Repeat a few times, if you like:

> I would like for you to be safe.
> I would like for you to be healthy.
> I would like for you to be happy.
> I would like for you to be at ease in the world.

When I attended one of Jack Kornfield's meditation seminars, he had his own creative lovingkindness meditation, which is an alternative to the above. He started the practice by having us sit quietly for fifteen or twenty minutes. The purpose of this meditation was to set an intention and repeatedly to plant the seeds of lovingkindnesses by using repetitive words and images. Kornfield suggested we begin by focusing on ourselves and then bring the focus to others. We began by holding the image in lovingkindness while repeating the following:

> May I be filled with lovingkindness.
> May I be safe from inner and outer dangers.
> May I be well in body and mind.
> May I be at ease and happy.

Kornfield told us that in addition to practicing lovingkindness during our daily meditation, we can also practice it anywhere—in line at a store, on an airplane, in the car, or during a social event. He said that the interconnected sense comes about naturally when practicing this meditation in the presence of others. We develop a wonderful interconnectedness with them and with our own hearts, which is the power of lovingkindness.

Guided Creative Visualization

Creative visualization is a technique in which you close your eyes and use your imagination to create what you want in your life. This can include everything from satisfying relationships, physical or mental health, and wealth to inner peace and harmony. For some people, creative visualization is an effective way to deal with psychological or physical wounds because it offers a way to cope with those traumatic events. Creative visualization can also open you up to new creative energies and transpersonal realms that can be good for your self-expression and writing.

Creative visualization may be initiated by a therapist, but you can learn to do it yourself; however, according to Siegel (1986) it is more effective if the image is chosen by the individual and is something with which the person feels completely comfortable. Years ago, when diagnosed with cancer, I was taught creative visualization techniques to elicit feelings of healing and empowerment. I was taught to imagine myself as a knight on a horse galloping up the beach, while the sharks were conquering all the cancer cells in my body. After doing this a number of times, I experienced a sense of control over the circumstances in which I found myself.

There are different methods of initiating creative visualization. The following one is adapted from Carl Greer's (2014) book, *Change Your Story, Change Your Life:*

Inhale and exhale and focus on your breath. Let go of any thoughts that enter your mind and imagine them fading away. Imagine that you are in a cave. You remove all your clothes and lie down. You feel moisture dripping from the ceiling, and its acidic nature begins to dissolve your skin, organs, and body systems. You become a skeleton, but your awareness is still present.

The sun comes out, and your awareness and essence are evaporated as water vapor. You feel the wind cleansing you as you move across the sky, and you become purified by the sun. It begins to rain. You become a part of the ocean, which continues to cleanse you. You sink into the sand and are then nurtured by the earth.

Suddenly, lightning strikes and reintegrates your physical body, and you feel as if you've become reformed—first your skeleton, then your body systems, and then your organs. You become human again and have returned to wholeness.

Writing Prompt 2:5 – Creative Visualization Review

Write about your creative visualization experience. What crossed your mind during the process? Did you feel healed or renewed in any significant way?

Hypnosis

Hypnosis works by altering the triggers in the brain. It has many applications. For example, it can be used to treat trauma; it can minimize self-sabotage issues; it can help with fears and weight-management issues; and it can help overcome a particular habit or help you to deal with denial. If you are being helped for a certain mental, emotional, or physical challenge, hypnosis can help you keep on track with the prescribed treatment. If you are trying to break a pattern of addictive behavior, for instance, the idea of hypnosis is that when you spend time concentrating on yourself and your inner workings, and focusing on what works and what does not work for you, then change and transformation is more apt to follow.

Over the years, I have had some positive personal experiences with hypnosis. As a result of being on bed rest with all three of my children, I inevitably gained excessive weight because of my lack of exercise. I had always been able to strike a healthy balance between eating and exercising and have always been mindful of good weight management. After my first child was born, I decided to seek the guidance of a hypnotherapist to help me lose weight. I saw him once a week for six weeks.

We all have preconceived ideas of what to expect before a new experience, and I was no exception. Before my first visit to the hypnotherapist's office, I was somewhat nervous and fearful that under his direction I would lose control of what I said or did. I had images of the hypnotherapist hanging a pendulum before me and of my falling asleep under his spell, unknowingly making silly comments. Thankfully, this never happened—at least I don't think so!

When I arrived, I noticed the hypnotherapist was wearing a ring on his middle finger. All I could see was a silver band. After an introductory conversation and before the actual session began, he turned his ring around and exposed a rather large turquoise stone that had been facing his palm. I soon realized that, instead of using a pendulum, he would use this turquoise ring to hypnotize me.

It is important to know that when you are hypnotized you will be completely awake and hear everything that is being said to you. If your experience is anything like mine, you will also feel quite relaxed. Some people have described the sensation under hypnosis as feeling completely limp. After each of my visits I felt extremely more or less stress free and looked forward to each of the five subsequent sessions.

A large part of the hypnosis entails creative visualization. Without revealing too much about my experience, I will say that the hypnotherapist began by encouraging me to take a walk in what he called a "magical forest." He told me to imagine myself looking into a deep pond to observe my reflection in the water. I was asked to imagine what I wanted to look like at the end of my weight-loss regime. This technique was very powerful, and, as it turned out, I used it by myself for many years to come.

My daughter, Regine, also had a good experience with hypnosis. During her teen years, she had had a fear of doctors—or anyone, for that matter—who wore a white lab coat. After graduating from high school, she asked if she could take a trip to Europe with her boyfriend. I told her I was concerned about her fear of doctors and the eventuality of what might happen if she or her friend got ill in a foreign country. She asked what I suggested and I recommended hypnotherapy, which had worked for me in the past. Being the open-minded person she was, and also badly wanting to make the trip, she agreed to see the same hypnotherapist I had seen. I was delighted to learn that at the end of the six sessions, she was able to walk into a hospital emergency room without feeling faint or sick; and now, more than fourteen years later, while pregnant with her first child she has no more issues in this area. The success of the treatment was remarkable.

For the writer, hypnosis can be a powerful tool to tap into creativity. Basically, it trains your mind to think in a more creative manner. It accomplishes this by clearing your mind of outside concerns so that you can focus on your writing. Hypnosis can help you tap into your unconscious mind, release the fear of writing, and become disciplined in your writing habits.

Hypnosis can also help remove mental blocks which hinder your creative flow. The block in creative flow has often been referred to as "writer's block," meaning the times when writers feel stuck and find that their words do not come easily. Hypnotherapists establish links between the mind and the times when your creative flow was at its best. In other words, they can train your mind to think of attaching the sense of being in the flow to times when you want to be in that state in the future. These are called anchoring techniques.

It is possible to engage in self-hypnosis, but it is probably a good idea to learn the technique from a trained hypnotherapist and then graduate to doing it yourself. The writer W. B. Yeats practiced self-hypnosis so that he could bring himself into a self-induced trance or the alpha state of mind. Once you are in this state, the real writing begins. The key is to make hypnosis part of your writing routine. It is about repeatedly saying to yourself, "When I sit at my desk, I will write, and I won't be distracted by other matters."

For self-hypnosis, you would do a fifteen-minute recording, telling your unconscious mind what it is you want to achieve or write and how you can make that happen. Then listen to the tape as a regular practice before sitting down to write. As author Anne Lamott says, "Writing is about hypnotizing yourself into believing in yourself, getting some work done, then unhypnotizing yourself and going over the material coldly" (1994, p. 114).

Breath Work

It is an obvious truth that we cannot live without breathing. The first thing we do when we are born is take a breath, and the last thing we do before we die is take a breath. Most of us take breathing for granted. Because it is so automatic, we rarely think about it. But to maintain a sense of optimal well-being and health, it is a good idea to be conscious of your breath because it keeps you in touch with your body and supports change and transformation.

There are a number of ways to become aware of your breath. The first way is to breathe in for the count of seven, exhale for the count of seven, and then hold your breath for the count of seven. Repeat several times.

Another breathing method, called yogic breathing, will help you relax and is particularly useful if you are stressed: Close off your right nostril with your right thumb and inhale through your left nostril; release and close off your left nostril with your middle finger and exhale through your right nostril. Once again, close off your right nostril, inhale through your left nostril, and exhale through your right. Repeat as many times as feels right for you.

Holotropic Breathwork is a transpersonal practice that initiates a conscious control of breathing, resulting in a therapeutic improvement of your emotional and physical state of mind. *Holotropic* is a term coined by Stanilov and Christina Grof that means "oriented toward wholeness." When LSD became illegal, Stanilov and Christina Grof discovered Holotropic Breathwork as a mind-altering technique leading to altered states of consciousness that can have a positive effect on your mental well-being. It involves sessions of altered breathing combined with loud, evocative music and body work. The emotions associated with the holotropic state vary greatly and range from feelings of ecstasy and bliss to despair, guilt, and other types of suffering. Most people experience very interesting insights when in a holotropic state, and they can revolve around metaphysical, philosophical, and/or spiritual issues.

Recalling Your Dreams

Our dreams are mirrors or doorways into our unconscious mind and our inner world. Sometimes they offer us guidance, self-discovery, and growth; and, in some cases, they can be healing. Our dreams can make offerings to our creative process and can help us make decisions and solve problems. One colleague of mine says that his dreams actually help guide him. Before he goes to bed at night, he writes down a question with the hope that his dreams will address it; and the following morning, he will have been given the answer. Other people might choose to meditate about a particular problem before they go to bed at night and stay focused on it before falling asleep. Obviously, not all dreams offer the answers we want, but it is good to be hopeful. There is no doubt that dreams can heighten your awareness about issues in your life.

Some might say that dreams are our soul's way of speaking to us—a way to give us messages. Freud's book *The Interpretation of Dreams*, published in 1900, paved the way for other investigations of the meaning of dreams and led to C. G. Jung's deeper analysis of dreams and exploration of the unconscious mind, both personally and in terms of the collective unconsciousness.

Years ago I taught journaling at the Santa Barbara Healing Sanctuary with Jungian analyst Robert Bosnak, who coined the term "embodied imagination," which is a therapeutic and creative way of working with dreams and memories. It is based on the principles of Jung's alchemy. Embodied imagination takes dreaming as the model for all images. Bosnak believes that, in a dream, we create an entire new world and explore the experiences we are living in the dream state. During analysis, participants are encouraged to write down or recall their dreams to the analyst in a hypnagogic state, which is between the dream state and the lucid state of consciousness. The analyst asks questions that help the person relive and reexamine the dream in order to understand its significance in the individual's life. This technique has proven to be very helpful for many people battling issues such as fear of aging, depression, weight gain, or arthritis.

Sometimes we wake up from a dream that seems so bizarre and out of context that we are unsure what to do with it. When that happens, the best thing is to pick up your dream journal and write down all that you remember about the dream. You might surprise yourself in that, once you begin writing, more details and information will emerge. Studies have shown that at least fifty percent of us have "lucid" dreams, meaning dreams in which you are actually aware that you are dreaming. These are often exhilarating experiences and can feel like a self-imposed trance. Lucid dreams usually end with the dreamer either waking up or losing their sense of lucidity. Lucid dreaming can be an effective way to achieve bliss because it can help reveal secrets and heighten your sense of self-awareness. In fact, I've used some of my lucid dreams in some of the poems I have written.

Some writers become inspired by their dreams' ability to transport them to a different world, the world of images that can enrich our imaginations with creativity. A good example is that of William Styron, who woke up from a dream featuring an image of a woman whom he had known in his early twenties. She was standing in a hallway with her arms full of books and a tattoo of blue numbers visible on her sleeve. When the dream occurred, Styron had been working on a story, but at that moment he decided to abandon it. He then went directly to his writing studio and crafted the opening lines of his famous novel, *Sophie's Choice.*

Also, novelist Isabel Allende says that she is very inspired by her dreams. She says that she always keeps a little notepad at her bedside for the purpose of writing her dreams down. Allende believes that we have a little storage room in our minds housing information that is only accessible during dreaming. With practice, we can bring this treasure of information into our conscious mind and use it in our writing. She says that sometimes when she reaches into her storage room and brings information out to write about, it then becomes true. She views this phenomenon as a sort of premonition, in the sense of a collective memory.

In fact, this happened to me about last year. I had a vivid dream celebrating my middle daughter's pregnancy. In reality, she had been trying to get pregnant for a very long time, but in the dream I was joyous and happy because I was making a party for her to celebrate a successful pregnancy. I was jumping for joy. When I woke up, I wrote about it. As it turned out, my daughter's older sister had a similar dream. A few months later we learned of her pregnancy in real life. My premonition had been most wonderful.

The best way to work with your dreams for your writing is to do as Isabel Allende does: upon awakening, jot the dream down in a journal that you keep at your bedside. Chances are that if you forget to write it down right away, it will drift back into your unconsciousness and you will forget it. After you record the details of your dream, remember also how you felt during and after the dream. Then try to make associations between the dream and what is happening in your actual life, presently or in the past.

After you have written down a number of dreams, it might be a good idea to meet with someone who specializes in dreams to help you understand the significance of yours and how they can help you rework your life. Bosnak (1986) suggests that when you are recalling the images and feelings of dreams, it is also important to sense how the dream feels in your body. Consider where in your body you have energy blockages, where it feels good, and where it hurts. Also consider what part of the dream captures your attention and what part bores you.

There are a number of ways to increase your recall of dreams. During the day, you could work on memory exercises, such as glancing around your room and getting a sense of everything in it. Try to fix in your mind the colors and position of the items you see. Then, close your eyes and see how much you recall about what you saw. Then try writing the things down without looking around the room.

Another way to facilitate dream recall is to make an intention to remember your dream before going to bed. Then, upon awakening but before arising, write down all that you remember of your dream in the journal that you keep at your bedside. Write whatever comes to you regardless of the order. The story line is not as important as are the images and how you felt during the dream.

To remember or get a sense of your dreams, some dream experts suggest setting your alarm for some time in the middle of the night. When the alarm sounds, shut it off and, without stretching or getting out of bed, immediately begin writing in your journal whatever you recall about your dreams. One of my colleagues sets the alarm for forty-five minutes before she plans to wake up and then uses that extra time to record her dreams. Of course, if waking up in the middle of the night or earlier than you plan to arise is not something you want to do, then definitely consider recording your dreams first thing in the morning, before going to the bathroom or having your very first cup of java.

Finally, another good way to facilitate remembering is to carry a journal at all times, because sometimes we recall snippets of dreams during the course of our day.

Writing Prompt 2:6 – Asking Your Dreams a Question

Think of a particular question or problem that you want addressed in your dreams. In the dream journal that you keep at your bedside, write this question down. Hopefully the question will make its way into your unconsciousness. First thing the next morning before getting out of bed, write down what you remember about your dream.

Writing Prompt 2:7 – Exploring a Vivid Dream

On another occasion, recall a vivid dream. Describe in detail the images in it. Note the feelings you associate with the dream. What does the dream remind you of in your present or past circumstances?

Knowing Your Shadow and Your Anima/Animus

Jung introduced the idea that we all have a shadow, which is the unconscious part of ourselves usually hidden from our immediate awareness. Because the shadow is composed of impulses that society views as unacceptable, our conscious mind does not want to claim ownership of those feelings or instincts and they become relegated to the unconscious mind. Some of those feelings might have to do with hatred, jealousy, aggressiveness, cruelty, and so on. Or maybe they have to do with walking around naked or spouting nasty comments or making love to everyone you find sexy. Regardless of the particulars, most people view the qualities that make up the shadow as the part of themselves that they would rather not think about.

Jung said that one of the best ways to get a handle on what your shadow qualities are is to think of what irritates you the most in other people. Then the idea is to accept that those same characteristics are true of you yourself. There is usually a huge payoff for this work! Jung considered the shadow to be pure gold, because getting in touch with it releases pent-up energy that can then be used in healthier ways, leading to your greater well-being.

In trying to confront or identify your shadow, you might discover that for years you have avoided paying attention to a part of yourself that you don't particularly like or are not proud of. It is important to know and also to write about your shadow side because, otherwise, it can be a roadblock to achieving bliss. Focusing on your shadow can make it feel more alive; and writing is an ideal way to do this as, in the process, other things might come to the surface, such as forgotten memories.

The opposite of the shadow or dark side of ourselves is the light that is a symbol for consciousness or what illuminates us. In order for healing and transformation to occur, it is important for you to bring your shadow into the light. There is great transformative power in facing your shadow and then understanding it. And writing is a great tool to help you shine the light of conscious observation in this process of acceptance. When you willingly look at your shadow and feel it, then you can become free from its grip.

Sometimes when we begin to visit those dark aspects of ourselves we can become sad or depressed. Some individuals might resort to addictive behaviors. This is what inspired my co-editor, James Brown, and me to compile an anthology called *Writers on the Edge: 22 Writers Speak about Addiction and Dependency* (2012). This collection shares personal stories of well-published writers who dig deep into their souls to discuss their addictions and dependencies and how they have affected their professional and personal lives. As writer and addict Jerry Stahl says in the book's foreword, "Through writing and other healing modalities some have been able to discover the light at the end of the tunnel, and others not." All the contributors to this book claim to have been healed and transformed through writing. Thus, we can say with some certainty that through writing, healing and transformation can occur because through writing we are able to see and possibly understand the reality of our situation.

You might wonder how to know what your shadow is. Reinekke Lengelle (2006), a professor at Athabasca University who has done shadow work, says that one way to identify your shadow is to realize that when you feel emotionally charged about what someone else did or is doing, there is a good chance that you are reacting because you have projected onto them a shadow trait of your own. So actually, the person is reflecting back to you an unconscious part of yourself. For example, those who call others judgmental are likely judgmental themselves. Another way you can identify your shadow is to become aware of when you may be in denial about something, as in, "I am not the jealous type." It might take some thinking or journaling to figure this all out, but it is worth the effort!

In the epilogue of the anthology *Meeting the Shadow,* co-edited by Connie Zweig and Jeremiah Abrams (1991), Abrams says,

> We each contain the potentials to be both destructive and creative. Admitting to the dark enemies within us is really a confessional act, the beginning of psychological change. Nothing about ourselves can change unless we

> first accept it and grant it reality. Shadow-work is the initiatory phase of making a whole of ourselves (p. 304).

Sometimes we are affected by the projections that other people make onto us. Since an early age, I remember being labeled as "beautiful." "You look so much like Elizabeth Taylor," people used to tell me. While most people would be honored to be called "beautiful" in this way, there are times when it bothers me. I have had to think long and hard about why, and only in my adult years have I begun to figure it out. As with many creative types, during my early school-age years socializing and daydreaming were a huge part of my classroom learning. I enjoyed observing people, which probably was the seed for my life as a writer and psychologist.

My grades were never stellar, but they were decent enough to get me into college. When I took standardized tests, I scored poorly, and my mother thought I would probably not be accepted into college. Her message to me was that I was beautiful but not very smart. From an early age, I intuited that I had street smarts, which as an adult I came to learn were much more valuable, anyway. As kids, we take our parents' messages as the gospel. We do not know any different. We often do not realize until we are older the deep damage that words and labels can cause. In many ways, my beauty might have led to a little love addiction; so therefore, in a small way, I resent being called "beautiful" and would much rather be recognized for my brain and called "smart." I spent a lot of time writing about this in my journal, and it felt good to do so.

Writing Prompt 2:8 – On Being Labeled

Think of a name or label someone has called you that really bothered you. Maybe you were called lazy, stupid, judgmental, stupid, short-sighted, or narcissistic. How has this label affected the person you have become?

Writing Prompt 2:9 – Inviting the Shadow

Find a quiet place to write. Close your eyes and ask your shadow to appear. Your shadow can be depressed, fearful or angry. Begin a conversation with your shadow and in your journal describe its characteristics. Write about how your shadow can have a positive effect on your life. (Adapted from an exercise in *Poemcrazy* by Wooldridge, 1996, p. 79)

In many ways, our shadow can inspire creativity. I have heard the shadow called "a sleeping giant," and it said that to write in the most compelling way, we must face the shadow head on and write openly about that side of us. Our shadow encircles us and lives in our mind, body, and spirit. We can increase our awareness of it by reflecting on our dreams or by getting into the flow of our writing. Sometimes those we choose as friends are those who can reveal our shadow to us, in that we often project our undesirable unwanted characteristics onto others.

In a sense, the poet Rumi's "Open Secret" discussed in step 1 is akin to the shadow in that each one of us tries to hide a secret. There is great power to be gained from sharing your secret, because it can begin a conversation about something you should or need to talk about. You just never know when you open that door who or what will be waiting on the other side.

Speaking of the other side, it seems like a good time to mention the *anima,* which according to Jungian psychology is the feminine part of a male's personality, and the *animus*, which is the masculine part of the female personality. Anima and animus are sometimes called soul images, and Jung says we typically and unconsciously project our own such inner aspect onto the opposite sex. A man's anima may be experienced or projected as feminine, whether in the form of a maiden, mother, witch, or prostitute. A woman's animus may be experienced or projected as masculine, manifested in terms of aggressiveness, physical power, and intellectual or spiritual strength, such as might be characteristic of a professor or a clergyman. In Jungian psychology and for the purpose of writing, the anima and animus may be considered a source of inspiration, vitality, and/or creativity. Another word for *anima* or *animus* might be the inner *muse.*

Muses for Inspiration

A large part of self-awareness is knowing yourself in a way so that you understand who you are and what or who inspires you. When entering into the creative zone, it is helpful to gather your muses about you, whether in the form of energies, photographs, or artifacts. Many writers have muses who inspire their creativity. In ancient times, when authors sat down to write they would invoke muses by calling them or singing to them. Many of my writing colleagues become inspired by reading the works of writers whom they admire. They might even call them "muses." Others garner individuals who inspire them, whether they are teachers, lovers, spouses, or friends.

Muses can change from time to time depending upon the project on which you are working, but sometimes you can have one muse who inspires all your work. For a long time my creative life has been inspired by Anaïs Nin, probably because we both began our literary career as a result of loss. On my office wall hangs a painting of her that my husband lovingly made for me for one of my birthdays. She's always watching me, exciting the thought process and calming any negative energy that wants to take over. No matter what, she makes me feel as if I am not alone. The shelf behind the desk where I write this book has two shelves of books by and about her, including *Café in Space*, which is an annual journal dedicated to her life and work and provided by the Anaïs Nin Trust. I've been blessed to have had a few poems and essays published in this volume.

There have been times when I've been told that I am someone else's muse, and this is such a gratifying feeling—to be able to inspire others. Kim Stafford in his book *The Muses Among Us* (2003) offers a wealth of ideas and words of wisdoms to inspire the muse within us. The basis of all the inspiration, he says, should be a deep sense of curiosity, and I couldn't agree more.

Step Three
Speaking Your Truth

The feeling is often the deeper truth,
the opinion the more superficial one.
—Augustus William Hare

Speaking your truth is not only healthy but also psychologically quite liberating. Releasing your stress by writing your thoughts is one way of speaking your truth. By speaking the truth, you are not writing to be right, you are writing to be "real." You are also thinking about what is important to you, what your values are, what inspires and drives you, and what gives your life purpose. Your truth is *your* truth and no one else's. In general, it is easier to be truthful than to avoid the subjects that might be more painful for you to write about. In the end, the rewards for speaking and writing the truth will be great.

The Art and Power of Storytelling

Storytelling dates back to the beginning of time. Stories hold up mirrors so that we can see ourselves. We tell stories because they fill the silence. Stories can help heal us. In telling our own story we learn the essence of our being. Most personal stories are told in the first person, using "I." Some writers prefer shifting their perspective and telling their story from the third-person stance, using "he," "she," or "they." Some people find it easier to tell stories this way from the viewpoint outside of themselves because it allows them to have some distance from the story.

There is much to be learned both from writing our own stories and from reading the stories about others. When hearing the stories of other people, we learn about both the tragedy and the comedy of life. Their stories become our story and can change the way we perceive and understand our own life. Other people's stories can also empower and enlighten us. Hearing other people's stories also make us feel less alone, confused, and troubled. For example, the power of story-telling is especially obvious in programs like Alcoholics Anonymous where people come together to tell and share their stories.

Stories are typically about people, animals, or things. In order to be called a story, something has to happen. As Flannery O'Connor wisely said, "If nothing happens, it's not a story." One of my writing mentors in graduate school shared a great tip in regard to writing stories about people. He said that when writing, always imagine or visualize the people in your story appearing on stage. And he, too, said that in a story there should always be something happening. In other words, the characters always need to be doing or saying something. The characters should not appear to be like stick figures moving about.

In a story, there also needs to be a conflict. In fact, some would say that the conflict *is* the story. Robert McKee, who has been offering workshops on "story," says that "conflict is to storytelling what sound is to music" (1997, p. 210). In personal essay or memoir, the conflict would likely focus on the people in your life engaged in a challenge or difficult situation that needs resolution. This might involve a power struggle or a difference of opinion concerning what action would be best to take. The conflict could also involve an inner struggle of yours, perhaps over something you want to do—in the face of other forces against you. Coming-of-age stories often involve some sort of inner conflict because the individual is in the midst of a life transition. A conflict in a story keeps the reader turning the page because they want to find out what happened. In a conflict, something might be gained or lost.

Cheryl Strayed's memoir, *Wild*, illustrates a good example of conflict. At the age of twenty-two, when her mother died, Strayed thought her life was also coming to an end, because her mother's death caused such a change in family dynamics. At about the same time, her marriage fell apart, resulting in very challenging times for her. Strayed decided to go for a hike alone across the thousand miles of the Pacific Crest Trail to try to "find herself." As a result of this experience, she became healed in a way that gave her the moral strength to forge ahead with her life. The conflict of this story (losing her mother and husband) created a degree of stress (loss of identity) necessitating and leading to an eventual resolution (finding herself).

Sometimes, stories begin with a conflict and other times the conflict comes in the middle. As the story progresses, the tension mounts, and then the lead character has a revelation, an illumination, or an epiphany. We all have different ways of handling conflict. For example, heroes are fighters, and cowards run from difficult situations. We admire those who overcome adversity or difficult times, and we become inspired by their stories. In the best case scenario, conflict results in change and/or transformation.

One thing to keep in mind is that when writing, there should be a reason for every detail that is included, and those details should move the story along. Take a minute to think about some of the best stories you have ever read or heard. What were the details that contributed to this effect? What were the characters' conflicts, and how were they resolved?

Even though the stories children tell are fragmented, children are typically great storytellers because their stories are compelling and spontaneous. They often choose images that are connected to emotions and are also often connected to accidents or incidents. When children share their stories, they usually do not censor the details, and this makes for stories that are even more compelling, because it is the details that bring a story to life. As Henry Miller once said, "The moment one gives close attention to anything, even a blade of grass, it becomes a mysterious, awesome, indescribably magnificent world in itself" (1964, p. 37).

When my kids were little, I kept a journal for each one, and each time they shared a colorful anecdote or story I tried to capture it on the page. They were just always so cute, innocent, and observant. I felt that if I did not document them at the time, I would forever miss the opportunity.

Stories connect people. Chances are that when there is a storyteller, there is someone listening to the story. This sense of interconnectedness extends beyond individuals. Stories are perhaps the strongest bonds we have with other nations, races, and languages. Australian aboriginals painted symbols from stories on cave walls to help the storyteller remember the story. The Egyptians were the first people actually to write down their stories, and the Romans were good at spreading stories. When a story is told well, the listener is transported on a journey to a new place. Hearing other people's stories gives us different perspectives of the world. Sharing our own stories through writing helps us figure things out and also helps others figure things out.

Another way to look at stories is through what Joseph Campbell called the "Hero's Journey." This is the journey we take from birth to death or from innocence to wisdom, and from stagnation to a new life. The hero's journey is also a path to learn about our authentic selves and our direction in life. During this journey we are continuously posing questions that are the seeds of awakening. Writing is the perfect place to pose the questions that are buried inside our psyches.

When we read or hear other people's stories, whether they are of heroes, heroines, gods, goddesses, or others, we learn that before the characters see the light, they enter darkness, whether through trauma or in a dark forest or barren desert. We learn that in order to be the hero of our own life we must go through challenging times. We also learn that such stories contain a universal message. This universal message can help provide meaning and understanding for our own lives. Writing our stories helps to foster an inner awakening and a transformation of the body, mind, and spirit. If you stop to think about it, every story you hear or tell is a story about transformation.

If you write from the perspective of the hero, then you are writing what Arthur Frank (1995) calls "the quest narrative," because you are meeting your illness, trauma, or troubling times head on. Sometimes you might have no idea what you are seeking in such writing; you just know that something important is to be found. This type of narrative most often becomes published because it offers different ways of being during difficult circumstances. If you decide by the end of this book to write a memoir, it may mean that you have been transformed by an experience you encountered and have chosen to write a quest narrative. Your readers will witness your transformation as a result of your challenging times (see step 5 for more on the quest narrative).

In my research on the transformative powers of memoir writing, writer Mark Matousek said that while writing his memoir, *The Boy He Left Behind* (2000), he was transformed by letting go of the pain from his past. When he began writing his memoir, he felt as if a part of him was missing because, as a child, he did not have a father living at home; but while writing his memoir he realized that there was really no reason for him to feel that way. Monika Wesolowska, in her memoir *Holding Silvan* (2013), said that while she began writing the memoir to heal from the loss of her son, by the time she reached the end of her book she had been transformed in that recounting her loss had helped her view her life in a much larger context. She also realized that, through writing, she had achieved a sense of closure regarding her son's untimely death.

In summary, it is very liberating to be able to tell your story. Carl Greer (2014) brilliantly said that when we write our stories we stop being confused about the events in our lives and thus begin to access the wisdom that we might have lost when we disassociated ourselves from any traumatic memories, feelings, or insights.

Writing Prompt 3:1 – Family Story

Recount a fascinating or compelling family story. Reread it and underline the most interesting parts. Go back and write more details about those sections. Remember, your story should have characters, a conflict, and a resolution of the conflict. Consider what is at stake for you or another family member.

Writing Your Emotional Truth

Writing with your emotional truth is about writing from your heart, rather than entirely from your mind. The emotional truth of a story is the truth of how you feel about the story. Each person has their own emotional truth. Your emotional truth might be different altogether from that of another person, even if that person lived through the same kind of experience you did.

When you write your story, whether in the form of journaling, an essay, a memoir, or a poem, make sure to write what you want to write, rather than what you think *others* want to hear. While writing, say to yourself, "Here is how I see it," or "Here is how it happened to me," or "This is my take on the story." The focus should be on the story and the details connected to it. Sometimes, small details must be added to liven up a story, but the important thing is that the emotional truth is present.

The point is that the story you are writing should remain true to the way you lived through your experience. Writer Pat Conroy, who died a couple of years ago of pancreatic cancer, said that truth is relative and that he didn't worry too much about it when writing his memoirs. He said that if you get wrapped up in what the absolute truth in a story is, then your story will not be told, and the silence around not telling your story is what can deplete an individual of bliss. In fact, he brilliantly said that it is the silence associated with untold stories that can get people into trouble. In other words, what is *not* said can be more harmful than what is actually said.

One thing to keep in mind when writing is that, over time, the details about experiences tend to become blurred or distorted. As you recall events from your past, you will discover certain emotional truths about yourself and your encountered experiences. Remember, you are writing your own emotional truth, no one else's. When you write, it is important not to think about pleasing those whom you are writing about. Otherwise, your writing will not be the best it can be, and it could also potentially ruin the story you *really* want or need to write.

Chances are that if you are not writing your emotional truth, then you are probably being careful to write in a way not to offend others. This type of writing will *not* lead to bliss. It might be writing that leads to publication, but not to bliss. This type of writing is like writing with a façade. The idea of a façade reminds me of my last trip to China in 2008, when they were preparing for the Olympics. In addition to trying to figure out how to minimize respiratory problems in the smog-filled Beijing, the residents were also working on creating a good façade to present to the world. The tour guide took us through some downtown residential areas, showing us how the outside of the buildings and apartment complexes were being refurbished, but when she took us inside we noticed that some of the conditions were below poverty level. She told us that it was very important to the Chinese culture that the outside of the buildings were refurbished, but what they looked like inside was less important. In other words, spending money on the façade to impress the visitors traveling to the Olympics was more important than were the actual living conditions of the Chinese people.

When I think of writing that does not get down to emotional truth, I think of that visit to China. Preparing a façade may be effective in getting a message across, but it is a phony message. Writing that does not represent emotional truth does not have energy or vitality. Basically, the writing becomes journalistic reportage, which is often not compelling. For your best writing to emerge, you must be willing to take risks, and that involves telling your inner truth. As Anaïs Nin says, "The closer a writer keeps to emotional reality, the more alive the writing will be." (1968, p. 83).

Writing Prompt 3:2 – Childhood Emotional Experience

Think about an emotional experience from your childhood. Write about it truthfully from your own perspective. Refrain from thinking about what you "should" write; instead, write about what you need to write.

Finding Your Authentic Voice

The truth is that when you find your authentic voice in writing you will know it, and you will also be on your way to finding your bliss. You will know it because the writing just feels right, and your words flow rather easily. You can always tell when someone is writing in their authentic voice because what they are saying rings true. Last year, I met with memoirist Mary Karr. When speaking about voice in memoir she shared that great memoirs can live or die based 100 percent on the voice of the writer. She said that all the great memoirists she knows sound on the page like they do in person and that their voices make you feel close to them, almost as if you are inside them.

Writing your emotional truth means being honest about your feelings. It is about allowing your inner voice to take charge. In other words, you are writing from your heart, not your head.

When I was in graduate school for writing, one of my mentors suggested that when writing I should make believe that I am seated across the table from my best friend. The writing, like the talking, should be personal and intimate. He also suggested that as part of my editing, I should read my work out loud. He advised that this is the best way to identify an authentic voice.

"I want to write like Mary Karr," a woman in one of my memoir-writing workshops once told me. When I asked her what it was about Karr's writing that she loved, she said, "It just flows so beautifully and poetically. It has such a nice rhythm. I can't put her books down." She went on to ask, "How can I do that?" I told her that she should start by rereading all of Karr's books and study what was specifically compelling. Then, she should read her favorite sections out loud and write or type them. Copying is one way to imbue us with the writer's style.

Before her passing in 2009, writer Barbara Moss Robinette shared with me that even though her MFA was in art, she had taught an MFA-in-writing program. She called herself a "self-taught writer." When I asked how she had taught herself to write, she said that after choosing her favorite books, she copied sections longhand in her journal. She believed that that was the best way to learn how to write. She said that it was her way to infuse herself with the voice of her favorite writers.

When you are in tune with your authentic or inner voice, you have a greater chance of tapping into your intuition and thus can become more alert to messages from the universe. Your inner, authentic voice gives you affirmation and advice. It might also arrive during altered states of consciousness, relaxation, or self-hypnosis. During difficult times, your authentic voice may become even louder.

Some creative individuals—such as authors, poets, musicians, and healers—are often thought of as people who are in touch with their intuition and inner voice. Gandhi admitted that he heard an inner voice that shared this message with him: "You are on the right track; move neither to the left nor the right, but keep to the straight and narrow." The more we trust our inner voice, the more quickly we will be led to our bliss.

One thing I learned in graduate school is that sometimes it takes a while to find your authentic voice. It also takes being confident about your subject matter. It is a good idea to write about what you know. When writing for bliss, chances are that you are writing about yourself, and there is no one who knows you better than you do. Some people find their authentic voice more easily than others do. When teaching my students, I speak about the "throat-clearing" sessions of writing. That is, when you sit down to write you might begin by rambling; you start to write about one subject and then the trajectory of your writing ends up somewhere else. This process is perfectly fine and sometimes essential for writing. What you may find is that your story actually begins on the third or fourth page. I call those first few pages "throat-clearing pages." In the final drafts of the manuscript revisions, these pages are sometimes discarded because they often do not move the story forward; however, they are nevertheless a vital part of the writing process. When you are "in your voice" you will speak from your heart. Your true voice emerges only after the throat clearing or false voice has been allowed to emerge.

For most people, it is difficult to write in their authentic voice and edit at the same time. Two different sides of the brain are involved in each of these tasks. Writing with your authentic voice is the voice coming from your body and not your mind. When you are in the practice of writing from your body, you will reap the rewards of a happy and blissful journey.

Thaisa Frank (1994) offers a number of suggestions and rituals to help cultivate the most natural voice for you. Some of the things she suggests include surrounding yourself with your favorite objects, writing when you are angry, humming as you write, and writing with the hand opposite to the one with which you normally write. She also suggests writing only fragments of a story or dialogue, writing in the dark, or dressing all in one color as a way to be different from the way you usually dress.

If you are writing about someone dear to you and you have a piece of their clothing, you might try having their clothing nearby when writing. Some years ago I was fortunate enough to receive a purple cape from a deceased writer whom I admire and whose essence inspires me. Instead of keeping the item hanging in my closet, my spiritual guide suggested that I wear it while writing. When doing so, I found that my creativity flourished and my voice became extremely authentic. It was as if words flowed more easily when I wore the writer's cape; perhaps in some ways, they might even have been flowing from her.

Writing Prompt 3:3 – On a Visionary Person

Think of someone whom you view as either intuitive or a visionary. Write about this person and why you think they are intuitive. What personal experiences have you had with them to make you view them in this way? How do you think that you can learn from their intuitive powers?

Writing Prompt 3:4 – On Your Authentic Voice

Write about what you believe your authentic voice is. Who is the person who wants to come through in your writing? Give examples of writers whom you want to emulate and what it is about their voices that you admire.

Writing Techniques

There are basic writing techniques which can help your writing be more compelling to read, such as using the active voice, using the senses in your descriptions, replacing verbs for nouns, simplifying what you are saying by deleting unnecessary words, replacing complex words with more simple ones, avoiding repetition, and writing like you speak.

But, there are also some more specific writing techniques which are available to writers to help writing come even more alive or to help you make the point you want to make. Certain techniques can make your writing become more powerful and alive. Below are some that can help in this way.

Embodied Writing

The most compelling personal narratives share profound emotions and incorporate what research psychologist Rosemarie Anderson (2011) calls *embodied writing*. This type of writing can be a powerful tool for transformation. It is a way for the reader to become deeply connected to the story being told. Anderson claims, and I agree, that the human experience is relayed from the inside out. In other words, to describe lived experiences, especially profound ones, embodied writing works to give the body a voice in a way that it may not have had before. While engaged in embodied writing, the writer becomes more involved in their own story because they feel the emotions of the experience in their physical being. Sometimes the actual experience is not as important as how the individual has reacted to or dealt with the experience.

The connection between and weaving of the body and mind is important. It has been known for a while that emotional experiences are linked with our physiological systems. Hence, what we sometimes call having a "gut feeling" about something. When you are engaged in embodied writing, you are listening to the messages of your body. It is important to listen to these messages because they are very connected to your inner truths. While writing, practice expanding the joy of following your heart, and give it the freedom to wander and think about all the possible "what ifs."

Anderson says that there are seven characteristics of embodied writing:

- The writing is true to life, inviting sympathetic resonance (feeling words in the body).
- The writing includes internal and external information about the experience.
- The writing is written from the inside out.
- The writing is concrete and specific and uses the senses.
- The writing is attuned to the living body.
- The narratives are embedded in experience and are usually written in the first person.
- The writing is poetic and literary.

Writing Prompt 3:5 – Being Aware of Your Feelings

Sit still with your eyes closed. Ask yourself how you are feeling today. Try to pinpoint where the emotion you are feeling is located in your body. Just feel it. Don't read into it or analyze it. Simply write about your experience.

Reflective Writing

Once you have provided the readers with the basic idea of your story, you may integrate reflective writing into it. Reflective writing entails sharing the thought processes associated with your lived experience. Thus, in addition to sharing your experience, you add your personal reflections about it. If you are writing about something that happened a long time ago, you might write about what you think the meaning of that experience was, and/or how it might have affected you over the years. You might reflect on how the experience changed or transformed you, and/or how you might have behaved differently at the time

As children, we tend to take events and situations for granted, but as we grow into adulthood we have a tendency to examine our lives more analytically and with a more reflective lens. This was my experience when writing my memoir, *Regina's Closet*. Using the few remaining relatives and my grandmother's retrospective journal, which she left for me in her closet, I began investigating and examining my grandmother's life. My reflection on both our lives helped me understand that childhood experiences—such as her being orphaned at the age of eleven and my own loss when she committed suicide—greatly affect the adults we become. Acknowledging this made me realize that I could close the door on the experience of finding my grandmother dead and move on in a state of well-being. Studying and reflecting on my grandmother's life transformed me in that it brought me a deep sense of resolve.

Freeman adds an interesting perspective to the art of reflective writing and examines the idea of *hindsight,* which he refers to as "a process of looking back over the terrain of the past from the standpoint of the present and either seeing things anew or drawing" various connections (2010, p. 4). He says that narrative reflection is a way to give meaning to the trajectory of events, experiences, and epochs, which happen to emerge in and through the act of hindsight. Hindsight, he claims, is at the core of self-understanding and consequently plays an important role in shaping and deepening our moral life. In his book called *Hindsight,* he explores how one, perhaps pivotal event that might have seemed inconsequential at the time becomes infused with meaning as we look back at it at a later date. This is exactly what happened to me with my grandmother's suicide. As a child, I took the experience in stride, but only when I got older and people asked how my grandmother died did I realize through narrative reflection the huge impact on me of having lived through such an experience.

Reflective writing is also a tool to connect you with your readers. It allows them to understand your experience and helps them resonate with the story. As Phillip Lopate (2013) deftly says, "There is nothing more exciting than to follow a live, candid mind thinking on the page, exploring uncharted waters" (p. 43). It is this thinking on the page in the most transparent way that will engage your readers. After all, don't we love being in another person's head?

Reflective writing is about digging deep down into your emotional truth. This means that you are digging deep into your heart's center to write about what you are *really* feeling, rather than about what you *think* others want to hear. Reflective writing is not the same as explaining, which is about telling or reporting a story; rather, reflective writing is filled with emotions about the experience. Just as painters use a variety of paint strokes, writers use techniques such as reflection to bring depth and insight into their stories. Reflection helps to bring the story alive. The best writing puts a lens on the story, up close and personal, and then pulls back and looks at it from a distance. If your writing does not have reflection, it will read like a journalistic reportage of what happened to you. Reflective writing helps you find meaning in your experience, especially if it was a chaotic one. It pushes you deeper into your understanding of your lived experience and its role in your life.

Sometimes when we reflect, we tend to speak directly to ourselves to offer advice or encouragement. Maybe the "silver-lining voice" or the voice that always looks for the good aspect of a situation starts to talk in the journal. In other situations, the reflective journal entry might even pose a question to ponder, such as, "I wonder what I really want out of my marriage?"

In his essay, "Finding the Inner Story of Memoir and Personal Essay," creative nonfiction writer Michael Steinberg (2012) says that memoir, in fact, has two stories—the story that you remember and the story of your thoughts about or reflection on your experience. In other words, what you are asking in reflective writing is: What do the facts in my story really mean, and what do I feel when I write the scenes associated with my story? The real question concerns how you interpret the story of your own lived experience.

Buddhist psychology differentiates between the stories we tell and the experiences we have. Our minds tell continuous stories combined with thoughts about the experiences that affect us. Buddhists remind us of the importance of being mindful of and acknowledging our thoughts but caution us not to become obsessed with or lost in them. Sometimes if we become lost in our thoughts, writing can help us make sense of them or disentangle them. Writing can also help us witness the details of our stories and help us distance ourselves from them.

When Kim Stafford was writing his memoir about his brother's suicide, he said that he was transformed by reflecting on the idea that his writing inspired him to dig deeper into understanding his own life. It also forced him to pose questions. Looking back and reflecting on his brother's life made him realize that relationships don't end with death; they go on forever, and sometimes they can even become magnified after someone has died. Stafford also found that only when his son transitioned into adolescence did he himself begin to reflect and consequently write about the circumstances surrounding his brother's life and death.

While reflecting on his experience, Stafford shared this in my interview with him about his memoir: "I can't protect my son from pain. Life will give him struggles. But I can be present to him and I can share dark secrets with him in a way that was not given to me as a child and that was not given to my brother."

Monica Wesolowska provided another example of reflection in speaking to me about writing about her son who died quite young. In reflecting on the way in which people receive terminal news, she said this:

> I just think that our sense of entitlement as a culture, our mythical idea that we all somehow deserve to make it big and that that's where we're all headed—we're all going to make more and more money—extends to the idea that we're all going to become more and more healthy and eventually not die. So with that paradigm, I think a parent with a very damaged child almost can't hear a doctor saying that it might be fatal. I just think people don't hear that and doctors often don't say it, in fact. People come home from getting a terminal diagnosis without understanding that they've been given a terminal diagnosis.

Reflection is simply a tool to help you understand your life as you look back at certain events and experiences. It adds an interesting dimension to storytelling—connecting the past to the present. The balance of telling your story and weaving in reflective writing varies from one piece of writing to another, but it is the correct balance that brings about compelling writing and transformation for both the writer and the reader.

The Challenges of Remembering and Not Remembering

Your memories are of everything you have experienced up to the present moment. This includes everyone you have met and spoken to and encountered. Without memories, it would be difficult to engage in personal writing.

The best personal writing will be written from your personal perspective incorporating your emotional truth, without someone else's point of view. Sometimes siblings are both writers and decide to write their memoirs, and it might be surprising that their stories sound so different. The reason is that they are both writing their own emotional truth about the story and how they saw it unfold.

Sometimes writers who write about true experiences want the liberty to fictionalize their story, either to make it more compelling and/or because they do not remember precise details from their past. One good example is *The Things They Carried* (2009) by my friend, Tim O'Brien. One of the most amazing things about this book is that it is fiction; like some fiction, it is written in the first person, but it reads just like memoir. It is based on O'Brien's Vietnam experience. When we visited together, we spoke a lot about memory—in fact, he wrote a great short story called, "How to Tell a True War Story," which is actually a work of fiction. But when you read it, just as when you read his novel, you could swear that it is a work of nonfiction. In his short story, he says—and I believe this also pertains to memoir writing—that one cannot tell a true war story because in the fog of war perceptions are altered, and the recollections and restorying depend on the person telling the story. In our conversation, he said that what is important in any story is not so much the details and the order of events but how the story is told and the emotional truth it is sharing, even if it is a matter of reimagining the truth.

Because memory is fallible, when writing we have no choice but to merge memory with imagination. In fact, because memory is unreliable, we need to depend upon our imagination as a way to fill in the gaps. As Tobias Wolff says, memory has its own story to tell.

Memory is the writer's most poignant tool. If you didn't have any memories, you couldn't write a memoir. That is why most memoirs are written by those of us in middle age and beyond: we have a lot to remember. The exception, of course, would be writers to whom something tragic or unusual has happened that they are compelled to write about, such as Lucy Grealy (2003) in *The Autobiography of a Face*. Memory is like a muscle, the more you use it the stronger it becomes.

Writing Prompt 3:6 – Your Core Truths

If everything were stripped and taken away from you—your body, your health, your family, friends, loved ones, and possessions—and you were left with your authentic self, what life experiences or lessons or truths based on your memories would you like to express or share with the world?

Writing Prompt 3:7 – Recalling Childhood Again

Close your eyes. Bring your attention inside. Bring yourself back to your childhood. Think about a memory you would like to write about. Write nonstop for ten minutes.

Writing Prompt 3:8 – Getting Inside a Memory

Close your eyes and imagine your life on a movie screen. Allow the memories to float in across the screen. Now choose one memory to write about in detail. Notice yourself in the memory and describe what you are feeling and seeing. How does your body feel? Try to immerse yourself inside the memory.

Memory and Imagination

Memory ends at the present moment. It is everything you have lived, experienced, seen, and felt up until this instant. Everyone houses their own set of memories. As I have mentioned, when we are telling stories verbally or on the page we might subconsciously fill in the gaps of what we remember to be true by using our imagination. In fact, one of the interesting things about the writing process is how it gives access to the unconscious mind. Fiction writers must master the art of making a good scene; the challenge of the memoirist is how and what to remember. Sometimes it might feel unnecessary to stick to the exact or literal truth of what happened, as long as the message or the meaning of the experience is portrayed. There is a lot of controversy regarding the line between fiction and nonfiction. When people write memoir, they typically write the truth to the best of their knowledge. However, memory plays tricks on us, and sometimes details get blurred. Typically, what we usually remember is whether we felt good or bad in response to an experience. When people read memoirs, they expect to hear nothing but the truth, but sometimes authors either write what they think to be true or add to the story to make it more compelling.

In other words, because memory is fallible and has gaps, the writer might fill in details by embellishing. A well-known example is the scenario around James Frey's memoir, *A Million Little Pieces,* and how he told it slant. For those who don't recall the story, back in 2002 *Smoking Gun* published an article claiming that Frey fabricated part of his memoir. This inspired many people to read his book, and, as a result, sales skyrocketed. When interviewed about what happened, Frey said that all memoirists alter minor details to increase the literary effect of their story. His comment began a nationwide discussion about the truth in memoir, something I had been discussing in my writing workshops for years.

In fact, my thesis for my MFA in writing was on this very subject—the interplay between memory and imagination. I compared two memoirs: Eudora Welty's *One Writer's Beginnings* (1995) and Mary McCarthy's *Memories of a Catholic Girlhood* (1972). In her book Welty compared her inner and outer worlds:

> The outside world is the vital component of my inner life. My work, in the terms in which I see it, is as dearly matched to the world as its sharer. My imagination takes its strength and guides its direction from what I see and hear and learn and feel and remember of my living world. But I was to learn slowly that both these worlds, outer and inner, were different from what they seemed to me in the beginning (p.76).

What I learned is that for the most part, writers set out to write truthful memoirs; but often, as in McCarthy's case, it does not take long before they realize the unreliability of their own memories. McCarthy gets lost in a labyrinth of confusing images from her past. She is unsure about the demarcations among her memory, her imagination, and her habitual childhood lying. She is not even sure if there is a clear boundary.

McCarthy shares her memories of the difficult times before her parents' death when she was six years old. At the time of the influenza epidemic, her family had to evacuate their home. She vividly describes the hotel in which they all spent an evening and its grim environment. She said that she remembered some of the things about her mother's death and how all the adults looked worried and uncertain; but she was unsure if she truly remembered all the details, because at the end of her passage she wrote, "...as I recall it." Her inability to check the facts gave her a strong sense of insecurity about her past.

One of my favorite essays on the subject is Patricia Hampl's "Memory and Imagination" (2002). I have read it many times and still learn from it. She says that what we remember is actually what becomes our reality. While some people might claim that those who write memoirs are self-involved, Hampl disagrees, saying that such writers are not self-absorbed but rather write memoir to find out what they don't know, in an attempt not only to find themselves but also to find (and share) a world.

Some writers use a memory box that helps guide their writing. Regarding some years, you might have only six boxes, or even three, because that is all you remember—and that's fine.

Here's how to make a memory box:

- Make a chart for any year of your life.
- Make a box for each month.
- Fill in each box with what you were doing at that time.

Look for stories in this timeline and then tell some quick ones. Chances are that there will be too many stories, but you will figure out which ones you are really compelled to tell. Sometimes you don't know what you will write until you actually sit down to do it. Think about the sound of your childhood and the adult you became. While you are doing this, it is important to keep little notebooks everywhere, because you might remember an incident that you want to put into one of your boxes, but by the time you get home you'll have forgotten it.

When the memoirist sets out to write a memoir, he or she quickly realizes that memoir writing is not merely a transcription of a life but rather a fictionalized version, sprinkled with reflection and perspective, fleshing out the gaps. In essence, the memoirist must be seen as an interpreter and a creator, as well as a preserver of history.

In studying the interplay of memory and imagination, I realized that in order to write a compelling memoir a balance must be struck between fiction and nonfiction. Nowhere is it written that memoirs are fact; memoirs ought to be about truth, which is often the by-product of memory mixed with imagination.

Writing Prompt 3:9 – Keys to Truth

Write for ten minutes about a memory from your childhood. After ten minutes, stop and reread what you wrote. Circle the images and feelings that are strongest or resonate the most with you. Write in more detail about one or two of the images you have circled.

Step Four
Examining Your Life

The meaning of life is to find your gift;
the purpose of life is to give it away.
—Pablo Picasso

Plato says that the unexamined life is not worth living. There is much we can learn by looking back and studying our lives; things that may not have seemed significant at the time become more meaningful as time goes on. The process of writing is a good one for examining our lives, hopes, dreams, and aspirations. The dance we do to discover our bliss and the stories we tell can help us focus on finding a life purpose.

Some people believe that your life patterns, purposes, and themes are written in your DNA, while others believe that we tend to have more control over our destinies. My sense is that it is a combination of both factors. At times we might feel as if we want something more out of life, but we don't know how to find out what that something is. For the most part, we all want to make an impact on the world. The place where we want to have impact is usually in areas that we feel passionate about. To have impact on or make a change in the world, we need to take initiative and be able to take a risk.

Most often your purpose is already present within you, it is just a matter of finding it. First, you need to know yourself and what has shaped your past and what inspires you to move forward. These are all pieces of information offering tools of awareness. Such knowledge can be very empowering.

Life Purposes and Themes

Your life theme concerns what drives you and what you are always searching for. It may be described as the trajectory or actions that your life has followed in the past and will probably continue to follow in the future. When the theme is right for you, you will feel a sense of flow, as if you are headed in the correct direction and everything feels right. You will feel as if your life has meaning. In his book *Flow* (2008), Csikszentmihalyi says that when life has meaning you feel as if there is a sense of harmony. During my teen years in the 1960s, someone would say, "Man, he's got his head together," which means that he really is doing what he was meant to do. This inner congruence results in a deep inner strength and sense of serenity.

Rather than following the path suggested by someone else, those "in the flow" appear to be living their chosen authentic dreams. When your theme is connected to your life purpose, you will feel motivated and intrinsically happy. While others may suggest what life theme or profession suits your personality, nobody can completely convince you what your life theme should be. You need to discover and nurture it on your own and find your own sense of purpose. As Csikszentmihalyi says, "Through trial and error, through intense cultivation, we can straighten out the tangled skein of conflicting goals and choose the one that will give purpose to action" (p. 225).

Sometimes life themes are established early in life and might be in response to childhood experiences. Perhaps the experience was a joyful one, or it might have been related to trauma or pain as a result of loss, abandonment, being orphaned, or being severely hurt physically or emotionally. Not everybody responds to challenging situations in the same way, and it is not so much the experience you had that matters but how you reacted to it and what its effect was on your life. Some people are blessed to be able to turn disorder into order, or to make good from bad, or to draw meaning from their lived experiences.

My life provides a good example: Because of my grandmother's suicide, my mother gave me a journal, and that journal became the springboard for my becoming a writer. My journal was and continues to be a place where I go to heal when I hurt, when I feel abandoned or confused. Many of my healer friends and colleagues have stories of turbulent earlier lives, whether it was from being reared in a dysfunctional family or because of other exposures.

Young adults often battle to discover their life purpose or what career path to choose. This can also happen in midlife. Even though I am not a clinician, people are often drawn to share their stories and woes with me. When they are at a crossroad in their life, the question I am compelled to ask them is: What brought you joy or bliss as a child? They are often surprised to be asked this question, and it is interesting to watch a smile spread across their face. They stop to reflect, and then I ask whether they have ever thought of revisiting their childhood passions. Inevitably, they say, "I haven't thought about that in so long." I suggest that they write about it and see what unfolds on the page—perhaps some juicy revelation or illumination. In many ways, I believe that our childhoods hold the keys to who we become as adults.

If you are at a crossroad, or even if your life path has been as a seeker, chances are that you will ask questions about your life purpose, your destiny, your right path, and how you discover it. These are indeed sacred questions. They are awakening questions, and they are questions that inspire us to transform. They inspire us to look for the messages elicited by our hearts that compel us to examine what matters most of us.

During the discovery process, you might notice untapped talents and desires of your heart. Sometimes, when we look closely at these sorts of questions, we can also come face to face with angst, confusion, and concerns that inspire us to dig deeper into our soul's quest. In either case, writing is a productive way to tap into the answers to these questions.

I love how Siegel, in his book, *The Art of Healing* (2013) describes the purpose of life. He says that he believes the purpose of life is to achieve the true balance we need to use our bodies and light to become soulful in our actions. He suggests that we think of ourselves as a candle with the flame reaching for the heavens in the hope that it connects with the Divine. He says to think of the wax and wick as our bodies, which help to keep us connected and grounded. While the candle burns, the flame consumes the wax fuel, and its quality is determined by how pure the flame is. This candle illuminates our world by sharing our love and light. "When we die, that light and love are handed to future generations. Therein lies immortality. The light from that candle becomes the pathway to learning about life, just as words are pathways to sharing and understanding ideas" (p. 193).

Part of my research on the benefits of writing for healing examined the impact on our life theme of early significant or pivotal experiences. The results were most interesting. When I was interviewing five esteemed writers, they admitted that early pivotal experiences not only inspired them to become writers but were clues to their life themes. Kim Stafford, author of *100 Tricks Every Boy Can Do* (2012), said that since childhood his life theme has been *kuleana*, or, as he describes it, "the freedom to tell stories." It has also been described as a "privilege," "concern," or "responsibility." When writing about his brother's suicide, Stafford realized that the experience of writing and telling his stories gave him a palpable freedom. Also, since childhood, he has posed a great deal of questions, and he admitted that while writing his memoir, he posed even more questions. Through writing he also realized the importance of transparency in his life, and he figured out why his father never discussed his brother's suicide. He suspected that it was due to his father's upbringing during the Great Depression; people thought differently in those days, and suicide was considered a taboo subject. Unlike today, it was rarely discussed.

Another writer in my study, Mark Matousek, called himself a seeker and said that his life revolved around posing questions. He admitted that the themes in both his memoirs focused on his deep sense of spiritual hunger. He said that with this hunger came a sense of wonderment and trying to figure out how to deal with the hunger in the most effective and productive way. One of his most interesting revelations through writing is that survivors are very often seekers and that the creative impulse is connected to a sense of longing.

Writing Prompt 4:1 – The Big Questions

Write one page about each of the following:
What really matters to you?
What is your soul's purpose?
What is life for?
To what do you want to consecrate your life?

The Meaning of Experiences

Central to our needs as humans is the need to understand the world around us. In knowing the causes and meaning of certain lived experience we come to understand the role and impact of those experiences in our lives. We can say that the search for meaning continues until the day we depart from this world. Often it takes some distance from a lived experience for us to be able to understand it. Some people reach out to religious or spiritual paths to help them gain such understanding. Some refer to writing as a spiritual practice because it cuts through the illusion of the self. Writing has been my own spiritual practice because it helps me release whatever is bottled up inside of me. It helps me find out what I do not know, and thus it helps me become more aware. It also helps me discover meaning and find a container for my experiences. Writing as a spiritual practice is very liberating and satisfying. It is liberating because when you release your secrets you become free and have more control over your life.

When diagnosed with breast cancer in 2001, I journaled my way to recovery. One of the things I realized is the brevity of life. I realized that there is no time like the present to seek bliss. I also realized that having toxic people in my life is a bliss deterrent, so as much as possible I try to surround myself with inspiring, positive, and loving individuals. "We are our friends," someone once told me, and I truly believe this to be true. When I slowly eliminated toxic individuals from my life, I felt so much stronger and empowered, and my healing path was much easier to maneuver.

In his research on writing for healing, Pennebaker (1990) found that half the participants in his study used certain words to explain how they felt after writing or what illuminations had come to them. Those words were *realize*, *understand*, *resolve*, and *work through*. He says that, intuitively, people tend to see writing as a way to understand and resolve their own personal upheavals, and that often their intuitions during writing are accurate.

As humans, we are complicated and affected by our environment (nurture) and by our genetics (nature). We are shaped by our experiences and the landscape of our childhoods, whether joyous or wounded. Essentially, we *are* our childhoods, and the patterns established during childhood often continue into our adult years. Throughout our lives, nature and nurture weave together, forming the landscape of who we are and what we respond to on our life path. We are forever shaped by these forces. As we evolve and move into our golden years, we are able to look back with the perspective to see these facets more clearly, knowing that no two people evolve in the same way.

Psychologist C. G. Jung coined the term *individuation*, which is the process of becoming self-aware of who we truly are. This is akin to the process of self-actualization. He maintained that our ability to find purpose and meaning in life is hugely dependent on the degree to which we individuate and on how we define and see ourselves. Midlife is a critical phase in a person's life, occurring between the age of forty to sixty, wherein the person enters a sort of transition of identity or an altered sense of awareness. It is a time when some people evaluate their path or position in life, reflecting on what they've accomplished and what they want to do with the rest of their lives. Some people become very stressed during this time and decide to do something completely different, whether it be to buy a luxury car, have an affair, buy a new house, or take a trip.

Jung also said that our personality is made up of two parts, the conscious and the unconscious. Our ego gives us our identity and is the center of our consciousness. It sets us apart from others. Our unconscious part, on the other hand, works in the background, bringing us into balance.

The Patterns in Our Lives

Knowing and understanding your life patterns can be a clue to determining your life purpose, which could put you on the path of bliss. Whatever it is that makes your heart sing, whatever brings you joy, whatever your priorities are—those are the things that are important for you to pursue. While this sounds like obvious advice, it is amazing how often people forget this truth and work in jobs or choose careers that don't inspire them or put joy into their hearts.

Looking into and examining our past—the patterns in our lives, where we came from, and where we are headed—is one way to understand who we are. Those who have participated in

Alcoholics Anonymous know that this kind of reflection is a huge part of the writing process. On the road to recovery, when AA attendees do personal writing they are advised to divide their writing into three parts:

- Their past
- What happened that might have led to addiction
- Who are they now (i.e. belief systems, strengths, and weaknesses)

They might then be advised to look for threads or themes running through all three writing subjects. Are there any patterns or commonalities? To take it one step further, they might be asked to identify any lessons they learned along the way and any insights that might have come to them. This sort of life review is a powerful way to paint a portrait of yourself.

Writing about Difficult Times

It has been said that writers turn to writing during difficult times because writing is a way of healing and softening the pain. As Lesser says in her book, *Broken Open* (2005), "If I could distill all the great writings on suffering down to a few words, I would simply say that suffering and crisis transform us, humble us, and bring out what matters most in life" (p. 89). Anyone who has faced their mortality understands the importance of this statement. Surely, being a cancer survivor, I completely agree with Lesser's statement.

In 2006, exactly five years after my breast cancer diagnosis, I returned to my oncologist for a routine check-up. Everything was normal about my visit, until I received a phone call from him telling me that I had to return for a repeat blood test because one of my immunoglobulins (IgA) was elevated. This immunoglobulin or antibody plays an important role in immune function for the body's mucous membranes. The repeat test also came back elevated, so he suggested doing a bone-marrow biopsy. While he was reluctant to tell me what he thought was the problem, he finally said that he suspected multiple myeloma, a rare form of bone-marrow cancer. The biopsy confirmed this diagnosis.

The news was absolutely shocking since, at the time, I was in my early fifties and had learned through reading that this disease most often strikes men in their seventies who had worked in the mining industry. I had none of the risk factors; and my oncologist was also stunned. Dr. Piro was a tall, well-dressed, wise, and handsome middle-aged man with a positive demeanor and energy. At my follow-up appointment after the bone-marrow biopsy, he looked deep into my eyes and said, "If this diagnosis doesn't rivet you, nothing will." While in the moment, there was little time to respond or to reflect upon his words, when I got home I did spend some time writing about his comment. Eventually, I acknowledged the wisdom of his words. More than ever before, I felt a deep sense the urgency to follow my bliss. I made the decision right then and there to remove all the toxins from my life—including people and food—and, as Lesser deftly stated, I tried to bring into my life what mattered most

Siegel (1989) has a similar thought in that he views "disease as a gift" (p. 190). Becoming ill makes you think about the way your life is unfolding and encourages you to push the reset button. Becoming ill alerts you to the priorities in your life — what is important and what is unimportant. It becomes a catalyst for change and transformation, and it also encourages you to reevaluate your life path, who is in your life, and what brings you the greatest feeling of bliss.

Wounded Healers and Storytellers

Many of those in the helping professions have had situations such as mine with cancer or others that challenged their psychological, emotional, or physical well-being. They might have become a doctor, nurse, or therapist to satisfy an inner need to help others and the need to be appreciated. Often these individuals have been called wounded healers because, in helping others, they unconsciously are healing an inner wound of their own. Sometimes these people become wounded storytellers and work to share their experiences and journeys with others. Actually, in shamanic cultures the most gifted healers are called "wounded healers" because they have been called to look deeply into the psyche. They use the pains and wounds of life in an alchemy of healing that is very empowering and has deep purpose.

Arthur Frank (1995) identifies three types of narratives written by wounded storytellers or those who write about difficult times—the *restitution narrative*, the *chaos narrative*, and the *quest narrative*. Personally, I believe that the type of narrative chooses you, in that it is greatly connected to who you are and your personality type. While at times I wrote narratives that could have slipped into any of the three categories, for the most, and even though many of my narratives were about the darker times in my life, I instinctively shined the light on those times, believing that from all bad comes good and that things will improve. Thus, my instinct has been to write the restitution narrative.

The restitution narrative. This type of narrative shares the story of difficult times, but through it runs the idea that, for example, "Yesterday I was healthy, today I am sick, tomorrow I will be healthy again." This narrative harbors positive thinking and bright undertones and is usually written by those who are dealing with acute, rather than chronic, illness. The focus tends to be on their improved health. The writer of this type of narrative minimizes his or her illness, assuming they will be "back to normal soon."

The restitution narrative is connected to another type of writing, the *reconstitution narrative*, in which the writer longs for a sense of acceptance of their trauma as a way to create a coherent story of themselves and their lives. In this way the traumatized person brings together the shattered or fragmented aspects of their experiences to form a meaningful bridge between the past and the present.

An example would be Monica Wesolowska's memoir, *Holding Silvan*, about her son who died during his first year of life. When I interviewed her for my study, she said that writing about her son's untimely death helped her look at life in a much larger context. Moreover, writing about him was one way to keep him alive. Sharing Silvan's story also gave her a sense of closure about his birth and short life. She said it helped that she completed the memoir after her subsequent two sons were born. Essentially, the writing process was transforming, because she felt that without the sense of closure she gained from it she could not have moved into the next phase of her life of rearing her other sons. At the same time, writing gave her a chance to reminisce about her own childhood and the losses inherent to it.

She examined and compared how others in her family dealt with losses. She was inspired to examine the patterns of loss in her own life—how they have accumulated and how they have made her the person she now is.

The chaos narrative. This narrative is the opposite of the restitution narrative in that the writers assume a position of illness or a problem with no hope or indication for improvement. They write as if they are doomed. They tend to illicit anxiety in themselves and in the reader. There seems to be less room for reflection in this type of narrative; everything about the writer's situation seems urgent and stressful. The perspective is a negative one, and the reader feels as if the writer is in freefall with no hope of returning.

The quest narrative. Those who write this type of narrative accept their illness or difficult situation and use it for their own growth and transformation. They meet their problem head on and use their difficulty as a way to forge ahead. Writing about difficult subjects makes you feel better afterwards because there's a relief about writing down what has been bothering or upsetting you. Writing can release you of the burden. In other words, "it gets it out of your system."

When discussing this type of narrative, I am reminded of my daughter Regine's comment when I was diagnosed with breast cancer at the age of forty-seven. She was sixteen at the time. When my oncologist phoned, I was seated in my home office. Regine happened to be walking past when she saw me hang up the phone with a distressed expression on my face. She knew I'd been waiting for the doctor's report from my breast biopsy and intuited that I had just received bad news. She slowly walked toward the sofa where I was seated. She sat down beside me, put her arm around me, put her head on my shoulder and said, "Mom, I think there's a book in this." I glanced at her and smiled at her ability to see the good in this potentially devastating news. By writing my breast cancer story, I would be transformed and empowered in the process.

Her comment surprised and delighted me. It was at that point that I realized she truly knew and understood the role of writing in my life, in that it was clearly a way of healing. Regine understood that I was a writer who capitalized on my difficult times. In all aspects of her life, her wisdom continues today.

My recovery from breast cancer was also around the time of the events of 9/11. I saw myself healing from two events—the loss of my breast and the loss to the city of my youth. I was dealing with a personal pain while also trying to cope with a universal one. From a physical and emotional standpoint, those times were quite challenging, and looking back I can hardly fathom that I made it through. I vividly remember having to shut off the television because the repeated viewing of the towers falling was injuring me over and over again. The pain became unbearable and too intense at times. Sometimes we have to know when just to take care of ourselves.

Sometimes, writing over and over about a difficult time or a wound buried deep inside can allow you to put that wound in a container and detach from it. It can allow you to stand back and reflect on the wound's effect on your life. Stepping back can give you a perspective that contributes to your well-being. Repeatedly thinking and writing about your difficult times can also allow you to become less emotional about them. For example, this happened for me in that I spent many years writing and talking about my narcissistic mother. My mother never wanted children and at times aired her resentment of me by ridiculing me in public. Her putting me down had a deep impact on my sense of self-esteem. As an adult, writing about how I felt, examining why she was like she was, and exploring its effect on me helped me to understand and cope with the situation.

Regardless of the type of narrative you choose to write, it is natural to incorporate self-reflection into your story. When using reflection in your writing, you will observe what is happening in both your exterior and interior world. This will help you understand yourself better, which is a key to transformation.

Self-reflection encourages you to examine your thoughts, feelings, attitudes, and beliefs. It might inspire you to set intentions as a way toward transformation. When other people read your self-reflective writing, they might be inspired to engage in their own self-reflection.

Pennebaker believes that although writing can be healing, there comes a point when you might need simply to stop because the writing could be opening up old wounds that have the potential of becoming tender. Sometimes reopening old wounds can backfire. In the end, it's all about finding a balance in your life as a way to achieve a sense of well-being.

Writing Prompt 4:2 – Trying out Narrative Styles

Choose a narrative method which resonates with you—restitution, chaos, or quest. Write about a troubled time you encountered. If you had an illness, write a letter to the part of you that was injured. If it involved a relationship or a loved one, write a letter to the loved one.

Sharing Stories to Heal

Sharing the stories of your difficult times can also guide others in navigating their own journeys. How you navigated your journey can serve as a road map for those who might feel lost during the process. They might be too close to their lived experience to be able to figure out how to handle it. Witnessing your experience can greatly help them.

Those who are deeply wounded physically, psychologically, or spiritually often lose their voice in the process, and sharing their stories helps them reclaim that voice as a way of healing. As Frank (1995) says, "The voice speaks the mind and expresses the spirit, but it is also a physical organ of the body" (p. xii).

There are not many people who have not navigated some difficult time in their lives. After encountering such times, you will see that telling your story is a way to healing and survival. Writing your story activates the narrating part of your mind and thus can increase your sense of well-being, whether you share your writing with others or not.

Viktor Frankl openly shared his Holocaust story in his book *Man's Search for Meaning* (1959). This book deeply resonated with me because my father was also a Holocaust survivor, having spent five of his most formative years, from the ages of fifteen to twenty, in the concentration camp at Dachau. When Frankl was asked why he wrote the book, he said that he wanted "to convey to the reader by way of concrete example that life holds a potential meaning under any conditions, even the most miserable ones." He added that sharing his story would be helpful even for those who were in despair.

Mortality as a Great Teacher

My mother was somewhat obsessed with the beauty of cemeteries. Whenever we passed one, she made sure to take me for a visit. In some way, you can say that, like my mother, I have been obsessed with death for a very long time. My first term paper in high school was about euthanasia. Many years later when I met with Eva Hoffman at a writing seminar in Key West, over a cup of coffee she told me that everyone has a life theme and that she thought mine was death. She was right. Even though people see me as bright, positive, and charismatic, under the surface there was a time when I was deeply obsessed with death, and I once read someone say, although I cannot recall who, that death is the prime condition of life. Indeed, a strange and macabre way to look at life, but at the same time realistic. You cannot have life without death. They just work together. Death does have a lot to teach us, and if you have ever been at a loved one's death bed, you know exactly what I'm talking about. My family sat vigilance for my father-in-law, and it was amazing to watch him transition.

One value of being aware of the reality of death is that it motivates you not to squander time. During the fall of 2001, after recuperating from my breast surgery, I was reminded of the brevity of life and the importance of pursuing our dreams. My husband, who has always encouraged me to follow my bliss, was even more emphatic this time, now that I had come face to face with my own mortality. I had always wanted to go to graduate school, so I applied and was accepted into Spalding University's charter class of its low-residency MFA program. I was very excited to begin in October, a little over a month after the happenings of 9/11. People had huge fears about flying at the time, but many of us thought that the increased security would make it safer than ever. There was talk that the school administrators would delay beginning the program, but they finally decided to move forward. They handled the situation beautifully, in that the faculty capitalized on it and had us do a lot of writing for healing, since we were all healing from the trauma to our country. We wrote many healing poems and essays and then shared them. This greatly contributed to the healing process.

Ever since writing in my journal became a way to heal after my grandmother's suicide, I have used writing to heal during difficult times. By the time I was sixty, I had not personally lived through any world wars, but I had lost many loved ones and had had some health challenges, all of which lead me to writing.

Sometimes it takes others to help us identify our life theme—as Eva Hoffman helped me identify my theme of death—but sometimes it also takes flipping through our filled journals to identify patterns in our writing over the years. There is a storyline that runs through your life, and writing can help you discover what it is; this process may be used as a springboard for growth and transformation. Knowing that thread or theme and writing about it can lead you to a sense of wholeness and harmony. In this way, we can more easily identify our bliss. It is the telling of who you are through storytelling that can ignite the flame of bliss. In the act, you release that flame into the universe.

Lesser says that there are three rules about dying: First, death isn't something only that happens at the end of life. She says that each day—in physical, emotional, and spiritual ways—we are born dying. Second, grief is good because it is a sign of how much we have loved. And third, the death of the body is the beginning of an adventure.

In her book, *Foolsgold*, Wooldridge (2007), refers to things that may have been lost, such as "a marriage, a child, a house, a city, a world. An idea of who we are. Whatever seems familiar, tried and true." (p.17). She says that loss leads to a sense of emptiness which often coincides with a time of silent reflection. During these quieter or silent times is when we might also get an inkling of something that lights up inside of us or something that can help us heal. During these times, it's important to just "allow" to see what emerges. This is an opportune time to write.

Writing Prompt 4:3 – Learning from Difficult Times

In writing about a difficult time, begin by writing at the top of your journal page, "I used to be, but now I am..." In your writing, share what you learned in the process and what words of advice you would give others who are walking a similar path.

Inner-Child Healing

In his book *Reconciliation* (2010), Thich Nhat Hanh says that inside each of us there is a young, suffering child, and that to protect ourselves from future suffering we try to forget the pain. He says that the cry we hear deep in our hearts comes from the wounded child within. Healing our inner child can help heal any negative emotions we might have. It is important to know that wounds exist in every cell of our bodies, in the same way that they house the DNA of our ancestors. Sometimes early wounds or experiences, according to Siegel (1989), can have consequences on our physical and emotional selves as we grow up. Sometimes we can ignore the pain from past experiences, but they will always be there. Sometimes we push aside any pain or suffering from our past as a way to cope during our present life, but every so often the pain resurfaces. At times, the resurfacing happens while writing and is an important part of your healing. Pain can also emerge during meditation, and that is perfectly normal and fine.

Sometimes the baggage we carry from childhood is difficult to shake, and some people become obsessed or possessed with traumas encountered during their childhood. Many people can function, but others could unravel in detrimental ways if they do seek ways to resolve the past pains through narrative. Whether writing narrative or expressing yourself verbally, embracing and acknowledging the wounded child is the first step in the healing process. When we put light in a dark room, we can see more clearly. Walking around in the dark brings with it more problems. You can talk to your inner child and say that you hear him or her and haven't forgotten that part of yourself. Thich Nhat Hanh suggests breathing in and saying, "I go back to my inner child," and breathing out and saying, "I take care of my inner child." Taking care of your inner child simply means being mindful of his or her presence. You can even try to write from your inner child's point of view.

Years ago when I was in therapy, my therapist told me to have a conversation with my inner child. She had me close my eyes and go back to the time when I felt pain. She told me to imagine where I was when I felt the pain and then to have a dialogue with that child in that place.

For me, my pain was my mother's lack of attention and ridiculing me in public, especially when we had visitors. In having a conversation with my inner child, I imagined myself as a shy four-year-old in my childhood kitchen, holding onto my mother's lower leg just before guests arrived for a dinner party. I tried to grasp on to the security of her presence, but at the same time I was scared, it because the sense of security was false. The therapist told me to talk to the child using my adult sensibilities. I told the child that everything would be okay and that she is loved and adored by many, especially her father. I told her that her mother had her own problems and could not deal with mine. I reminded her to look for security elsewhere and said that my mother would never be the quintessential mother seen in television soap operas. I reminded my inner child to look for and appreciate my mother for the strengths she did have. After all, she was an educated woman who brought me my first journal, which probably planted the seed for my life as a writer. I told my inner child that I should be grateful for this and for my deep passion for books, which was probably the result of my mother having frequently taken me to bookstores when I was a child. I also told my inner child that unfortunately my mother was an emotionally detached person and that it was not my problem to deal with.

This dialoging exercise taught me a lot about acceptance: people are who they are and carry with them certain traits that we need to honor and appreciate. This type of role playing served as a huge step in my own healing process from the childhood trauma of verbal abuse. I ended up writing about it, and a lot more was revealed in the process.

What I learned through journaling, reflective writing, and meditation is that my mother also had an inner wounded child that she had passed down to me in my DNA. Her generation never learned how to heal their wounds; they were immigrants and survivors. Practicing mindful meditation and paying attention to the breath during different times in the day help us to recognize, heal, and transform inner-child pain. We must remind ourselves that wherever there is pain, there are also seeds for transformation, understanding, awakening, and healing. Writer Jesmyn Ward shares many wise insights about writing, one of which is, "You get the most powerful material when you write toward wherever it hurts. Don't avoid it. Don't run from it. Don't write toward what's easy. We recognize our humanity in those most difficult moments that people share" (2016, p. 242).

Step Five
Finding Your Form

There's nobody in the world that doesn't have memories worth writing about.
—Flannery O'Connor

While personal writing takes many forms, many people say that in order to figure out the genre that most fits your personality you should consider what you like to read. Chances are that that should be your genre of choice. One of the first questions I ask students in my memoir-writing classes is what their favorite memoir is, or what the last memoir they read was. I am shocked when some people tell me that they don't read many memoirs. I tell them that the first line of business before writing a memoir is to read as many memoirs as they can get their hands on. If you don't like reading memoir, you should not be writing one.

If you find an author whose voice and story resonates with you, then you should read all their work and examine what it is about their writing style you like. Study them well.

After you become inspired by a writer, consider using the inspiration to craft your own writing. As is true regarding any other skill, practice makes the master. The more you write, the better you will become. When you are ready, you can share your writing with others—either friends or in a writer's group—but only share when you yourself are happy with your work, because chances are that people won't read your work twice.

Journal Writing

The art of journal writing dates back to when our ancestors wrote on cave walls. Later, the tenth-century Japanese court lady Sei Shonagon kept a famous writer's notebook in which she recorded a miscellaneous catch-all of things that were charming and annoying, descriptions of nature, odd facts, and malicious observations of countrymen. Now considered a classic, Shonagon's *The Pillow Book* can also be considered an early blog.

The first published journals were those kept by Samuel Pepys in the seventeenth century. Between 1666 and 1669 he wrote an eleven-volume diary that was published after his death in 1825. The journals of the Lewis and Clark expedition appeared in the late 1700s and early 1800s. Then came James Swan, a Native American who wrote extensively about whaling practices in the mid-1800s. Walt Whitman wrote in his journal in the mid-1860s, and Ralph Waldo Emerson wrote about activities and friends of special interest to him, including Henry David Thoreau. In 1885, when Susy Clemens, Mark Twain's daughter, was thirty years old, she wrote a memoir about her experience of being the daughter of a celebrated author.

A journal, diary, or notebook—whatever you choose to call it—can play many roles. It can serve as a vehicle for self-expression, a tool for clarity, a repository for observations, and a container for thoughts. A journal may also be a powerful tool for comfort during difficult times. The words you jot in your journal give life to what you see, feel, hear, and want. This process helps bridge your inner and outer worlds. Writing in a journal is a way to set intentions and present manifestations in your life. Journals and journal writing have often been described as one's best friend or confidant. Journal writing can be as calming and grounding as meditation is. It can orientate you and stabilize your emotions. My friend and colleague Tristine Rainer says in her book, *The New Diary* (1978):

> The diary is the only form of writing that encourages total freedom of expression. Because of its very private nature, it has remained immune to any formal rules of content, structure or style. As a result, the diary can come closest to reproducing how people really think and how consciousness evolves" (p.11).

For years, many friends and colleagues have called me the "journaling guru." There are a few reasons for this. First, people always see me holding a journaling, and second, I often write and teach about the healing power of journaling. While I advocate that novices journal every day, most seasoned journal keepers and/or writers tend to journal when inspired. My passion for keeping a notebook was sparked by the diarist Anaïs Nin, who began writing, as I did, at a time of loss.

As I have mentioned, when I was ten years old my mother gave me a journal of Kahlil Gibran's to cope with my grandmother's suicide. My mother was an English major at New York University and believed in the power of the written word. Since I had already shown an interest in reading and writing, she thought giving me a journal would be a good form of self-therapy and self-expression. At the time, seeing a grief therapist—or any kind of therapist, for that matter—was not commonplace. Little did my mother realize that her gift of the journal was to inspire in me a lifetime of writing. I've been keeping journals now for over fifty years.

Many other writers have begun journaling as a result of trauma or life transitions. These can include the loss of a loved one; health issues; relationship changes (breakups, divorce, or widowhood); job changes; or other life upheavals. For example, Anaïs Nin began keeping a diary when she was eleven and was having a difficult time after her father abandoned the family. Nin began her journal as a letter to her father, which she never actually sent, but she felt that it was the best way to communicate what was on her mind. The journal was simply a great place to moan, complain, muse, reflect, ruminate, and create and/or direct concerns.

Nin called her journal her "opium pipe." She told her journal everything. She had no filters or fears, which is one of the reason she was such a compelling writer. She was filled with transparency, which sets compelling writing apart from writing that is ordinary. She admitted that it was in her journals that she discovered how to capture what writer Virginia Woolf coined as "moments of being" in her life. Nin's journals included the mundane reporting of everyday life, but they also included significant confessions and self-reflections about her life, loves, and pursuit of happiness.

Journal writing can be a springboard for other kinds of writing. My book, *Writers and Their Notebooks* (2010), is a collection of essays in which esteemed writers share their stories about how journaling has helped them. Essayist Lopate in the book's introduction says, "The writer's notebook is an invitation to the Muse. The phonic similarity between the words *muse* and *musing* seems suddenly to make perfect sense. We call to our better self (another name for Muse) with these intimate scribbles" (p.viii).

The practice of keeping a journaling can:

- Improve communication skills
- Begin a dialogue with the self
- Increase awareness
- Increase sense of gratitude
- Be empowering and energizing
- Provide emotional release
- Foster exploration and self-discovery
- Help track patterns in your life
- Help work through illness or trauma
- Help to cope with stress
- Foster creativity
- Help tap into intuition
- Build self-confidence
- Be a place to practice your writing
- Be a container for sentiments, hopes, and dreams
- Capture moments that you don't want to forget
- Help discover and tap into the authentic voice
- Help manifest intentions
- Help foster mindfulness
- Help you detach from and let go of the past

For years I have been advocating journal writing and sharing my passion with others by gifting my loved ones with journals for holidays and birthdays as well as when they encounter difficult times. I once received an email from a woman who worked at an organization that empowers young girls at high-risk to write. This woman has begun blogging about her own turbulent journey and feelings regarding her own serious health matters. Even though I rarely share personal emails, because she has gone public I feel comfortable sharing this letter, without using her actual name:

> Hi Diana,
>
> I hope you're doing well! I'm writing because I wanted to thank you for helping me in a way you may not be aware of. I'm not sure if you've heard from [Jane, a mutual colleague], but I was recently diagnosed with stage-1 invasive breast cancer, and I'm starting aggressive treatment next week.
>
> I'm only thirty-two, so this came as a major shock to me. Although my prognosis is good, I'm HER2 positive and I have two tumors, so I will be getting a double mastectomy with reconstruction, followed by four months of aggressive chemo and eight months of a milder chemo. I feel like this diagnosis has turned my whole world upside down, and the only thing I could think to do about it (besides cry a lot!) has been to write.
>
> I started journaling immediately and felt the urge to share my experience with others through a blog. But I hesitated as I thought about the personal nature of all this and worried about how others might judge me for my weaknesses, both physical and emotional. I went to my local bookstore and couldn't find any books about anyone's personal experiences with breast cancer; all I could find were the cold textbook-type books written by doctors.
>
> Then I remembered the day in August when my boss and I drove out to Santa Barbara to meet you for lunch. I had spent that morning researching your past work and read that you had written about your experience with breast cancer. Thinking back to that day, I realized if a highly respected and talented writer like you felt brave enough to write about this, then I could, too.
>
> I started gathering my notes and journal scribblings and put them into a blog, paired with photos I've taken. It's been a really wonderful way to preserve the writer/

> photographer part of my identity while I adopt this new "cancer-patient" role. And the response from my friends and family has been a huge reward in itself.
>
> I'm currently reading your book *Healing with Words*, and I feel so empowered by your honesty and candor. I also love your poetry and I think I'm going to try to write a little poetry myself, though that is not my specialty!
>
> I really don't think I would have started my blog if it weren't for you. Even though I'm always encouraging our teens to tell their stories, I sometimes need a reminder myself. You are helping me strip away the shame and embarrassment and fear of breast cancer and allowing me to discover my strength and creativity instead.

This letter is a testament to how our writing, if we decide to share it, can not only help us heal but can also help others heal on their own similar journeys. For this young woman, writing helped her understand and come to grips with her journey. It also helped release her deep fears and feelings of anxiety.

If you have navigated difficult times or encountered a transition in your life, you know how helpless you can feel. Writing can help bring back a sense of control in your life. At the same time, it can transform negative energy into positive energy, and this can be very empowering.

My own journaling practice has greatly evolved over the years. As a young girl, I wrote my deepest sentiments about what was happening at a given moment in time. As a teenager, I wrote about my angst in growing up as an only child of immigrant parents who had no idea what it was like to grow up in the United States. My thoughts of isolation and loneliness accumulated in my journal resulted in my experimenting with illicit drugs during the 1960s hippie movement. While this brought me closer to my peers, it isolated me even more from my parents. My journal was also a place where I experimented with poetry. These days, my journals have become a potpourri of musings about the present, past, and future. While my focus is to be mindful of the moment, it is difficult to be a sexagenarian and not reflect on how the past has influenced my present-day perspective.

My journal now includes books I want to read, poetry written by me and by famous authors, first lines for future poems, article and book ideas, quotations, recipes, and restaurant business cards accumulated during my travels, especially during my spiritual retreats to Maui. My journals have become a sort of collage or scrapbook of what moves me during the course of my day—both in the world and in my creative mind. For example, some years ago, after first moving to California, I jotted down all the creative ways hungry or homeless individuals asked for money using their handmade signs. I thought that some were quite ingenious and wondered if accumulating all the sayings might result in a book one day. However, that project, like so many others, never really evolved. The fact is, you never know which jottings in your journal could result in a long-term project, so it's important to write down everything of interest.

Another reason to jot in your journal when you can is that the writings serve as a landmark to which to return when you want to know how you were feeling at a particular time in your life. It can reaffirm your feelings; it can also help you identify your patterns of thinking and what obsesses or concerns you. Although we often tend to have the same themes in our writing, it is interesting to read back through your journals to learn and reflect about what your themes are. When I returned to peruse my cartons of old journals, I realized that over the years I had done a great deal of writing about loss—loss of loved ones, loss of health, loss of a positive spirit.

Brenda Stockdale, in her book, *You Can Beat the Odds* (2009), studied the importance of the body-mind connection, especially when confronting trauma. She is a huge journaling advocate when it comes to dealing with the stress of trauma. Her work suggests techniques to control stress and help your body calm and heal itself. She says that journaling can help you identify psychological stressors that can affect your mood and your body. When stressed physically or emotionally, and you journal your symptoms, you are better able to connect the dots. She suggests that, once a week, "you look back on what you've written and notice any connections between events, moods, and symptoms" (p. 169). In doing so, you can identify any patterns your symptoms have, what leads to them, and how you can conquer them. As an advocate of stream-of-consciousness writing, she says that if you write in this way, "What needs to come out usually does" (p. 173). Thus, she adds, you are increasing your self-awareness and problem-solving skills.

Many writers use their journal to bring awareness to their situations and as a way to document their experiences to be used for future published works. In my doctorate research on the healing power of writing memoir, I interviewed writer Monica Wesolowska, who said that she began keeping a journal to record the experience of her son's difficult beginnings. As she was already a writer, it was clear that this traumatic experience would lead her to write the story of Silvan's life, and that this would both help heal her and empower her realization that if you love someone you need to let them go—thus her inspiration to write *Holding Silvan* (2013).

Writer and poet Susan Wooldridge views her journal as her centering place.

> I slip into a quiet world where I zero in on what's within and around me. It's a wide, private, empty canvas to carry everywhere, welcoming possibility. In the shelter of its covers I form, shape, hold, and dabble with who I am. I've been tracking my life, working things over and out, writing poems, making lists, taping things down, and scribbling with black ink since I was fourteen (2007, 42).

While I am an advocate of using a pen and a journal, there is usually at least one student in my workshops who will confess that they have awful handwriting and wonder if it is okay to journal on the computer. I reply that while there are benefits to the hand/eye coordination required for writing in a journal, writing on a computer is better than not writing at all. I share an article I read years ago in *The Wall Street Journal* (Bounds, G., 2010) in which some physicians say that writing by hand can be a good cognitive exercise for baby boomers who want to keep their minds sharp as they age.

Tools for Journaling

In view of the fact that manual journaling is more powerful, here are some basic suggestions for journaling tools to keep in mind. While everyone may already have what they consider the best tools for their own journaling habit, the suggestions below are from those who have been journaling for a long time or have been successful with this art form.

Notebook

In my classes, I suggest that my students always have some writing material on them, because they simply never know when an idea will strike or the muse will arrive. I've been known to pull aside while driving on the freeway to write down an idea for an article or jot down a line for a poem I want to write. The notebook is good for this because it can snatch thoughts in the moment about which you can go back and write more deeply when you have the time.

Choose a notebook or journal that feels good to you. It should be something you feel comfortable with and want to pick up and hold. It should be a book that reflects your personality. It is important that your journal lies flat while you write. There's nothing more frustrating than having to wrestle with the book binding in order to write.

You might prefer a spiral-bound book or one with a colorful cover to emulate style. Some people prefer lined pages, while others prefer unlined ones. It's a personal thing. I used to prefer lined journals, until by accident before leaving for vacation one year I bought an unlined one. To my surprise, I ended up liking it because I found it less restrictive. My default journals are Moleskins, which come in a variety of colors and styles. Some months ago, I wandered into a Moleskin store in Soho in New York. I was like a kid in a candy store. I thought I had died and gone to heaven. They also now have pens that easily clip onto the notebooks, so that there is no excuse not to write. Whatever inspires your best writing is the way to go. Continue to experiment during your creative life.

Writing Instruments

Your pen should be comfortable in your hand and should flow easily. I personally prefer the gel pens. I also like using purple ink. You might well have your own preference, or you might want to experiment with a variety of colored pens. Lately, I've enjoyed using fountain pens to write in my journals. I was happy to discover that you can now purchase clickable fountain pens.

Place

Establish a good place to journal. Sacred spaces are discussed in step 1. You might already have a special space in which to write, but if you don't, it is fun to create an imaginary one—a safe place where you can tap into your creative energy.

Twentieth-century author Virginia Woolf coined the idea of "a room of one's own" and wrote a book with that title. I love this idea. Woolf was referring to a figurative room, which is a deeper concept than a literal, physical space. Essentially, she was referring to someplace where you can feel safe and comfortable—a place that offers a blanket of support. To establish such an imaginary place, please re-visit "Creating a Sacred Space" (pp. 33–35)

Stream-of-Consciousness Writing

Not lifting your pen off the page when you write is a good way to tap into your authentic thoughts and voice, and it is your authentic voice from which your best journaling will arise (see step 3). This type of writing is sometimes called "free writing" or "stream-of-consciousness" writing; surrealist Andre Breton called it "automatic writing." He described it as writing that just keeps flowing regardless of where the words lead. The pen keeps moving or the keyboard keeps tapping. The surrealist idea was to unlock inhibitions to allow the irrational or creative mind to step in. Here are the steps to begin the practice of this kind of journaling:

- Find a centering ritual, such as meditating, lighting a candle, having a cup of coffee or tea, going for a walk, or doing yoga.
- Gather your materials—a writing instrument and a journal.
- Choose a time of day when you can write uninterrupted for at least fifteen to thirty minutes.
- Date your entries.
- Begin to write freely about whatever drops into your mind. Refrain from censoring and editing.
- Remember that grammar and spelling do not matter.
- Give yourself permission not to be perfect.

- Try using different colors of ink in your journal depending upon your mood.
- Put the judge aside. Do not edit.
- Remember that, unlike in writing an essay, in journaling there is no beginning, middle, and end. It is okay to start on one subject and end up some place else. The most important thing is that you release what is in your heart.

In summary, in the same way that tennis players practice serving and musicians practice their scales, writers must practice writing. As Virginia Woolf said, "The habit of writing for my eye is good practice. It loosens the ligaments" (1953, p. 13).

Writing Prompt 5:1 – Let the Words Flow

On the top of your journal page write: "I remember. Use stream-of-consciousness writing, without lifting your pen off the page. Write the first thing that pops into your mind. Keep your words flowing by repetitively using the words, "I remember." Your sentences do not have to connect as they would in an essay, in which there must properly be a beginning, a middle, and an end.

Types of Journals

When I first began journaling, I had a journal for each subject—one for my daily musings, one for gratitude, one for dreams, and one for my travels. The problem was that it seemed as if I never had the right journal at the right time. Life was stressful and complicated enough, so I finally decided to keep only one journal. Now I keep all my thoughts under one roof in one journal. However, I still find it convenient to have a designated dream journal. Some people might prefer having different journals for different reasons, and this is perfectly fine. You must find what works for you.

Dream Journals

Dream journals record your dreams as a way to explore your unconscious mind. They can help you see the patterns in your life, especially if you have recurring dreams. Sometimes you may find that your dreams are difficult to remember, but if you keep a journal at your bedside and write before getting out of bed in the morning, your recall will increase (see step 2). As I grow older, I have found that I have to focus more on the remembering. It does not happen naturally. I have to allow myself enough time in the morning to recall my dreams; or, if something happens during the day that reminds me of a dream, I have to take the time to stop and write.

It is best to write the dream down before you are completely awake. Some people even write in the dark with one of those pens that light up at night. (I sometimes use those in the cinema to jot in my journal compelling lines from the movie.) Write as much of the dream as you can remember, with as many details as you can, including feelings and images. Write whatever you remember, even though it might not seem significant at the time. Be open to what pops into your mind, and write in a stream-of-consciousness manner (see step 2).

You can either write down the dream or draw the key images, whether they are objects, animals, symbols, or scenes. If you draw, try to do some free writing about what you drew. What in the image resonates with you? You can also create a conversation with the dream.

Gratitude Journals

Gratitude encompasses love and appreciation. It is important that we all feel and express and cultivate gratitude in our lives. Gratitude is a key component for living a spiritual life. We never know what circumstances will confront us, but we *do* know that every day we are presented with the miracles of life. As poet Pablo Neruda says, "You can pick all the flowers, but you can't stop the spring." There are many reasons why it is important for you to feel gratitude and express it when you are able. Expressing gratitude is important for your happiness. A sense of appreciation makes other people like you because you will appear to be less self-centered.

As a two-time cancer survivor, I keep a gratitude journal to remind me of all the positive aspects of my life—and we all have them but often forget them. I will never forget what the oncologist who diagnosed my second cancer said: "This is the time to look for the joy in your life and have it encircle everything you do." This really helped me come to grips with my situation.

Writing Prompt 5:2 – More Gratitude

Take a few minutes to list ten things for which you are grateful. Now choose one thing on your list, and write for ten minutes about that topic.

Travel Journals

When I travel, I usually take a journal dedicated to each particular trip. It's just nice to look back to get a perspective. The best way to keep a travel journal is to write as if you are writing a long letter to a close friend. By writing it for someone else, you will probably have the tendency to write specific details, such as names and sights. Writing "beautiful view" is not as compelling as writing, "We sat on the veranda of our hotel overlooking the aquamarine Mediterranean Sea as palm trees lining the street swayed back and forth."

Actually, keeping a travel journal can enrich your journey. It's fun to stick postcards, menus, and travel tickets into the journal to jog your memory when you later reread the journal. Sometimes, I place these artifacts into a large envelope in the back of my journal. I absolutely love postcards. I know someone who collected them and lined the walls of her bathroom, thus making wallpaper.

Organizing Your Journal

You don't have to organize your journal, but some people prefer to do so for easy future access. You might want to begin by making sections, such as a general musings and gratitude quotations. I love using quotations as springboards for my writing, so I collect my favorite ones in a designated section of my journal. On the last page of my journal I keep a list of books to read, often suggested by others during conversation.

Letter Writing

Writing a letter to someone is a good, old-fashioned way to express your concerns and to get your feelings out. Sometimes writing a letter helps you practice expressing your feelings to someone before actually having a conversation with them. You can write a letter to someone with whom you might be having difficulty communicating. And even though you write a letter, you don't have to send it. My father died in 1991, but I still write letters to him on the anniversary of his passing. It is my way of connecting with him and telling him what's been happening in my life. I know he'll never read my letters, but that's not the point. The point is that it is cathartic for me to write him.

Writing Prompts 5:3 – More Gratitude

Write a letter to someone deceased or to someone who is alive but with whom you are unable to talk.

Write a joy letter expressing your happiness about knowing and being with a particular person and how they make you feel.

Write a blessing letter to someone who has blessed you and changed your life, expressing that you don't know how you could have lived without that person.

Essay Writing

The personal essayist is an observer of the world. The French word *essai* means "trial" or "attempt." While the memoir typically focuses on the past, in the personal essay the writer examines his or her own past, present, and future in the context of the universal subject of the essay.

For some people, writing an essay is an ideal art form. The subjects can be broad and can encompass political, social, and personal issues as well as the natural world or travel. The big appeal in personal essays is that they interweave one's own personal opinion or experience with a universal truth that resonates with readers. The personal essay forces you to examine, in depth, a particular subject or concept. You might begin by having a certain opinion about the particular subject you are examining; but, through the anecdotes and observations you include, by the end of the essay your view of the subject might have changed or become magnified.

While sharing a personal story, you bring out a larger perspective that moves your writing beyond its personal aspects to a more universal one. The charm of personal essays rests in the writer's reflection on a particular subject. Reflection is what sets the personal essay apart from other short forms. Without reflection, an essay would just be a report or recording of the goings on in the writer's life. In the personal essay, the writer tries to find meaning in his lived experience or the chaos of his life or the life around him. The reflective quality of an essay is the creative aspect. Reflecting on the past is not the same as explaining it.

One of the best books on the personal essay was written by a dear friend of mine and master personal essayist Lopate, who edited and wrote *The Art of the Personal Essay* (1995). The book's introduction is like a book in and of itself. Lopate says that the hallmark of the personal essay is its "intimacy." What Lopate means is that the writer is put up against her memories. The personal essay is a difficult genre in which to write because of its potential complexity, given that it needs to share what happened and what it means in the context of a human life. People read essays to get a perspective about a subject or to learn something about other people's experiences and viewpoints.

Writing Prompt 5:4 – Letters of Joy and Blessing

Think about a subject of an essay. In a stream-of-consciousness manner write down a list of subjects about which you would like to write. Consider subjects you are emotional about—subjects that make you feel anger, frustration, grief, fear, love, joy, or wonder. Your opening paragraph should set the scene for the essay and should immediately reveal to the reader the essay's focus. The format of an essay is the same as a book in that there should be a beginning, a middle, and an end.

If you want to write essays, it is a good idea to read the works of the best essayists, such as Phillip Lopate, Virginia Woolf, Edward Hoagland, Annie Dillard, David Sedaris, Lia Purpura, Nancy Mairs, and E. B. White, to name a few.

Blogging

The term *blog* represents a contraction of *web log*. Basically, a blog is a shared online journal in which a person can post entries about their personal stories, business, news, politics, health, opinions, sports, or any other areas of interest. Many blogs offer a commentary about a particular subject or sometimes even professional advice. Sometimes bloggers hire ghost writers or use guest bloggers (experts who post on particular subjects). Some blogs include text, images, video, or audio and sometimes also provide links to other websites.

Many people wonder about the distinction between *diaries*, *journals*, and *blogs*, words that are sometimes used interchangeably. Each one is a form of personal or individualized writing. In my opinion, a *diary* is a more old-fashioned term we baby boomers used when we were teens. Diaries are often dated, chronological recaps of what happened during the course of a day. The term is derived from the Latin word *diarium*, or "daily allowance." A classic example of a diary is *The Diary of Anne Frank*, a personal book holding deep secrets and feelings.

Some bloggers document and comment on their own daily events, while others might blog less frequently and address issues of broader interest. More often today, bloggers have a theme to their blogs, and they try to stick to it. The advantage thereby is that they have probably secured a regular following, whether it is of foodies, baby boomers, readers, writers, gardeners, or history buffs. While the layout and format of the blog is important, I believe that the theme or content of your blog is even more important, because it is the content that inspires readers to return to your blog.

Anyone can blog. You can begin by opening a free account on Wordpress.com, Blogger.com, or Typepad.com. When blogs first emerged, many were written in stream-of-consciousness style. In those early days of blogging, people viewed blogging as public journaling, but I believe that many blogs have evolved into something greater.

If you write a blog or are considering starting one, it is a good idea to keep a journal. The journal can be a storehouse of ideas possibly to share on your blog. If you have a product or are writing a book, a blog is a good place to establish a community of people with similar interests. A few of my colleagues have begun food blogs in which they have posted recipes that evolved into a cookbook.

The blog is also a place where writers can draw support from others. For some people, it can be a stepping stone for publishing a book. Many books, fiction and nonfiction, have begun as blogs. Either the blogger creates a book from all the blogs, or a publisher approaches the blogger about writing a book.

Writing a blog is a place not to boast or brag but rather to show and tell in a way that will resonate with readers. Successful bloggers teach readers something and can possibly make a difference in their lives. I am always honored to receive comments on my blog. Without those comments and the ones I receive in private emails, I have no idea how or if my words affect others.

The blogging world is quite competitive. In 2014, there were over 250 million blogs, and that just includes WordPress and Tumblr (Houghton, 2014). A good idea before beginning a blog is to decide on your theme and your audience. A first-rate reference book on beginning a blog is *Blogging for Writers* by Robin Houghton (2014).

Memoirs, Biographies, and Autobiographical Writing

A memoir is a first-person account chronicling a *slice* of life, not an entire life. It is a subjective recollection from one's own perspective. Typically, it holds the thread of a theme or focus throughout the book. What sets a memoir apart is that it weaves the story as it happened and includes reflection. An autobiography, in contrast, is also written in the first person, but it is written about the *entire* life of the author. It shares what happened based on historical facts but, unlike memoir, does not include reflections or descriptions about why something happened or what it might mean in the context of one's whole life.

Most autobiographies are written by celebrities. Biographies are also usually about famous people, but they are written in the second person by someone other than the subject. An example would be *A Beautiful Mind* (1998), written by Sylvia Nasar about John Nash.

The best memoirs have been written by those who have allowed enough distance between their lived experience and the writing about it. This distance provides a much appreciated additional perspective. According to Freeman (1993), when an individual writes about an experience, especially in the form of memoir, it offers the opportunity to give a new meaning to that lived experience by understanding it through the present-day lens.

There are many reasons people might be inspired to write a memoir. Often it is because of a burning need to do so. The memoirists whom I interviewed for my research claimed that they had a story to tell and felt that they were the only one who could tell it. Others might have secrets to share, or maybe they want to write a memoir to study or understand a situation. Other reasons to write a memoir include to preserve the family's legacy, learn more about the family, search for personal identity, gain some insight into the past, or heal from a traumatic experience. Writer Andre Aciman believes that people write memoirs because they want a second chance to make another version of their lives. When you write a memoir, you are writing *your* version of what you think happened from your own perspective. Someone else might have another version, and years and years later your perception of an incident might eventually change.

When I interviewed Maxine Hong Kingston regarding her two published memoirs, she said that her inspiration had stemmed from her reflection about what had happened historically to her family as immigrants and about the ghosts from her Chinese past, particularly regarding her aunt's suicide after her aunt had been ostracized from the community for having an illegitimate child. The fact that her aunt was born into and then forgotten by the family grated on Kingston's psyche for many years. While her mother wanted her to communicate her stories with the world, Kingston was told to hold on to the secret about her aunt's suicide. Kingston wrote *The Woman Warrior* (1989) as a way to explore these conflicting messages.

Memoirist Mark Matousek said that his inspiration for writing his first memoir, *Sex, Death, Enlightenment* (1996), stemmed from his transcendent experience of the realization that his life as a busy writer for a large New York magazine was taking a psychological toll on him. He felt a deep desire and need to slow down his life from the fast track. It was as if a voice inside him gave him this message. For him, writing the memoir was a personal, mystical, and spiritual exploration, and in the process, he found himself transforming in a positive way.

Throughout her life, Linda Gray Sexton, daughter of celebrated poet Anne Sexton, who committed suicide when she was in her forties, has struggled to come to terms with losing a mother in such a way. Writing her two memoirs, *Searching for Mercy Street* (1994) and *Half in Love* (2011), has helped her to heal and to reconcile herself to the trauma of her childhood. Writing has also helped her deal with her own emotional demons. In the latter book, Sexton said that writing helped her to come to terms with her mother's death and to disentangle herself from the strong tentacles that the suicide had attached to her own life. Having a family member who has committed suicide affects your family history in a way that is difficult to shake. Linda Gray Sexton's writing is powerful, not because she uses the written word as a vehicle to express revenge or anger, but because she uses it as a way to release and come to terms with her own demons.

In my own research, I found that the participants in my study had a passion for posing questions, and this quality suggested a particular personality trait inherent to writers, especially memoirists. Posing questions is inherent to wanting to understand our past experiences. Frank said that "the post-modern memoirist writes to discover what other selves were operating, unseen, in a story that is the writer's own, but that writer is several selves" (1995, p. 70).

Some years ago at an Associated Writers and Writers' Programs (AWP) conference, I attended a panel with writer Mindy Lewis, who wrote the memoir *Life Inside* (2002) about having been incarcerated in a psychiatric hospital from the ages of fifteen to eighteen. She spoke about how in her narrative she had had to face shame and how it separates people. She said that while writing her memoir, she had a chance to go back and take a closer look at her experience. She said that for a long time she avoided writing her story because she was afraid to be engulfed by painful memories that she had worked so hard to put behind her. She said she began to write out of outrage and blame. As she wrote, she got to recreate all the people in her life—the ones she loved and missed. She even got to have sex again for the first time. She claimed that writing gave her the distance she needed from her story, and she found it more healing than therapy because it depended less on interpretation than on experience itself. In summary, she said that when we write our stories and read the stories of others, we are bearing witness to what has been recorded by the inner observer who emerges. The illumination that occurs dispels the shame we may have felt when we have avoided painful aspects of our story in the past. We are essentially connecting what Virginia Wolff called our "moments of being" as we see our lives in the larger context.

It is important to mention that one reason *not* to write a memoir is for the purpose of revenge. Revenge does not serve anyone well. In fact, the best revenge is to live a good life. It is also difficult to read a memoir that judges rather than reflects upon the past. Take Frank McCourt's *Angela's Ashes* (1996) for example: he had a horrific childhood; and, after reading his book, you truly feel sorry for him, but you don't pity him. He wouldn't have wanted that. Other wonderful and inspiring memoirs are Vivian Gornick's *Fierce Attachments* (1987), Lucy Grealy's *Autobiography of a Face* (2003), Mary Karr's *The Liar's Club* (2005), Dave Eggers's *A Heartbreaking Work of Staggering Genius* (2001), Tobias Wolff's *This Boy's Life* (2000), *Townie* by Andre Dubus III (2012), and *Winter Journal* by Paul Aster (2013).

When writing a memoir about painful experiences, here are some things to remember: If you are writing for publication, you should know that readers are drawn to and fascinated by dramatic stories that are fast moving and sensational. However, you should refrain from whining in your narrative and avoid self-pity and the "woe is me" point of view. After a while, that perspective becomes tiring for the reader to read. Remember, the reader wants to see how you grew from or were transformed by your experience, not so much how you wallowed in it. They want to know how the experience *changed* you.

For me, writing *Regina's Closet*, my memoir about my grandmother who died when I was ten, has been one of the best experiences of my life, because I got to learn so much about my past that I might not have learned otherwise. The idea of writing a memoir has been a burning need inside me for a long time. My sentiments are similar to those of the poet Pablo Neruda, who says that for him writing is like breathing. Personally, I cannot live without writing. I live to write. Most memoirs are written by those who have lived a number of decades.

Reflection is an important part of writing a memoir. My cancer diagnosis led to a great deal of reflection. Trauma or illness leads us to reflect upon our ancestors—their lives and their health. What inspired me to write my memoir was my mother finding my grandmother's journal, which she wrote after immigrating to the United States in 1939. She was orphaned during World War I in Poland, and then, after a life of hardships, she took her life in 1964. The fact that she was a writer also intrigued me.

I believe that, besides illness or mishaps providing the inspiration for writing a memoir, when you reach a certain age you begin thinking about writing because you have finally gained enough distance from events that occurred during your childhood. I read somewhere that many writers need to wait at least ten years before writing about an event that happened to them. The interval gives us time to reflect and to add those reflections to our memoir, which is essential to make it compelling. Sometimes it takes longer than a mere decade. My father died twenty-six years ago, and I am just now able to write about him comfortably.

William Zinsser, in his book *Writing about Your Life* (2004), beautifully states, "We come from a tribe of fallible people, prisoners of our own destructiveness, and we have endured to tell the story without judgment and to get on with our lives."

How to Make a Memoir Compelling

Did you ever wonder why some memoirs are so easy to read, while others you can't wait to finish? There are many things to keep in mind when writing your memoir:

- Write in storytelling style. It is interesting to hear about people's lives and struggles and to listen to them try to achieve some understanding of a problem. That's why I wrote my memoir—to try to understand why my grandmother had taken her life. By the time I had read and digested her journal and integrated it into the book, I had a clear picture why she was so depressed.
- Show, don't tell. To show the event the writer would begin, "It was a hot, sultry day in the city when we packed up our minivan with kids and dog, raw hamburger and sliced bread, and headed for the lake." Help the reader visualize it. Put the scene on stage.

- Incorporate a good balance of scene and summary. According to Judith Barrington in her classic book, *Writing the Memoir* (2002), "It is scene and summary that make for a good story, while musing in some form makes it layered and thought provoking" (p. 91).
- Use a good balance of narrative, scene, dialogue, and reflection. A good memoir has lots of dramatic tension, dialogue, and scenes. There should be movement from chaos through crisis to peace. For a memoir to be interesting to anyone besides the writer, it needs to be crafted as a story with enough suspense to keep the reader reading. Each scene should move the story forward. The most common problem with memoir writing is an absence of dramatic structure and an overabundance of episodic structure. Sometimes the episodes are just strung together and going nowhere. This type of writing does not capture the reader because, generally, it lacks a story arc—a beginning, middle and end.
- As you begin writing your memoir, notice where your strengths and weaknesses lie. Do you like writing scenes? Musings? Character descriptions? It is a good idea to push yourself to write what comes least naturally. It will make your memoir stronger if you make yourself work on those areas to which you are least drawn.

Some Essential, Personal Writing Tips

1. *Set a schedule for yourself.* Promise yourself that you'll write for a certain amount of hours each week. Writing, like working out, is a discipline. It is hard to start, but once you do you are glad you did, or—maybe like me—you won't be able to stop. Writing is my daily vitamin. My family knows that when I am grouchy they need to send me off to my office to write, and then later I come out refreshed and able to face whatever each day has to offer. You should write every day, but if you can't, then you

should at least be thinking about your writing project.

2. *Each day, try picking a specific topic to write about.* Give yourself an assignment. For example, the first day, write about a childhood memory, such as when you rode a two-wheel bike for the first time, what your first birthday present was, who gave you your favorite book. It is daunting to face a blank page, but if you give yourself an assignment it will be easier. The following day you can write about your wedding and then about when your first child was born. Then one day write about your experience with hurricanes in Florida or any other significant experience.
3. *Read what you wrote the day before.* I always begin each day of writing by first reading what I wrote the day before. This helps me get into the flow of my thought and sometimes gives me an idea of what to write about. I always finish my day's writing in mid-thought, so I have an easy starting point for the following day. Because of this, I rarely have writer's block. I just pick up where I left off and run with it.
4. *Make sure you are not bored when you read your work.* If you are bored, chances are that others will be, too. Sometimes when I find my writing boring, my work at the time is also boring. When that happens, I pick a book by a writer whom I admire and read a few pages. Then I return to my own memoir, hoping that the other writer's style will rub off on me and bring me new-found inspiration.
5. *Decide for whom you are writing.* There is a difference between writing for yourself and/or your family and for publication. Who your audience will be will affect how much you revise or edit. If you hope to write for publication, then it's a good idea to find a writing or critique group in your area. When I moved to Orlando twenty years ago, the first place I visited was Barnes and Noble. I asked about their writing group, which as it turned out

met once a month. Sometimes you have to keep searching until you find the right group for you. It has to fit like a shoe. Keep trying until you feel comfortable with the people in the group. A lot of the process is trial and error.

6. *Be careful not to sound like a fact teller.* In other words, don't merely list the way events happen, as that is not interesting to read. Instead, try being a storyteller (see step 3). Writing memoirs depends on storytelling, not a chronology of what happened. Imagine your story as a screenplay. Successful memoirs read like novels. They use novelistic techniques, such as dialogue and scenes. A writing professor of mine once told me to put my characters on stage. This good piece of advice has helped me to write scenes. It is a good idea to mix the scenes in your story with your reflections and innermost feelings about it, as the reader wants to know, not only what happens, but also what you *think* about what happens.
7. *Do research.* When doing personal writing, remember that your memory will play tricks on you. You cannot remember everything. Try to speak to family members, pull out family albums, read up on the history of the time—anything that will give you a more grounded idea of your subject. When I wrote about my grandmother, I called the few remaining family members for phone interviews. I also went online to study World War I and to get a clearer picture of what things were like in her time. She lost both her parents to cholera in Poland, so I studied cholera.
8. *Remember to show, not tell.* To show is to take a reader's hand and walk them through an event. They should hear, smell, touch, and see what you have experienced. This is done by creating scenes with dialogue, action, descriptions of people, settings, and—most important—sharing the sensory experience of the narrator. The best memoirs strike a balance between showing and telling.

Writing Prompts 5:5 – Transformative Moments

Make a list of some of the most transformative moments in your life. Choose one to write about in great detail.

Write about a time in your life when you felt a great deal of joy. What do you need to bring that joy back into your life at this moment in time?

Writing Fiction

Most writers of fiction or nonfiction say that they can find a story anywhere. It can be based upon your life or the life of someone you observe. When writing fiction, there always seems to be a blending of fact and invention. Some people say that you should write about what you know, while others suggest that you should write about what you *don't* know. Some people write stories based on their dreams. You can get stories just by talking with people and hearing *their* stories. You might be intrigued by a story you hear and begin to daydream a story around it.

Some people choose to write fiction to hide the identities of people they want to write about. I joke to my fiction-writing friends that they are "hiding behind the veil of fiction." Perhaps you want to write about a bad experience you had as a child but do not want to expose the names of those involved. Fiction is an option. A friend of mine who was sexually abused as a child wrote a novel about sexual abuse.

For some writers, writing fiction liberates them from their stories, and allows them to delve deeper into their imagination. When it comes to writing about difficult times, fiction writing can be as healing or maybe more healing than writing non-fiction writing. When writer Stephen Jay Schwartz's was twenty, his physician father committed suicide. He felt that was a time when his writing really matured because he had serious issues to explore in his life—his long-term intrigue with prostitutes and his struggle with sex addiction. He'd been fascinated by writers living on the edge, such as Charles Bukowski, Jack Kerouac, and Henry Miller, and to develop his writing, he took to the streets to meet prostitutes first-hand. As time went on, he wrote stories about his experiences, and in conjunction with therapy to save his marriage from the tribulations of sex addiction, he decided to write a novel, *Boulevard*

(2009), which was actually a popular thriller with the protagonist being a sex addict. Under the umbrella of fiction, he was able to explore all his own issues using a fictitious character as his alter-ego. "Writing the book helped me through the process and, to a certain degree, kept me sober" (2012, p. 101). He admits that writing the book became a sort of catharsis for both he and his wife.

Another example of using fiction to heal through difficult times, was one of my students wrote a novel about falling in love with her therapist. In the novel, she blended her imagination in it by saying that she ended up joining an ashram in India to heal. One rule is that fiction must always include conflict; if you can develop the sense of conflict, then you can create a short story or a novel.

Just as regards any other genre, if you want to write fiction, then you should read fiction. Sometimes the format or style of the work you read is one that you might want to emulate, and there is nothing wrong with that.

Writing Prompt 5:6 – From Emotion to Character

Think of one intense emotion that you have experienced at some point in your life—joy, greed, lust, envy, jealous, anger. Give this trait to a fictional character. Create a scene with this character and the emotion. The character should not be you, but it can resemble you in some way. Incorporate another character into your scene. This could be a seed for your story.

Step Six
Unleashing with Poetry

Musicians must make music, an artist must paint, a poet must write if he's to be ultimately at peace with himself. What one can be, one must be.
—Abraham Maslow

Poetry is the voice of the soul. Poets help us see a slice of the world in a way in which we might not have observed it before. They highlight details to cast a light on a feeling, an image, or an event. Poetry also helps offer insight into both the human psyche and human behavior, and it is a place where the imagination can roam free. Freeman (1993) says that, except for their bodies, humans would not exist if they were unable to imagine who they have been and who they are. "Kill the imagination," he says, "and you kill the self."

Writing and reading poetry can be a springboard to growth, healing, and transformation. When you read or write a good poem you will be forever changed and not the same person you were before. The poems that change us the most are those that touch us intimately.

Another advantage of reading and writing poetry is that it can improve your writing because it forces you to use images and figurative language that help writing come alive. Dylan Thomas said, "Poetry is what makes me laugh or cry or yawn, what makes my toenails twinkle, what makes me want to do this or that or nothing!" (1952, p. xxii).

Reading and writing poetry also encourages a certain interconnectedness and helps to establish a sense of community between yourself and others. In other words, poetry can help us feel as if we are part of a larger picture and not just living in our isolated little world. We learn that other people have traveled similar journeys and have similar feelings about where they've been and where they're going. "Reading poetry is a way of connecting through the medium of language—more deeply with yourself even as you connect more deeply with another. The poem delivers on our spiritual lives precisely because it simultaneously gives us the gift of intimacy and interiority, privacy and participation" (Hirsch, 1999, p. 5).

David Richo (2009) says that writing poetry is a spiritual and psychological event because we need to live in the moment and identify with what is important. When writing poetry, you have the chance to unleash your unconscious mind. Sculpting your feelings and thoughts into a poem can take you on a journey where your conscious mind actually takes a little holiday. Writing poetry is a time to loosen up and allow yourself the freedom of expression at a time when self-expression is probably needed the most. Writing poetry allows you to tap into your authentic voice, which can lead to self-realization. Writing poetry can also be a form of meditation because it encourages a sense of mindfulness and tapping into what you are feeling, seeing, and experiencing at the moment of writing. Henry David Thoreau once said that if you sit in a clearing long enough, the animals will come out of the woods and present themselves. Figuratively speaking, this also happens when you write poetry. All sort of surprises can follow suit when you put your mind to writing poetry.

What is Poetry?

Poetry is a genre of writing in which succinct, vivid, and intense language is given to feelings, images, and ideas. It is a snapshot written from the inside out. William Wordsworth defined poetry as "the spontaneous overflow of feelings; it takes its origin from emotion recollected in tranquility..." Typically, a poem has a distinctive rhythm. Poetry can also share transformative moments or revelations. Regardless of the type of poem, poetry uses an economy of words, and every word in a poem is important. The more specific the poem, the better it will be. Barry Spacks, the first poet laureate of Santa Barbara, said in conversation that a poem "wants to charm, fascinate, and compel attention. It offers a fresh path through long-known places, a way of going that's odd, new." A poem draws you in; it is evocative, and it seduces you to read further. The best poetry is written about concerns and inspires the reader to reflect, dream, reminisce, observe, and fantasize. Poems are written in fragments, and each line should have a single image and feeling.

Types of Poems

There are many, many types of poems; below are some of the more popular ones. The most commonly used poems in writing for healing and transformation are the narrative and prose types.

- Narrative poem: a poem that tells a story. An epic poem is one example.
- Prose poem: the merging of a short story and a poem.
- Persona poem: a poem in which the poet takes on an identity as someone or something else.
- Sestina: a poem that consists of six stanzas with six lines each, with a short concluding stanza.
- Villanelle: a nineteen-line poem with two repeating rhymes and two refrains. It has five stanzas of three lines and one stanza of four lines.
- Haiku: a Japanese form consisting of three lines with a syllable count of five-seven-five.
- Cento: a patchwork poem made up of lines from other poets.
- Ode: an ancient form to commemorate someone or something, often philosophical or personal.
- Ars poetica: a poem that praises poetry; written about poetry or about a poet.
- Acrostic: a poem in which the first letters of each line form a word or phrase if written vertically.

Writing Prompt 6:1 – Playing with Acrostics

Choose a word of meaning to you and generate an acrostic poem. Write the word vertically on your page. Now write words beside the letter that best describe the word and illuminate your feelings or thoughts about the word. Thus, each line represents one letter. For example, in using the word, lonely:

L=left by oneself but wanting people

O= often off and about in the forest

N= never feeling the love of others

E= escaping from the hustle and bustle of the city

L= lingering alongside socialites makes it worse

Y= yearning for companionship and love

Poetry as Inspiration

Reading poetry can inspire the writing of poetry. Reading poetry encourages a link between the writer's voice and the mind and heart of the reader. Jane Hirshfield in her book, *Ten Windows* (2015), talks about how great poems transform us and also bring us hope, and a sense of community—they feed into our thirst for connection, while at the same time they bring us tears. She also says, and I agree, that "they promise that these are banquet recognitions we may enter and eat of, if we look and feel through even the briefest poem's eyes" (p. 271).

We feast on the words and they feed and nurture us. These are some of the many reasons I always return to poetry. As a young girl, I remember having little poetry books that I slipped in my pocket or purse and pulled out to read for inspiration. I did this whether I was feeling melancholic or was waiting in the car while my parents ran errands. I can't remember all the names of the poets whom I read back then, but Robert Frost, Emily Dickinson, and Walt Whitman surely come to mind. Reading poetry was my form of spirituality and provided a bond with my subconscious mind. I wasn't mature enough to talk about it, but, on reflection, that's exactly what it did.

As a teenager, I became entrenched in the poems of Rod McKuen. My first introduction to him was through his book, *Listening to the Warm* (1967). That orange book cover filled me with the warmth that I badly needed to help me navigate the turbulence of that time—I being a flower child of the sixties, burning incense, and reading on my bed with the black light shining onto the posters on my wall. I vividly recall the themes of McKuen's poems as focusing on love, spirituality, and the natural world—all subjects that compelled me then and continue to inspire me. McKuen opened me up to feelings that I didn't know I had until I read his poems.

I owned all of McKuen's poetry books, and I was sad to learn that my parents sold them when they moved from my childhood home in the eighties. But lo and behold, a few years ago when roaming around my local used bookstore—Bart's in Ojai, California—I stumbled on McKuen's entire poetry collection. If I remember correctly, it was a few days before my birthday, and I treated myself to an early gift. I cracked open the first book, and memories of my adolescence flooded in. For most people, adolescence is a time of rebellion, a time when we question our parents, our teachers and the rules instilled by society. For many people, it's a tumultuous time. While reading McKuen, I had flashbacks of writing from places of pain—sometimes palpable, other times not. There is no doubt that McKuen's words probably inspired my passion for writing for healing and for getting down to emotional truth, as this poem clearly illustrates:

> It's nice sometimes
> to open up the heart a little
> and let some hurt come in.
> It proves you're still alive.
>
> —Rod McKuen (1967, p. 56)

For the next little while I reread all McKuen's books; and, when scanning the Internet, I learned that he had been a songwriter, something of which I was unaware as a teenager. In my heart of hearts, I suspected that he had probably died, but being the optimistic and hopeful person I am, I searched for venues where he might be performing. I had a faint glimpse of optimism that I would get to hear him—fantasizing about the young man who had brought so much joy into my adolescence. In essence, I was refusing to acknowledge the passage of time. Then one day, the coolest thing happened. I opened the newspaper and noticed that McKuen had just passed away at the age of eighty-one.

While much of McKuen's earlier poetry focused on love, in his later years his poems turned to areas of darkness as he acknowledged his own aging, just as we must all do one day. I also realize that those who love music often also love poetry. There is a connection between them and the lyrics. People are less intimidated by music than they are by poetry. My hope is that by the time you reach the end of this chapter you will feel much more comfortable reading and writing in the form.

Reading Poetry

Just as is true of any other type of writing, if you want to write poetry you need to read plenty of poems. When reading a poem, it is more important to experience what the poet is saying than it is to understand what the poem means. Try to suspend your disbelief and accept the poem on its own terms. Go with the flow and rhythm of the poem. If you feel perplexed while reading, that's okay—try to remain open to all eventualities. Maintaining what Buddhists call "the beginner's" or "don't know" mind (discussed in step 1) is important when reading poetry. Try to let go and just read. Having a beginner's mind is giving yourself the freedom to allow the poem to speak to you freely, remembering that poems don't have to be interpreted. A poem might mean one thing to you and another thing to someone else, and that's fine. We all come with different backgrounds and perspectives that cast a light on how we see or understand the poem or the experience being addressed. There is no right or wrong way of reading or understanding poetry. Trust that your experience is your own experience and that it is good.

When reading and rereading the poem, listen for its feel, its rhythm, and its tone. Also, look for the word choices and the line breaks. See if you can identify what is *not* said. What is the poet saying in the blank spaces between the lines? Read the poem out loud. In your journal, jot down how the poem made you feel. Did you feel happy, sad, warm, confused, inspired, scared, or enlightened? Did you want the poem to go on and on, or were you ready for the poem to end? Did the poem remind you of something? Write all your impressions in your journal.

Sometimes our own poems erupt when we read poems written by others. Allow this to happen. Some years ago I saw an intuitive who suggested that I read the love poems of Pablo Neruda and gave me an assignment to respond to his love poems with one of my own poems. Coincidentally, Neruda is one of my favorite poets. The intuitive did not know of Neruda, but the name just came to him. I took his advice and went home to read some of my favorite Neruda love poems; as a result, some of my best poems emerged.

Poetry and Healing

Healing is often done alone as a path to wholeness. As Rumi says, "The wound is the place where the light enters you." As we move through the years, we become filled with memories. Some of the memories may be good ones, while others may be a result of past wounds. Sometimes it takes years for wounds to heal, and other times it could take a lifetime, if at all. Richo, who facilitates workshops on personal and spiritual growth, says that these wounds can take many forms and often fit into one or more of the following categories, which he calls the five As: attention, acceptance, appreciation, affection, and allowing. Our body never forgets, and sometimes memories emerge in the most unconscious ways. One way to release the wounds of the past is to write them down. Poetry helps us access these wounds, which can lead to healing and transformation.

Richo, who has written poetry related to the loss of his father, believes that there is a process for healing emotional wounds. That process involves four steps: addressing our concerns; processing our issues; preparing for resolving; and finally, integrating all the new realizations.

Healing can occur between the wounded and their loved ones and also between the wounded and the community at large. Many indigenous cultures view illness and trauma as the person falling into a certain amount of disharmony with their community. For healing to occur, it needs to happen in the self and within and as a part of the community.

Poet Audre Lorde began writing and reading poetry during childhood as a way to deal with growing up in Harlem as an

African-American woman of two parents with emotional walls between them and their children. During her childhood, she secretly wrote poems in her private journal, yearning to escape from the tension at home, especially that between herself and her mother, whom she felt hated her. By the time Lorde was twelve, she had memorized many famous poems. Writing and reading poetry was her way of healing and coping with the difficulties she encountered at home. *Warrior Poet,* a biography by Alexis de Veaux (2004), provides a comprehensive depiction of Lorde's genesis and life. For years I have felt a deep connection with Lorde because of some similar experiences. It feels as if we are kindred spirits. We both were born to mothers whom we felt did not want us and who refrained from nurturing the women we really were. As I did, Lorde lost a friend to suicide and, like me, was also diagnosed with breast cancer in midlife.

Maya Angelou is a powerful example of a woman and poet who was liberated and healed through writing. Following a traumatic event in her childhood, she found her voice through her love of language. Her famous poem, "I Know Why the Caged Bird Sings" celebrates her courage and dignity and the strength she found in the written word. Here's an excerpt of that poem:

> The caged bird sings with a fearful trill
> Of things unknown but longed for still
> And his tune is heard on the distant hill for
> The caged bird sings of freedom.
>
> (Angelou, 1983)

Writing Prompt 6:2 – Your Life as a Poem

Write a prose poem that is an autobiography of your life. Focus on the highlights and end with a revelation, a summary, or an epiphany. Reread and remove any unnecessary words, phrases, adverbs, and adjectives that take away from the intensity and rhythm of the poem.

Poetry as Therapy

Poetry is used as therapy in a number of clinical situations as a way to facilitate healing and transformation. Poetry is a powerful means to get feelings on paper and a way to tap into what is going on inside the self or in the unconscious mind. Confessional poets are ones who use poetry in this way. Poetry is also a great container for deep feelings. It's been said that writing poetry tends to break a silence that needed to be broken. This is one way in which poetry can be healing.

Often poetry therapy involves narrative poetry because this poetic form, which has been around for a long time, tells a story. The voice of the poem is the speaker, and typically it is quite distinctive. When writing narrative poetry, keep in mind that it needs to be in the form of cause and effect: something happens and then, as a result, something else happens.

Poetry is often used in conjunction with therapy because everyday occurrences and events become transformed in a poem. By using vivid language, we merge the intellectual and the emotional parts of ourselves. Years ago, when I realized that the loss of my grandmother might have had a deeper effect on me than I had realized, I sought the assistance of a therapist. Knowing I was a writer, and after we had gotten to know one another a bit, she gave me an assignment: "I want you to write a poem as a letter to your grandmother." While I had been writing poetry for years, I had never thought of writing about or for my grandmother. The therapist asked me to bring the poem to my next appointment. Instead of my reading it to her, she read it out loud to me. I found this to be an amazing exercise, because I heard my words in a different way. Having someone else read your poetry out loud seems more poignant than reading it yourself. Here's the poem, which was later published in my poetry collection, *Dear Anaïs: My Life in Poems for You* (2008).

To Dettner

You took your life in the house where

we lived together forty years ago.
I was ten and you sixty.

Your ashen face and blonde bob
disheveled upon white sheets

on the stretcher held by paramedics
lightly grasping each end, and tiptoeing

down the creaking wooden stairs
you walked up the night before.

But now your body descended to the ambulance
and sirens swarmed like vultures

around the place I once called home.
I wonder why you left in such a way,

as the depression gnawed
at your gentle heart, which cared for me

since my very first push into the world.
I've learned from you

never to give up, but to find
a passion and thank you

I did
I live to write

so I shall never die.

I often begin my poetry workshops with Rumi's poem, "The Guest House," because it describes emotions and inner experiences and gives listeners permission to create their own poem. It elicits, joy, shame, and, most importantly, the idea of being open to "unexpected visitors." We should always be open minded while writing, allowing the muse to infiltrate our psyche. This poem also reminds the listener that there is something to learn from all the visitors in our lives. In other words, whomever we are in contact with has the capacity to teach us, whether they treat us nicely or in a not-so-nice manner. This poem has invited and liberated my workshop participants to open up and speak their minds.

The Guest House

This being human is a guest house.
Every morning a new arrival.

A joy, a depression, a meanness,
some momentary awareness comes
as an unexpected visitor.

Welcome and entertain them all!
Even if they are a crowd of sorrows,
who violently sweep your house
empty of its furniture,
still, treat each guest honorably.
He may be clearing you out
for some new delight.

The dark thought, the shame, the malice.
meet them at the door laughing and invite them in.

Be grateful for whatever comes.
because each has been sent
as a guide from beyond.

—Rumi, translation by
Coleman Barks (1995, p. 109)

Often the professions we choose are a reflection of our childhood interests and experiences. They don't often arise out of the blue, especially if we are doing something we really enjoy doing. A dear friend, Perie Longo, PhD, who has been a registered poetry therapist for over twenty years and is the author of *Healing Effects of Poetry*, remarked that her interest in poetry began during childhood when she sat in school daydreaming and looking out the window tapping her feet to a rhythm. "The more I would fall into the rhythm, the more complex it would become, and then words and images would swim to my mind." Only years later did she realize that entering into the space of rhythm is where poetry lives. At the same time, she acknowledges that the focus of poetry for healing is basically self-expression and individual growth, as opposed to the focus of poetry as an art form, which is the poem itself.

Longo has come to believe that poems come from the indefinable place that she calls the "secret place." From this place emerge little gems that are clues to what is going on in the subconscious mind. Some classically trained poets might snarl at the idea of writing from this "secret place," or creating what we might call "confessional poetry," because they are formalists whose poems are sometimes difficult to understand. I prefer more accessible poems in which there is resonance between the reader and writer and more of a chance for the reader to be moved by the poem.

The Courage to Write Poetry

In step 1, I spoke about the importance of fearlessness and the courage to write in all the genres, including poetry. Perhaps writing poetry requires the most bravery, because the best poetry is written from the heart, and every word counts. Each word has to be specific and clear.

Writing poetry can often involve overcoming a sense of fear, and fear is a creativity blocker. Buddhist poet Kimberley Snow has some great tips for overcoming the fear of writing and of writing poetry in particular, such as:

1. Visualize and describe a private and safe place to write and return to it whenever you want to write.
2. Doodle all over your page.
3. Try to locate "fear" in your mind, and then feel where it lives in your body. Write about where you think it originates.
4. After being seated at your desk, visualize a peaceful scene. Now visualize one of your favorite writers. Become inspired by that person and pick up your pen and write.
5. Meditate before writing.
6. Gather photos of fearless people and animals and have them in your writing space.

Many people begin writing poetry from a place of pain, loss, or grief. In his poem, "Sunday Morning," Wallace Stevens says, "Death is the mother of beauty." This is a very spiritual way to look at poetry, because it is true that death encourages us to recognize the power of someone's beauty. We might examine their bothersome features but more often their beauty. Poetry encourages us to look closely at a life and perhaps bring it back into view through words. It has been said that a great deal of our sense of beauty, in fact, comes from our relationship to mortality.

Gaining courage happens over time, but it also happens when you read the work of other courageous writers. One reason Anaïs Nin has been such a huge influence on my own writing is her transparency and ability to express her deepest sentiments without focusing on what others will think of what she writes. She completely let her guard down when she wrote. Her writing has resonated with me for a long time. Even though she never wrote poetry, her words were very poetic; and she had a dear friend, Daisy Aldan, who was a poet and who wrote a beautiful poem that she read at Nin's memorial service after Nin passed on January 14, 1977. Nin seemed always to be saying what I felt, and the best writers do that—articulate what the reader cannot. As Nin deftly puts it, "The role of a writer is not to say what we can all say, but what we are unable to say" (Nin, *Diary*, vol. 5, pg. 171).

Poets whose writing you find compelling are probably those who most open up with their emotional truth. My favorite poets in this respect include Billy Collins, Anne Sexton, Pablo Neruda, Sylvia Plath, Adrienne Rich, and Laure-Anne Bosselaur. Many of my students ask if poetry is closer to fiction or nonfiction, and I also sometimes discuss this issue with my fiction-writing friends. For the most part, I say that it is closer to fiction because, when you write poetry, you can take the liberty of letting your imagination roam free and using "poetic license."

Poetic license means that you have the freedom to exaggerate or abandon the facts of what you are writing about and do whatever is necessary to create a compelling poem. You are the ultimate authority of your own poem. In your first draft, you should just let it rip and leave the cutting and revision for a later date. If you edit while you write, you risk severing some of your creative flow and energy. When that happens, chances are that you are not writing from your heart, you are writing from your brain; and often the brain tends to censor, which doesn't always translate into the best poetry. This process also applies to prose writing. For example, in creating the first draft of this book I simply wrote and moved forward to the end. Then I went back to read and edit my words.

Letting Go and Beginning

Letting go is about just allowing life and experiences to unfold as they are meant to unfold. This also applies to writing poetry. When writing poetry, try to release or let go of your rational mind and let your sensations and emotions take over. Letting go is also about slowing down and pausing while being mindful of what is stirring inside you. For some people, beginning a poem is the most difficult, but with practice it will become easier. When writing a poem, think of it in fragments. Each line is a fragment. Put the line breaks as a natural pause to your thoughts. Keep the focus of each line to one single image. For me, beginning a poem is the easiest part, because I fill my journal pages with first lines and then take it from there.

Susan Wooldridge who has been shaping words into poems since the age of fourteen says that poems simply arrive, and there's a certain magic when they do.

> "They hide in feelings and images, in weeds and delivery vans, daring us to notice and give them form with our words. They take us to an invisible world where light and dark, inside and outside meet" (1996, p. xii).

As you string words together, feel the poem erupt from deep inside you. Begin by writing about something about which you feel strongly. Writing in this way will help reveal you to yourself. It will transform you and direct you down a path of bliss. Over time, you will learn what inspires you to write poetry. Everyone is different. As David Starkey wisely says, the brain is a mystery, and we know that poetic inspiration is unpredictable. He adds that most poets will say that they try writing poems, fail, and keep trying before they come up with poems they are happy with. "So write, write, write!" (2014, p. 71).

Life provides all of us much material to write about. In addition to our memories, reflections and fantasies mentioned earlier, this wealth of material can also include the books or articles you read and the movies you've watched. Poet Robert Frost deftly says,

> "A poem begins with a lump in the throat: a homesickness or a love sickness. It is a reaching out toward expression: an effort to find fulfillment. A complete poem is one where an emotion has found its thought and the thought has found the words" (Frost, 1964, p. 199).

Poems come to me when I least expect it, but most often when I am in the midst of doing something else. Sometimes an image or a title drifts into my mind, and that's where I begin. There are many ways to begin; however, as I mentioned earlier, to write poetry you should read a lot of poetry. Reading the works of other poets is a wonderful way to invite in the muse because it fills you with random thoughts and invites rhythm into your own poetry. It might also inspire you to go to poetry readings or to listen to poems being read audibly. My book, *Lust,* for example, is read by actress Kate Udall, and she does a terrific job of bringing the poems alive.

Pablo Neruda shares how he came to poetry in his poem called "Poetry." Here are a few lines from the poem:

> And it was at that age . . . Poetry arrived
> in search of me. I don't know, I don't know where
> it came from, from winter or a river.
>
> —Pablo Neruda (1970, p. 457)

At other times, great poems erupt when I go into a sort of trance while writing—when the title or image comes to me and I need just to begin writing without stopping. Writers dream about moments like this, but it is not always easy and in fact nearly impossible to initiate such a trance. When trying to get into the zone of writing a poem, consider some of the tips offered in step 2 on developing self-awareness. It might be that you want to light a coffee-scented candle, burn incense, listen to a particular type of music, or maybe go for a walk. You might be the type of person who begins your writing day by saying a prayer, meditating, or inviting in the muse. Try a variety of measures to tap into your creative side. One writer friend of mine used to write letters to his father before he sat down to write poetry. Feeling his father's presence inspired him and invoked feelings that he was then ready to write about.

While rearing my three children, I re-immersed myself into poetry when I didn't have large chunks of time to write long essays or books but did know that I needed some creative time. Without creative time, it was much more difficult for me to deal with the emotional and physical challenges of rearing three children. Writing poems seemed to fit perfectly in-between making dinner and helping with math homework. At the same time, it was fulfilling because I had created something. My toolbox included a little journal and a pen, something I would keep in my jean pocket because I never knew when that line or image would come to me. Then I got hooked all over again as I had been as a teenager. The more I wrote, the more I wanted and needed to write. I would think of poem titles while on the freeway and have to pull aside and jot them down in my journal.

When inspiring my workshop participants to write a poem, I hand out two fortune cookies. I suggest that they use the line of one fortune cookie for the first line of their poem and the line of the second one for the last line of the poem. The point is that the first line of your poem doesn't have to be dramatic or flashy. All it has to do is set the scene with an image or a description of something. You want to capture the readers' interest enough so that they will read on.

Writing Prompt 6:3 – Inspiration from Other Poets

In considering poetry as a meditation, find a quiet time to be by yourself for twenty minutes. Find a poetry anthology and read the poetry of many poets. Find the poet whose voice and sensibility resonates with you. Read a poem by that poet a few times, first to yourself and then out loud. Feel the poem's rhythm; see its images and ideas. Choose your favorite line from the poem, and let it be the first line of your own poem. Write it at the top of your journal page. Now continue writing lines in connection with it.

Put your pen down and reread what you wrote. Do you discover new emotions or feelings you never realized you had before? Reflect upon this.

Writing Prompt 6:4 – The Wisdom of Uncertainty

Begin a poem with, "I do not know."

Writing Compelling Poetry

The best poets master details in their writing. For example, instead of saying "tree," they'd say "elm tree," or instead of saying, "bird," they'd say "robin." The idea of poetry is to create an image with words, and this is sometimes difficult for beginning poets. If you want to create an image, then begin with an idea or thing and take it from there, one step at a time.

When writing poetry, it is important to be in touch with and use all five of your senses—seeing, hearing, feeling, touching, tasting, and smelling. In using your senses, you enable readers to imagine alongside you what you see, hear, smell, taste, and touch. They can better feel your experience with an image or a situation, person, or thing. For example, when you are talking about a perfume, use adjectives such as *musty*, *floral*, or *pungent* to describe how the perfume comes across to you. Detailed writing also uses metaphors and refrains from using clichés. In the writing world this is called "showing" as opposed to "telling." Make believe that your poem is like a movie in which everything is visual and has to be shown. When you are explaining an emotion, describe how the person's personality comes through—in terms of facial expressions, gestures, and motions. Here are some examples of the difference between telling and showing:

Telling	**Showing**
You are pretty.	Your face glows like the evening's moon.
The teenagers were excited.	Giggles and yelling filled the concert hall.
The pizza was delicious.	The pizza's gooey cheese and tomato sauce begged to be eaten.
You snore very loudly.	Your snores sound like a bullhorn.

Here are some examples of adjectives that use the senses:

- **Sight**: shimmering, blotchy, mauve, glazed
- **Sound**: tinkling, screeching, rumbling
- **Taste**: tart, sour, sugary, bitter

- **Touch:** rough, sticky, plump
- **Smell:** stinky, pungent, aromatic

One of my favorite poets is Billy Collins because his poetry is so accessible. Hearing him read during graduate school changed my life. It was then that I realized that anyone can write poetry as long as they have keep observational skills and tap into sentiments inherent to humanity. It is unnecessary to analyze, dissect or interpret his poems. For the most part, they are poems most of us can relate to. Collins vividly writes about everyday occurrences, using vivid imagery. In his poem, "The Fish" he writes about a waiter serving him a fish and how the fish stared up at him. Here are a few lines from the poem:

> I feel sorry for you, it seemed to say,
> eating alone in this awful restaurant
> bathed in such unkindly light
> and surrounded by these dreadful murals of Sicily.
>
> —Billy Collins (2008, p. 92)

Duende

The word *duende* refers to a spirit or the quality of passion and inspiration. When it comes to writing poetry, duende is about writing with soul or in a heightened state of emotion. If you are in a state of duende, then the poem you're reading or writing is making you laugh, cry, or reflect. It is giving you a sort of bodily reaction. The feeling may be of anger, excitement, or deep sadness. Some singers elicit duende, such as Bob Dylan, Tom Waits, and Leonard Cohen. All good love songs and poems must have duende, because love is never free of sadness. The best poetry examines the dark side while viewing the light. The contrast between the lightness and the darkness is what brings poignancy to the poem.

Lorca says "the duende is a force not a labor, a struggle not a thought. "The duende, then, is a power, not a work. It is a struggle, not a thought… the duende surges up, inside, from the souls of the feet, not a question of skill, but of a style that's truly alive: meaning it's in the veins: meaning, it's of the most ancient culture of immediate creation" (Lorca, 1998). He says that when the duende comes it is followed by radical change, a sort of religious enthusiasm. Lorca believes that all the arts—especially music, dance, and poetry—are in touch with duende, basically because they need to be expressed and then interpreted.

One of my favorite poets, and known for his love poems, Pablo Neruda is a poet who can transport the reader from darkness to light, which is illustrated in many of his works, using his own life and beliefs as inspiration. The poet and the reader become transformed by his passions, loves, memories, regrets, and accessible sensibilities. This excerpt from his poem, "From Every Day You Play" is an illustration:

> My words rained over you, stroking you.
> A long time I have loved the sunned mother-of-pearl of
> your body.
> Until I even believe that you own the universe.
> I will bring you happy flowers from the mountains,
> bluebells,
> dark hazels, and rustic baskets of kisses.
>
> —Pablo Neruda (1970, p. 27)

Speaking of duende, Neruda once said that "nothing remains except that which was written with blood to be listened to by the blood." In fact, it was Lorca who introduced Neruda to his contemporaries in Madrid. When I was first introduced to Neruda's poetry, his words deeply inspired mine, as I felt a deep-seated passion rise up in me, wanting to be heard.

I view duende as a sort of fire or deep passion inside a creative individual. If you think of duende as a life force, then I can say that it has visited me many times and is forever prevalent. This sense began during my childhood, when I wrote a lot of poetry because I had a lot of emotions trapped inside. I felt like an old soul in a child's body, and the only way to release this frustration was through writing. My mother's attitude that children should be seen and not heard pushed me deeper and deeper into the realm of poetry, where I could release myself freely.

Creativity and inspiration pulls you toward duende, in which state the muse comes through you. The best art keeps the fire and ecstasy alive in the writer. For me, writing about sexuality has always been healing. Maybe those who have been molested during childhood always feel this way. Looking back on my adolescence, I realize that now I want to celebrate my body and not condemn it—as I might have had to do subconsciously after being molested by my science tutor. Only after entering my fourth and fifth decades did I begin to have the courage to tap into the fire burning inside me. The walls of fear began dissipating. Finally, the "me" that I wanted to share with the world emerged in my fifth poetry collection, *Lust*, which was a culmination and merging in words of my sexual encounters and my fantasies about them.

Writing Prompt 6:5 – Your Passion, Your Personhood

At the top of your journal page, write, "I confess." Write a poem about something you feel passionate about, incorporating duende. Keep writing and see where the poem takes you.

Metaphor

A metaphor is a figure of speech that applies a word or phrase to an object or action to which it does not literally relate. It can also be described as a way to compare two dissimilar things. Using metaphors in poetry can be a powerful way to express yourself. Metaphors provide images for the reader, and in this way the poet can easily get his or her point across. If a picture is worth a thousand words, then so is a metaphor for a wordsmith.

Coming up with metaphors is not always that easy. Here's a trick I learned in graduate school: Think of what you want to express with a metaphor. Let's say you want to describe rain in your poem. Think about all the characteristics of rain and what else might have those properties—for example, rain dancing across the street, rain-washed sun light, tears from the heavens, and the showers of the spirits.

One of my favorite metaphors is a train as an image for life. Yes, it moves fast, but try to think of riding in a train and visualize how your life stretches out in front of you and behind you on the tracks. You are the passenger on the train, and you have the choice to get off at certain stops or to stay on the same track. When you get off, you have the opportunity to explore and discover new routes, new places, and new people and encounter new experiences. In examining your life, you might want to get off and explore at a particular stop, or perhaps slow down or speed up at certain times. Doing this exercise can be very transformative and lead to new avenues. Changing your route could offer you a chance to get on the right track or offer you the opportunity to discover something you might not have discovered had you remained on the same route.

Geri Giebel Chavis (2011) has identified metaphor therapy in her psychotherapy practice, in which she has found that her clients have compared themselves to various things such as chameleons, tornadoes, packhorses, or ghosts. One of her clients who had been sexually abused by her father and emotionally abused by her mother said that there were times in her life when she was afraid that others would "take a piece" of her away or that her mother still had "pieces" of her that she could never get back. In working with clients, Chavis goes deeper into the metaphor, asking them what they saw, heard, smelled, tasted, and felt in connection with the metaphor they are describing. She repeats these descriptions out loud and then invites the client to jot down the words and write for five or ten minutes about them. In giving this assignment, she rarely uses the word *poem*, because the idea of writing a poem is daunting for most people, although what she finds emerges is usually the poetic expression of the client's true emotions. Going deeper into the metaphor helps Chavis explore the client's deepest sentiments. It reinforces the idea that we are living at the crossroads of the past and present and that exploring memories through metaphors helps to tap into unresolved conflicts.

Robert Frost's great, poem, "The Road Not Taken," elicits thoughts on transformation and the choices we make and how they can affect everything else in our lives. Here's an excerpt:

> Two roads diverged in a yellow wood,
> And sorry I could not travel both
> And be one traveler, long I stood
> And looked down one as far as I could
> To where it bent in the undergrowth;
> Then took the other, as just fair,
> And having perhaps the better claim
> Because it was grassy and wanted wear,
> Though as for that the passing there

Had worn them really about the same.

He uses the circular method of writing poetry and ends the program by bringing us back to the beginning;

I shall be telling this with a sigh
Somewhere ages and ages hence:
Two roads diverged in a wood, and I,
I took the one less traveled by,
And that has made all the difference.
—Robert Frost (1943, p. 270)

Writing Prompt 6:6 – Poetry as Pathfinder

Consider your life as a train ride. Write a poem about your personal journey. Write about when you stayed on the train and when you took a risk and got off at an unknown stop and what happened. This poem is all about finding your path. Some paths are longer, some scarier, some more tenuous than others.

Reading and writing poetry brings us closer to our true essence and leads to self-discovery, self-realization, and, ultimately, a sense of bliss. The best poetry both read and written is about what concerns or inspires you, whether it is connected to memories, dreams, observations, or fantasies. "Just let it rip," as my writing mentor once told me.

Step Seven
Sharing Your Writing

If you're not afraid of the voices inside you,
you will not fear the critics outside you.
—Natalie Goldberg

For many writers, sharing their stories is one of the most rewarding aspects of writing, both personally and universally. From a personal standpoint, writing releases us from our stories and empowers us toward healing and transformation. It also helps us transcend our own experiences. Writing begins the conversation about our past and helps inform our future decisions. From a universal standpoint, sharing our writing helps others navigate their own personal journeys.

When interviewing Mark Matousek for my research, I asked him what motivated him to write his two memoirs. He told me that he'd always been inspired by higher forces and aspirations. In making public his own personal struggles and growth, he felt as if he were working for the higher good. In this way, according to humanistic psychologist Abraham Maslow, Matousek was metamotivated. His writing may have originated from what Maslow called D-creativity, meaning writing that serves the purpose of filling a void in someone's life or of being a means to survival. In Matousek's case, he needed to share his story because of the loss of his father to the family unit. During the writing process, this D-creativity led to B-creativity—having to do with being connected to a higher level of growth—because the more Matousek wrote, the more he realized how dependent his existence was on sharing his story with the universe.

Some writers, like Monica Wesolowska, tend to oscillate back and forth between D- and B-creativity. Writers such as Kim Stafford, the son of the esteemed poet, William Stafford, admitted when I interviewed him that he began writing as a way to feel connected to a higher level of growth; but, while writing his memoir, he found that it was his means to survival and a way to understand his brother's suicide.

Until I returned to graduate school more than three decades after my grandmother committed suicide, I had no idea of the deep impact her death had had on my life. After my first memoir, *Regina's Closet*, was published in 2009, I received many emails from others who thanked me for sharing my story because it had also helped them cope with the suicide of their loved ones. I had bestowed the gift of writing on those who knew me, and as well as on those who were strangers to me.

Only when I began writing and sharing my story did I feel the intensity of my loss, and I began to integrate it into my life. Sharing my story helped me not only to see beyond it but also to see it in the perspective of all else happening in the world. I learned how depression affects so many people and about the deep sense of desperation. I realized how, like many other survivors, my grandmother had tried to be resilient; but sometimes there comes a time when a human being simply surrenders to deep psychic pain.

From the perspective of preserving a legacy, writing can be a gift to loved ones.

Telling our stories for future generations to read creates a bridge from the past and present to the future. It is also a way to honor our ancestors and can help guide future generations.

Writing about Others

When writing about your own life, it is nearly impossible to do so without writing about the lives of others. Joy Castro says that in her memoir, *The Truth Book* (2012), she wrote extensively about her family members. She did archival research about her father and grandfather that included reading transcripts from audiotapes in Spanish. When the book was eventually published, many in her family were no longer alive, but Castro was still able to share the book with her brother, proving to him that she was proud and respectful of him for all the violence he had endured.

Instead of using her brother's real name in her manuscript, Castro chose to refer to him as "my brother." However, when he eventually read the manuscript he told her that she could use his real name because he was proud of the life he had lived. In the published book, Castro decided to honor his sentiment. She also shared the books with her father's first girlfriend, whom Castro had never met. The girlfriend wrote to say how much she loved the portrait Castro painted of the girlfriend's relationship with the father and how much she appreciated the clarity and closure that the book brought her, following as it did the father's mysterious disappearance from the girlfriend's life.

I received a similar response when I shared my memoir, *Regina's Closet*, with my mother. My mother was a poor historian and unable to provide a good description of my grandmother's experience as an orphan during World War I. Therefore, in addition to doing archival work, I had to do extensive research with the few remaining family members. I only showed the memoir to my mother after it was published. While she had read avidly in her earlier years, she was no longer a reader, so I didn't think she'd actually read the manuscript and have anything significant to add. But she not only read the book, she also told me that she didn't realize the impact that my grandmother's suicide had had on me. She admitted that she was so busy dealing with her own grief that she never truly acknowledged mine. My memoir was quite revealing for her; she admitted to having learned things about her mother that she never knew or had forgotten. In the end, she actually admitted that she was proud of me for having written the book and that my grandmother would also have been proud.

As Castro deftly summarized, writing her family's story was a way to gain illumination and understanding. It was also a way to help and honor others. That is a privilege, she said, that comes when we expand our memoirs to include the lives of other people as they relate to our own. On the other hand, if you are uncomfortable writing about some of the more unpleasant sides of your loved ones (and we all have such sides), you have choices: you can decide to keep your writing private; you can change the names of the people in your life (even though they'll probably figure out who is who, anyway); and, of course, you can wait to publish until they have passed away. This last option would probably make the situation somewhat less complicated.

There are different ways to tell a story about others. Some people tell it all; others access their fiction licenses, and, for whatever reason, omit particular segments. Everyone makes their own choices. Dinty Moore believes that it is the writer's duty to view the world without filters over the eyes or rose-colored glasses that tend to distort the truth. "Let the scales fall away," he says (2013, p. 92). There is no place for political correctness when writing family stories. "The quarry of family secrets has a deep end, full of darkness and uncertainty, and writers who dive down into that material are going to have to learn to swim, and breathe underwater, while still holding their eyes wide open" (2013, p. 94).

My friend Philip Lopate, the guru of the personal essay and the author of the classic anthology, *The Art of the Personal Essay,* told me once, "You can insult someone by writing too much about them or not enough." He shared the story of once having written an essay about his mother, who had an affair when he was a little boy. After reading the essay, she said she was disappointed in what he wrote. "It isn't that I didn't do that," she said. "It's just that I've changed," she said.

What to Include

Deciding what to tell and what not to tell is one of the most challenging aspects of writing publishable personal stories. My belief is that what we should include are those elements that are relevant either to the story or to our own personal growth and transformation. If you begin writing by having a few questions in mind about your life and making those your focus, then any scenes or information that don't inform those questions can be deleted.

It has been said that if you are a friend or family member of a writer, you are doomed—your story will be told. Having said this, I should share that people often sense a kind of duality while writing—in terms of their roles as a writer and as a family member. The stakes are sometimes high when writers are completely transparent about their stories, and often the decision of what to include and what not to include is not an easy one. Often, the answer emerges during the writing and revision stages. I suggest not to stress out during the writing process but to "let it rip" in the first draft; then in the second draft, allow yourself the opportunity to delete sections of the manuscript that you feel are unimportant or for which you have not received approval from those about whom you are writing. Doing this is a way to obtain a sense of comfort and perhaps make all individuals involved happy. Writers such as Meghan Daum say that in the first draft you should just write without thinking about other people's feelings. In other words, "Write now, worry later"; and I agree that the first draft should be uncensored without thinking of what the readers' reaction will be. As Daum says, "Don't overthink it" (2016, p. 87).

Everyone approaches writing about others differently. For example, Edwidge Danticat (2016, p. 63) says that when she writes about herself, she always imagines her reader as a close family member or someone with whom she has an intimate relationship. In this way, she reminds herself that there is an eager audience wanting to hear her stories. When writing *Regina's Closet*, I had a photograph of my grandmother on my desk, as a reminder that I was writing to and about her. That is what guided me.

In her memoir, Castro was driven by two essential questions: What compelled her father to shoot himself, and why, when she was interviewing for an academic position, did a professor she had known only for a day tell her that she had no personality? Anything that answered those questions remained in the book, and any information that didn't was deleted in subsequent drafts. In this way, Castro was on a path to growth, transformation, and—ultimately—bliss, because her questions would be answered. Many writers of personal stories believe that, regardless of the genre, the process is a voyage of discovery; if we already know the answers to our questions, then there is no point in writing. This precaution is one way to avoid complacency.

It is normal to wrestle with your inner and outer voices that may simultaneously urge you to stay silent, become defiant, and claim the right to your truths. In the end, what you write is your decision and depends on what you're comfortable with. Moore admits that, despite his parents' imperfections and mistakes, he truly honors both of them. He believes that straightforward telling of family stories has value and that "more people have been harmed over time by secrets and concealment than by candor and revelation" (2013, p. 91). One of the most important aspects of sharing personal stories is acknowledging that, while you are sharing your own personal story, you are also offering the world a larger perspective, thus moving the writing beyond the personal toward a more universal message that can be read and understood by those who might have encountered similar experiences.

Including controversial aspects of other people's lives into your book can always be navigated. One way to avoid conflict with your loved ones is to let them read an early draft of your work that doesn't include any negative or controversial material. Although Joyce Carol Oates mainly writes fiction, like most fiction writers she draws from her real-life experience. When I once her speak, she confessed that she never offered her manuscript to her husband to read prior to publication. It seems to have worked for them, but this might not be a rule of thumb for everyone. Since my husband is my first reader, it probably wouldn't work for me. My dilemma over my memoir about my grandmother was that my mother was still alive at the time of writing. Even though my mother had made some unpleasant comments over the years, I toned them down for the sake of publication. I would never want to hurt her unnecessarily. More importantly, what I omitted didn't affect the flow of the story that I wanted to tell. This is a decision only the writer can make. As it turned out, once the book was published, my mother never even read it cover to cover. She just skimmed it!

Years ago, I did have a dilemma when writing my essay, "Tough Decisions," about my eldest daughter's difficult adolescence, battle of being an artist, and encounters with illicit drugs. While she survived and thrived through those turbulent times, the details continued to be somewhat embarrassing to her, especially when she became a young parent herself. While I knew that it was important to share her story with the world because it would help others deal with their own scenarios, I labored over writing and publishing the essay. I considered changing her name in the essay but still using my name as the by-line, but I realized that readers who knew me would figure things out. My daughter didn't feel comfortable with the idea of my publishing her story, and so I decided to honor her request and not publish it. It would not have been worth the anguish or the stress on the relationship. I knew that I would have plenty more of great stories to write.

The decision to write about our families is instinctive, and what to include and exclude should be something you feel in your gut, especially if others are going to read your work. As I mentioned earlier, writers of personal stories are usually motivated by a deep sense of urgency, desire, and passion, and this is from where the best writing emerges. Many family members are proud of having an in-house writer and enjoy reading their works, while others are deeply bothered by knowing that any of their stories can be shared, sometimes with notice.

Often, writers assume that another person does not mind that we share their story, only to learn that it could really bother them. A good example is Phyllis Rose's encounter when writing her memoir, *The Year of Reading Proust* (1999). In this book, she tells the story of her brother-in-law, who was a Benedictine monk in France. She described him as charming and beloved. She once spent about seven hours speaking with him about his life; and, as is common practice among writers, after their meeting she took copious notes. When it came time to write her memoir, she realized that because it was interesting, she wanted to include some of her communication with him. She intuited that he had spent so much time speaking with her because he wanted to share his story with the world. But in the end, this was not the case.

It is unclear whether Rose assumed inaccurately or whether her brother-in-law changed his mind once he read what she had written. In any event, after he read her manuscript (which was sent by someone else), he wrote her to say that he was appalled at what she wrote and took offense at what she had shared about his life. In fact, he felt betrayed by her. Indeed, she was surprised by his reaction, and she decided to comb through the manuscript together with him to remove any of his objections. While Rose felt that her intentions in her writing had been good ones, they weren't interpreted in that way. The moral of the story is that sometimes it is easier to clear the air before publication than it is to wait for things to blow up when the book hits the bookstore shelves.

Jane Taylor McDonnell said in *Living to Tell the Tale* (1998) that when writing her memoir, she also offended her family members. She decided not to have all her family members read the book, because if she did she would never have completed or published it. Some people told her that they were offended by how she portrayed her extended family, especially when she mentioned relative poverty and how it was deemed shameful. After much contemplation, she realized that she couldn't come up with a creative way to tell her story differently. In making the decision to publish her book, she realized that there were some individuals who would be insulted and knew that she would have to live with that.

Writing about Family Secrets

One of the most challenging aspects of writing and publishing personal stories is the decision to reveal or keep family secrets. There are not many families who don't have secrets, and because we all see the world differently, everyone has their own versions of that secret and the truth connected with it. Because memory gets distorted over time, so do the details of a family secret. As mentioned in an earlier chapter, everyone has their own emotional truth, and this does not mean that one person is right and another is wrong; it just means that the perspectives are different.

Maxine Hong Kingston, who was part of my research on writing for healing, confessed that she was unable to share her family story until everyone involved passed away because she was holding a family secret about her aunt having had a child out of wedlock. In writing her memoir, *The Woman Warrior,* about growing up Chinese-American, Kingston analyzed her aunt's life within the cultural history of her Chinese village as compared to Kingston's own life in growing up in the United States. The book opens with Kingston's mother telling her, "You must not tell anyone... what I am about to tell you. In China your father had a sister who killed herself. She jumped into the family well. We say that your father has all brothers because it is as if she had never been born."

Kingston calls her deceased aunt the "No Name Woman" and held onto this secret long enough to tell the story—until everyone had passed away. In this way, she could bring her aunt alive again in sharing her story with the world. During the writing process, Kingston realized how writing about her aunt's life was a way to reconnect with her past without hurting anyone's feelings, inasmuch as the people she was writing about were all gone. This was the only time at which Kingston would have felt comfortable writing about them.

Making rules for writing about family secrets is difficult, especially if you're aiming for publication, but I can offer some suggestions. As Kingston's story illustrates, the easiest path to take is to wait until the people involved in the secret have passed away. If they have *not* passed away, then it is probably a good idea to consult with them for clearance. After you are happy with the version of the story you have portrayed, you may choose to share with a select group of family members for their approval. Sometimes the family members will give you their own emotional truth about the story, which may be different than yours. At that point, it's your choice whether to include their perspective as part of your story.

Writing Prompt 7:1 – Safe Draft: Family Secrets

Write about a family secret as if you were not going to show anyone. Reread it and edit away the sections you think will offend.

Writing Prompt 7:2 – Safe Draft: Someone Disliked

Write a portrait of someone you dislike, knowing that what you are writing will never be read by that person. Write it again, knowing that the person will read it.

Now reread what you have written. When you are comfortable with the piece, ask yourself if the portrait you've created is enhancing. Reflect on the question of how, if you were to publish the story, you might revise it so that you don't upset anyone unnecessarily. Keep in mind that sometimes simply writing the story is more important than the side effects of hurting another person's feelings.

Writing about Sex and Intimacy

Sex and intimacy is one subject I wanted to include in this book, because for me bliss is very much tied to intimacy. Many people refrain from writing about sexuality, but I believe that when and if you decide to do so, then you will become liberated. This liberation goes hand in hand with personal transformation or the process of becoming aware of, facing up to and taking responsibility for your thoughts, feelings, and actions. This self-realization is optimized through communication with others as a way to form a connection. Intimacy and sexuality is a way to connect, and I also think that a good sexual life inspires creativity.

In his book, *Against the Stream (*2007) Levine talks about how Buddha spoke about sexuality and that it is one of the strongest energies accessible to humankind. Having feelings of sexuality and sensuality can be very empowering and can lead to a blissful state, which in turn can make us feel real good about ourselves. What Buddhism does not advocate is the sense of attachment some people might feel to sexual desire, which could lead to extreme and harmful behaviors, often equated with sexual addiction.

My first exposure to the importance of sexuality was just after my first gynecological visit with my family doctor. It was the 1960s and specialists were rare. The family doctor offered comprehensive medical care. At the end of my office visit, Dr. Robbins sat me down at his desk and handed me a book called, *Love and Will* by Rollo May. He told me I should read it cover to cover. At the time I was sixteen years old, and in all honesty, did not understand what May was really saying. I shelved the book and years later, pulled it down from my book shelf to realize what a gem it really was. May, an American humanistic psychologist who believed that Eros was the life force, and the fundamental energy behind Will. He believed that Love directs our Will toward our highest potential. He saw Eros as the spirit of life, not to be confused with sex drive. He believed that sex drive seeks gratification and release of tension, where Eros drives us toward self-realization. This sense of Eros has been a major driving force in my own creative life.

The art and power of communication about intimate moments, whether verbally or on the page, cannot be overstated. Body language reveals what is transpiring, both consciously and unconsciously. Watching peoples' actions while listening to what they say, and then writing about it, helps you get to know them and helps to identify what is important to them and the relationship.

There are many good books that take a poetic view of intimacy, and, if you're interested in engaging in this type of writing, for inspiration you might want to check them out. Some of my favorites include *Intimate Kisses* and *The Poetry of Sexual*

Love, both edited by Wendy Maltz. Also, my own recent poetry collection, *Lust,* shares musings about and during intimate moments. Each intimate moment should be identified as a profound human experience, a glimpse into the psyche of another person that results in a deeper understanding of who they are and who you are with them. This connection forms the deepest type of desire and joy.

Years ago, while wandering through the local shop of a bookstore chain, I stumbled upon Sallie Tisdale's book, *Talk Dirty to Me: An Intimate Philosophy of Sex*. At first glance, the cover looked like a buttock; but on closer examination, I could see that it featured someone holding an apple. However, the reason the book caught my eye was not so much the cover but its subject. The first chapter, entitled "Desire," began by saying, "We talk about sex all the time, we moderns." It went on to allude to the idea that sexuality and intimacy are communicated in both verbal and nonverbal ways. For example, by putting your arms around someone's waist while kissing, you express that you want to be drawn in with that person. You want to be one with him or her. If someone tries to kiss you and your arms are crossed about you, it is surely an indication that you are not interested in being kissed. The more intimate and longer kisses portray a deeper connection and desire between two people. Writing about kissing can help you learn about your own preferences and desires. In my writing workshops, one of the participants' favorite prompts is when I tell them to write about their first kiss, something many of them have not thought about in years. I share my writings about my own first kiss when I was thirteen and of how my boyfriend David and I linked braces and had to wiggle ourselves free. It was quite the scene and very amusing to write about and share.

Writing about intimate encounters and subjects can be done in the genre of your choice, whether it is nonfiction, fiction, or poetry. As discussed in an earlier chapter, writing poetry is both a psychological and a spiritual endeavor because it taps into the practice of mindfulness by encouraging the poet to remain in the moment with their words. Poetry about sensuality and sexuality can be very powerful, whether you write it for yourself or a loved one. The best poems show the poet tuned into their internal and external landscape by sharing specific details about observations, situations, images, or feelings.

Writing erotic fiction is an option for those who might want to use their imagination when writing. Reading and writing erotic fiction can be liberating, but it can also be stimulating for couples to do together. Examples of coming-of-age erotic fiction include *The Story of O*; early young-adult erotic fiction includes the works of Nancy Friday, such as *My Secret Garden*; my favorite erotic fiction is pertinent from the 1920s onward and includes the works of Anaïs Nin, such as *The Delta of Venus* and *Little Birds*. Henry Miller's *Tropic of Cancer* also falls into this category. Nin's works are more erotic fiction than pornography because she writes beautifully and with poetic flair.

While these published writers were comfortable writing about the subject of sexuality, others might not initially feel as comfortable. That's why erotic *fiction* is an option for many, in that you can fictionalize real-life events. In this way, your imagination can come into play. Desmond Morris in his book, *Intimate Behavior* (1971), identifies twelve stages of the progression of intimate behavior. While these behaviors are geared mainly toward heterosexual Homo sapiens, they definitely can have a broader appeal to many alternative lifestyles.

Any one of these stages may be written about, depending upon what resonates with you. Also, your writing doesn't necessarily have to occur in this particular order. Obviously, it's highly individualized. The progressive stages of intimate behavior include the following kinds of contact:

1. Eye to eye
2. Eye to body
3. Eye to voice
4. Eye to hand
5. Arm to shoulder
6. Arm to waist
7. Mouth to mouth
8. Hand to head
9. Hand to body
10. Mouth to breast

11. Hand to genitals
12. Genitals to genitals

Writing Prompt 7:3 – Perfectly Safe Sex

Write a poem or a short story following the progression of intimate behavior.

Writing Love Letters

Writing love letters is another way to express intimate feelings with our loved ones. A few years ago, I was honored to attend a fundraising event for Antioch University in Santa Barbara, featuring a performance of the A. R. Gurney play, *Love Letters*. It was originally a Broadway production in the 1980s, but the stars in the current show—Carol Burnett and Brian Dennehy—had also performed the play in 1993 in Telluride, Colorado! This was truly an iconic performance by two powerful octogenarians.

Andy and Melissa, the characters in *Love Letters*, had been childhood friends who had maintained a lifelong correspondence through notes, cards, and letters, which were read back and forth between them onstage. Even though the two had been romantically involved way back when, their lives had gone in different directions with various partners. Nevertheless, over the years they served as one another's confidant and, so to speak, "life anchor."

Through the correspondence, sometimes just informative, other times intimate, the audience learned about the deep bond between these individuals. We only realized the depth of the relationship when, at the end, Andy wrote a letter to Melissa's mother after hearing of Melissa's passing. One saw how spiritually connected the two were, although we never found out if they had actually been physically intimate.

This play was a reminder of the importance of passionate and sexy communication with someone you've known, either for your entire life or even for just a short period of time. It's also a reminder of the playfulness of letters, which can be initiated with present-day lovers. E-mail correspondence has taken over our lives, but it might be fun to consider writing an old-fashioned love letter to your beloved.

Writing passionate or sexy letters is one of the many ways a couple can be romantic with one another. Sometimes it's easier to jot down our feelings without being distracted by looking at the object of our affection. Receiving a passionate love letter allows us more easily to enter into the drama and emotions that are part of an intimate relationship. Every love letter is different and expresses feelings that are unique to the bond between the lovers.

The idea of passionate love letters has been around for centuries; but, as a literary form, it probably began during the Renaissance as a way to keep the embers hot even when lovers were not in close proximity to one another. Women in Victorian times often wrote love letters as a way of intimately expressing themselves to their suitors.

Like the characters portrayed by Burnett and Dennehy, some lovers may not have the opportunity to become intimate and find instead that their relationship revolves around letter writing. This was also the case with writer and prophet Kahlil Gibran, who had a twenty-seven-year affair with a schoolteacher through love letters alone. Here are some tips for writing a sexy, passionate love letter:

- Remember that the idea is to inform, amuse, explore feelings, and express love.
- Imagine the person being seated across from you. Think about what you'd like to say.
- While writing, place a photograph of your beloved on your desk.
- Be honest and sincere.
- Write from your heart.
- Make a list of what you love about the person and tell him or her what those qualities are.
- Be playful.
- Use terms and scenarios special to just the two of you.
- End the letter with a tease, or a seductive thought or fantasy.
- Spray cologne or perfume on the envelope.

- Seal your envelope with a kiss.

Like a good book, the first lines of letters should be captivating and draw your beloved in. Here are some sexy openings to famous love letters:

- "I will cover you with love when I next see you, with caresses, with ecstasy." (Gustave Flaubert to Louise Colet)
- "You have me completely in your power. I know and feel that if I am to write anything fine and noble in the future I shall do so only by listening to the doors of your heart." (James Joyce to his wife)
- "Even when I am in bed my thoughts rush to you, my eternally beloved, now and then joyfully, then again sadly, waiting to know whether Fate will hear our prayer—To face life I must live altogether with you or never see you." (Beethoven to the Immortal Beloved)
- "You have been wonderful, my Juliette, all through these dark and violet days. If I needed love, you brought it to me, bless you!" (Victor Hugo to Juliette Drouet)
- "Please, please don't be so depressed—we'll be married soon, and then these lonesome nights will be over forever—and until we are, I am loving, loving every tiny minute of the day and night." (Zelda to F. Scott Fitzgerald)

Revising and Editing

Writers write what is called a "draft," which is a version of the entire writing project, whether it's a short story, novel, memoir, essay, or nonfiction book. I remember writing my first book—a self-help memoir, *Getting Pregnant and Staying Pregnant: Overcoming Infertility and Managing Your High Risk Pregnancy,*—in the 1980s on a Smith Corona typewriter before this type of book was even popular. Drafts were different in those days. It was commonplace to crumple up two dozen pieces of paper revising one single page. Writing and completing books took much longer back then. Flaubert when he was writing *Madame Bovary* spent five years devoting days to one single paragraph and sometimes hours to a single line, but in the end he wrote a masterpiece.

Most writers, even the most well-published and greatest of them, create many drafts of their work before the actual publication date. For the most part, there might be as many drafts for the emerging writer as there are for the accomplished writer. As mentioned earlier, in the first few drafts it's a good idea just to "let it rip" and to write without being self-critical or analytical. Don't worry about spelling or grammar. Try to put yourself into the creative, trance-like flow of your work. There is no suggested or magical number of how many versions it will take to make your writing publishable. My best advice is to revise, revise, revise. If you break down the word *revision*, you are technically *re*-visioning your work, or seeing it again and again.

Many of my students ask me how many drafts they should write when working on their books, and I tell them as many drafts as it takes. Once I heard an esteemed writer say that his comfort zone was three drafts, and that's been my general rhythm, as well. It's been said that the first draft is about conception, the second draft about development, and the third draft is about polishing the manuscript.

Revision is essential to the writing process and probably the most important part of writing. Nonfiction writer Moore says that revision is "the place where discoveries are made and ideas are polished, where the good becomes very good, and the very good become excellent" (2007, p. 27). Fiction writer Raymond Carver admitted to have done twenty or thirty drafts of his stories and never less than ten or twelve. It might sound daunting to the novice writer, but revision is an integral part of the writing process. One writer friend says that she almost enjoys the revision process more than she does writing the initial draft, because she finds it to be a more creative process.

Everyone has their own revision style, and you need to find out what works best for you. It's always a good idea to do your writing and then let it sit for days or weeks and then return to it for editing. One way to begin revising is to check for the voice and the point of view of your writing. Try to distance yourself from your work and read it as if you aren't the author.

Before letting anyone else read your work, make sure that you've reread it many times and it is as perfect as can be.

A large part of editing nonfiction is rearranging so that the story flows. Just because you wrote something in a particular paragraph for your first draft doesn't mean that in subsequent drafts you cannot shift sentences or paragraphs around. When I was working on my MFA thesis, my mentor, Philip Deaver, taught me the art of "chunking" to help with organization. This was particularly useful for sections of the book in which I found that there was no natural flow and that paragraphs were not connecting. Phillip told me to sit on the floor, lay out all the pages of one chapter, and then cut out each paragraph and leave it on the floor. Then I was to rearrange all the paragraphs, making sure to create connecting sentences so that each paragraph would flow into the next one.

I once had a writing mentor who told me to cut at least 10 percent of what I included in the first draft. Just as when dressing, less is more. In such work, however, it is important not to delete or cut anything that is essential for moving your story along. When revising, try to keep the spark going and to recapture the excitement you felt when you began writing your book. Trust your intuition. Here are some basic rules for making revisions:

- Remember that chances are you will be doing a lot of rewriting.
- During your first read, revise primarily for structure.
- When rereading your work, remove yourself from the narrative; make believe that it is someone else's writing.
- Mark the sections you find most interesting.
- Consider deleting the sections you find boring; chances are that your readers will also find them boring.
- Make sure that each word is right and clear
- Write with authority.
- Be mindful of your punctuation. Semicolons connect two sentences that are closely related, and commas give the reader a chance to pause.

- You must have a sense of what is interesting to people. Cut everything else. If it doesn't add to the story's momentum, then cut it.

Other things to look for:

1. Are some paragraphs too long?
2. Are there unnecessary details that do not push the story forward?
3. Is there a dearth of short sentences?
4. Are some paragraphs too long?

Showing Drafts to Others

For as long as possible, try to refrain from showing others your work. Also, try not to show your work too early in the writing process. And I don't suggest talking about your project too often, either, because it tends to dissipate the energy of the piece and might even bore your readers. I believe that the first draft is for your eyes only. Writer Stephen King calls the first draft a "closed-door draft." Often the first draft, because of its rawness, is laden with things you might not want your readers to see. Only a seasoned reader will be able to see past all the mistakes, and it is unlikely that they will offer to read the book a second time. Sometimes not sharing your work is difficult because you want to know if you're on the right track, but the wrong feedback from a first draft can shatter your self-esteem.

Anne Lamott says that she always shows her work to one or two people before sending to her editor or agent. Getting feedback from someone she is close to builds her confidence and gives her time to improve sections that need improvement. She said that she has two people who usually read her work; one is another writer and best friend, and the other is a librarian who reads a lot. However, Anne only gives her work to them when she feels comfortable and happy with it herself.

Also, you should be careful to whom you show your work. Some people can be either too ruthless or too nice. My preference is to show my work to an editor who is an experienced reader or who gets paid to read. These individuals are savvy about what sort of things to comment on. Always keep in mind that writing is not a team sport. It is your project, and you can take what suggestions you believe in and leave the rest by the wayside.

Publishing Basics

It has been said that we all have at least one book inside us. That does not mean, however, that writing or publishing that book will be easy. Like any other endeavor, it takes a great of energy, tenacity, patience, and perseverance. When I tell people I am a writer, nine out of ten people respond by saying, "That's so cool. I always wanted to write a book." I usually smile in the knowledge that either they will never do it, or they will find out that it's not as easy as they thought to write a book.

In terms of getting your work published, I don't have all the answers or a magical wand, but I can share my own experiences and those of my colleagues. One thing is for sure: if you write from your heart and write what you are passionate about, the chances of getting your work published and enjoyed by others are greater than if you write about a given subject because you think you *should*. Writing from your heart will also be a much more enjoyable way to write for you. The power of the word is so strong, and it is good to know that you can transform others by the virtue of your word.

One of my inspirations to become a writer has been that I was silenced as a child. My mother, of Austrian heritage, believed that children should be seen and not heard. While that might sound like a horrible constraint to bestow on a child, it actually empowered me to become a writer. I felt as if there were insights and feelings locked up inside me that needed to be released. In view of the thought that from all bad comes good, her attitude encouraged me to sit long hours in my room reading the works of great writers and writing my own words on the page. Intuitively, I knew that I had something valuable to share with the world, and I was not going to let my mother's sentiments get in my way. I filled volumes and volumes of journals that later evolved into published books.

Part of my inspiration to get published was to share my experiences, but it was also an unconscious way to seek approval from my publishers and readers. If we did not feel human worth as children, then we often look to receive it from others. Many are continually searching for signs of self-worth.

Creativity is an amazing way to seek self-worth and also helps to build self-esteem. It is a very powerful force of nature. Creative acts, whether writing, playing music, making art, or making love should bring joy and beauty into our lives. The most important part about writing is having it be real and being written from the heart.

What resonates with you might resonate with someone else; but it might not resonate with everyone, and that's perfectly okay. The most important thing is that you write for yourself, and in doing so your most authentic and best voice will emerge.

Choosing Where to Submit Your Work

There are many reference books that suggest places to submit your work. *Writer's Market* is a great resource.

Go to a bookstore and peruse the books that might be similar to yours. Approach those publishers or see what agents those writers use. These days it is not essential to have an agent for nonfiction works, but you can if you choose to. If you are a good networker, you probably don't need an agent.

Writing Prompts 7:4 – Writing about Writing

Write about the moment you first decided to sit down and write and what your inspiration was.

Write a few pages about your longing to be accepted, loved, and embraced.

Writing Prompt 7:5 – Getting Ready to Publish

Write a few pages about a time when you imposed requirements on other people—how they might have felt and how you felt in doing so.

Appendix: Additional Writing Prompts

- My life has taught me that ...
- The guiding principle in my life is ...
- Tough times have taught me that ...
- I am different from my parents in that ...
- I have the power to ...
- I am making the most of what I have by ...
- My family will remember me for ...
- Five years ago, I didn't know ...
- My way of expressing compassion is ...
- If I had only one day to live, I would ...
- Looking forward, I can hope ...
- I want to tell my younger self that ...
- The gifts I can offer the world include ...
- My attitude to money comes from ...
- I have everything I need except ...
- What I want most is ...
- I am sorry about ...
- I am not sorry about ...
- I'd like to be more generous, but ...
- If I were a better person, I would ...
- To describe my creativity in less than two hundred words, I would say ...
- The talent I would develop if I had half the chance is ...
- The thing I regret most about my life is ...

- If I could accomplish one more thing, I would ...
- The accomplishment I am most proud of is ...
- If I could live anywhere in the world, I would choose ...
- The saddest moment in my life was when ...
- My favorite childhood memory is ...
- The thing that scares me the most is ...
- What I most appreciate about my life is ...
- I am making the most out of what I have by ...

Other suggestions for topics:

- Write your obituary.
- Write down your ambitions.
- Write about how you think you come across to people.
- Write about one of your favorite places in the world.
- Write about a place you remember well and want to share with others.
- Write about an important event from your childhood.
- Write a letter to someone who is no longer in your life.
- Write a letter to someone you hurt.
- Write about your first experience in a library.
- Reminisce about how things have changed since you were a child.
- Write about how you have changed or remained the same since you were a teenager.
- Write about the first time you were kissed.
- Write about the first time you rode a bicycle.
- Write about the first time you had sex.
- Write about someone you had a crush on but who didn't like you.
- Write about three things you want to keep and three things you want to lose.
- Write about a family ritual and your thoughts about it.

- Write a poem about fixing something that's broken.
- Write about a machine or piece of technology you've loved or hated.

References

Almond, S. (2012, March 25). Why talk therapy is on the wane and writing workshops are on the rise. *New York Times Magazine*. Retrieved from www.nytimes.com.

Anderson, R., & Braud, W. (2011). *Transforming self and others through research*. Albany, NY: State University of New York Press.

Aster, P. (2013). *Winter journal*. New York, NY: Picador.

Barrington, J. (2002). *Writing the memoir: From truth to art; a practical guide to the craft, the personal challenges, and ethical dilemmas of writing your true stories*. Portland, OR: The Eight Mountain Press.

Bosnak, R. (1986). *A little course in dreams*. Boston, MA: Shambhala Publications.

Bounds, G. (2010, October 5). How handwriting trains the brain: Forming letters is key to learning, memory, ideas. *The Wall Street Journal*. Retrieved from www.wsj.com.

Byron, T., translator. (1976). *The Dhammapada: The sayings of the Buddha*. New York, NY: Borsoi Books.

Campbell, J. (1988). *The power of myth*. New York, NY: Anchor Books.

Castro, J. (2012). *The truth book*. Lincoln, NB: The University of Nebraska Press.

Chavis, G. G. (2011). *Poetry and story therapy: The healing power of creative expression*. London, England: Jessica Kingsley Publishers.

Collins, B. (2008). *Ballistics: Poems*. New York, NY: Random House.

Csikszentmihalyi, M. (1996). *Creativity*. New York, NY: Harper Perennial.

Csikszentmihalyi, M. (2008). Flow: The psychology of optimal experience. New York, NY: Harper Perennial Modern Classics.

Danticat, E. (2016). In M. Maran (Ed.), *Why we write about ourselves: Twenty memoirists on why they expose themselves (and others) in the name of literature* (pp. 59–72). New York, NY: Plume.

Dass, Ram (1971). *Be here now.* New York, NY: Crown Publishers.

Daum, M. (2016). In M. Maran (Ed.), *Why we write about ourselves: Twenty memoirists on why they expose themselves (and others) in the name of literature* (pp. 73–87). New York, NY: Plume.

DeSalvo, L. (1998). *Breathless*. Boston, MA: Beacon Press.

DeSalvo, L. (2000). *Writing as a way of healing: How telling our stories transforms our lives*. Boston, MA: Beacon Press.

DeSalvo, L. (2002). *Vertigo: A memoir.* New York: NY: The Feminist Press at CUNY.

De Veaux, A. (2004). *Warrior poet: A biography of Audre Lorde.* New York, NY: W. W. Norton.

Dubus, A. III. (2012). *Townie.* New York, NY: W.W. Norton.

Eggers, D. (2001). *A heartbreaking work of staggering genius*. New York, NY: Vintage.

Frank, A. W. (1995). *The wounded storyteller: Body, illness, and ethics*. Chicago, IL: The University of Chicago Press.

Frank, T., & Wall, D. (1994). *Finding your writer's voice: A guide to creative fiction*. New York, NY: St. Martin's Press.

Frankl, V. E. (1984). *Man's search for meaning: An introduction to logotherapy*. New York, NY: Simon & Schuster, Inc.

Freeman, M. (1993). *Finding the muse: A sociopsychological inquiry into the conditions of artistic creativity*. New York, NY: Cambridge University Press.

Freeman, M. (2010). *Hindsight: The promise and peril of looking backward.* New York, NY: Oxford University Press.

Frost, R. (1943). *The road not taken*. New York, NY: Henry Holt and Company.

Frost, R. (1964). Letter to Louis Untermeyer on January 1, 1916. In L. Thomson (Ed.), *Selected letters of Robert Frost* (p. 199). New York, NY: Holt, Rinehart and Winston.

Goldberg, N. (2013). *The true secret of writing: Connecting life with language*. New York, NY: Atria Books.

Gornick, V. (1987). *Fierce attachments*. Boston, MA: Beacon Press.

Grealy, L. (2003). *Autobiography of a face*. New York, NY: First Perennial.

Greene, G. (1980). *Ways of escape*. New York, NY: Simon & Shuster.

Greer, C. (2014). *Change your story, change your life: Using shamanic and Jungian tools to achieve personal transformation*. Scotland, UK: Findhorn Press.

Hampl, P. (2002). Memory and imagination. In R. Root (Ed.), *The fourth genre: Contemporary writers of/on creative nonfiction* (2nd ed.). (pp. 259–268). Upper Saddle River, NJ: Pearson Education.

Hanh, T. N. (2001). *You are here*. Boston, MA: Shambhala Publications.

Hanh, T. N. (2010). *Reconciliation: Healing the inner child*. Berkeley, CA: Parallax Press.

Hirsch, E. (1999). *How to read a poem and fall in love with poetry*. Durham, NC: Center for Documentary Studies at Duke University.

Hirshfield, J. (2015). *Ten windows: How great poems transform the world*. New York, NY: Knopf, Borzoi Books.

Houghton, R. (2014). Blogging for writers. Cincinnati, OH: Writers Digest Books.

Kaplan, J. (2015). *The gratitude diaries: How a year looking on the bright side can transform your life*. New York, NY: Dutton.

Karr, M. (2005). *The liars club*. New York, NY: Penguin.

Keyes, R. (1995). *The courage to write: How writers transcend fear*. New York, NY: Holt Paperbacks.

King, S. (2000). *On writing: A memoir of the craft*. New York, NY: Pocket Books.

Kingston, M. (1989). *The woman warrior.* New York, NY: Vintage International Edition.

Lamott, Anne. (1994). *Bird by bird.* New York, NY: Anchor Books Doubleday.

Lengelle, R. (2006). Writing the shadow: An exercise in exorcising the demons within. In G. Bolton, Field, V., & Thompson, K. (Eds.), *Writing works: A resource handbook for therapeutic writing workshops and activities* (pp. 167-171). London, England: Jessica Kingsley Publishers.

Lesser, E. (1999). *The seeker's guide: Making your life a spiritual adventure.* New York, NY: Villard Books.

Lesser, E. (2005). *Broken open: How difficult time can help us grow.* New York, NY: Villard Books.

Levine, N. (2003). *Dharma punx.* New York, NY: HarperCollins.

Levine, N. (2007). *Against the stream.* New York, NY: HarperCollins.

Levine, N. (2014). *Refuge recovery.* New York, NY: HarperOne.

Lewis, Mindy. (2002). *Life inside.* New York, NY: Washington Square Press.

Longo, P. (n.d.). *Healing effects of poetry.* Retrieved June 22, 2016, from http://www.allthingshealing.com/ Psychotherapy/ Healing-Effects-of-Poetry/6350#.

Lopate, P. (Ed.). (1995). *The art of the personal essay: An anthology from the classical era to the present.* New York, NY: Anchor Books.

Lopate, P. (2013). *To show and to tell.* New York, NY: Free Press.

Lorca, G. (1998). *In search of duende.* New York, NY: New Directions.

Maslow, A. H. (2011). *Toward a psychology of being.* Blacksburg, VA: Wilder Publications.

Matousek, Mark. (2000). *The boy he left behind: A man's search for his lost father.* New York, NY: Penguin Putnam, Inc.

Matousek, M. (1996). *Sex, death, enlightenment: A true story.* New York, NY: Riverhead Books.

May, R. (1975). *The courage to create.* New York, NY: W. W. Norton.

McCarthy, M. (1972). *Memories of a Catholic girlhood.* Orlando, FL: Harcourt, Inc.

McCourt, F. (1996). *Angela's ashes.* New York, NY: Simon & Schuster.

McDonnell, J. (1998). *Living to tell the tale.* New York, NY: Penguin Group.

McKee, R. (1997). *Story: Substance, structure, style and the principles of screenwriting.* New York, NY: HarperCollins Publishers, Inc.

McKuen, R. (1967). *Listen to the warm.* New York, NY: Random House.

Miller, H. (1964). *Henry Miller on writing.* New York, NY: New Directions.

Moore, D. (2013). The deeper end of the quarry: Fiction, nonfiction, and the family dilemma. In J. Castro (Ed.), *Family trouble: Memoirists on the hazards and rewards of revealing family* (1st ed.). (pp. 88–94). Lincoln, NE: University of Nebraska Press.

Moore, D. (2007). *The truth of the matter: Art and craft in creative nonfiction.* New York, NY: Pearson Education Group.

Morris, D. (1971). *Intimate behavior.* New York, NY: Doubleday.

Neruda, P. (1970). *Neruda: Selected poems.* New York, NY: Houghton Mifflin.

Nin, A. (1931–1974). *The diary of Anaïs Nin* (Vols. 1–7). Orlando, FL: Harcourt Brace Jovanovich.

Nin, A. (1968). *The novel of the future.* Athens, OH: Swallow Press.

O'Brien, T. (2009). *The things they carried.* Boston, MA: First Mariner Books.

Pennebaker, J. W. (1990). *Opening up: The healing power of expressing emotions.* New York, NY: The Guilford Press.

Pennebaker, J. W. (2004). *Writing to heal: A guided journal for recovering from trauma & emotional upheaval.* Oakland, CA: New Harbinger Publications, Inc.

Raab, D. (2007). *Regina's closet: Finding my grandmother's secret journa*l. New York, NY: Beaufort Books.

Raab, D. (2008). *Dear Anaïs: My life in poems for you.* Austin, TX: Plain View Press.

Raab, D. (2010). *Writers and their notebooks.* Columbia, SC: University of South Carolina Press.

Raab, D., & Brown, J. (Eds.). (2012). *Writers on the edge: 22 writers speak about addiction and dependency.* Ann Arbor, MI: Modern History Press.

Rainer, T. (1978). *The new diary: How to use a journal for self-guidance and expanded creativity.* New York, NY: Penguin Group.

Richo, D. (2009). *Being true to life: Poetic paths to personal growth.* Boston, MA: Shambhala Publications.

Rilke, R. M. (2000). *Letters to a young poet.* Novato, CA: New World Library.

Rose, P. (1999). *The year of reading Proust.* Berkeley, CA: Counterpoint.

Rumi, J. (1995). In C. Barks (Trans.), *The essential Rumi.* New York, NY: Quality Paperback Book Club.

Sacks, O. (2015). *Gratitude.* New York, NY: Borzoi Books, Knopf.

Sarton, M. (1980). *Recovering: A journal.* New York, NY: W. W. Norton.

Schönfelder, C. (2013). (Re-)visions of the buried self: Childhood trauma and self-narration in Margaret Atwood's *Cat's eye.* In G. Rippl, P. Schweighauser., T. Kirss., M. Sutrop., & T. Steffen (Eds.). *Haunted narratives: Life writing in an age of trauma* (pp. 257–274). Canada: University of Toronto Press.

Schwartz, S. J. (2009). *Boulevard.* New York, NY: Tom Doherty Associates, LLC.

Sexton, L. (1994). *Searching for Mercy Street: My journey back to my mother, Anne Sexton.* Berkeley, CA: Counterpoint.

Sexton, L. (2011). *Half in love: Surviving the legacy of suicide.* Berkeley, CA: Counterpoint.

Siegel, B. S. (1986). *Love, medicine and miracles.* New York, NY: William Morrow.

Siegel, B. S. (1989). *Peace, love and healing.* New York, NY: Harper.

Siegel, B. S. (2013). *The art of healing*. Novato, CA: New World Library.

Snow, K. (2014). *Writing yourself awake: Meditation and creativity*. Santa Barbara, CA: Bluestone Books.

Stafford, K. (2003). *The muses among us: Eloquent listening and other pleasures of the writer's craft*. Athens, GA: University of Georgia Press.

Stafford, K. (2012). *100 tricks every boy can do: A memoir*. San Antonio, TX: Trinity University Press.

Starkey, D. (2014). *Creative writing: An introduction to poetry and fiction*. Boston, MA: Bedford/St. Martin's.

Steinberg, M. (2012, May 29). *The fourth genre: The art and craft of creative nonfiction*. No. 3 [Web log message]. Retrieved from http://www.mjsteinberg.net/blog.htm? post=857003.

Stockdale, B. (2009). You can beat the odds: Surprising Factors behind chronic illness and cancer. Boulder, CO: Sentient Publications.

Suziki, S. (1976). *Zen mind, beginner's mind*. Boston, MA: Shambhala Publications.

Thomas, D. (1952). *Notes on the art of poetry:* Austin, TX: The University of Texas.

Ward, J. (2016). Jesmyn Ward's wisdom for memoir writers. In. M. Maran (Ed.), *Why we write about ourselves: Twenty memoirists on why they expose themselves (and others) in the name of literature* (pp. 231–242). New York, NY: Plume.

Welty, E. (1995). *One writer's beginnings*. Cambridge, MA: Harvard University Press.

Wesolowska, M. (2013). *Holding Silvan: A brief life*. Portland, OR: Hawthorne Books.

Wilson, T. D. (2011). *Redirect: Changing the stories we live by*. New York, NY: Little, Brown and Company.

Wolff, T. (2000). *This boy's life*. New York, NY: Grove Press.

Wooldridge, S. (1996). *Poemcrazy*. New York, NY: Three Rivers Press.

Wooldridge, S. (2007). *Foolsgold: Making something from nothing and freeing your creative process*. New York, NY: Random House.

Woolf, V. (1953). *A writer's diary*. New York, NY: Harvest.

Zinsser, W. (2004). *Writing about your life: A journey into the past*. Cambridge, MA: Da Capo Press.

Zweig, C., & Abrams, J. (Eds.). (1991). *Meeting the shadow: The hidden power of the dark side of human nature*. New York, NY: Tarcher.

Further Reading

General Books on Writing

Abercrombie, B. (2002). *Writing out the storm.* New York, NY: St. Martin's Press.

Abercrombie, B. (2007). *Courage and craft: Writing your life into story.* Novato, CA: New World Library.

Ackerman, A., & Puglisi, B. (2012). *The emotion thesaurus: A writer's guide to character expression.* CreateSpace Independent Publishing Platform.

Barrett, A., & Turchi, P. (2004). *The story behind the story: 26 stories of contemporary writers and how they work.* New York, NY: W. W. Norton.

Bolton, G. (2011). *Write yourself: Creative writing and personal development.* London, England: Jessica Kingsley Publishers.

Brande, D. (1981). *Becoming a writer.* Los Angeles, CA: Tarcher.

Csikszentmihalyi, M. (1996). *Creativity.* New York, NY: Harper Perennial.

Csikszentmihalyi, M. (2008). *Flow: The psychology of optimal experience.* New York, NY: Harper Perennial Modern Classics.

Frank, T., & Wall, D. (1994). *Finding your writer's voice: A guide to creative fiction.* New York, NY: St. Martin's Press.

Goldberg, N. (1986). *Writing down the bones: Freeing the writer within.* Boston, MA: Shambhala.

Goldberg, N. (1990). *Wild mind: Living the writer's life.* New York, NY: Bantam Books.

Goldberg, N. (2000). *Thunder and lightning.* New York, NY: Bantam Books.

Goldberg, N. (2004). *The great failure: My unexpected path to truth*. New York, NY: HarperCollins.

Goldberg, N. (2007). *Old friend from far away: A practice of writing memoir*. New York, NY: Free Press.

Goldberg, N. (2013). *The true secret of writing: Connecting life with language*. New York, NY: Atria Books.

Gornick, V. (2002). *The situation and the story: The art of personal narrative*. New York, NY: Farrar, Straus, and Giroux.

Hall, D. (2003). *Life work*. Boston MA: Beacon Press.

Harrison, K. (2008). The forest of memory. *Truth in nonfiction: Essays*. David Lazar (Ed.). Iowa City, IA: University of Iowa Press.

Hemingway, E. (1999.) *On writing*. New York, NY: Touchstone.

Lamott, A. (1995). *Bird by bird: Some instructions on writing and life*. New York, NY: Anchor.

Lee, J., & Miller-Kritsberg, C. (1994). *Writing from the body*. New York, NY: St. Martin's Press.

Lopate, P. (Ed.). (1995). *The art of the personal essay: An anthology from the classical era to the present*. New York, NY: Anchor Books.

Lopate, P. (2013). *To show and to tell*. New York, NY: Free Press.

McClanahan, R. (1999). *Word painting*. Cincinnati, OH: Writer's Digest Books.

Miller, B., & Paola, S. (2004). *Tell it slant: Writing and shaping creative nonfiction*. New York, NY: McGraw-Hill.

Moore, D. (2007). *The truth of the matter: Art and craft in creative nonfiction*. New York, NY: Pearson Education Group.

Palumbo, D. (2000). *Writing from the inside out*. New York, NY: John Wiley & Sons, Inc.

Rainer, T. (1978). *The new diary*. New York, NY: Penguin Putnam.

Rainer, T. (1998). *Your life as story*. New York, NY: Penguin Putnam.

Rico, D. (2000). *Writing the natural way*. New York, NY: Tarcher/Putnam.

Rose, P. (2008). Whose truth? In D. Lazar (Ed.), *Truth in nonfiction: Essays* (1st ed.). (pp. 31–41). Iowa City, IA: University of Iowa Press.

Rule, R., & Wheeler, S. (1993). *Creating the story: Guides for writers.* Portsmouth, NH: Reed Elsevier, Inc.

See, C. (2002). *Making a literary life: Advice for writers and other dreamers.* New York, NY: Random House.

Starkey, D. (2014). *Creative writing: An introduction to poetry and fiction.* Boston, MA: Bedford/St. Martin's.

Steinberg, M. (1996). *Those who do, can.* Urbana, IL: National Council of Teachers.

Steinberg, M. (2012, May 29). *The Fourth genre: The art and craft of creative nonfiction.* No. 3 [Web log message]. Retrieved from http://www.mjsteinberg.net/ blog.htm? post=857003.

Tiberghien, S. M. (2007). *One year to a writing life: Twelve lessons to deepen every writer's art and craft.* New York, NY: Marlowe & Company.

White, E., & Strunk, W. (1999). *The elements of style* (4th ed.). New York, NY: Pearson.

Wooldridge, S. (2007). *Foolsgold: Making something from nothing and freeing your creative process.* New York, NY: Random House.

Woolf, V. (1942). *Women and writing.* Orlando, FL: Harcourt.

Zinsser, W. (1996). *On writing well: The classic guide to writing nonfiction.* New York, NY: HarperCollins.

On Writing Fiction

Burroway, J. (2011). *Imaginative writing: The elements of craft.* New York, NY: Penguin Academics.

Burroway, J., & Stuckey-French, E. (2006). *Writing fiction* (7th ed.). New York, NY: Pearson Longman.

Gardner, J. (1999). *On becoming a novelist.* New York, NY: Norton.

Hood, A. (1998). *Creating character emotions.* Cincinnati, OH: Story Press.

Roorbach, B. (1998). *Writing life stories.* Cincinnati, OH: Story Press.

Stein, Sol. (1995). *Stein on writing*. New York, NY: St. Martin's Press.

Tharp, T. (2006). *The creative habit: Learn it and use it for life*. New York, NY: Simon & Schuster.

On Journaling

Adams, K. (1990). *Journal to the self*. New York, NY: Warner Books.

Capacchione, L. (2015). *The creative journal*. Athens, OH: Ohio University Press.

Nin, A. (1978–1984). *The early diaries of Anaïs Nin* (Vols. 1–4). Orlando, FL: Harcourt Brace & Co.

Progoff, I. (1992). *At a journal workshop*. New York, NY: Penguin Putnam.

Rainer, T. (1978). *The new diary*. New York, NY: Penguin Putnam.

On Writing Memoirs

Andrew, E. J. (2005). *Writing the sacred journey: The art and practice of spiritual memoir*. Boston, MA: Skinner House Books.

Barrington, J. (2002). *Writing the memoir: A practical guide to the craft, the personal challenges, and ethical dilemmas of writing your true stories*. Portland, OR: Eight Mountain Press.

Birkerts, S. (2008). *The art of time in memoir*. Saint Paul, MN: Graywolf Press.

Castro, J. (2013). *Family trouble*. Lincoln, NE: University of Nebraska Press.

Frank, A. (2002). *At the will of the body*. New York, NY: Mariner Books.

Freeman, M. (1993). *Rewrite the self: History, memory, narrative*. New York, NY: Routeledge.

Freeman, M. (2010). *Hindsight: The promise and peril of looking backward*. New York, NY: Oxford University Press.

Goldberg, N. (2007). *Old friend from far away: The practice of writing memoir*. New York, NY: Free Press.

Gutkind, L. (2008). *Keep it real.* New York, NY: W. W. Norton.

Heilbrun, C. (2002). *Writing a woman's life.* New York, NY: Ballantine Publishing Group.

James, C. (2009). *Unreliable memoirs.* New York, NY: Norton.

Karr, M. (2015). *The art of memoir.* New York, NY: HarperCollins.

Maran, M. (Ed.). (2016). *Why we write about ourselves: Twenty memoirists on why they expose themselves (and others) in the name of literature.* New York, NY: Plume.

McDonnell, J. (1998). *Living to tell the tale.* New York, NY: Penguin Group.

Murdoch, M. (2003). *Unreliable truth: On memoir and memory.* New York, NY: Seal Press.

O'Shea, S. (2008). *Note to self.* New York, NY: HarperCollins.

Polking, K. (1995). *Writing family histories and memories.* Cincinnati, OH: Betterway Books.

Rainer, T. (1998). *Your life as story.* New York, NY: Putnam.

Rippl, G., Schweighauser, P., Kirss, T., Sutrop, M., & Steffen, T. (2013). *Haunted narratives: Life writing in an age of trauma.* Toronto, Ontario, Canada: University of Toronto Press.

Silverman, S. (2009). *Fearless confessions: A writer's guide to memoir.* Athens, GA: University of Georgia Press.

Stafford, W. (1978). *Writing the Australian crawl.* Ann Arbor, MI: University of Michigan Press.

Woolf, V. (1942). *Women and writing.* Orlando, FL: Harcourt.

Zinsser, W. (1998). *Inventing the truth: The art and craft of memoir.* New York, NY: Mariner Books.

Zinsser, W. (2004). *Writing about your life.* Philadelphia, PA: De Capo Press.

On Writing Poetry

Addonizio, K., & Laux, D. (1997). *The poet's companions: A guide to the pleasures of writing poetry.* New York, NY: W. W. Norton.

Bishop, W. (2000). *Thirteen ways of looking for a poem: A guide to writing poetry*. Boston, MA: Addison Wesley Longman.

Dury, J. (1991). *Creating poetry*. Cincinnati, OH: Writer's Digest Books.

Fox, J. (1995). *Finding what you didn't lose: Expressing your truth and creativity through poem-making*. New York, NY: Penguin Putnam.

Gillian, M. (2013). *Writing poetry to save your life: How to find the courage to tell your stories*. Tonawanda, NY: Miroland.

Kooser, T. (2007). *The poetry home repair manual*. Lincoln, NE: University of Nebraska Press.

Peacock, M. (1999). *How to read a poem*. Collingdale, PA: Diane Publishing.

Raab, D., & Brown, J. (Eds). (2012). *Writers on the edge: 22 writers speak about addiction and dependency*. Ann Arbor, MI: Modern History Press.

Richo, D. (2009). *Being true to life: Poetic paths to personal growth*. Boston, MA: Shambhala.

Rumi, J. (1995). *Essential Rumi*. New York, NY: HarperCollins.

Stafford, W. (1978). *Writing the Australian crawl*. Ann Arbor, MI: University of Michigan Press.

Wooldridge, S. (1996). *Poemcrazy*. New York, NY: Three Rivers Press.

Wooldridge, S. (2007). *Foolsgold: Making something from nothing and freeing your creative process*. New York, NY: Random House.

On Writing for Transformation and Healing

Barron, A., & Barron, C. (2012). *The creativity cure: How to build happiness with your own two hands*. New York, NY: Scribner.

Bonnett, K., & Butler, M. (2012). *Writing alchemy*. Milbridge, ME: Knowledge Access Books.

Brosmer, M. (2009). *Women writing for (a) change*. Notre Dame, IN: Sorin Books.

Davey, J. (2007). *Writing for wellness.* Enumclaw, WA: Idyll Arbor.

Frank, A. (2002). *At the will of the body.* New York, NY: Mariner Books.

Jepson, J. (2008). *Writing as a sacred path: A practical guide to writing with passion and purpose.* New York, NY: Ten Speed Press.

Lepore, S. J., & Smyth, J. M. (2002). *The writing cure: How expressive writing promotes health and well-being.* Washington, DC: American Psychological Association.

Lesser, E. (2005). Broken open: *How difficult times can help us grow.* New York, NY: Villard Books.

Metzger, D. (1992). *Writing for your life.* New York, NY: HarperCollins.

Pennebaker, J. (1990). *Opening up.* New York, NY: Guilford Press.

Raab, D. (2014). Creative transcendence: Memoir writing for transformation and empowerment. *The Journal of Transpersonal Psychology, 46 (2).*

Sestito, J., & Thurman, R. (2009). *Write for your lives: inspire your creative writing with Buddhist wisdom.* New York, NY: Sterling.

Snow, K. (2014). *Writing yourself awake: Meditation and creativity.* Santa Barbara, CA: Bluestone Books.

Solly, R., & Lloyd, R. (1989). *Journey notes: Writing for recovery and spiritual growth.* New York, NY: Ballantine.

Vogler, C. (1998). *The writer's journey: Mythic structure for writers.* Studio City, CA: Michael Wiese.

On Buddhism

Chödrön, P. (2001). *The places that scare you: A guide to fearlessness in difficult times.* Boston, MA: Shambhala.

Dogen. (2004). *Beyond thinking: A guide to Zen meditation.* Boston, MA: Shambhala.

Epstein, M. (1999). *Going to pieces without falling apart: A Buddhist perspective on wholeness, lessons from meditation and psychotherapy*. New York, NY: Broadway Books.

Hanh, T. N. (1992). *Peace is every step: The path of mindfulness in everyday life*. New York, NY: Bantam.

Hanh, T. N. (1999). *The miracle of mindfulness: An introduction to the practice of meditation*. Boston, MA: Beacon Press.

Hanh, T. N. (2006). *Present moment wonderful moment: Mindfulness verses for daily living*. Berkeley, CA: Parallax Press.

Richo, D. (2009). *Being true to life: Poetic paths to personal growth*. Boston, MA: Shambhala.

Suzuki, S. (1973). *Zen mind, beginners mind*. Boston, MA: Weatherhill.

Tiberghien, S. (2007). *One year to a writing life: Twelve lessons to deepen every writer's art and craft*. New York, NY: Marlowe & Company.

Watts, A. (1999). *The way of Zen*. New York, NY: Vintage.

On Psychology and Spirituality

Abrams, J., & Zweig, C. (1991). *Meeting the shadow*. New York, NY: Penguin Putnam.

Bolen, J. (1985). *Goddesses in everywoman*. New York, NY: Harper.

Boorstein, MD, Seymour. (1996). *Transpersonal psychotherapy (2nd ed)*. Albany, NY: State University of New York Press.

Bosnak, R. (1986). *A little course in dreams*. Boston, MA: Shambhala.

Campbell, J. (Ed.). (1971). *The portable Jung*. New York, NY: Viking.

Campbell, J. (1972). *The hero with a thousand faces*. Princeton, NJ: Princeton University Press.

Csikszentmihalyi, M. (1996). *Creativity*. New York, NY: Harper Perennial.

Csikszentmihalyi, M. (2008). *Flow: The psychology of optimal experience*. New York, NY: Harper Perennial Modern Classics.

Daniels, M. (2005). *Shadow, self, spirit: Essays in transpersonal psychology*. Charleston, VA: Imprint-Academic.

Freeman, M. (1993). *Finding the muse: A sociopsychological inquiry into the conditions of artistic creativity*. New York, NY: Cambridge University Press.

Grof, Stanislav. (2000). *Psychology of the future*. Albany, NY: State University of NY Press.

Johnson, R. A. (1991). *Owning your own shadow: Understanding the dark side of the psyche*. New York, NY: HarperOne.

Jung, C. G. (1989). *Memories, dreams, reflections*. New York, NY: Vintage.

Kornfield, J. (2002). *The art of forgiveness, lovingkindness, and peace*. New York, NY: Bantam Dell.

Pearson, C. (1991). *Awakening the heroes within*. New York, NY: HarperCollins.

Richo, D. (2009). *Being true to life: Poetic paths to personal growth*. Boston, MA: Shambhala.

Shapiro, D. (2010). *Devotion: A memoir*. New York, NY: HarperCollins.

Shapiro, D. (2013). *Still working: The perils and pleasures of a creative life*. New York, NY: Atlantic Monthly Press.

Shapiro, R., & Shapiro, A. (2012). *Writing—the sacred art: Beyond the page to spiritual practice*. Woodstock, VT: Skylight Paths.

Siegel, B. S. (1993). *How to live between office visits*. New York, NY: Harper.

Recommended Memoirs

Ackerman, D. (2012). *One hundred names for love*. New York, NY: W. W. Norton.

Allende, I. (1996). *Paula*. New York, NY: First HarperPerennial.

Allende, I. (2003). *My invented country*. New York, NY: HarperCollins.

Allison, D. (1993). *Bastard out of Carolina*. New York, NY: Plume.

Almond, S. (2004). *Candyfreak*. Chapel Hill, NC: Algonquin Books.

Angelou, M. (1969). *I know why the caged bird sings*. New York, NY: Random House.

Baker, R. (1984). *Growing up*. New York, NY: Signet.

Brown, J. (2003). *The Los Angeles diaries*. New York, NY: HarperCollins.

Burroughs, A. (2002). *Running with scissors*. New York, NY: Picador.

Burroughs, A. (2003). *Dry*. New York, NY: St. Martin's Press.

Burroughs, A. (2016). *Lust and wonder: A memoir*. New York, NY: St. Martin's Press.

Cantwell, M. (1995). *Manhattan, when I was young*. Boston, MA: Houghton Mifflin Co.

Cheever, S. (2001). *As good as I could be: A memoir of raising wonderful children in difficult times*. New York, NY: Washington Square Press Publication.

Conroy, F. (1977). *Stop time*. New York, NY: Penguin Group.

Danticat, E. (2008). *Brother, I'm dying*. New York, NY: First Vintage Books Edition.

Didion, J. (2005). *The year of magical thinking*. New York, NY: Alfred A. Knopf.

Dillard, A. (1988). *An American childhood*. New York, NY: Perennial Library.

Dubus III, A. (2011). *Townie*. New York, NY: W. W. Norton.

Dufrechou, J. (2002). *Coming home to nature through the body: An intuitive inquiry into experiences of grief, weeping, and other deep emotions in response to nature* (Doctoral Dissertation). Retrieved from ProQuest Dissertations and Theses Database. (UMI No. 3047959)

Edelman, H. (2009). *The possibility of everything.* New York, NY: Ballantine Books.

Eggers, D. (2001). *A heartbreaking work of staggering genius.* New York, NY: Vintage Books.

Ensler, E. (2013). *In the body of the world: A memoir of cancer and connection.* New York, NY: Picador.

Fisher, M.F.K. (1937). *The art of eating.* New York, NY: Harper & Brothers.

Frank, A. (2002). *At the will of the body.* New York, NY: Mariner Books.

Gilbert, E. (2007). *Eat, pray, love.* New York, NY: Penguin Books.

Gordon, M. (1996). *The shadow man: A daughter's search for her father.* New York, NY: Random House.

Gornick, V. (1987). *Fierce attachments.* Boston, MA: Beacon Press.

Gosse, E. (1983). *Father and son.* New York, NY: Penguin English Library.

Grealy, L. (1994). *Autobiography of a face.* New York, NY: Houghton Mifflin.

Grossman, S. (1993). *Making peace with my mother.* Manchester, CT: Knowledge Ideas & Trends.

Hall, D. (2006). *The best day the worst day.* New York, NY: First Mariner Books.

Hampl, P. (2009). *The florist's daughter.* New York, NY: First Mariner Books.

Harrison, K. (1997). *The kiss.* New York, NY: Random House.

Haskell, M. (1990). *Love and other infectious diseases: A memoir.* New York, NY: William Morrow & Co.

Hemmingway, E. (1964). *A moveable feast.* New York, NY: Charles Scribner's Sons.

Hoffman, A. (1997). *Hospital time.* Durham, NC: Duke University Press Books.

Hoffman, E. (1989). *Lost in translation.* New York, NY: Penguin Books.

Hornbacher, M. (1998). *Wasted: A memoir of anorexia and bulimia.* New York, NY: HarperCollins.

Jamison, K. R. (1996). *An unquiet mind.* New York, NY: First Vintage Books.

Jamison, K. R. (2009). *Nothing was the same.* New York, NY: Alfred A. Knopf.

Karr, M. (1995). *The liar's club.* New York, NY: Penguin Books.

Karr, M. (2000). *Cherry.* New York, NY: Viking Penguin.

Karr, M. (2009). *Lit.* New York, NY: HarperCollins.

Kaysen, S. (1994). *Girl, interrupted.* New York, NY: Vintage Books.

Kingston, M. (1989). *The woman warrior.* New York, NY: Vintage International.

Kingston, M. H. (2004). *The fifth book of peace.* New York, NY: Vintage International.

Knapp, C. (1996). *Drinking: A love story.* New York, NY: The Dial Press.

Kübler-Ross, E. (1998). *The wheel of life: A memoir of living and dying.* New York, NY: Touchstone.

Kumin, M. (2001). *Inside the halo and beyond.* New York, NY: W. W. Norton.

Lamott, A. (1993). *Operating instructions.* New York, NY: Pantheon Books.

Lauck, J. (2001). *Blackbird.* New York, NY: Washington Square Press.

Lauck, J. (2001). *Still waters.* New York, NY: Pocket Books.

Lesser, E. (2016). *Marrow: A love story.* New York, NY: Harper Wave.

Levi, P. (1998). *The drowned and the saved.* Ontario, Canada: Summit Books.

Levine, Noah (2003). *Dharma punx.* New York, NY: HarperCollins.

Lopate, P. (1995). *The art of the personal essay.* New York, NY: Anchor Books.

Lopate, P. (1996). *Portrait of my body.* New York, NY: Anchor Books.

Lopate, P. (2003). *Getting personal.* New York, NY: Basic Books.

Lott, B. (1997). *Fathers, sons and brothers.* Orlando, FL: Harcourt Brace & Co.

Mairs, N. (1989). *Remembering the bone house.* Boston, MA: Beacon Press.

Marquez, G. G. (2004). *Living to tell the tale.* New York, NY: Vintage Books.

Matousek, M. (1996). *Sex, death, enlightenment: A true story.* New York, NY: Riverhead Books.

Matousek, M. (2000). *The boy he left behind.* New York, NY: Riverhead Books.

McBride, J. (1997). *The color of water.* New York, NY: Riverhead Books.

McCarthy, M. (1957). *Memories of a Catholic girlhood.* Orlando, FL: Harcourt, Inc.

McCourt, F. (1999). *Angela's ashes.* New York, NY: Touchstone.

McCourt, F. (2005). *Teacher man.* New York, NY: Scribner.

Moss, B. (2001). *Change me into Zeus' daughter: A Memoir.* New York, NY: Touchstone.

Nabakov, V. (1989). *Speak, memory: An autobiography revisited.* New York, NY: Vintage International.

Oates, J. C. (2011). *A widow's story.* New York, NY: HarperCollins.

Plath, S. (1971). *The bell jar.* New York, NY: Harper & Row.

Raab, D. (2007). *Regina's closet.* New York, NY: Beaufort Books.

Raab, D. (2010). *Healing with words.* Ann Harbor, MI: Loving Healing Press.

Rapp, E. (2007). *Poster child.* New York, NY: Bloomsbury USA.

Rapp, E. (2013). *The still point in the turning world.* New York, NY: Penguin Press.

Ray, D. (2003). *The endless search: A memoir*. Brooklyn, NY: Soft Skull Press, Inc.

Russo, R. (2013). *Elsewhere*. New York, NY: Vintage Books.

Sachs, A. (2000). *The soft vengeance of a freedom fighter*. Oakland, CA: University of California Press.

Sarton, M. (1977). *Journal of a solitude*. New York, NY: W. W. Norton.

Sebold, A. (1999). *Lucky*. New York, NY: Scribner.

Sedaris, D. (1997). *Naked*. Boston, MA: Little, Brown and Company.

See, C. (1995). *Dreaming: Hard luck and good times In America*. New York, NY: Random House.

Sexton, L. G. (1995). *Searching for Mercy Street*. New York, NY: Random House.

Sexton, L. G. (2011). *Half in love: Surviving the legacy of suicide*. Berkeley, CA: Counterpoint.

Shapiro, D. (2000). *Mom's marijuana: Life, love, and beating the odds*. New York, NY: Vintage Books.

Shapiro, D. (2010). *Devotion*. New York, NY: HarperCollins.

Skloot, F. (2003). *In the shadow of memory*. Lincoln, Nebraska: University of Nebraska Press.

Slater, L. (1996). *Welcome to my country*. New York, NY: Random House.

Slater, L. (1998). *Prozac diary*. New York, NY: Random House.

Slater, L. (2000). *Lying: A metaphorical memoir*. New York, NY: Random House.

Sontag, R. (2008). *House rules*. New York, NY: HarperCollins.

Spiegelman, A. (1986). *Maus*. New York, NY: Pantheon Books.

Stafford, K. (2012).*100 tricks every boy can do*. San Antonio, TX: Trinity University Press.

Stahl, J. (1995). *Permanent midnight: A memoir*. Los Angeles, CA: Process.

Steinbeck, J. (1962). *Travels with Charlie*. New York, NY: Viking Press.

Strayed, C. (2012). *Wild*. New York, NY: Alfred A. Knopf.

Styron, W. (1992). *Darkness visible.* New York, NY: Vintage Books.

Styron, A. (2011). *Reading my father.* New York, NY: Scribner.

Tan, A. (2003). *The opposite of fate.* G.O. New York, NY: Putnam's Sons.

Walls, J. (2006). *The glass castle.* New York, NY: Scribner.

Wasserstein, W. (2000, February 21). Complications. *The New Yorker.*

Welty, E. (1995). *One writer's beginnings.* Cambridge, MA: Harvard University Press.

Wesolowska, M. (2013). *Holding Silvan: A brief life.* Portland, OR: Hawthorne Books.

Whitman, W. (1961). *Walt Whitman's Civil War.* New York, NY: Alfred A. Knopf.

Wiesel, E. (2006). *Night.* New York, NY: Hill and Wang.

Williams, T. T. (2001). *Leap.* New York, NY: Vintage Books.

Williams, T. T. (2001). *Refuge.* New York, NY: Vintage Books.

Williams, T. T. (2012). *When women were birds.* New York, NY: Sarah Crichton Books.

Williams, W. C. (1978). *I wanted to write a poem: The autobiography of the works.* New York, NY: New Directions.

Winterson, J. (2001). *Why be happy when you could be normal?* New York, NY: Grove Press.

Wolff, G. (1979). *The duke of deception: Memories of my father.* New York, NY: Random House.

Wolff, T. (1989). *This boy's life.* New York, NY: Harper & Row.

Woolf, V. (1927). *To the lighthouse.* Orlando, FL: Harcourt, Inc.

Woolf, V. (1985). *Moments of being.* Orlando, FL: Harcourt, Inc.

Wright, R. (1966). *Black boy.* New York, NY: Perennial Library.

Wurtzel, E. (1994). *Prozac nation: Young and depressed in America.* New York, NY: Riverhead Books.

Permissions

Page viii: Excerpt from *The Diary of Anaïs Nin, Volume Two:* 1934–1939. Copyright © 1967 by Anaïs Nin and renewed by Rupert Pole. Reprinted with permission of Houghton Mifflin Harcourt Publishing Company. All rights reserved.

Page 39: "Chinese art and Greek art" by J. Rumi, (an excerpt) from p. 122 in *The Essential Rumi,* translated by C. Barks (New York, NY: HarperCollins, 1995). Reprinted with permission of Coleman Barks.

Page 146: "Caged bird," from *Shaker, why don't you sing?* by Maya Angelou, copyright © 1983 by Maya Angelou. Reprinted with permission of Random House, an imprint and division of Penguin Random House LLC. All rights reserved.

Page 149: "The guest house" by J. Rumi, from p. 109 in *The essential Rumi,* translated by C. Barks (New York, NY: HarperCollins, 1995). Reprinted with permission of Coleman Barks.

Page 156: "The fish," in *Ballistics: Poems* by Billy Collins, copyright © 2008 by Billy Collins. Reprinted with permission of Random House, an imprint and division of Penguin Random House LLC. All rights reserved.

About the Author

Diana Raab, MFA, PhD, is a memoirist, poet, blogger, workshop facilitator, thought provoker, and award-winning author of seven books and over a thousand articles and poems, as well as the editor of two anthologies. Her passion and expertise is in writing for healing, transformation, and self-empowerment. She is very interested in creativity and what drives the creative process. Her early inspiration came from reading the journals of Anaïs Nin, as she was impressed by Nin's candor and honesty. Raab has been writing since childhood, when her mother gave her a Kahlil Gibran journal to help her cope with the loss to suicide of her beloved grandmother.

Raab's MFA is in nonfiction writing from Spalding University, and her PhD is in Transpersonal Psychology from the Institute of Transpersonal Psychology (aka Sofia University), where she researched the healing and transformative aspects of memoir writing. She is also a registered nurse and was a medical journalist for more than twenty-five years.

For decades, Raab has been a motivating force, inspiring others to write the stories and narratives of their lives. She has worked with those from all walks of life, including esteemed writers, business people, published and emerging writers, cancer survivors, and those surviving various types of trauma.

A world traveler, Raab was born in Brooklyn, New York, and has lived in Montreal and Florida. She currently resides in Southern California with her husband of four decades. She has three grown, creative, and entrepreneurial-driven children and two grandchildren. When not writing or offering workshops, she may be found meditating, hiking, nurturing her bonsais, or sitting on a cliff or by the sea crafting poems and musings in her journal.

Raab serves on a number of boards, including that for Poets & Writers, and she is a trustee at the University of Santa Barbara (UCSB). She blogs regularly for *Psychology Today, PsychAlive,* and *The Huffington Post.*

For more information, visit www.dianaraab.com.

Index

Unique Insights into Writers and their Addictions

Writers On The Edge offers a range of essays, memoirs and poetry written by major contemporary authors who bring fresh insight into the dark world of addiction, from drugs and alcohol, to sex, gambling and food. Editors Diana Raab and James Brown have assembled an array of talented and courageous writers who share their stories with heartbreaking honesty as they share their obsessions as well as the awe-inspiring power of hope and redemption.

"Open to any piece in this collection, and the scalding, unflinching, overwhelming truths within will shine light on places most people never look. Anyone who reads this book, be they users or used, will put it down changed. And when they raise their eyes from the very last page, the world they see may be redeemed, as well."

—Jerry Stahl, author of *Permanent Midnight*

"*Writers On The Edge* is a thoughtful compendium of first-person narratives by writers who have managed to use their despair to create beauty. A must-read for anyone in the recovery field."

—Leonard Buschel Founder, Writers in Treatment

ISBN 978-1-61599-108-2

A Writer Carves a Path to Healing with her own Words

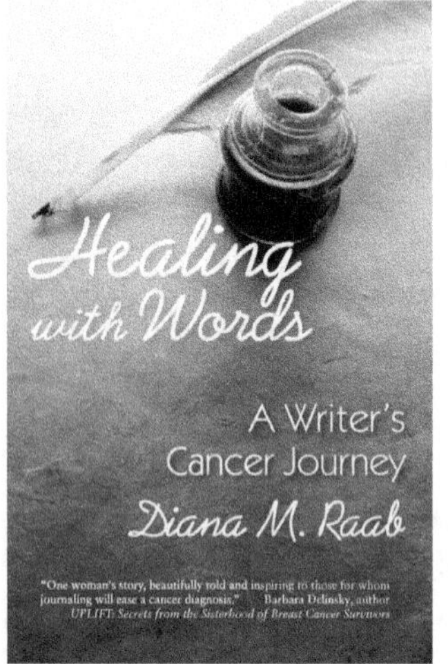

Healing With Words: A Writer's Cancer Journey is a compassionate and wry self-help memoir written by an award-winning prolific author, nurse and poet, who at the age of forty-seven found her life shattered first by a DCIS (early breast cancer) diagnosis and five years later by another, seemingly unrelated and incurable cancer—multiple myeloma. The book includes the author's experiences, reflections, poetry and journal entries, in addition to writing prompts for readers to express their own personal story. Raab's journals have provided a safe haven and platform to validate and express her feelings. Raab views journaling to be like a daily vitamin—in that it heals, detoxifies and is essential for optimal health.

Readers will learn to:

- Understand the importance of early cancer detection and how to take control of their own health
- Discover the power of writing to release bottled-up emotions
- Learn how the process of journaling can facilitate healing
- See how a cancer diagnosis can be a riveting event which can renew and change a person in a unique way

ISBN 978-1-61599-010-8

CPSIA information can be obtained
at www.ICGtesting.com
Printed in the USA
LVHW041556220119
604810LV00017B/1017/P

9 781615 993239